Kansas Baseball, 1858–1941

Kansas Baseball, 1858–1941

Mark E. Eberle

WITH A FOREWORD BY
DOROTHY SEYMOUR MILLS

University Press of Kansas

Published by the University Press of Kansas (Lawrence,
Kansas 66045), which was organized by the Kansas
Board of Regents and is operated and funded by
Emporia State University, Fort Hays State University,
Kansas State University, Pittsburg State University, the
University of Kansas, and Wichita State University.

Library of Congress Cataloging-in-Publication Data
Names: Eberle, Mark E., author.
Title: Kansas baseball, 1858–1941 / Mark E. Eberle ; with
    a foreword by Dorothy Seymour Mills.
Description: Lawrence : University Press of Kansas,
    [2017] | Includes bibliographical references and index.
Identifiers: LCCN 2016047598 | ISBN 9780700624393
    (cloth : alk. paper) | ISBN 9780700624409 (pbk. : alk.
    paper) | ISBN 9780700624416 (ebook)
Subjects: LCSH: Baseball—Kansas—Wichita—History.
Classification: LCC GV863.K22 E34 2017 |
    DDC 796.35709781423—dc23
LC record available at https://lccn.loc.gov/2016047598.

British Library Cataloguing-in-Publication Data is
available.

Printed in the United States of America

10 9 8 7 6 5 4 3 2 1

The paper used in this publication is recycled and
contains 30 percent postconsumer waste. It is acid free
and meets the minimum requirements of the American
National Standard for Permanence of Paper for Printed
Library Materials Z39.48–1992.

Contents

Foreword

DOROTHY SEYMOUR MILLS

Most historians—even most baseball historians—pay scant attention to early amateur and semipro baseball in American towns except as a forerunner of what interests them more: the big-league teams and players in large cities. When they talk about nineteenth-century and early twentieth-century baseball, they really mean the professionals in the big leagues. They quickly describe what amateur play was like in general so that they can move on to their real interest: the major leagues and their professional players. Writers love to take on a subject like a famous professional player or team. Do you know how many biographies of Mickey Mantle have been published? Do we really need thirty?

Mark E. Eberle is one of the few who understand and recognize the importance of early baseball as it was played in towns around the United States beginning right after the Civil War, not just as a prelude to the establishment of the major leagues but for itself. With this book, Mr. Eberle joins the ranks of the few who have concentrated on the kind of baseball that was for many years—and is even now—played by amateurs and semipros in the small towns of America. This kind of baseball is closer to our everyday lives. In early town ball, the man who makes a home run today turns out to be your butcher or barber or schoolteacher tomorrow, so you already know him.

Amateur baseball was for many years an integral part of everyday living. Studying that kind of play requires a different kind of research. Instead of checking the *New York Times* and the *Boston Globe*, a researcher like Mr. Eberle must scour early newspapers with names like the *El Dorado Daily Republican*, the *Fort Scott Daily Monitor*, and the *Chanute Tribune*. He must consult old books like *Beadle's Dime Base Ball Player* (1867), which often mention small-town baseball. With this kind of research he adds himself to an exclusive group looking not for names like Mickey Mantle but for the long-forgotten names of clubs and players in an obscure town in the southwest part of his state. The result is a kind of micrographic work that brings us up close to the players and their teams.

The small group of scholars that Mr. Eberle has joined includes Todd Peterson, who wrote *Early Black Baseball in Minnesota* (2010); Jeffrey Michael Laing, author of the biography *Bud Fowler: Baseball's First Black*

Professional (2013); David Vaught, who wrote *The Farmers' Game: Baseball in Rural America* (2012); L. M. Sutter, author of *New Mexico Baseball: Miners, Outlaws, Indians and Isotopes, 1880 to the Present* (2010); and Thomas K. Perry, who wrote *Textile League Baseball: South Carolina's Mill Teams, 1880–1955* (1993). A film producer who belongs in this group is Mark Honer, who produced a documentary called *Town Teams: Bigger than Baseball* (2016). The kind of books and films these writers create is the kind that reveals for us what our early forebears were doing and thinking.

In his book Mr. Eberle shows us that early baseball history in small towns has an importance beyond being the background for the big-league teams that attract so many writers as well as fans. A town's social life often centered on its own small baseball park, where the team named after the town played and where visiting teams provided the challenge needed for a town's progress.

Amateur baseball, often called town baseball, even when it has stopped being played, has left its mark on our towns in the form of the old-time baseball park, with flimsy wooden grandstands, uncomfortable bench seating, and sometimes rickety fences. These baseball parks have a long history with the building of towns. As Mr. Eberle shows, they were important gathering places for the people who built this country. In many cases they were the reason a town grew into a respectable, prosperous, and attractive place to live. Eberle gives us some solid verifying quotations from newspaper reporters of the time about the value of a town baseball team, which was well recognized—like this one: "One of the very best advertisements a town can have is a good base ball team. There will be no questions over that point."

A baseball park was one of the first things townspeople talked about building as soon as they had established the basics like homes, a water supply, a school, a general store, and a church. In a few areas of Kansas, baseball took a while to become an acceptable activity because the residents thought it encouraged idleness, and idle, lazy youths were deeply distrusted. But in most Kansas counties, the people saw no harm in the game. They soon tired of the obstacle-filled pastures where they played at first (when they weren't working) and dreamed of the ballparks with smooth diamonds, grandstands, and fencing that they knew were being built in some eastern states.

By the end of the 1800s many Kansas towns had constructed ballparks with grandstands, some of them with roofs to protect fans against bad weather. As soon as they could, they fenced in the parks, so that they could charge admission—maybe ten cents—and therefore recoup some of the money they had invested in these parks. For these structures, as Mr. Eberle shows, were generally built at the expense of the residents, sometimes through taxes, but often through the contributions of businesses and civic organizations like the Elks Club, and even with individual gifts. Town residents recognized that a ballpark was meant for everyone to enjoy, so its residents contributed to keep it operable.

Teams were established in each town by groups made up of friends and neighbors, coworkers, coreligionists, and people who knew each other through some organization. Everyone in town was allowed to play, but the best players were soon discovered. They made up the team named for the town. And sometimes the best players were discovered in unexpected places, for town baseball immediately reflected the astounding diversity of Americans at play. A team might become desperate to win an important game and would hire a ringer so that winning would be practically assured. Eberle has found that this ringer might be a highly skilled African American player who could be paid to play for any white or African American club that needed him. If any Mexican Americans lived in the area, Mexican American teams formed and played against teams of white men. If any African Americans lived there, African American teams formed and played against teams of Mexican American and white players. Some American Indian teams passing through also played local white town teams.

If you doubt any of this, read the histories of the individual Kansas towns that Mr. Eberle has visited and studied. The early town newspapers are full of reports covering these interethnic games. Although a reporter might use stereotypical descriptions of players and their clubs of different ethnicities, the writer's expressions seem not to have affected the enthusiasm with which the outsiders were welcomed.

And if you doubt that women and girls played baseball in these early days, check Mr. Eberle's many references to their games that he found published in the town newspapers of Kansas. Like women's teams in the early colleges of the Northeast, some of the Kansas women's teams formed in the early colleges. Women often formed teams in town, too. Eberle has even found evidence of a women's baseball league established by five towns in the Topeka area. Although some townspeople seemed startled to discover that women played baseball, Eberle reports no opinions like major league club owner Albert Spalding's decision flatly forbidding women to play.

The stories Eberle has found in which Kansas residents welcomed visiting teams of foreigners like Japanese teams are more evidence of early townspeople's openness to diversity. Towns gladly hosted traveling black professionals, too, like the famous Kansas City Monarchs, as well as traveling Mexican teams from Mexico, traveling American Indian teams like those made up of army scouts and those from Indian Schools like Haskell, major league teams who occasionally presented exhibition games in towns, and traveling "bloomer girl" teams from many states.

Some of these traveling teams, like some of the Kansas town teams, were integrated. Women's teams played against either women's or men's teams. Some women's teams included a male player or two in their lineups. Although some Kansas newspaper reporters seem to have been surprised by encountering women's teams, that did not stop the women. Occasionally, a reporter admitted that a women's team beat a men's team.

This willingness of Kansas townspeople to host teams of persons unlike themselves was good for town business, for it multiplied the number of existing teams in operation. The railroads recognized early what baseball meant to a town and knew that establishing train stops at these lively towns would be good for their own business. Think how pleased a prospective newspaper publisher would be to have so much happening in town to write about! Baseball and other forms of intertown rivalry sold papers.

The local baseball park was a social center, as Mr. Eberle demonstrates. When an important traveling team like the Kansas City Monarchs came to town, businesses closed and everybody turned out to see the famous black team. If the park was full, boys and men climbed trees or nearby buildings to get a view of the game. On holidays, like "Old Settlers' Day," baseball became the headline event, after a bronco-busting contest, a baby show, and a horse race. At one of these celebrations, the umpire wore on his hip what a reporter described as "an enormous six-shooter." No doubt he expected trouble, because everyone was excited.

There was no lack of variety in the teams that arose in small towns. Towns produced muffin teams, military teams, church teams, and young girls' teams. Doctors played lawyers. Incarcerated men played outsiders. The House of David sent teams around the country to play town teams. So did the Ku Klux Klan.

Town teams could join any league that seemed right for them. One town had its own five-team league; three teams were composed of white players and two of black players. There were town amateur leagues, semipro leagues, professional leagues, minor leagues, twilight leagues, boys' leagues, and college leagues. Some were set up for businesses (one business per league, or several), and some by civic organizations like the YMCA.

The leagues were often short-lived. They came and went depending on whether the town teams could afford to be members, and that depended on their income and community support, which varied. Teams tended to reorganize every year because whether they could play often depended on donations, promotions, and benefits held by fans. Towns might drop out of a league for the wheat harvest, which needed all hands, or not even start the season until the harvest was over. The situation was unstable, but while it lasted it was varied and colorful.

The boys who lived in towns had the advantage over city boys in that they could see and even talk every day to the players who displayed their baseball talents in the local games. In big cities, boys became hero worshippers who knew of the players' skills and successes only at a distance. In the towns the boys needed only to walk down the street to hail the baseball stars. They knew that the fellows who won and lost the games were not heroes. Heroes are people who accomplish a deed that helps others even if it means they are putting themselves in danger. The First Responders are therefore heroes. Baseball players are not. They are skilled baseball players, some of them star players. City boys who saw baseball players as heroes were living in a fantasy world. Town boys who knew they were just men like any men, except for their baseball skills, were able to live closer to reality.

It was in the thirties that the towns knew they needed help in keeping their baseball parks in good enough shape to operate or in building a new one. The government stepped in, with the Works Progress Administration (WPA) building entire parks or refurbishing old ones. The WPA built more than 3,000 baseball parks around the country. Sometimes federal, state, and local agencies combined to collect the needed funds, and often local residents contributed their time, labor, and money as well. After all, the local baseball park was an emblem of their town, and they wanted a winning team playing in a nice-looking baseball park.

In the twenties and thirties, large organizations arose offering town teams and other independent teams participation in important national tournaments: the National Baseball Congress (NBC), for semipros; the American Amateur Baseball Congress (AABC); and the Denver Post Tournament. These tournaments welcomed some "amateurs" and "semi-pros" who were really professionals. Clubs wanted to compete in these tournaments because of the attractive cash prizes (this was the Great Depression), but they might find themselves competing against a famous professional team led by Satchel Paige himself.

The viability of the town teams came into question before World War II. Town teams were failing to attract enough customers for them to pay for equipment and travel. Eberle explains the new models of play created with the rise of youth leagues, high school leagues, and collegiate summer leagues, as well as the changes in American culture with the advent of new forms of entertainment and communication, like the radio. All of these changes made town baseball lose money at the gate. But the beloved town baseball parks were often saved, refurbished, and repurposed.

Eberle analyzes the reasons for which so many of the old town ballparks still remain in recognizable form. He explains that the town ballpark (or even its former site) appeals to a community's view of itself. Generations of fans (like Eberle himself) view it as a historical property, full of memories for everyone, like the memory of "the day Satchel Paige played here," the kind of moment in history Eberle brilliantly christens a "historical waystation." Millions of Americans have had this sort of connection with the town ballpark.

So Eberle set out to visit the oldest remaining town baseball parks in his state and find out how they came into existence, as well as how they are doing now. Historians like to put their eyes on places they write about and find out where the actions of history take place. They get a feeling for what life there was like, a feeling that "puts clothes on" the people and makes them real.

In the course of his research, which is dizzyingly thorough, Mr. Eberle found the parks and took the time to study their history. His goal in writing this book was to provide a context for the continued preservation and use for these parks, which he views as "living history."

In preparing this history of early Kansas baseball, Mr. Eberle has given us a valuable approach to understanding who we are as Americans. Our past is there, inside ourselves as shared memories. All we need to do is bring it to the foreground.

While reading Mr. Eberle's book, I was startled to realize that I had found in it a way of reconnecting with my own earliest relationship with baseball—not in Kansas, but in Cleveland, Ohio, my hometown. My first job, which I began in the fall of 1950, was as a kindergarten teacher at Dunham School. Every morning I took a Hough Avenue bus to East 66th Street, where I got off, walked past a boarded-up building on the corner, and then entered the school next door, where I met with a roomful of five-year-olds to begin their formal education.

It was not until the next spring, when I read about the imminent demolition of the failing structures inside the board fencing, that I realized that every weekday I had been walking past the remains of the famous baseball site called League Park, where, since the late nineteenth century, famous and not-so-famous players had entertained thousands of fans. The Cleveland Indians baseball club had just built Lakefront Stadium, although they still used League Park afterward. They stopped using it shortly before I began my job as a teacher and discovered the identity of the fenced-in property. The Hough Avenue district had fallen into deep disrepair, and so had League Park.

It took years, but community leadership rescued the League Park site, and the Hough Avenue district has revived with it. League Park underwent a transformation that Mr. Eberle would approve: it has become a recreation facility that includes a community baseball diamond, the Cleveland Baseball Heritage Museum, and a community park with walking trails. It is part of a neighborhood restoration that has transformed a declining section of the city into a vital area where, as one woman resident put it, "there's some place for people to go in the community." A man who loved to play baseball claimed that he could "feel the presence" of former players there because "there has been greatness before us on that field." All this is happening because some people cared about history.

We must all be grateful for work like that of Mr. Eberle's, which readjusts our view of early baseball as valuable in itself instead of just as a prelude to the major leagues. I hope it inspires many others to open their own hometown history and find what has been going on in relation to the town baseball park there, and then take the time to share it all with us. I think they will find treasures that the rest of us will appreciate.

Acknowledgments

AROUND THE HORN

In my pocket, I carry a British £2 coin that has engraved into its narrow rim a phrase traced back to Bernard de Chartres in the twelfth century and made famous by Sir Isaac Newton in 1676: "Standing on the shoulders of giants." It is a reminder that all scholarship and other accomplishments of human society are founded on the work of our predecessors. In this spirit, I thank all the authors (some of them anonymous authors of newspaper reports) who recorded or analyzed the information upon which this summary is based. Even authors who wrote text decades ago that we now find rude or abhorrent in its tone or words provide us with valuable historical insight into how our society has changed and give us a perspective by which to better appreciate and admire those people who persevered in the face of intolerance and bigotry. I am also grateful to those who endeavor to make historical resources ever more accessible through archives, libraries, and websites. However, I exclude from this general acknowledgment anyone who claims that extraterrestrials are in any way responsible for the construction of the grandstands featured in this book. Baseball has enough myths as it is, and they are much more interesting.

I am especially grateful to Dorothy Seymour Mills, who graciously agreed to write the foreword. Her third volume (*Baseball: The People's Game*) in the three-part history of the sport, coauthored with her late husband, Harold Seymour, covered segregated teams at the national level that are included in this book about a single state. She is both knowledgeable and kind in equal measures.

Jan Johnson was an invaluable guide through the early history of Kansas baseball. She pointed me toward interesting stories and critiqued much of the text. When it comes to the history of baseball in the state, she is not only the most knowledgeable person on the subject, she is also generous in sharing that knowledge and passion. Jan and I were connected by Mark Honer while he worked on his 2016 documentary, *Town Teams: Bigger than Baseball*, which recounts the nature of the game in Kansas during the period covered in this book. He also introduced me to Dorothy Seymour Mills and others as we worked on our concurrent projects. It was a fortuitous nexus of several independent pathways crossing the same territory.

I am grateful to the following individuals and the staffs of libraries and museums who assisted with my research. They all offered invaluable assistance by providing documents, directions for further inquiries, or other insights that improved the content of this book. Of course, any errors in fact or interpretation rest solely with me. John Kovach and Barbara Gregorich (with the Maud Nelson story); Patricia Osborne (Blue Rapids Historical Society); Joan Weaver (Kinsley Public Library); Ed Carlson; Mark Metcalf; Sam Leben (El Dorado Baseball Hall of Fame); John Washington (Garden City Recreation Commission); Steve Cottrell (Garden City Engineer); Jan Coulter (Finney County Historical Museum); Jeff Boyle (City of Hays Parks Department); Connie Schmeidler (Fort Hays State Historic Site, Hays); Betty MacDonald (Ellis County Historical Society, Hays); Becca Hiller (Santa Fe Trail Center, Larned); Richard Schwartzkopf (*Larned Tiller and Toiler*); Angela Bates; Bill Hesse; Joe Tomelleri; Kevin Williams; Phil Dixon; Lynn Womack; Chanute Historical Society Museum; Kansas Oil Museum (El Dorado); Hays Public Library; Humboldt Historical Museum; Geary County Historical Society and Museums (Junction City); Jordaan Memorial Library (Larned); Harvey County Historical Museum (Newton); Kauffman Museum at Bethel College (North Newton); Sumner County Historical and Genealogical Society (Wellington); Wellington Public Library; and the Hastings (Nebraska) Museum of Natural and Cultural History.

In addition to those who offered assistance with the text, I thank the following people, libraries, and museums who granted permission to reproduce historical photographs and other images used in this book. While an author's goal is to create a full and accurate mental image with his or her prose, a picture is still worth a thousand elegant words. Don Musil, DVM (Blue Rapids); Patty Nicholas and Sherry Severson (Forsyth Library, Fort Hays State University, Hays); Pete Felten (Hays); Sylvia Augustine and Mark Metcalf (Independence Historical Museum and Art Center); Kurtis Russell (Allen County Historical Society, Iola); Joan Weaver (Kinsley Public Library); Ray Olais (Newton); and Nancy Sherbert (Kansas State Historical Society, Topeka).

Lastly, I would like to thank Kim Hogeland, my editor at the University Press of Kansas, who was more than patient with me during the publication process. In addition, I am grateful to copyeditor Amy Sherman and to the reviewers of the book proposal and manuscript, who provided valuable advice. They helped me to understand exactly what story I was trying to tell and how to explain it clearly. And I appreciate all of the work the staff at the University Press of Kansas put forth to design and produce a high-quality book.

I am standing on the shoulders of giants.

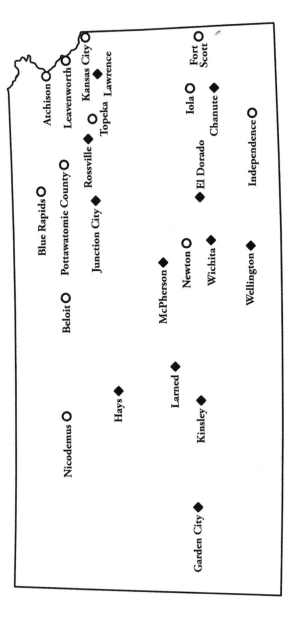

Selected sites mentioned in the text. The diamonds (◆) are towns with historical baseball parks.

Prologue

Walt Whitman once said, "I see great things in baseball.
It's our game, the American game. It will repair our losses and
be a blessing to us." You could look it up.
Bull Durham

base-ball is our game: the American game:
I connect it with our national character.
Walt Whitman, 1888*

I attended grade school during the 1960s in Olathe, Kansas, one of the suburbs of Kansas City. At the time, several families with young children populated our neighborhood on the margin of the growing town. Two blocks to the west was a railroad embankment—an earthen wall that separated us from the farmland beyond and impounded two large ponds to the north and south of our block. Where the paved streets of our neighborhood ended, a gravel road continued over the top of that barrier and provided us with access to the rural countryside. We lived on the interface of the vanishing rural landscape and the ever-expanding suburban sprawl that characterized the decades following the Great Depression and Second World War. A half century later, sentimental memories render this an idyllic environment in which young boys could spend their summers, clad in white T-shirts, blue jeans with rolled-up cuffs, and canvas sneakers. The new suburban neighborhood provided a relatively large cohort of young children on a single block, while the ponds and nearby countryside provided ample opportunities for exploration. With no internet, no cell phones, no cable, and only black-and-white televisions for the three broadcast channels, the colorful outdoors stimulated all our senses and was the focus of our recreational activities.

On summer days, those activities included playing baseball in the back yard, with the requisite collateral damage of four bare patches of dirt on the grass lawn and occasional broken windows. Football was fine from the perspective of a young fan (the Chiefs came to Kansas City in 1963), but playing football or even basketball was more challenging for youngsters because the balls were much larger. For a boy of six or seven years, a baseball could be more easily handled in a way that allowed us to emulate our sports heroes, at least in our imaginations. Baseball was also the summer sport, when a three-month break from school gave us full days for outdoor activities.

In addition to playing among ourselves, we also rode our bicycles up and over the railroad tracks to search the ditches along gravel roads for discarded glass pop bottles. If undamaged, these could be returned for the deposit of 2¢ apiece at the neighborhood grocer, housed in a small wooden building of narrow aisles, relatively dim lighting, and rough wooden floors that was entered through a wooden screen door—a family business that has been replaced by charmless convenience stores. Three bottles meant you had enough for a nickel pack of five baseball cards, packaged with a stick of stale gum, and a penny in change. Upon completing our transaction, we rushed outside to open our package under the shade of the leafy trees surrounding the store, bemoaning the presence of cards we already had and celebrating any that were new, especially those of prominent players or any member of the Kansas City A's. Trades were sometimes conducted on the spot. Being fans of our beloved but perennially weak A's in the days before the National and American Leagues were parceled into divisions with interleague games, we were loyal supporters of whatever team represented the American League in the World Series.

This was a time when televised baseball games during the regular season were limited to the Saturday afternoon game of the week, which usually did not feature the A's. Radio was the means of enjoying a live ballgame away from the ballpark. This was also before World Series games were played at night—that did not happen until 1971. The relatively late date for the first night game during the World Series explains why my grade school chums and I had to spend afternoon recess huddled around a small transistor radio, hoping the battery would not give out, to enjoy a live World Series game on weekdays. When recess was not in session, we occasionally received updates during class from someone with a radio and clandestine earphone or from a sympathetic teacher. Decades later, I look back fondly on this intersection of my life with baseball.

Baseball nostalgia also contributed to this project, which grew quite unintentionally from simple curiosity. Now a longtime resident of Hays in western Kansas, I was familiar with the old grandstand constructed of limestone and concrete at Larks Park. It is the local baseball field used by the collegiate summer league team (the park's namesake Hays Larks), the Fort Hays State University baseball team, and American Legion teams. A brass plaque mounted on an exterior wall commemorates its construction by the Work Projects Administration (WPA) and the City of Hays in 1940. Seeking context, I wondered: what is the oldest baseball park in the state?

I knew from my experience searching for the oldest baseball parks in North America that there are many claims but precious little documentation and occasionally too much misinformation, repeated enough times so as to take on the guise of fact. To satisfy my curiosity, I followed *Bull Durham* character Annie Savoy's advice to "look it up." I wanted to get it right, and I wanted to document the answer, so no one would have to simply take my word for it, just as I wanted to quote Walt Whitman's view of baseball as accurately as possible.

And what about the other historical ballparks in Kansas? Just how many remained? My original question transformed into a broader quest. I would search for all the historical ballparks in Kansas where the game is still played and then travel to see each one, so I could document what they had become as well as what they had been. How well had they survived the decades? Did they still host America's summer pastime, or had they been abandoned or replaced by those who inherited them from their proud builders? Only a few old baseball grandstands remain, but there are some real treasures among the state's historical ballparks.

I began my search online. Were any towns or groups bragging about their old ballparks? A few were. Then I used Google Earth to search for signs of a baseball grandstand in the larger towns of all 105 counties, *large* being a relative term when contrasting metropolitan areas around Kansas City and Wichita with the extensive rural areas of Kansas. From the beginning, I intentionally excluded any ballparks that lacked a grandstand. Most baseball diamonds in Kansas have only relatively small, prefabricated bleachers with no roof, if they have any seating at all. I was only interested in those ballparks that exhibited permanence. Who had cared enough to build a grandstand of wood, brick, stone, or concrete, and who had cared enough to preserve it?

With my list in hand, I visited all the old ballparks. I also visited local libraries, history museums, and government offices, as well as the archives at the Kansas State Historical Society's Kansas Museum of History in Topeka, reading old newspaper stories and searching for old documents, photographs, and artifacts. Some newspapers were accessed online through the Library of Congress, Newspapers.com, Newspaper Archive, Google News Newspaper Archive, Gateway to Oklahoma History, Illinois Digital Newspaper Collections, State Historical Society of Missouri, and the Wamego Public Library. Newspaper reports were typically biased in favor of the home team and its ballpark, but they sometimes criticized both for their faults. They provide an invaluable source of information about the sport and its venues that is both geographically comprehensive and accessible, if viewed with a critical eye. Books, journal articles, and other documents provided additional historical information and context. All are cited within the text through endnotes and the bibliography. ("You could look it up.")

With the search for historical ballparks well in hand, I sought additional context. Who had built these ballparks, and what had preceded the long-lasting structures still in use today? Who had played on these diamonds and under what circumstances? History has a trajectory that provides valuable insight into later events. For example, the story of baseball prior to the Second World War, when these old ballparks were constructed, was a time of segregation on and off the ball field. In addition to the town teams or minor league teams composed almost exclusively of white males, there were teams of women, African Americans, American Indians, and Mexican Americans. All played in Kansas, and all shared a passion for baseball. It would be impossible to fully appreciate the histories of the old ballparks without understanding something of the communities who built them and the people who spent their summers—and occasionally their winters—playing the national pastime for their own pleasure and for the enjoyment of fans watching from the grandstands.

As I conducted this research for my own enlightenment, I met a number of people who shared a similar curiosity about the history of baseball and the old ballparks in Kansas. Sharing this story is why the results of my personal journey were compiled for this book. I hope it will entertain and inform people with an interest in baseball and history. I also hope it will offer support for people interested in preserving the state's few remaining historical ballparks. What follows are brief narratives and photographs of historical baseball sites in Kansas, introduced by a history of the early game in the state—the local game. All of the baseball parks look better in person, especially during a ballgame, so any effort to experience them for yourself is worthwhile. It is a pleasant way to spend a summer evening. This guide is merely an introduction to the long histories of the ballparks and the sport in the state—a sample of the many people, places, and events. Enjoying a bit of living history in person is the ultimate experience.

Introduction

Pushing the Abner Doubleday myth aside, we now understand that baseball was derived from a variety of ball games dating back centuries, as summarized in books such as those by David Block (*Baseball before We Knew It*) and John Thorn (*Baseball in the Garden of Eden*). The game we know today came to us through New York in the early 1800s. Ball clubs such as the Gothams of the 1830s and the Knickerbockers of the 1840s compiled written rules that borrowed from existing games, with some important changes. For example, they eliminated the practice of putting a runner out by hitting him with the ball as he ran between bases (soaking). This meant that harder balls could be used, and harder balls could be hit and thrown farther than their predecessors. The New York rules also incorporated a concept from earlier ball games that designated foul territory (as used today), but the penalty for hitting a foul ball was no longer an out (the first two fouls later became a strike, as did a third foul on a bunt attempt). This reduced the size of the field in an effective way compared to similar games of the time in which the ball could be hit in any direction (as is true of cricket). In 1857 baseball clubs in New York formed the National Association of Base-Ball Players, which became the guardian of the rules as they continued to evolve, until 1870. These rules were published, which meant they could easily be carried elsewhere, allowing a reasonably consistent sport to spread through other regions. This contributed to the rise of the New York game across the United States and Canada at the expense of two other popular ball-and-stick games of the period—the Philadelphia game (what is now often referred to as town ball) and the Massachusetts game (sometimes called round ball).[1]

Baseball spread from New York to the Midwest during the 1850s, as recounted for the state of Michigan by Peter Morris. The story of Kansas baseball that begins in 1865 could slip comfortably within his narrative of the transition from teams organized as gentlemen's clubs to amateur town teams, with their more diverse mix of players, and eventually to the increasingly professional teams.[2] While his Michigan tale of this formative period for the sport ends in 1875, the story of Kansas baseball presented here continues through the end of the century and into the early 1900s. Setting these sorts of boundaries for what is covered in a book is not unlike teams and umpires meeting prior to a game to cover the local ground rules that accommodate the unique attributes of each ballpark.

This history of Kansas baseball spans the years between the US Civil War and the Second World War. Using major wars as temporal boundaries for a history of baseball might seem an odd choice, but there are connections. In the years leading up to the Civil War, settlers arrived in the Kansas Territory from other parts of the country, including the Northeast. Although they brought an interest in baseball and its siblings with them, the challenges of the period delayed the organization of baseball clubs until after that horrible conflict had ended. Following the Civil War, soldiers were also sent from the eastern United States to Kansas, where they engaged in wars to dispossess American Indians of their lands. These soldiers were among the first to play baseball in the state.

Eighty years later, following the end of the Second World War, baseball began to change dramatically. The decades prior to that war were a time of segregation, when the fallacy of separate but equal, including baseball teams, generally ruled life in the United States. While this is a book about baseball rather than a treatise on cultural history, the story about the segregated nature of the sport cannot be ignored. The history of baseball not only reflects much of the country's history,[3] it encompasses the entire history of the state, including some of the ugliness of an evolving society and the indomitable spirit of the people who drove that evolution toward a more inclusive society. This was also a time when watching a baseball game could only be done in person, which resulted in the organization of hundreds of local teams throughout the state. These aspects of the game began to change after 1945, albeit slowly. The era of segregation began to pass, while watching major league teams play live baseball became possible through a variety of formats, beginning with television, which contributed to reduced interest in supporting local adult baseball teams. The Second World War also ended the extensive building projects of the Great Depression, which included several Kansas stadiums, a few of which are still in use. In addition to telling the story of early baseball in Kansas, stories are recounted here for nine ballparks constructed prior to the Second World War that provide tangible connections to this history.

Although this book summarizes the history of baseball when it was still largely a local game, it is not possible to include histories for all of the hundreds of teams in Kansas, and I apologize if your hometown team has not been mentioned in these pages. However, this summary might provide a useful background for local enthusiasts who choose to compile the histories of these town teams.

Despite the nearly ubiquitous baseball teams in the state, there has never been a major league team based in Kansas. Even Kansas City, Missouri, did not have a long-term major league team until the Philadelphia Athletics moved west in 1955. (The 1884 Kansas City Cowboys played in the Union Association during its only season, and the 1914–1915 Kansas City Packers played in the similarly short-lived Federal League.) However, numerous players in the major leagues have been associated with Kansas through birth, residency, or membership on a Kansas baseball team. Only a few of these players receive brief mentions on these pages because the emphasis here is local baseball, and information about many of these players is already available in a 1988 article by Thomas Busch in the journal *Kansas History* and a 2014 book by Tony Hall, both of which are listed in the bibliography. Several major league players from Kansas are also the subject of book-length biographies or shorter biographies posted online through the Society for American Baseball Research (SABR). Others are still waiting for an author.

Even though baseball boasts a wealth of statistics, or perhaps because of these data, it is the nature of baseball fanatics to debate various aspects of the sport and its history. Which was the best team? Who was the best player at a particular position? Who was the best hitter? The list is seemingly endless, and one of the common questions is, which baseball park is the oldest? Given the long history of baseball and the changes occurring in the sport, the answers for many of these questions come with caveats. Although there might be no unambiguous answers to resolve all the questions to everyone's satisfaction, this is actually a blessing rather than a curse. It allows baseball fans to engage in friendly debate about the relative merits of the answers they choose to support. It engages fans in the sport and its history. Accordingly, I need to define some of my caveats before I provide the answers I choose to support regarding the list of the oldest ballparks in Kansas. You might think compiling such a list for a state or the country would be a clear, straightforward process. You would be wrong.

For perspective on the oldest baseball parks, Fenway Park in Boston, Massachusetts (1912), is the oldest ballpark still in use in the major leagues. Wrigley Field in Chicago, Illinois (1914), is a close second.[4] The oldest ballpark with its original grandstand is Rickwood Field in Birmingham,

Alabama (1910). As with other baseball questions, the answers offered to the question of which baseball park is the oldest come with caveats, as illustrated by the answers Fenway Park (limited to the major leagues), Rickwood Field (with its original grandstand), and other examples in table 1. A common distinction among the various claimants to being the oldest is the difference between historical baseball grounds and historical baseball parks.

First, it will help to distinguish between the two principal types of structures used for seating. According to *Merriam-Webster's Collegiate Dictionary* (11th ed.), a grandstand is "a usually roofed stand for spectators," whereas a bleacher is "a usually uncovered stand of tiered planks providing seating for spectators." I make use of the leeway granted by the dictionary—the qualifier "usually" in each definition—to further define a grandstand as a substantial building set on a foundation and used for spectator seating. A bleacher, on the other hand, has the look of portability, even if it is anchored to the ground. Of the nine oldest grandstands included in this book, six have a roof over the seating area, and three do not, but this list still conforms to the dictionary definition of a grandstand—it "usually" has a roof. Using this definition of a grandstand, I can distinguish between a baseball park and a baseball ground. The term *baseball park* as used here refers jointly to a playing field and a grandstand. *Baseball ground* refers only to a playing field. With these definitions in mind, I can add the final caveat—age—to define historical baseball grounds and historical baseball parks.

For the purposes of this book, historical baseball grounds are sites used for baseball prior to the Second World War and still in use for the sport today. Historical baseball parks also have grandstands constructed prior to the Second World War, when most such construction projects were suspended. Given that these grandstands are more than seventy-five years old, they have undergone restoration, renovation, or both, some more extensively than others. Restoration involves work to preserve the historical structure in a condition as close as possible to the original, while renovation involves work that substantially modifies the existing structure compared to the original. Despite any restoration and renovation, however, the integrity of the original structure is intact. Nine such grandstands exist in Kansas.

Using these caveats, the criterion for establishing the sequence of the oldest ballparks in Kansas used in this summary is reasonably straightfor-

Table 1. Oldest baseball parks and baseball grounds in North America, with various caveats

Oldest Baseball Park (historical grandstand)

still in use by a major league team	Fenway Park, Boston, Massachusetts (1912)
with the original grandstand	Rickwood Field, Birmingham, Alabama (1910)

Oldest Baseball Ground (historical field with newer grandstand)

in continuous use with the same field orientation	Fuller Field, Clinton, Massachusetts (1878)
in continuous use with different field orientations	Labatt Memorial Park, London, Ontario (1877, 1883)
where the game is currently played, but not continuously through its history	Hartford Base Ball Grounds at Colt Meadows, Hartford, Connecticut (1874)

ward. It is based on the ballpark's historical grandstand, which I have dated by the dedication of the ballpark or its first use for a baseball game. The nine grandstands in Kansas were constructed between 1924 and 1940. In some instances, the baseball ground predates the current grandstand, and the oldest grounds in the state have been used for baseball since the 1890s. This offers opportunities to those people who wish to advocate that these baseball sites are the oldest in the state. However, I am focusing on ballparks, not ball grounds—grandstands, not just the playing fields.

Sadly, only nine historical ballparks still host baseball games after more than seventy-five years. Yet nine is a fitting number, given its central importance to the game played at these ballparks—nine innings in a standard game and nine players on each team (not counting the designated hitter, which was not used during the years covered in this book). Though few in number, there are some real historical treasures in the state on a par with any smaller ballparks in the country, and each has a unique character expressed through its architectural details. With a little care, it is possible that all the historical baseball grandstands—some recently restored—will survive to celebrate their centennials.

In addition to these nine historical baseball parks, there are numerous historical baseball grounds in the state. These historical ball grounds have no associated structures or only the most basic structures (perhaps a backstop and a few bleacher seats), or they have grandstands that are relatively recent constructions. Documenting every historical baseball ground used in Kansas since the late 1800s would be a tremendous—probably impossible—challenge, involving more time and resources than were available for this project. Hundreds of pastures and open fields were regularly used for baseball games in the late 1800s and early 1900s, and their exact locations are often uncertain, or they have been lost to development as towns grew. Such research is left to local enthusiasts, who can better document these sites. However, a few historical baseball grounds are mentioned in the appendix of this book for the benefit of people who enjoy visiting such sites. Three baseball parks with grandstands constructed between 1947 and 1966 (more than fifty years old) are briefly described—an honorable mention list to complement the first nine.

In summary, this is a sample of the sport in Kansas that conveys what baseball was like in those early years for the communities that chose to build the baseball grandstands still with us decades later. It is a guide that can be tossed into a vehicle on a trip to a ballpark, much as bird watchers carry their field guides on trips to a wetland during the spring migration. Hope springs eternal in baseball. My hope is that documenting the legacy of the sport and these historical sites in the state will provide a context for their preservation and continued use by future generations who enjoy America's summer pastime as players and spectators. These sites are not just part of our past. They are part of our future. They are living history, in which everyone is still welcome to participate.

PART I

Early History of Baseball in Kansas

The youth of the land are encouraged by teachers and parents to
become proficient in [baseball], as an athletic sport healthful to mind and
body. Its popularity, however, is due largely to the fact that it is spectacular, and
brings more enjoyment to those who witness it than to the players themselves.
Justice Silas W. Porter, Supreme Court of Kansas, 1909*

Baseball fields would not exist if there were no teams to play on them and
no fans to watch them. Thus, we begin with a sample of the teams that
played baseball in Kansas from 1858 to 1941, when the nine oldest grandstands were constructed. Although full summaries of the teams and players at each ballpark are beyond the scope of this project, a few anecdotes
are included to provide context about the people who first used these early
baseball fields. The historical grandstands, the ball diamonds, and the
game of baseball itself connect us to them.

Baseball in Kansas has featured teams that are often assigned to various
categories, especially as the game existed prior to the Second World War.
As elsewhere in the country, there were teams representing towns, businesses, churches, schools, military units, and prisons. There were men's
teams, and there were women's teams. There were teams segregated by
race, and there were integrated teams. There were teams for adults, and
there were teams for youngsters. Much of this variety across the nation
was described by Dorothy Seymour Mills and Harold Seymour in *The
People's Game*, the third volume in their excellent multivolume work *Baseball*. Presented here is the story of these teams from the more detailed
perspective of a single state.

In addition to the various groups who played baseball in Kansas, teams differed in the level of compensation received by the players. There were amateur teams, semiprofessional teams, and professional teams. To clarify these three terms regarding payments to the players, *amateur* is reasonably straightforward and refers to teams whose players were not paid a salary to play baseball—although the team, which was usually represented by a formal association or other organization, might have received money for expenses from sponsors, gate receipts, or prizes. The term *semiprofessional*, however, has been somewhat loosely applied. It could refer to a team on which only some of the players were paid, often the pitcher and possibly a catcher hired for an entire season or a specific game. The term could also apply to an entire team whose members played part-time and were paid a portion of the revenue earned during the season, perhaps from a particular game or tournament. A third use for the term refers to players who were paid to ostensibly work for the company sponsoring the team, often with paid time off for practice and games. Professional players received a salary to play baseball full-time, although most sought other employment during the offseason in the period covered here. It was not unusual for professional players in the state to turn down offers to join major league organizations and stay in Kansas to play baseball, where they could earn more money. Some of the amateur and semiprofessional teams in Kansas played in local leagues, and some of the state's professional teams were members of various minor leagues.

Although some towns had multiple teams, the primary focus of the townspeople was the team that represented them against nearby towns—the "town team." Most town teams were amateur or semipro teams, but there were a few independent, professional town teams in Kansas (such as the Beloit Leaguers described later). Minor league teams are treated here as distinct from town teams. An accurate count of just how many towns in the state have hosted a town team has not been documented, but several towns in nearly all 105 Kansas counties hosted teams during at least one summer. Thus, it can safely be stated that town team baseball was played in Kansas by hundreds of teams on hundreds of baseball diamonds that varied from simple grass fields around which spectators stood or sat on the ground, to fine ballparks with substantial grandstands covered by a roof to protect fans from the afternoon sun in the days before night baseball. The chapters that follow explore this variety. They do not include every category of baseball team that could be imagined, but they include those categories of teams that played in towns across the state through most of the late 1800s and early 1900s. For example, prison teams at the federal penitentiary in Leavenworth, the state penitentiary in nearby Lansing, and similar facilities had obvious constraints on travel, so their contributions to Kansas baseball history were limited to their immediate neighborhoods. Thus, they are not covered here but are left for others to document.

The story here begins with the early town teams organized across Kansas. Although this opening chapter deals primarily with teams of white males, some of the topics about the nature of local baseball, such as municipal bans on Sunday baseball, are also relevant to the segregated teams covered in subsequent chapters. The people playing the game might have been segregated by race or sex, but they all played the same game. Acknowledging and understanding this aspect of our past is important. The long history of segregation is the ghost in the room that cannot be ignored. The lessons we learn from this history should inform our actions in the present to help us avoid the harm caused by the actions of the past, so the ghost will not haunt us into the future.

CHAPTER 1

Town Teams and the Early Game

Possibly the first published mention of "base ball" being played in Kansas was in an Emporia newspaper on New Year's Day 1859—two years before Kansas became a state. The newspaper story described Christmas day celebrations in 1858 that helped people escape, however briefly, the turmoil of Bleeding Kansas in the years leading to the US Civil War. After four years of murders, threats of violence, widespread skirmishes, and political intrigues of national importance following the passage of the Kansas-Nebraska Act—all set against the backdrop of the everyday hardships of frontier life—there was a respite on Christmas day.

> But *the* feature of the observance was a huge game of "ball" in the public square. Nearly all the male bipeds of the place—old and young—participated in the sport, which commenced in the morning and continued until dark.—The fun and excitement were great, and doffing, for the time, the gravity and dignity of every-day life and business, all were "boys again," and entered into the spirit of the game with a relish and vigor that would have done credit to their younger years.—The discussions which grew out of this revival of "the days when we were young," have been very numerous, covering the whole range of "ball science," and many are the learned disquisitions we have listened to in regard to the merits and demerits of "base ball," bull-pen, cat-ball, etc., with the proper mode of conducting the game.[1]

As the newspaper story suggests, there were several types of games at the time involving a ball and stick.[2] For example, American Indians in Kansas played lacrosse, sometimes referred to as Indian baseball (described in chapter 4). In 1870, "the last surviving thirteen of the Old Artillery, challenge[d] any thirteen in the world, or elsewhere, to play a game of regular old-fashioned town ball" in Lawrence. A game was quickly arranged "near the brewery," in which the Flying Artillery successfully defended their challenge.[3] Another game of town ball featured prominently in a story reprinted by a Kansas newspaper in May 1860, purporting to tell how Abraham Lincoln learned of his nomination for president of the United States:

> When the news reached Springfield, his friends were greatly excited and hastened to inform "Old Abe" of it. He could not be found at his office or at home, but after some minutes a messenger discovered him out in a field with a parcel of boys having a pleasant game of town ball. All his comrades immediately threw up their hats and commenced to hurrah. Abe grinned considerably, scratched his head and said, "Go on, boys; don't let such nonsense spoil a good game."[4]

In January 1860, a Topeka newspaper reported that the young men of the city, which had been incorporated only three years earlier, indulged in "the pleasant recreation derived from a game of ball. It is no unusual occurrence here, even now, in the dead of winter."[5] What type of ball game the young men were playing was not described, nor was there any suggestion that teams had been formally organized.

Cricket: The Fading Competitor

Perhaps the first ball club in Kansas, organized in April 1860, was not a baseball team but a cricket club, in Leavenworth.[6] The club was short-lived, however, as the Civil War erupted a year later. After the war, another cricket club was organized in Wyandotte (Kansas City, Kansas) in late 1866, and it persisted until 1869. By January 1867 the Wyandotte City Cricket Club had purchased "5 acres of beautiful ground from M. B. Newman . . . within the city limits, south of O. H. Mitchell's property."[7] However, they played their first match, a contest between single and married members, at "Mr. Buesche's Grove on Fifth Street" on July 4, 1867, as part of the club's daylong celebration.[8] As the only cricket club in the state at the time, they also played baseball against outside competition. In these instances, they were referred to as the Wyandotte City Cricket Nine, which would distinguish them from a cricket team of eleven players.[9] Other cricket clubs followed, typically in towns with immigrants from Great Britain.

In 1871 the Bala Cricket Club was organized at "this enterprising Welsh colony" in Riley County. The club in Bala accepted a challenge from a team in Wakefield and invited the Junction City town club to a friendly match.[10] Whether the clubs in Wakefield and Junction City were cricket clubs or baseball clubs who could add two players for a cricket match was not stated, although Wakefield did have a cricket club in the 1880s. In 1874 the Capital Cricket Club was organized in Topeka and scheduled its first "grand match . . . between the English and American members of the club" for April. At a practice match the following month, spectators were invited to "roost on the neighborhood fences, watch the progress of the game, and at the same time engage in handkerchief flirtations with the seminary girls."[11] However, by July, a Topeka newspaper wondered, "Where is the cricket club, whose 'overs' were so much admired in the early springtime? Have they faded away under the summer sun? And why don't the boys go out any more to play?"[12]

Cricket did persist—sporadically—in a few Kansas towns into the early 1900s. In September 1874 "a large number of people" at the Salina ball grounds watched a cricket match between the local cricket club and the Smoky Valley Base Ball Club.[13] The following year, a Lawrence Cricket Club was organized and played on the open fields opposite the baseball grounds.[14] A decade later, an Emporia cricket club was organized in 1885 and 1886.[15] However, cricket was most persistent in Topeka, where clubs were organized periodically from 1874 to 1914, with much of the support coming from employees of the Atchison, Topeka and Santa Fe Railroad (the 1914 Topeka team was named the Santa Fe Cricket Club).[16] Topeka cricket clubs traveled to play matches against the Emporia Cricket Club in 1886 and a Kansas City club in 1914.[17]

A peak of sorts for cricket in Kansas occurred in 1889, when there were at least three clubs, with a fourth club possibly playing in Topeka. The club in Medicine Lodge in south-central Kansas was isolated from its peers in Clay Center and Wakefield in northeastern Kansas. While most cricket clubs played matches between teams picked from among their members, Wakefield defeated Clay Center in an intercity match in August. Despite the loss, a Clay Center newspaper expressed the wish that its club could accept an invitation to play at the state fair in Topeka the following month and "transfer the championship from Topeka to Clay Center."[18] Hope springs eternal in cricket as well as in baseball.

In 1900 Florence was apparently the only town in the state with a cricket club,[19] although Topeka continued to organize clubs periodically after the turn of the century. Among all the ball-and-stick games, cricket was the only potential competitor for baseball played in Kansas during the early years of statehood. In addition to the cricket teams periodically organized in the state, numerous stories were published in Kansas newspapers about cricket teams and matches in the northeastern United States and Great Britain. However, limited interest among the citizens of Kansas for participating in cricket as players or spectators meant that the sport could not compete with baseball for long. When a baseball game and a cricket match were held simultaneously on adjacent fields in Topeka in 1895, "like a two ring circus, it was impossible to 'keep tab' on both games at the same time, and the novelty of cricket soon wore off among those who looked on the first game they had ever witnessed, and a stampede was made by the spectators for the game they understood."[20]

Early Baseball Teams

After the Civil War, soldiers stationed in Kansas played baseball to pass the time. Among these troops were members of the recently organized Seventh US Cavalry, stationed in western Kansas. Officers played baseball while camped west of Fort Hays during the summer of 1868.[21] That same spring at Fort Wallace, near the Kansas-Colorado border, troopers of the Seventh Cavalry and soldiers of the Fifth US Infantry played at least two games featuring teams named Keogh (for Captain Myles Keogh of the Seventh Cavalry) and Beecher (for Lieutenant Frederick Henry Beecher of the Third US Infantry).[22] Later in the summer of 1868, two companies of the Seventh Cavalry, under the command of Captains Robert West and Frederick Benteen, crossed paths while on separate patrols in the Solomon River valley of north-central Kansas. They paused to play a baseball game, with pickets posted "to prevent being surprised by Indians." It was the second time the two companies had played a game "under similar circumstances."[23] Baseball for the Seventh Cavalry continued in the Dakota Territory during 1873–1876, as the troopers played teams from other units and civilian teams. The professional baseball aspirations of a few of these players ended with wounds received in June 1876 at the Battle of Little Big Horn (the Battle of the Greasy Grass).[24]

With the demands on time, resources, and lives during the years of

Bleeding Kansas and the Civil War, it is not surprising that the history of baseball played by organized clubs in the state apparently began after the close of these conflicts, perhaps stimulated by the baseball experiences of soldiers or former soldiers who served during the war and carried the sport westward across the Kansas frontier. The sport also received a boost from immigrants to the state from the Northeast and Midwest, where some of these settlers had played baseball. For example, the town of Kinsley was established in the 1870s, and an early baseball team featured several transplanted players among its new residents. Earl and Frank Spencer reportedly had played professional baseball in Ithaca, New York, and Charles Snapp had played for a professional team in Chicago, Illinois. Some of their teammates apparently had played on teams in Ohio, Pennsylvania, and Wisconsin before moving to Kinsley.[25]

The first baseball club organized in Kansas was the Frontier Base Ball Club (BBC) of Leavenworth, which was among the ninety dues-paying clubs listed in the summary of the National Association of Base-Ball Players (NABBP) convention held in New York in December 1865.[26] Founded in 1857, the NABBP was the first formal organization to govern baseball across several states. Colonel Thomas J. Moonlight, formerly of the Eleventh Kansas Cavalry, served as acting secretary and pitcher for the Frontiers, and he occasionally umpired games between other teams.[27] In the summary of the December 1866 convention, a Kansas club from Fort Scott was on the list of teams paying dues.[28] This was probably the Lincoln Base Ball Club, which had been organized earlier that year.[29]

Although they did not pay dues to the NABBP, the University Base Ball Club of Lawrence and the Wyandott [sic] Base Ball Club were also founded in 1866.[30] In October and November of that year, the Frontier BBC and the Wyandott BBC played a pair of games, one in each city (referred to as a home-and-home series), "for the championship of Kansas." The Frontiers won both games.[31] In 1867, the Wyandott BBC moved their baseball ground "from the levee to the Huron place," a parcel of land that included the Huron Indian Cemetery (now the Wyandot National Burying Ground).[32] It is perhaps the oldest site of a baseball ground in Kansas still maintained, in part, as a public park, although it lacks a baseball diamond. Later that year, a third team in Wyandotte—the Anderson Base Ball Club—was organized by railroad employees, who "ranged from sturdy brakemen and bronzed engineer to the dapper conductor and 'wiry' telegraphist." Thus, teams representing towns and companies both had their origins in Kansas from the beginning, just as they were developing elsewhere in the country. And so it came to pass in 1867 that a gentlemen's baseball club, a cricket club, and a railroad company's baseball team vied for the baseball championship of the city. The Anderson BBC claimed the honor after the deciding game in a close contest with the Wyandotte City Cricket Nine.[33]

A story published by a Kansas City, Missouri, newspaper in 1927 told of a game supposedly played by another Kansas baseball club in 1866. According to the story, the team was named the Atchison Pomeroys. At the time, Samuel C. Pomeroy of Atchison was a former mayor of the city (1858–1859) and a sitting US senator from Kansas (1861–1873).[34] Republican senator Pomeroy sits on the wrong side of history with respect to his prominent role in unsuccessful efforts to unseat President Abraham Lincoln in 1864. On the other hand, in December 1871, Pomeroy introduced a bill in the US Senate establishing the Yellowstone region as the country's first national park. In March 1872 President Ulysses S. Grant signed the bill into law.[35]

The 1927 story of the baseball game supposedly held in August 1866 had the visiting Atchison Pomeroys playing a third game in a series with the Kansas City (Missouri) Antelopes. To prevent the sort of violence that had marred the second game, the person reportedly asked to umpire the third and deciding game was James Butler "Wild Bill" Hickok. According to the story, none of his decisions during the game were challenged, and the Antelopes were said to have won the game by a score of 48–28. It would be a great story, if it were true. However, the legend of Hickok's service as umpire in this instance is a myth given life by the newspaper story published sixty-one years after the supposed event and embellished in later retellings, some that were clearly fictional.[36] No contemporary sources for the event are known, and there are several errors in the 1927 article that taint its credibility. Hickok's biographer, the late Joseph Rosa, pointed out that Hickok almost certainly was not in Kansas City in August 1866 based on his employment with the military that year. Rosa also noted several other incorrect details in the published story.[37]

In addition to the problems noted by Rosa, there is evidence that Atchison had no baseball club in 1866. An Atchison newspaper published a plea the following spring on May 16, 1867, for the organization of the town's first baseball club:

Base ball seems to be in great vogue everywhere throughout our country, for sport out of doors—wicket and cricket being laid aside for the present. . . . Have we not enough interest in such health giving games to have a Base Ball Club in Atchison? Let some one put the ball in motion, and see if there are not enough jolly fellows among us to pursue it with a hearty good will.[38]

The plea was answered, and the newspaper reported on May 30 that the "Base Ball Club will meet at 2 o'clock p.m. to-day on their grounds in West Atchison." Challenges for games were soon issued and answered in the newspaper. These games were usually played against other nines from Atchison, plus a team in Saint Joseph, Missouri, which defeated Atchison 53–15. The team continued to be known as the Atchison Base Ball Club until August 1867, when they chose the name Ad Astra Base Ball Club, derived from the state motto, *Ad Astra per Aspera*.[39] The new name was retained in 1868 and again in 1870, when the ball club reorganized.[40] The first reference in Kansas newspapers to a baseball club named the Atchison Pomeroys was not published until 1884, when the Atchison Delmonicos were reorganized as the Pomeroys. The name was retained a couple more years and was a tribute to J. P. Pomeroy, a local businessman and sponsor of the team, not the former senator.[41] Unlike the Pomeroys, the Kansas City Antelopes were indeed an organized team in the late 1860s, making them the only part of the story that clearly stands true. The 1927 article also mentioned that the Antelopes had defeated the Leavenworth Frontiers in 1866, which is possible, but there is no assertion or evidence that Hickok was a participant in a game between the two teams.[42]

In addition to the Ad Astras of Atchison, other baseball teams in Kansas were organized in 1867, including the Prairie Base Ball Club of Olathe, the Junction City Base Ball Club, and three teams in Topeka (the Shawnee, Prairie, and Capitol baseball clubs), among others. Second teams were organized in Fort Scott (the Central club), Lawrence (the Kaw Valley club), and Leavenworth (the Quartermaster Department—QMD—club at the fort).[43] In 1868, the two Fort Scott clubs merged to become the Phoenix Club.[44]

While most early town teams were in the more populated region along the eastern border of Kansas, a baseball game was played farther west on the frontier, near the center of the state, in September 1867. Quartermaster clerks at Fort Harker made up the Bradley Base Ball Club, named in honor of their commander, Captain G. W. Bradley. Their opponents were the Smoky Hill Base Ball Club of the nearby town of Ellsworth. The Bradleys won the game 60–22 on a windy day.[45]

Following the first tentative steps toward town team baseball in Kansas during 1865 and 1866, the number of teams had quickly expanded in the young state by 1867. In August, a Lawrence newspaper declared, "Kansas is 'on it.' Clubs are being organized all over the state, challenges fly from one town to another, match games are played, and the 'noble game' is in a very vigorous state of health."[46] However, the permanence of amateur baseball teams in these early days of the sport continued to be uncertain. For example, in June 1868 a local newspaper wondered, "What has become of the Base Ball Club of Olathe?"[47]

Initially, gentlemen who owned local businesses, held political offices, or otherwise had the freedom to set their own schedules constituted several of the early baseball clubs in the state. These men could more easily arrange time to practice and play matches during the afternoon while most people were at work through the early evening, six days a week. Club members included men such as the aforementioned Thomas Moonlight in Leavenworth, who was serving as the federal tax collector in northeastern Kansas in 1867 while he was acting secretary of the Frontier Base Ball Club. In Lawrence, Dudley Haskell and his brother owned a store where they sold shoes, hats, and other goods. Haskell later represented Kansas in the US House of Representatives. As the owner of a shop, he could leave his clerks to run the store while he engaged in baseball during the late afternoon with other members of the Kaw Valley BBC. Similarly, members of the University BBC at the State University (now the University of Kansas) in Lawrence could set aside time in the afternoons for practice and games.

These and other baseball clubs were clubs in the truest sense of the word. They elected officers, and their secretaries issued formal challenges to other teams. Following a friendly match, the host club often entertained their guests with supper, music, or a dance. After defeating the Lincoln BBC of Fort Scott, the club in Carthage, Missouri, entertained their guests with a grand ball, "where all the beauty and elite of the city were present."[48] The Lincoln and Central baseball clubs in Fort Scott formed a joint association that provided for activities in addition to baseball, including a furnished reading room that was initially funded by proceeds from a dance sponsored by the teams. The Lincoln BBC also placed a photograph of their first nine—their top players—among the items in the cornerstone of the Fort Scott Masonic and Odd Fellows Hall.[49] The newspaper account of an 1867 match in Leavenworth between the Frontiers and the Kaw Valleys gives a sense of the festive nature of club baseball:

> A special train of two cars [from Lawrence] had been secured for the occasion, but on the departure it was found they were entirely inadequate to convey all who wished to join the excursion. Fortunately, Mr. Noble, Assistant Superintendent, was present, and with his usual gentlemanly courtesy, immediately furnished them with an extra car, obviating the difficulty. One car was almost entirely filled with ladies, who were out in force, giving the whole affair a very animated and gala appearance. The well-known and popular conductor, Jake Brinkerhoff, was in charge of the train, which was a sufficient guaranty that everything possible would be done for the comfort and pleasure of the party.

The match lasted a little over three hours, and updates were telegraphed back to Lawrence. The score was tied 41–41 after eight innings, but Lawrence pulled away, winning 50–44.[50] The return train ride to Lawrence was presumably just as festive.

Although early baseball clubs were often composed of "merchants, clerks, and professional men, who have stated times for out door [sic] exercise at this invigorating game,"[51] people from all walks of life enjoyed baseball, and more and more people began to play the game. Much of the recent history written about the origin and early development of baseball focuses on urban teams and the path to major league baseball rather than rural teams, such as those organized in most of Kansas.[52] Yet, as befits a sport later referred to as the national pastime, the early history of baseball was a mix of urban and rural teams. During the late 1800s and early 1900s in many of the smaller communities in Kansas and elsewhere, teams were organized for competition with other teams in the same city or from neighboring towns.[53] Some teams played an occasional game simply for the fun of it, such as a pair of autumn games in McPherson among three crews of grain threshers.[54]

In addition to teams playing for fun and exercise, an amateur or semi-professional team often represented the entire town, especially in rural communities too small to support more than one team. (Many towns actually had a second team segregated by race or sex, as will be described in subsequent chapters.) Most of these town teams only played their counterparts in towns that were nearby because the means of transportation at the time limited how far they could travel for a ballgame. However, the Lawrence Kaw Valleys made a trip to Saint Louis, Missouri, to play the Empire and Union Base Ball Clubs in 1868, losing both games. Round-trip train tickets were $12.65, a substantial expense at the time.[55]

Yet even if they were restricted to playing in a relatively small region of the state, baseball offered players the opportunity to represent their broader community—either their town or their profession—as part of a team. It also provided players the opportunity to achieve individual success. Just as young towns in Kansas struggled for economic advantage and survival, with many becoming ghost towns, some men sought economic advancement and status in the community for themselves through a new start on the frontier after leaving the eastern United States or Europe.

Baseball is unique among major team sports in the United States in several regards. For example, there is no time limit for a game, although darkness sometimes brought games to an end in the years before lights were installed at ballparks. In addition, baseball differs from other team sports such as football, basketball, and hockey in that the team controlling the ball (or puck) is on defense, not offense. The pitcher puts the ball in play and, with the help of eight teammates, attempts to defend against the lone batter's efforts to contribute to his team's score (sometimes assisted by base runners). The defense never confronts the entire offense collectively. This places substantial attention on a single offensive player—the batter. In any given game of baseball, the team could succeed while an individual does not play well, or vice versa, although success at both levels is certainly the goal.[56] These opportunities for success at two levels integral to baseball contributed to its wide popularity during its early years in Kansas, and the eclectic nature of those who enjoyed playing the game was noted in an 1870 Leavenworth newspaper, which reported that "the interest in what is now called the National Game has seized upon nearly all classes of people in America, and we hear of matches between all trades and professions—fat and lean, rich and poor, sturdy farmer boys and delicate dry goods clerks—all have taken a hand at it."[57]

Thus, the game of baseball played by clubs of gentlemen during the late 1860s and 1870s transitioned quickly into a sport played by town teams whose members represented a broad cross-section of the local community. This change in team membership occurred as the rules of the game were also changing. Early baseball rules differed in several ways

Photograph of men apparently ready to play baseball while wearing street clothes; photo taken at Tribune between 1900 and 1909. Two players are holding baseball bats, and one is holding a baseball. The fourth man from the left is the only one not wearing a hat, because he is wearing a catcher's mask (and a tie but no vest or jacket). Courtesy of the Kansas Historical Society, Topeka.

Baseball game in Tribune, July 4, 1908, photo taken from the outfield. Buildings in the background constitute a portion of the town, which had a population of 158 people in 1910. Their opponent in this game was a team from Towner, Colorado, about eighteen miles to the west. Courtesy of the Kansas Historical Society, Topeka.

from those used today. The "bound catch" had been one of the more contentious issues of the late 1850s and early 1860s. This rule allowed an out to be recorded if the ball was fielded on the fly or after its first bounce. However, the rule was eliminated before the 1865 season, immediately prior to the organization of the first teams in Kansas.[58]

Yet several other differences from the modern game remained. For example, according to the rules adopted by the NABBP in December 1866, the pitcher had to use an underhand delivery, while keeping his arm straight and perpendicular to the ground as it passed his body. In addition, the striker (batter) was not subjected to called strikes unless he refused to swing "at good balls repeatedly pitched to him." In other words, the pitcher "must deliver the ball as near as possible over the center of the home base, and *fairly* for the striker," giving him every opportunity to put the ball in play.[59] An early player in Lawrence explained that the pitcher "was compelled to deliver the ball where the striker wanted it. Knee Ball, Hip Ball, Shoulder Ball or High Ball." However, the striker was out if he swung and missed three balls that were pitched fairly, and if the catcher caught the third strike before the ball hit the ground or after only one bounce (as in today's rules, the batter could attempt to reach first base if the ball on the third swing and miss was not caught). The striker was also out if a foul ball was caught in the air or after one bounce, another holdover from the discarded bound catch rule.[60]

Other rules in the early years also favored the striker, such as one allowing longer bats. A bat fifty-five inches long—thirteen inches longer than allowed today—is in the collection of the Kansas Museum of History in Topeka.[61] It was presented in 1869 to Dudley Haskell, who used it in a game when he played for the Kaw Valley BBC.[62] Although the striker was standing virtually alone against the defense of nine opponents, the rules gave him several advantages in the early days of baseball. The overall goal of the game was to put the ball in play and run.

The rules that minimized the role of the pitcher compared to their current status changed in the early 1880s. Pitchers began to throw with their arms swinging out from their bodies, and by 1884, overhand pitching was allowed.[63] Yet even as late as 1887, pitchers were placed at a disadvantage. For that year only, four strikes were needed for a strikeout, rather than three. Remarkably that year, Independence pitcher Newt O'Rear "struck out sixteen men under a four strike rule" in a game against Coffeyville.[64]

However, as overhand pitching became legal and balls were thrown with various speeds and movements, the importance of the pitcher was enhanced, and this created the one-on-one competition between the pitcher and the batter that we now recognize as the heart of the game.

Before pitchers gained this importance, scores could be much higher than they are today. In an 1867 game between two of the better clubs in Kansas, the Lawrence Kaw Valleys defeated the Leavenworth Frontiers 29–21.[65] Exceptionally high scores were recorded in games between the Topeka Shawnees and Lawrence Universitys in 1867 (96–57) and the Lawrence Unions and Leavenworth Independents (two African American teams) in 1868 (90–58).[66] Teams that did not score in an inning were said to be "whitewashed," and newspapers often reported the number of innings a team was whitewashed as an accomplishment or an embarrassment, depending on which team they supported.

Once the importance of the pitcher was elevated, the position became so important to a team's success that a star pitcher was often brought in from another town—and often paid—to supplement a team otherwise composed of local amateur players. In an extreme example from 1920, the town of Little River sent an airplane on a 140-mile round trip east to Florence to bring in a pitcher for a game because the pitcher hired from the team in Beloit, over eighty miles to the north, was unable to travel due to heavy rains. The effort was apparently worth it. Little River defeated Lyons.[67] The days of friendly match games between gentlemen's clubs were ending, and competitive town teams became the standard. Professional teams soon followed in several towns.

Early Baseball Fields

In addition to the evolving rules, differences among baseball grounds added variation to the game. The quality of some fields was poor, being little more than a relatively flat pasture or plowed field, which placed the fielders at a disadvantage. Newspapers often bragged about the high quality of their local ballparks and occasionally complained about inferior baseball grounds in other towns. An 1890 baseball ground in Larned was said to have an old tombstone for home plate.[68] Unique conditions at a ballpark often were addressed in what were referred to as "ground rules" that governed situations not covered in the standard rules.[69] For example, at an 1897 game in Topeka, a ground rule stipulated that because there were two inches of water standing in right field, any hit to that field would be limited to a single.[70]

In August 1906 two Salina teams—the Lees and Athletics—agreed to a ground rule that any ball striking a tent set up by the Seventh-Day Adventists near the diamond would be limited to a single. A week later, the same two teams played on one of the most unusual baseball fields, requiring some even more unusual ground rules. They played on a "railroad right of way . . . among box cars, telegraph poles and wires[,] and railroad tracks."

> It was a great game, and was witnessed by a fairly good crowd. Because of the numerous box cars all the players were not in sight all the time and consequently the spectators saw only parts of the game. . . . The game resulted in a victory for the Lees by a score of 13 to 0. There was some heavy hitting, but ground rules prevented home runs and everything more than a single base. The ball was lost half the time either in or under a box car. Swift grounders that ordinarily would have been good for two or three bases were frequently cut off by the ball striking a rail and bounding back into the diamond. The game was played under the greatest difficulties of any game this season, but it was interesting.[71]

There were often no fences around early ball fields. Fans could line the base paths and occasionally ringed the outfield, sometimes crowding the players and interfering with the game. Ground rules usually limited a hitter to a double if a ball were hit into a crowd of spectators or vehicles ringing the outfield.[72] The term *ground rule double* is still used today for a ball that lands beyond the outfield fence after first touching fair ground on the playing field (it is actually not a ground rule, because it applies to all modern ballparks).[73] In an unusual interpretation of this rule in a 1908 minor league game in Wichita, a locally unpopular umpire awarded a Joplin, Missouri, player a home run on a ball hit down the third base line that rolled under the bleacher wire in left field because the local ground rule simply stated that a "ball hit into the bleachers shall count as a home run." The people establishing this ground rule likely assumed this would result from the ball going over the fence, not under it. Two police officers had to escort the umpire from the ballpark and onto a streetcar.[74]

Conversely, short outfield fences sometimes led to ground rules stating that balls hit over the fence on the fly would be ruled a double instead of

Baseball game in Barton County in central Kansas sometime between 1910 and 1920. The photograph shows a field of vegetation that is not evenly mowed, as would be expected today. Many games were played on rough fields, while others were played on fields that had been scraped, rolled, and mowed. Courtesy of the Kansas Historical Society, Topeka.

a home run. Such was the case at the "Broom Corn grounds" in Wichita for fly balls hit over a wire fence in left field erected to protect an onion patch. However, a left fielder managed to catch a fly ball hit into the onion patch by "going under the fence, [and] spearing it [the ball, not an onion] with one hand." Nonetheless, the umpire awarded the hitter a double.[75] A few outfield ground rules were even more elaborate, such as one at a game in Ottawa. If the ball went to the left of a "certain buggy" and into the line of vehicles, a runner was allowed only one base. If the ball went to the right of the buggy, whether it went into the line of vehicles or not, a runner could advance as many bases as possible.[76]

Fences behind the plate also presented challenges. In one game in Iola in 1911, the local minor league team hosted the town team from nearby Humboldt. In a moment of hubris, Iola established a ground rule for the game that runners could take as many bases as possible on any passed ball (a ball going past the catcher). Typically, runners could advance no more than one base on a passed ball or an overthrow at first or third base, but the leaguers, being a professional team, assumed they would benefit most from their atypical ground rule when playing against a lowly town team. The game turned out to be a pitchers' duel, with few hits. As if scripted by fate, a batter for Humboldt struck out swinging, but the ball got by Iola's catcher and slipped under the grandstand. By the time the Iola players retrieved the ball, the Humboldt player had circled the bases, scoring the only run of the game, which gave Humboldt and their African American pitcher, Pomp Reagor, a 1–0 victory.[77]

The absence of an outfield fence and constraining ground rules at many early baseball grounds meant that a home run could be achieved on a batter's speed around the bases or perhaps when a well-hit ball went "rolling into a corn field."[78] In a 1921 game in Chanute, with one man on base, Claude Spafford drove the ball "into the alfalfa between deep center and right. Spafford romped around the bases for all he was worth and after denting the pan walked over to the bench with a broad smile, expecting to receive congratulations. Instead Manager L. R. Somers remarked, 'That did not look like a bunt to me. You are fined the price of a smoke for not sacrificing when you were told to.'"[79] In other instances, ground rules diminished the excitement by limiting the hitter to a double if the ball made its way into an agricultural field.[80]

It was not only outfields bordered by crops that presented a challenge for fielders.[81] During a game in Chanute in 1904, the ball was hit into a "lagoon" near the baseball diamond and remained in play. Charley Fields of the Chanute Black Diamonds, an African American team, jumped into the chest-deep water to retrieve the ball and threw out a runner at home trying to score from first base.[82] At a Burlington baseball ground, the "outfield was restricted by trees," and any ball hit into the trees remained a live ball according to the ground rules. Apparently, the home team was adept at placing the ball within the branches.[83] At a game in Onaga, the home team's third baseman chased a foul ball and "became tangled up with a chicken" but still made the catch (which the local newspaper reported with the obvious pun).[84]

Umpires

In addition to the players, the umpire was an integral part of baseball games. The names of umpires were often listed with game summaries published in newspapers, and comments on their skills and impartiality (or lack of either) were sometimes recounted in those summaries. When no squabbles occurred during a game, the umpire might be credited with providing satisfaction to all parties. Yet when arguments marred a game, the umpire was often blamed for being the "tenth man" on the opposing team and was sometimes subjected to physical violence. A young girl in Kinsley learned from newspaper accounts of ballgames that "umpires are very bad men one day and very good men the next day." As reported by her mother, she was "greatly disturbed because they are not good all of the time." In 1866, Henry Chadwick noted the difficulties faced by umpires: "The position of an Umpire is an honorable one, but its duties are any thing but agreeable, as it is next to an impossibility to give entire satisfaction to all parties concerned in a match."[85]

Despite these challenges, some umpires gained local or national notoriety as consistently excellent arbiters. Most prominent among the umpires from Kansas was Ernest "Ernie" Quigley, born in New Brunswick, Canada, in 1880, but a longtime resident of Saint Marys and other cities in Kansas from early childhood. Quigley was an umpire in the National League from 1913 to 1936 and served as the league's first supervisor of umpires in 1937–1940. In addition, he refereed about 400 football games and 1,500 basketball games. His brother Larry Quigley also was an umpire in Kansas.[86]

Initially, the opposing captains agreed upon an umpire, as stipulated in the 1866 rules of the NABBP. Similarly, an umpire could only be changed during a game through mutual consent of both teams. This usually happened because an umpire was injured or because one or both teams were dissatisfied with an umpire's performance. Although not always the case, the umpire was expected to be "a player familiar with every point of the game." This might be someone from one of the teams who was not playing that day, a former player, or a player from a third club. In the early days of baseball there was only a single umpire, but each team provided a scorer. According to the 1866 rules, the position of an umpire on the field was "to the right of, and between, the striker and catcher, in a line with the home and third base." Sometimes they stood behind the pitcher. As the pitcher gained more importance and it became necessary to call each pitch as a ball or strike, the umpire moved behind the catcher, who moved closer to the plate. Later, a second umpire was frequently used to make calls in the field.[87]

The selection or replacement of umpires by mutual consent persisted into the early 1900s for town teams, although it was usually the home team that arranged for an umpire. For especially noteworthy games, efforts were made to have an impartial umpire, perhaps from another town. When white town teams played teams of African Americans or American Indians, white umpires were sometimes suspected of being biased toward the white team. In some instances the bias was so obvious that even white publishers of local newspapers would acknowledge the absence of impartiality. The Nebraska Indians barnstorming team even provided a second, white umpire in an attempt to ensure fairness. On rare occasions, an African American or American Indian ballplayer served as the sole umpire in games where one or both teams were white. In a game between two women's teams in Wichita, the female umpire was singled out, along with a pitcher, for the professionalism of her work. As minor leagues and local leagues were organized, they typically hired umpires to work their games—thus, semiprofessional umpires joined the semiprofessional teams on the playing field.[88]

Box Scores

Scorebooks (or scorecards) were used by the official scorer (there were two at early games, one provided by each team) to record the relevant data regarding the game. These have become progressively more detailed as the sport has grown. Box scores were developed and improved through time as a means of recording data to document each game—the performances of the teams and individual players—for presentation in the narrow columns of newspapers. They were derived from similar summaries used for cricket. The first known newspaper box scores for baseball matches were published in New York newspapers in October 1845 and contained three columns—a list of players' names and their corresponding numbers of outs and runs scored. Henry Chadwick, a native of England who immigrated to the United States as a youth with his family and eventually adopted baseball (without relinquishing cricket), was prominent in improving early scorebooks and box scores. This is but one contribution of many he made as a pivotal figure in the growth, development, and promotion of the game during its early years. Chadwick included early examples of scorebooks and box scores in the annual *Beadle's Dime Base-Ball Player*, along with standard abbreviations to be used, such as the now iconic *K* for a strikeout. Box scores continued to evolve into the twentieth century, as shown in the following examples from Kansas newspapers.[89]

CLAY PARK'S SIDE.

	Runs	Outs
H. C. Park, C.,	10	4
R. Miller, C. F.,	10	1
W. Williams, 2d B.,	9	3
A. Fulton, P.,	12	2
C. Knapp, L. F.,	12	1
— Bogen, 3d B,	9	4
W. C. Higginson, R. F.,	11	3
J. H. Sawyer, S. S.,	10	3
C. West, 1st B.,	10	3
	93	24

Fly balls caught, 2; do. missed, 8.
Passed balls, 9.
Outs on fouls, 5.
Home runs—Park 1, Knapp 1, West 3.

GREENEWALD'S SIDE.

Greenewald, C.	6	4
W. Hoover, 2d B.,	9	0
V. W. Parker, 1st B.,	8	2
J. Hoover, P.,	6	1
T. Hughes, S.S.,	6	4
— Munn, 3d B.,	7	3
F. Stanley; C. F.,	5	4
J. McFall, B. F.,	2	4
H. Bird, L. F.,	5	2
	54	24

Fly balls caught, 4; do. missed, 7.
Passed balls, 18.
Out on fouls, 6.
Home runs—W Hoover 2, J Hoover 2.
Time of game 4 hours—closed at 8th inning, owing to approaching darkness.

U. R. SMITH, Umpire.
S. H. CHISHOLM. Scorer.

A. An 1867 box score summarizing runs and outs for each player, along with a few other totals. Both the umpire and scorer are listed. Note that the eight-inning game lasted four hours, and 147 runs were scored. Games through the 1870s could have much higher scores (and more passed balls) than were typical after the pitcher was allowed to throw overhand (and catchers started wearing gloves). Source: Atchison Daily Champion, 30 July 1867.

MUTUALS.	R	O	PICKED NINE.	R	O
W H Glancy, c	2	3	F Allen, p	3	3
D H Houghton, p	3	3	A D Glancy, 1b	2	3
G Benning, lf	2	4	C Hetherington, cf	3	3
F McCready, 2b	4	2	G E Scoville, lf	4	2
W Kehler, 3b	3	3	F Hardwicke, ss	4	3
F Cobb, cf	3	2	W Coplan, 3b	4	3
McFadden, 1b	1	4	Joe Stringfellow, 2b	3	2
F Von Wardenburg, rf	1	4	G B Hooper, c	4	3
C C Ponsenby, ss	4	2	W Howe, rf	2	3
	23	27		26	27

Innings,	1	2	3	4	5	6	7	8	9	
Mutuals	0	1	5	6	8	2	0	1	6	—23
Picked Nine	1	1	7	4	4	1	0	1	1	—26

Umpire—McPheron. Scorer—Frank Everest.

B. An 1874 box score summarizing runs and outs for each player, along with a line score of runs per inning for each team. For many game summaries, only the line score was given, sometimes with the names of the pitchers, catchers, and umpire. Source: Atchison Daily Champion, 16 May 1874.

WHITE STOCKINGS.

Innings	1	2	3	4	5	6	7	8	9
Church, c	1	1	2	1	2	0	0	0	0
Reddington, s.s.	1	1	0	1	3	0	0	0	0
McGilian, 2d b.	1	0	1	2	1	0	0	0	0
D. Austin, 3d b.	0	0	1	2	1	0	0	0	0
McLinden, 1st b.	1	0	1	2	2	0	0	0	0
H. Grant, c. f.	0	0	1	2	2	0	0	0	0
McMillan, l. f.	1	0	1	2	2	0	0	0	0
J. Grant, p.	0	0	2	2	1	0	0	0	0
A. Austin, r. f.	0	1	1	1	2	0	0	0	0

Total No. runs, 5 3 10 15 16—49

GREELEY CLUB.

Innings	1	2	3	4	5	6	7	8	9
McFadden, c	1	0	0	0	0	0	0	0	0
Tippin, 1st b.	1	0	0	0	0	0	0	0	0
Lyon, l. f.	0	0	0	0	0	0	0	0	0
Cantrell, 3d b.	0	0	0	0	0	0	0	0	0
Wheeler, c. f.	0	0	0	0	0	0	0	0	0
Calvert, 2d b.	0	0	0	1	1	0	0	0	0
Blunt, p.	0	0	0	0	0	0	0	0	0
Fields, r. f.	0	0	0	1	0	0	0	0	0
Taylor, s. s.	0	0	0	0	0	0	0	0	0

Total No. runs, 2   2 1—5
Umpire—J. W. Mort.

C. Unusual 1877 box score summarizing runs per inning for each player. No scorer is listed, as was typical of later game summaries. Source: Garnett Journal, 14 July 1877.

Evolution and variation in early box scores designed to fit in newspaper columns. Continued on next page.

TOPEKA.

	A.B.	R.	1 B.	T.B.	P.O.	A.	E.
Miles, 3d b	4	0	1	1	2	1	0
Fowler, 2d b......	4	0	1	1	4	0	0
Fogarty, l. f......	4	0	0	0	0	0	0
Weaver, c.........	4	0	1	1	8	1	0
Butler, s. s........	4	0	0	0	2	6	3
Haddock, c. f....	3	1	0	0	1	0	0
Sullivan, 1st b...	4	0	0	0	10	0	0
Pettiford, p......	4	0	0	0	9	0	0
Fahey, r. f........	3	0	0	0	0	0	0
Totals..........	34	1	3	3	27	10	3

LEAVENWORTH.

	A.B.	R.	1 B.	T.B.	P.O.	A.	E.
Hall, c. f........	4	0	3	3	4	0	0
Cahill, 2d b......	4	0	1	1	1	1	1
Twineham, 3d b..	4	0	1	2	0	3	0
Hurley, r. f.......	4	0	0	0	0	0	1
Bohanan, c........	4	0	0	0	8	1	0
Pitsch, 1st b......	2	0	0	0	13	1	0
Snyder, l. f.......	3	0	1	1	11	0	0
Welch, s. s........	3	0	0	0	0	1	0
Hart, p..........	3	0	0	0	0	9	1
Totals..........	31	0	6	7	27	16	3

SUMMARY.

Runs earned—None.
Two-base hits—Twineham.
First base on errors—Topeka, 5; Leavenworth, 4.
Left on bases—Topeka, 7; Leavenworth, 6.
Passed balls—Bohanan, 2; Weaver, 2.
Wild pitch—Hart, 1.
Struck out—By Hart, 4; by Pettiford, 3.
Time of game—One hour and fifty-five minutes,
Umpire—Finning.

D. An 1886 box score for a game between two town teams that summarizes four types of offensive data (at bats, runs, hits, and total bases) and three types of defensive data (put outs, assists, and errors) for each player, along with other game details. Source: Topeka Daily Commonwealth, 6 May 1886.

TOPEKA WHITE SOX.

Players—	AB	R	H	P	A	E
Cole, lf....................	4	0	0	2	0	0
Murray, cf................	4	0	1	1	2	0
Downs, 2b................	4	0	1	2	4	1
Cooley, 1b................	4	0	0	14	0	0
Andrews, 3b............	4	0	0	2	1	1
Henry, c..................	3	1	1	6	1	0
Abbott, rf...............	2	1	1	2	0	0
Reagan, ss...............	2	0	1	0	3	1
Forrester, p.............	1	0	0	0	5	3
Howey, p.................	1	0	0	0	3	0
Blackburn	1	0	1	0	0	0
Total 30	30	2	6	27	20	6

CHICAGO WHITE SOX.

Players—	AB	R	H	P	A	E
Green, rf................	4	0	0	3	0	0
Vinson, lf...............	4	0	2	1	0	0
Hart, c..................	4	0	1	6	0	0
Isbell, 2b................	4	0	0	3	1	1
Dundon, ss..............	3	0	0	3	2	0
Clark, 3b................	3	0	1	0	1	1
Pennell, 1b..............	4	0	1	6	1	1
Welday, cf..............	4	0	0	2	0	0
Ruger, p.................	2	1	0	0	0	0
Patterson, p.............	2	0	0	0	3	0
Total 34	34	1	5	24	8	3

Topeka ....0 0 0 0 1 0 1 0 *—2
Chicago ....0 0 1 0 0 0 0 0 0—1
Summary: Two base hit—Murray. Sacrifice hits—Clark, Abbott, Reagan. Double play—Forrester to Henry to Cooley. Base hits—Off Ruger, 3; off Patterson, 3; off Forrester, 2; off Howey, 3. Struck out—By Ruger, 3; by Patterson, 2; by Howey, 1. Bases on balls—Off Forrester, 3; off Howey, 1. Passed ball—Henry. Umpire—Meyer. Attendance—700.

E. A 1906 box score for an exhibition game between the minor league Topeka White Sox and major league Chicago White Sox. The box score follows the typical format of the early 1900s. It is similar to the 1886 example but omits the total bases. However, it includes a line score, and the summary at the bottom begins to include more information about offensive and defensive data. Source: Topeka Daily Capital, 31 March 1906.

Trophies and Financial Rewards

With the increasing number of baseball clubs after the Civil War, a tournament was organized in Lawrence at the Kansas State Fair in September 1867, with the intention of diversifying the attractions. In the end, a fierce rivalry was born. After a series of games, the Kaw Valleys of Lawrence were proclaimed the state champions, and the team was awarded an engraved silver ball, which is now in the collection of the Kansas Museum of History in Topeka.[90] The rules of the NABBP called for losing teams in match games to surrender a leather-bound baseball to the winning team, so awarding a silver ball mimicked that practice.[91] In 1868 the Leavenworth Frontiers claimed the silver ball by default when the Kaw Valleys failed to arrive for the game to determine that year's champion, reportedly because the appointed day was stormy. However, the Lawrence team refused to surrender the trophy without a game being played.[92] The dispute dragged on for a year, until it was time to determine the following year's champion in the autumn of 1869. The championship trophy remained in Lawrence after the Kaw Valleys again defeated the Frontiers.[93] In fact, it was never relinquished by the city and remained in the possession of one of the early club members in Lawrence more than fifty years after it was first awarded (along with Haskell's bat).[94]

Silver balls were considered elite trophies awarded to early championship baseball teams, although the cost tended to limit their use to special occasions. Cash prizes (also referred to as premiums or purses) were

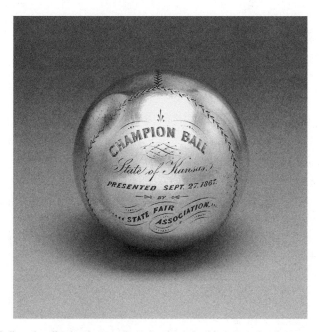

Silver baseball trophy offered to the state champion determined by games played among teams at the Kansas State Fair. The traveling trophy was awarded to the Kaw Valley Base Ball Club of Lawrence in 1867 and never relinquished by the team. Courtesy of the Kansas Historical Society, Topeka.

offered more frequently for special games at fairs or similar celebrations and might have been more appreciated by the players, who could all take a share of the money or use it to pay the team's expenses.[95] Yet silver trophies were still prized. Into the early 1900s, prior to the Great Depression, silver balls and bats (often in miniature) and silver cups, typically provided by local jewelers or other businessmen, were presented periodically to top teams or individuals.[96]

As club baseball was replaced by town team baseball, some of the town teams briefly continued the practice of early baseball clubs by issuing challenges to potential opponents through newspaper announcements, letters, or telegrams.[97] Likewise, through the 1880s, when a town team traveled by train to another town, the host team sometimes treated the visitors to a meal and possibly a dance in the evening. This practice declined as games became more numerous and rivalries intensified.[98] Still, the host team sometimes used a portion of the money from admission fees charged at the game to help pay the visiting team's travel expenses—what were sometimes referred to as team guarantees.[99] To encourage players to perform at their best, a split of gate receipts was also common, with 60 percent of the revenue awarded to the winning team and 40 percent to the losers. However, the Kansas Supreme Court ruled that this was a form of gambling.[100] Gambling among spectators and even players was widespread, but its full extent is difficult to gauge, given the lack of documentation.

Promoting the Town and Supporting the Team

As had happened with military units, town team baseball followed the settlers westward across the entire state. Baseball was not only one of the earliest forms of local entertainment in the days before radio and television, it was a social event that brought neighbors together during the summer, when the days were longer and the weather generally permitted leisure activities outdoors. Town teams composed of local players, especially in rural areas, generated loyalty among their neighbors and relatives, who were willing to support them through attendance at games and money to cover expenses. Railroads (and, later, electric trolleys) improved the opportunities for intercity competition, and railroad companies sometimes ran special trains or offered special fares for fans traveling from one town to another for ballgames.[101]

In many towns, the local baseball team was an important source of

Poster for an 1883 agricultural fair in Hays, Kansas. As major entertainment events in rural Kansas, fairs often included horse races, baseball games, and music, in addition to exhibits of agricultural products. The premium of $100 awarded to the champion of the baseball tournament was a substantial sum in 1883. Soldiers from nearby Fort Hays were to parade and participate in a "sham battle" during the fair. Courtesy of the Kansas Historical Society, Topeka.

community pride and unity, perhaps even a surrogate for the competition among towns vying for advantages in economic growth and prosperity.[102] This was perhaps more important in Kansas than in villages east of the Mississippi River, which had been founded much earlier and were already well established by the late 1800s as baseball became the national game.[103] Competition on the baseball diamond was certainly preferable to the violent clashes of the "county seat wars" that occurred in western Kansas from 1887 to 1893 between towns literally fighting each other to host the county offices, sometimes to the point that the state militia was dispatched to quell the violence.[104]

Local newspapers, whose accepted functions included overt boosterism, sometimes spearheaded the organization of town teams and encouraged local businesses to support them.[105] Although most newspapers mentioning baseball supported the sport as good publicity for their young towns, the support was not universal. Some newspapers provided little or no mention of local baseball teams or their games. A few were quite blunt in their condemnation of the sport, as evident in the sentiment expressed by a Junction City newspaper in 1870:

> Some fellow by the name of Sacket sends us a dead-head ticket to a Base Ball Tournament at Topeka, and wants us to publish a quarter of a column notice of him. If getting up such things is all Sacket has to do, he should be arrested as a vagrant. If we ever get to be King of this country, it will be difficult for us to determine who to hang first, base ballists or advertising agents.[106]

That "fellow" was O. Sackett, a newsagent in Topeka, who sold fruits and nuts in addition to newspapers. He also endeavored to be an active promoter of various theatrical and sports entertainments in eastern Kansas. A Lawrence newspaper described him as "incomparable, irrepressible, and invincible, and [he] will carry out whatever he undertakes." However, Sackett was apparently better at promising events than making appropriate arrangements to serve as agent for some of the prominent speakers, who refused to work through him. After failing at the lyceum business, he opened a "dime museum," first in Kansas City and then in Denver.[107] Sackett also did not receive permission to serve as the agent for the Shawnee BBC of Topeka, who disclaimed any relationship with him in area newspapers. However, he apparently did help arrange trips to Kansas in 1870 and 1871 by the Forest City BBC of Illinois, and tried unsuccessfully to arrange for the Cincinnati Red Stockings to visit the state.[108]

Despite the antipathy of some newspaper publishers, baseball thrived across the state, although town teams initially played relatively few games against their peers during the course of the summer. Travel by horse-drawn buggies or steam trains to other towns was a time-consuming venture for rural teams and their fans. In an extreme case, the Junction City baseball team lost a game 10–9 in Emporia and then returned home not on a passenger train, but on a freight train distributing railroad ties, which took fifteen hours to travel between the two towns, a distance of approximately sixty miles.[109] Limits on the number of games also were imposed by the fact that at least some, if not all, of the players on the early town teams were amateur sportsmen who worked in local businesses or on farms, which restricted the length of time and the days they could be gone to play baseball.[110]

In addition, the cost of the few pieces of equipment used in the early days—balls, bats, and a glove for the catcher—and the costs of uniforms were often beyond the personal means of the players on a town team, although the prices seem inexpensive by today's standards.[111] In July 1907, when a "genuine cast iron Natural Gas Range . . . with five lid burners, two double oven burners and pilot light" could be purchased for about $20.00, an advertisement for E. N. Woodruff and Company in Leavenworth announced that they were

Overstocked With Base Ball Uniforms And Have Marked All
$4.00 Suits $2.75
$3.00 Suits $2.25
$2.50 Suits $1.95
Boys' Suits 75c
$3.00 Base Ball Shoes $2.45.[112]

Construction and maintenance of a ball field and a grandstand would have been even more costly undertakings for towns that sought to support teams for the long term.

To raise money for expenses, the teams and their supporters relied on subscriptions (donations from local boosters), admission charges to games, and special fund-raisers, such as dances and talent shows.[113] In 1905 a merchant in Leavenworth sold tickets for $1 apiece in a raffle for a new two-passenger Cadillac automobile, which the winner could upgrade to a model with a back seat by paying $150. The raffle proceeds went to the local baseball association.[114] In 1909 proceeds from the opening night of "moving pictures and illustrated songs" at Larned's new Happy Hour Airdome (a theater enclosed on the sides but open to the sky) were donated to the town team. This was in addition to one Saturday's sales of cigars in the morning and sodas in the afternoon at a local drugstore, proceeds from one night each at two billiard and pool halls, proceeds from one evening at the local skating rink, and money earned through the team's sponsorship of a weeklong carnival.[115] In a precursor to modern marketing on sports clothing, new baseball uniforms for the Rossville town team were purchased by several local businesses, and the back of each uniform sported the name not of the player, but of one of the businesses that had donated money.[116]

Even baseball games were used as fund-raisers. "Muffin matches" had been played by inexperienced teams for pleasure and exercise in Kansas since the 1860s (*muff* referred to an error).[117] Soon, similar games featuring local men and women were used to raise money for their respective town teams and for other causes. For example, in what cynics might view as a contest between good and evil, the Wichita preachers scheduled a game against the Wichita lawyers for the benefit of the local hospital. The preachers practiced openly at the minor league ballpark, while the more competitive lawyers had "secret practice" at the corner of 15th and Market Streets.[118] Games between "fats and leans" were the most common pairing in benefit games. When weight limits were set, the two groups of players were generally distinguished as men weighing more than 200 pounds, on the one side, and less than 140 pounds on the other. As with the Wichita hospital in the game between the preachers and lawyers, most recipients of the funds raised at the ballgames were local, but in June 1889 teams of fats and leans in several Kansas towns donated the funds to victims of the devastating Johnstown flood in Pennsylvania.[119]

Sunday Baseball

In the days before night baseball, finding a time to play ballgames when the largest numbers of spectators could attend also presented a challenge. Initially, when games between teams from different towns were infrequent, they were sometimes played on weekday afternoons, and businesses were asked to close early to increase attendance, often through mutual consent, so no one would lose business to a competitor who remained open during the game.[120] As games became more frequent, they were increasingly played on Sunday afternoons, nestled between church services in the morning and evening. This was typically the only day of the week when businesses were not open and more people—both players and spectators—could enjoy leisure activities during daylight hours. A Hays newspaper noted in 1905, "People are enjoying these Sunday afternoons [at the ballgame], finding it a pleasant place to spend an hour, having no carriage to go riding in, while it lets the players forget their daily labor and exercise themselves."[121]

Views on baseball (and other sports) played on Sundays varied among the early residents of Kansas and elsewhere. Some people favored quiet rest, while others wanted to enjoy leisure activities such as baseball.[122] The connection between the day and the sport has a long history in the state. On May 17, 1868, Captain Albert Barnitz of the Seventh Cavalry wrote his wife, Jennie, from their encampment along Big Creek west of Fort Hays to say, "Have not been to church, because there was none to attend—but in lieu of this all the officers, including a half dozen from Fort Dodge, who were here on a visit, participated in a social game of base ball!"[123] While most people would not consider baseball an alternative to church, the Reverend S. E. Busser of Kinsley presented what local newspapers referred to as a Sunday evening ["discourse on the 'Moral Teachings of Base-ball'" or the "Religion of Baseball"] in June 1884. Reverend Busser also served as scorekeeper at a local baseball game.[124]

Yet the Puritan philosophy of engaging in rest rather than secular amusements on Sunday persisted, and there was strong sentiment into the early 1900s opposing any type of organized recreational activities on the Sabbath.[125] Some people considered baseball especially immoral. Referring to a "riot" associated with a Sunday baseball game in the town of Nebraska City along the Missouri River in southeastern Nebraska, an evangelist was quoted in a Kansas newspaper as saying, "Over ninety per cent of the people there either want saloons, gambling, Sunday ball-playing and the like, or are afraid to say anything against it."[126]

In Kansas, the general statutes of 1901 provided that "every person who shall be convicted of horse-racing, cock-fighting, or playing cards or game of any kind, on the first day of the week, commonly called Sunday, shall be deemed guilty of a misdemeanor, and fined not exceeding fifty dollars." Some prosecutors and other officials in the state considered baseball to be one of the banned activities. The law was originally passed by the "bogus legislature" of the Territory of Kansas in 1855, copied from an 1835 law in Missouri. The 1855 Kansas legislature was considered bogus by "free staters"—Kansas immigrants opposed to slavery—because large numbers of proslavery Missouri residents had crossed the border into Kansas to vote illegally. The Kansas law banning games on Sundays was repealed in 1859 (along with all other laws passed in 1855), but the ban on Sunday activities was reenacted in 1868.[127]

There were advocates both for and against the interpretation that applied this law to Sunday baseball. One member of the 1883 Atchison Blue Stockings played under a false name, as "it is said that his folks object to his playing on Sunday, and being a dutiful son he deceives them."[128] A Clay Center newspaper expressed ambivalence about the subject in 1895: "There is some talk of Sunday base ball in this town. Guess it won't hurt; our club cannot play good enough to break the Sabbath."[129] Rather than filing charges as a deterrent to Sunday baseball, the law was generally enforced, if at all, through attempts to prevent violations before they occurred.

In the autumn of 1903, Sunday baseball games were banned on the state-owned campus of the Western Branch of the State Normal School (teachers' college—the name taken from the French *école normale*; now Fort Hays State University) in Hays, which was established in 1902. Perhaps not surprisingly, the young students were undeterred, and in the spring of 1904 they were caught playing Sunday baseball on the adjacent Fort Hays Experiment Station property (now the Western Kansas Agricultural Research Center–Hays), which was also state property. That, too, was quickly banned by local administrators.[130] However, Sunday baseball in the city of Hays was still allowed, and a 2–0 victory in one such game in June 1904 by the Hays town team over the visiting team from Chapman (about 130 miles east by rail) was attended by more than 600 people, netting $125 in gate receipts, a sizable sum for the day.[131] In contrast, several players in Iola were charged that same year with violating the law by playing baseball on Sunday. However, the jury acquitted them because the state law did not specifically ban baseball.[132] Given these varied interpretations of the law across Kansas, resolution of the issue began its inevitable journey through the judicial system to the state supreme court in 1907.

It began when the Johnson County attorney filed a complaint in district court alleging that Ernest Prather "unlawfully and wilfully with divers other persons whose names are . . . unknown" played "a certain game, to wit, a game of baseball, the same being played with balls and a bat and with nine players on one side matched against nine players on the other side" on Sunday, July 14, 1907. Unlike the case in Iola three years earlier, Prather was convicted, and the case was eventually appealed to the Kansas Supreme Court. The state supreme court overturned the conviction in February 1909, ruling that the vague ban on "games of any kind" on Sundays would, if broadly interpreted, also "apply to every game—to authors, whist, chess, checkers, backgammon, and cribbage, even when played in the privacy of one's home." The word *game* in the context of the statute was interpreted as referring specifically to gambling, rather than purely athletic activities.[133] However, the sentiment against Sunday baseball persisted.[134]

Attempts were made to pass a state law that would specifically ban baseball on Sundays, and efforts to fight any such ban were equally vigorous.[135] Two years after the supreme court's ruling, 154 petitions either for or against a ban on Sunday baseball were submitted through the Kansas House of Representatives. By comparison, eighty-five petitions were submitted regarding women's suffrage, the other contentious topic of the day.[136] The effort to enact a ban on Sunday baseball in the state statutes failed, although similar bills continued to be introduced in subsequent years. On the other hand, the 1911 state legislature did approve an amendment to the state constitution providing women's suffrage in the state, and it was approved by voters in 1912, making Kansas the eighth state to do so.[137]

With no state law on the subject, the decision about permitting or prohibiting Sunday baseball rested with individual cities, where strong debate continued. As a result, baseball diamonds were sometimes placed beyond the city limits of towns officially opposed to Sunday baseball.[138] The city limits of Girard were even altered slightly to move the ball diamond on the edge of town outside the city to avoid the consequences of any potential municipal ban on Sunday baseball.[139] However, strong opposition in a town could still doom Sunday baseball through low attendance, as people opposed to Sunday sports stayed home.[140] In towns where baseball was not banned on Sundays, players sometimes refused to play except on weekdays.[141]

Intertwined decisions about how to fund teams and whether or not to play baseball on Sundays played a role in the short-term success of one of the premier independent town teams in Kansas prior to the Second World War. In 1919, I. O. "Ike" Sewell, a banker in Beloit, organized the Beloit Leaguers, a professional team that was arguably the state's best independent team. Despite the name, they were not part of any league. Organized to bring favorable attention to Beloit, the team's roster was drawn from young men returning from service during the First World War. Businessmen in Beloit supported the team through the Baseball Association, even arranging for the construction of a new ballpark christened Sewell Park. Larry Quigley, brother of well-known umpire and referee Ernie Quigley, served as the umpire for many of Beloit's home games until he had to return to his job at Kansas Wesleyan University in Salina that autumn. Before they had even established themselves as a premier baseball team, Sewell offered to pay any team that could defeat them $200. Few could claim the prize. The leaguers did not play games on Sundays, and they took a weeklong break in early July so the players could help with the local wheat harvest. Their season ran from June through October, and they compiled a record of 51–4 (plus one tie) against other independent teams. They closed the season by playing a series with the Western League (Class A) team from Omaha, Nebraska. Beloit's record against the Rourkes was 4–9. This was followed by a nine-game series with the Kansas City Blues of the American Association (Class AA), who won all but one of the nine games. The Baseball Association ended the year about $3,500 in debt, which was blamed on the cost of building the new ballpark and hosting the two minor league teams, which attracted few fans because of less than ideal autumn weather. Nonetheless, the decision was made to cover the debt and organize the team again in 1920.[142]

The Leaguers again played well, compiling a record of 71–24, including a record of 4–7 against the Kansas City Monarchs of the newly organized Negro National League. The Beloit Leaguers even made a trip west to play teams in northeastern Colorado. However, attendance at home games was less than expected, to the point that even women were encouraged to attend a meeting of the Baseball Association, where "equal suffrage" was promised. Operating the team was estimated to cost $1,800 to $2,000 per month, so increased gate receipts were essential to the team's viability. Late in the season, the decision was made to play Sunday games in an attempt to boost attendance. Encouragement for the team by local clergy early in the season gave way to a prayer meeting held as a protest against Sunday baseball "to keep Beloit from being advertised as a wide open town on the Lord's Day." Given the financial challenges of the team's first two years, the Baseball Association decided "home talent" would make up the Leaguers in 1921, and the players would earn their own pay as best they could from gate receipts or prizes. Games continued to be scheduled on Sunday afternoons, and attendance at home games was about the same as it had been during the previous year. However, the cost of operating the town team was much lower. As the members of the 1919 and 1920 Leaguers drifted away to play with other teams in Kansas and nearby states, Beloit was represented in 1922 by a strictly amateur team of local players, the least costly of their options for a town team.[143]

Having town teams that could not play the national pastime on Sundays presented a challenge in Kansas towns through the early 1900s. Lighted fields for night baseball did not arrive until the 1930s and 1940s, and businesses were open until early in the evening on the other six days of the week. That left little time in the evenings to play a full nine innings before it became too dark. Time spent traveling to another town would only add to the difficulties. Thus, some towns organized what were referred to as twilight leagues, composed of several teams within the town. Games typically were scheduled to start at about five or six o'clock in the evening and perhaps last fewer than nine innings. The late sunsets of summer aided in the completion of games, although they occasionally ended early when it became too dark to continue.[144]

Local businesses, civic groups, and churches typically sponsored the teams in twilight leagues, which were usually composed of white males, but not always.[145] For example, American Indians of Haskell Institute (a government boarding school) had a team in a Lawrence twilight league, and the Colored Giants played in an Osage City league.[146] Churches were sometimes the only team sponsors, and they saw the twilight leagues (sometimes referred to as Sunday school leagues) as a way to compete with—and possibly eliminate—Sunday baseball. They also saw the leagues as a way to increase attendance at Sunday school by requiring players to attend a certain number of Sundays to be eligible to play.[147] Players on church teams that played for another team on a Sunday could be banned from playing again on the church team.[148]

However, twilight leagues were essentially recreational leagues that typically offered a lower level of competition than provided by town teams, and strong competition was still of interest to large numbers of people in some towns. Teams that sought to play against opponents from other towns found it extremely difficult to avoid playing on Sundays, when they could potentially draw the largest crowds of paying fans to underwrite the team's expenses.[149] In Chanute, the African American team established in the 1890s had been playing intercity games on Sundays, but during a revival meeting in the winter of 1908–1909, "most of the ball players were converted" and chose to play no more baseball on Sundays. They reorganized and agreed to play only on weekdays.[150] It did not last, and there was no African American team in 1910. However, a new team was organized in 1911, and their first game at the local ballpark was a featured social event during Easter Sunday celebrations.[151] Sunday afternoon baseball games remained important social events in both African American and Mexican American communities through the early 1900s.[152]

Attempts were even made to organize a few Sunday-only leagues, although a team in Leavenworth was concerned it would have to compete for fans with two other teams in town that played on Sundays—one from the Soldiers Home at the fort and the other from the Catholic League.[153] When asked about Sunday baseball, Father Kelly responded,

> I would far rather have my boys out playing a clean game of baseball than out in the back yard shooting craps or doing something equally as sinful. I'm going to encourage the boys in this league and I am going to attend every game to show them that it is a good, pure thing for them to be doing. Church is always first and foremost, but . . . baseball come[s] next.[154]

On May 12, 1912, the minor league teams from Wichita and Topeka were invited to be "guests of honor at a special baseball service at the St. Paul's M. E. church" in Wichita. The Sunday service was attended by more than 300 baseball players from the two professional teams, plus several local amateur and semiprofessional teams, along with baseball fans. The talks that morning centered on a bold proposal for a "half holiday" to be set aside on a weekday across the United States that would allow baseball to be viable without playing games on Sundays. The manager of the Topeka team said baseball players would welcome the holiday, but without it, "baseball could not live without the Sunday games." After the services that Sunday afternoon, the two teams were scheduled to play a league game.[155] Fourteen years earlier, in August 1898, players from the minor league teams in these two cities had been arrested in Topeka for playing on a Sunday, although a jury acquitted them a few days later.[156]

Separate from the debates over Sunday baseball, city leagues were first discussed in Kansas during the closing years of the nineteenth century, when interest grew in baseball as a purely recreational activity. As with twilight leagues, various employers and organizations sponsored teams. Initially, the independent teams informally scheduled games among themselves. Formalizing these schedules as part of a city league was more efficient and provided for regular competition, with the added incentive of developing potential rivalries. Some of these teams, especially in larger cities, were sponsored by business owners, who began to see baseball teams as one way to improve employee morale, as much for the employer's benefit as for the employees'.[157] For example, the Cudahy Packing Company in Wichita sponsored both a white team and an African American team, and built its own baseball field with a grandstand.[158]

City leagues usually did not displace town teams or minor league teams, but they sometimes provided local baseball when these teams were absent. Competition among city league teams was even seen as a possible way to generate sufficient interest in the sport to later support a professional team.[159] City leagues were not organized solely in larger cities,[160] but some smaller towns preferred to organize intercity leagues among nearby communities, such as the "trolley leagues" composed of teams from towns connected by interurban rail lines in southeastern Kansas and southwestern Missouri. Similar leagues were organized in western Kansas along the Santa Fe Railroad and in "county leagues."[161]

Despite all the challenges confronting teams in the late 1800s and early 1900s, baseball remained the national pastime, and it continued to be played in many towns throughout Kansas, albeit sporadically. In the early years, teams were organized on a year-by-year basis. Sometimes teams were organized early in the spring and sometimes not until midsummer. The season could be delayed or interrupted by cold springtime temperatures, floods, or the absence of players and spectators when crops were being harvested. Some years, teams were not organized at all due to apathy or a major event, such as the absence of players who were serving in the military during the First World War.

While baseball persisted across the state, it assumed a variety of forms. In 1887 George Hancock of Chicago developed what was known initially as indoor ball, because it could be played indoors during inclement weather. This modified form of baseball involved a larger, softer ball and could be played on a smaller field. Through the early 1900s, the game evolved with myriad rules and various sizes of balls. The game was also referred to by names such as playground ball and kitten ball, but it was renamed softball in 1926, and that name gained wide acceptance during the 1930s.[162] The sport caught on slowly in most of Kansas, and early games were usually played indoors by men's teams during the winter at least as early as 1890.[163] An outdoor version of indoor ball was played under gaslight in 1905 between the host team from Concordia and the victorious Haskell Indians from the boarding school in Lawrence.[164] Three years later the first indoor baseball equipment exhibited in Emporia included lighter bats comparable to what a "10-year old-boy would use to play outdoor ball" and "official balls . . . in three sizes, the largest being three times the size of an ordinary Spaulding's [sic] outdoor ball."[165] In 1916 Spalding's sold indoor balls that were ten, fourteen, and seventeen inches in circumference (for comparison, modern softballs for adults have a circumference of twelve inches, and a baseball is nine inches).[166] The larger ball did not travel as far when hit, and it was easier to see in the evening, especially in games played under the dim lights used in the early 1900s.[167] Softball presented a challenge to baseball, primarily to the recreational city leagues (as noted in chapter 9), and it became an important feature of some Mexican American communities (the topic of chapter 5). However, much of the variety of early baseball was founded not on the sizes of the balls, but on cultural prejudices prevalent at the time.

CHAPTER 2

Hometown Women's Teams and Barnstorming Bloomer Girls

In the late 1800s exercise was encouraged not just for men but also for women, especially at colleges, although competition was often deemphasized for women.[1] Initially, tennis and basketball were considered suitable sports for women as participants, while baseball was generally viewed as overly strenuous and contrary to Victorian expectations of appropriate behavior by ladies. However, women were often encouraged, in the form of lower ticket prices or free admission, especially on scheduled ladies' days, to attend men's baseball games. Their presence at the game was meant to lend respectability to the sport and to subdue the often rowdy behavior of the male spectators. Gate receipts were also on the minds of team officials, and women typically were admitted free or at discounted prices only if accompanied by a paying male fan.[2] Nonetheless, American women and girls played baseball as early as the 1850s, although they were often ridiculed for doing so.[3]

College Intramural Teams

Among the better-known teams in the mid-1800s were those organized at colleges. In 1866 Vassar College, a school for women in Poughkeepsie, New York, apparently was the first college to have intramural women's baseball teams. Baseball games held on the campus of a women's college, where male spectators were not allowed, made it possible to avoid some of the protests against women playing baseball that likely would have been much more vehement if the games had been open to the public. The number of teams at women's colleges in the northeastern states increased through the late 1800s, but Victorian stereotypes persisted and diminished this activity.[4]

What began at women's colleges in the East spread to colleges in the West, including coeducational schools in Kansas, where women occasionally played intramural games. Most of the earliest teams were organized at colleges founded by churches, not the public schools. Perhaps the first college women's teams in the state were organized at Washburn College (now Washburn University) in Topeka in February 1886. The college had admitted women and minorities since its founding as Lincoln College by members of the Congregational Church in 1865. Two decades later, "the young ladies have organized themselves into two baseball clubs, Miss Bowles commanding one and Miss Boltwood the other. The shrill cry of 'put 'er home' may be heard most every pleasant afternoon."[5]

In 1894 a "ladies' base ball club" was reportedly organized at Ottawa University, a Baptist institution founded in cooperation with the Ottawa Tribe in 1865. Three years later, "an exciting event promised" at the university's annual field day was "a young ladies' base ball game" played by "a bevy of eighteen pretty young college girls."[6] Haskell Institute, a boarding school for American Indians, also had a women's baseball team in 1894.[7] Near the end of the century teams were organized at the state's two Methodist colleges. In 1897 a baseball game was played in Baldwin City "between nines of young women from Baker university [founded in 1858] who were clothed in bloomers."[8] That contest was followed two years later, in April 1899, by a pair of teams composed of female students at Kansas Wesleyan College (now Kansas Wesleyan University) in Salina (founded in 1886). A "large crowd witnessed the game and the young ladies showed excellent training in the handling of the ball."[9]

Women at Kansas colleges, eventually including the public institutions, continued to play intramural baseball periodically as the calendar rolled into a new century. At the State Normal School (teachers' college; now Emporia State University) in Emporia, a large number of girls took up baseball in the spring of 1906, but apparently did not play in public.

The girls have organized baseball teams, and dressed in bloomers, were out in force to practice last night. The practice was conducted behind barred gates and a high board fence, with Normal guards perched on top to watch the game and keep the prying eyes of the curious town boys from the scene. There were enough girls . . . to make four baseball nines with a substitute or two for each team.[10]

Six years later there was again talk of organizing girls' teams at the school and forming a league if there was sufficient interest.[11] The school had been established in 1863, and the first graduating class in 1867 included two women.[12]

By 1911 women's collegiate baseball had made its way to Wichita:

The young women of Friends University, a Quaker institution, are organizing a couple of baseball teams and the maids, clad either in knickerbockers or skirts reaching only to their knees, are spending hours at practice. Never before have the girls of the college taken to the sport and the faculty of the staid old institution is at a loss as to how to regard it all. The girls[,] innocently enough, however, are planning class games and even games with outside schools if any other girls' teams can be found. Enough players for two full squads are practicing and some of the girls are showing surprisingly good form.[13]

Talk of forming a women's baseball league at the University of Kansas in 1913 had the support of the women's athletic director, and women's baseball arrived at the State Agricultural College (now Kansas State University) a few years later. Women's teams also formed occasionally at county normal institutes, where local teachers were trained.[14]

Women's baseball also made its way to the westernmost state college. Founded in 1902, the Western Branch of the State Normal School in Hays initially conformed to the prejudice favoring basketball over baseball as a team sport for women. In fact, the women's basketball team was the first athletic team organized at the school.[15] They sometimes traveled to neighboring towns with the men's baseball team and played an outdoor basketball game on the field before or after the baseball game.[16] The "young married ladies" of Hays also organized a basketball team—the Juno Ladies Basket Ball Club—in 1902.[17]

Men's baseball began at the school in 1903, and the "Normal School girls talk very seriously of organizing a base ball team. They have so many applications, that they agreed to have a few practice games . . . to decide who the best players are."[18] Nothing seems to have been sustained from this interest, but in 1914 female students fielded two intramural baseball

Women's basketball game at the Western Branch of the Kansas State Normal School (now Fort Hays State University) in Hays during the 1904–1905 academic year. The limestone building is the central section of what is now Picken Hall, the first building on campus. The women's basketball team sometimes played on the same athletic field immediately before or after the men's baseball game. Courtesy of the University Archives, Forsyth Library, Fort Hays State University, Hays.

teams, the Shamrocks and the White Sox.[19] In April of the following year, male students at the Normal School constructed a baseball diamond and tennis court for the female students to use.[20] The girls could play baseball among themselves, but not with the boys.

Independent Women's and Girls' Teams

Despite the association of early women's baseball in Kansas and elsewhere with colleges, independent baseball teams of local women predate them. The first independent women's teams were organized at least as early as 1873 in Wichita. The city was incorporated in 1870, and its first men's baseball club was organized in 1872, only one year before the first women's team.[21] Most women's teams were organized for the pleasure of playing, despite receiving little or no support from their community. For example, in 1889, one newspaper writer commented on high school girls in Newton playing baseball, stating that he "thought it was proven several years ago that female baseball playing was a physical impossibility."[22] On the other hand, women's teams that played for the benefit of a local project often would receive substantial community support. For example, two teams of "ladies" in Herington raised $101 in 1903 for the public library fund by playing a five-inning game "in the presence of 500 admiring spectators" who were "astounded" by their skills.[23]

In some cases, the brief newspaper accounts of teams of female players between 1873 and 1906 make it difficult to determine whether the players were girls or young women, being variously referred to as "females," "girls," or "ladies," just as teams of young men were often referred to as "boys." Though not universally, newspapers tended to refer to unmarried players as "girls" and married players as "ladies" or "women." These accounts rarely provided summaries of any games, and box scores were virtually unheard of. The organization of a women's team, not the game itself, was considered the principal news story.[24]

Intercity baseball games for women's teams were rare in Kansas. In 1902 in Atchison, a team of African American "girls" was organized, who would have been doubly challenged to find opponents given the racial and sexual prejudices of their time. They confronted the challenge by scheduling their first game against local African American men over fifty years of age.[25] Most early women's baseball teams followed the more typical route to avoid cultural biases against women's baseball—having enough players to field two nines.

An early attempt at an intercity game between women's teams occurred in central Kansas in July 1889. Two nines were organized in McPherson, and in August they "played an interesting game . . . in which some of them used considerable skill in manipulating the ball and bat." That same month, an apparently unsuccessful attempt was made to arrange a game between the McPherson and Marion women's baseball teams at Chingawasa Springs, a short-lived spa. However, nearly twenty years later, a women's team in McPherson did get to play an intercity baseball game.[26]

On May 4, 1907, residents of the small town of Windom in McPherson County attended a baseball game between the "Windom ladies and the school girls." The schoolgirls won 26–21. The local newspaper even published a photograph of the two teams, each team wearing uniform outfits of headscarves and cumbersome-looking dresses that reached to the ground. The novelty of female baseball teams is evident in the fact that the newspaper offered this picture as a souvenir postcard for 5¢ through the rest of the summer. At the time, the Windom boys' team had not been enjoying much success. That May the Windom boys defeated Conway 18–11 for their first victory in three years. Meanwhile, the Windom

FAIRIES

		P.O.	Scor	Left on bases
8	Mrs. L. C. McMurray	3	0	0
5	Mrs. J. Grattan	1	2	0
1	Mrs. Dallas McMurray	2	1	0
4	Miss Mary Bridgeman	1	2	0
9	Miss Ina Haight	1	0	1
6	Miss Gladys Hapgood	0	0	2
3	Miss Lottie Brubaker	0	1	0
7	Mrs. Bomberger	0	1	0

Bench—Mrs. Heithecker.

BONBONS

		P.O.	Scor	Left on base
1	Mrs. Hayes	0	3	0
8	Frances Hensmyer	0	1	0
3	Mrs. Ragland	2	0	1
4	Mrs. Harry Hapgood	1	1	1
7	Miss Bertha Haberlein	3	0	0
6	Miss Mayme Coons	1	1	0
9	Miss Mar. Bridgeman	0	1	0
5	Miss Bes Bridgeman	1	0	0

Bench—Mrs. Geo Steel and Miss Clara Colline.

Fred McMurray caught for both sides and Chester Nelson umpired a good game.

Newspaper box scores for women's games were almost unheard of in Kansas. This 1906 box score summarizes put outs and runs, and includes an unusual column for "left on bases." This might refer to the number of baserunners who did not score when that person batted, but based on the accompanying description of the game, its meaning here is unclear. The numbers to the left of the players' names refer to their positions on the field (1 = pitcher, 2 = catcher, 3 = first base, 4 = second base, 5 = third base, 6 = shortstop, 7 = left field, 8 = center field, and 9 = right field). Given that a man caught for both teams, they apparently used a female "designated hitter" to bat for the catcher. Note that the married women were listed under their husbands' first names (or no first name).
Source: McPherson Daily Republican, 9 August 1906.

schoolgirls disbanded their baseball team after the game, but the ladies intended to continue playing after reportedly receiving challenges from teams in Castle Hill, Little River, Marquette, and Wheatland. However, the intercity game that received the most press coverage was between the Windom ladies, outfitted in their long red dresses, and a McPherson women's team in July. Windom easily defeated McPherson 40–3 in seven innings. For their efforts, Windom received the winner's share of 50 percent of the gate receipts, McPherson 40 percent, and the McPherson fairgrounds 10 percent for the use of their baseball field. A portion of the proceeds awarded to the McPherson team was donated to the city's band.[27]

Of course, a baseball game involved more than just players. Although mention of early female umpires in Kansas newspapers was even rarer than the mention of women's games, in 1908 the first game of the newly organized West Side Girls' Baseball Club of Wichita was reported as "as good an exhibition of the sport as is often given by some of the boys' amateur teams. The features of the game were the pitching of Esther Welsh and the umpiring of Nancy Chance."[28]

The continued resistance to even organizing female baseball teams was evident in 1908, when rumors spread that the Independence Shamrocks "young ladies" team was quietly being organized. "If the Shamrocks had been a man's organization, why, the plans of the club would have been heralded . . . before maturity." The organizational meeting had been announced in the newspaper only two days earlier simply as an attempt to form "a Shamrock Club," with no mention of baseball. Nonetheless, the Shamrocks did organize, and the newspaper published the names of the club's officers and the team's roster with their positions, but nothing about any games.[29]

And then came 1911. That was the year the Kansas legislature approved an amendment to the state constitution providing for women's suffrage— the right to vote in statewide elections. Similar proposals had failed in 1867 and 1894; however, from the first days of Kansas statehood in 1861, women could vote in district school elections, and they gained the right to vote in municipal elections in 1887. On the third attempt for statewide women's suffrage initiated in 1911, male voters approved the constitutional amendment in the 1912 election, making Kansas the eighth state to address this injustice.[30] It was during the campaign actively waged for approval of the women's suffrage amendment that Kansas apparently had its first informal women's baseball league. There is no evidence that the young women were making a political statement by organizing their teams as the vote loomed for the amendment. Apparently, they did it simply for the fun of playing baseball.

In Pottawatomie County, northwest of Topeka, teams of young women were organized in five towns—Belvue, Louisville, Onaga, Wamego, and Westmoreland. There were also rumors of women's teams organizing in Blaine, Pleasant Hill, and Saint George, but there are no known reports of games involving teams from these villages.[31] According to the US census in 1910, Wamego was the largest town in this rural county, with 1,714 residents. Other towns included in the census that year were Louisville (246), Onaga (759), Saint Marys (1,397), and Westmoreland (484). There were also several villages in the county not specifically mentioned. For example, Belvue was not included in the federal census until 1920. Saint Marys, the second-largest town in the county, was the only one listed in the census that did not organize a women's baseball team in 1911.

Pottawatomie County was a hotbed of baseball that summer. A dozen town teams of white males were organized, some with second nines, who also played rivals in the county. In addition, the first nines played teams from other counties, including an African American team from Frankfort in neighboring Marshall County. There were also several benefit games (muffin games) featuring teams of men who were not playing on the town teams, as was common in the early days of baseball. A newspaper in Westmoreland, the county seat, published the win–loss records for all the town teams each week, although there was no formal league.[32] Unlike most newspapers in the state up to that time, several Pottawatomie County newspapers also covered their women's baseball teams, which had an informal arrangement of intercity competition similar to that of the men's teams.

For the women of Pottawatomie County, playing baseball in 1911 began when a team of "unmarried girls" from Wamego was organized to play a team of "married young women" to raise funds for iron benches to be used at the city park during the town's annual Fall Festival in September. Almost 500 spectators attended the benefit game on July 1, which began at six thirty in the evening and ended after four innings because of darkness. Most of the players wore bloomers, which were "just as natty as the players were nifty in handling the bat, glove and ball." The base paths were shortened by five feet. It was not specifically mentioned whether the ball was pitched overhand or underhand, but a later article mentioned a rumor that a pitcher for Westmoreland "shoots in curves that would confuse any old league professional." Wamego's unmarried girls defeated the married young women either 13–12 or 14–12, depending on the report.[33]

During the next two weeks, the women put in "considerable practice" for a rematch on July 14. A local newspaper advertised the game under the banner, "Did You Ever See Women Play Base Ball?" The unmarried girls were again victorious 15–12 or 15–13. This game lasted five innings and attracted "the largest crowd that ever went to the City Park to witness a ball game," estimated at more than 600 people. The parks board provided concessions, and the Wamego band provided music. The offensive highlight of the second game was provided by Bulah Axtell, who "hit a long fly to left field that was lost in the crowd" for a home run. It "set the six hundred fans wild, and . . . will never cease to be the important topic when base ball affairs are being discussed here." The women's baseball teams raised $136 that summer for the park benches (equivalent to more than $3,000 in 2016).[34] What was perhaps not anticipated, however, was that the team of unmarried girls would continue to play through late September as other teams in the county were organized.[35] "Some how or other the people like to see the ladies play the national game, and since Wamego has made a start in this direction other neighboring towns are organizing teams."[36]

The women's team in Louisville began practicing on July 10, after the first game in Wamego was featured in local newspapers. They played the Wamego team in the county's first intercity women's baseball game of 1911 on July 21. A Wamego newspaper ran a large advertisement for the game and predicted that attendance would "tax the holding capacity of the park." Once again, more than 600 fans attended the game, including numerous supporters traveling from Louisville. As was often the practice at baseball games during this period, Wamego won the game and claimed the winner's 60 percent share of the gate receipts, which exceeded $50. The two teams played a return game in Louisville on July 28.[37]

As the second game between Wamego and Louisville was being arranged, a team "composed of several of the young ladies and a few of the younger married ladies" of Onaga was organized. The "ladies are putting in considerable practice[;] in fact, they are practicing every evening on the ball grounds."[38] At the same time, Westmoreland "girls and some of the married women" also practiced baseball every evening and talked of "organizing two teams [to] make some money for the fall festival fund."

On August 5, the Westy girls defeated their married counterparts 26–1. The married women had only eight players, so they were allowed to have one man on the team.[39] The Belvue women's team was organized in late August and played in only two games. They hosted the team from Louisville on August 29 and played a return game in Louisville on September 1. Although they played only briefly, the community supported their efforts. Between forty and fifty people from Belvue traveled to Louisville "to cheer their girls." Belvue and Louisville split their two games but did not play a tiebreaker.[40] Similarly, Onaga played only two games with Wamego in September, despite being organized in July.[41]

Studio photographs of the Wamego, Onaga, and Westmoreland teams posing with their bats, gloves, and balls were published in the *Topeka Daily Capital*, one each month in August, September, and October.[42] The photograph of the Wamego team was first printed in a large advertisement in the *Wamego Reporter* for the game against Westmoreland. The photograph of the Onaga team first appeared in the *Onaga Herald*.[43] In the photographs, most of the women wore what look like high school uniforms for physical education or similar activities (one of the Onaga players has "OHS" across the front of her jersey).

Newspapers in towns that fielded these women's teams published summaries of several games, along with the names of the players, which was often not done for teams of white males. The highest attendance reported at the games was an estimated 700 spectators at a game in Wamego won by the visitors from Westmoreland.[44] The games were usually played in the evenings and typically lasted three to five innings, with darkness ending at least some of the games.[45] Although the games were shorter, the women played hard and took them seriously. The umpire at some of the Wamego games, Dr. M. D. Hill, "was entirely surrounded by the ladies and his gentle voice was drowned by the rapid fire objections" to some of his calls. Jennie McCabe, the pitcher for Onaga, was injured sliding into third base, "and the aid of a physician was necessary," although she had recovered from her unspecified injury by the following day.[46] Despite a rain shower during a game between Wamego and Louisville, the women continued to play until it became too dark. "The girls certainly have the grit. They took no notice to the rain and played as long as they could see."[47]

The women on these baseball teams also displayed their independence away from the ball diamond. In 1911, travel from one town to another—and life in general—moved at a more leisurely pace than we are accus-

Onaga girls' baseball team wearing athletic uniforms and posing with their baseball equipment. Onaga was one of five towns in Pottawatomie County to have a girls' baseball team that played home-and-home games against each other during the summer of 1911. The teams were well supported by their local communities and received substantial positive coverage in local newspapers, contrary to what was typical of the day. Photographs of the teams from Onaga, Wamego, and Westmoreland were published with their stories in a Topeka newspaper and picked up by newspapers across the country. Courtesy of the Kansas Historical Society, Topeka.

tomed to a century later, which partly reflected the quality of the unpaved roads and the vehicles available at the time. Thus, on some of their trips through the county, the women's teams would spend the night on the road, but not in hotels or similar accommodations. Instead, they camped at city parks in the company of a chaperone, usually a married woman. Such excursions were becoming more common among groups of young women. The Louisville team even enjoyed a weeklong camping trip at Moodyville, established in 1882 as a park and health spa associated with mineralized springs, although by 1910 the population of Moodyville was only thirty-three people. During this outing, the Louisville girls traveled the four miles into Westmoreland for a game.[48]

Westmoreland claimed the county title at the end of August after defeating Louisville and Wamego twice each with no losses.[49] However, Wamego and Onaga played a pair of games in September. Wamego defeated Onaga

13–10 at the Onaga Stock Show and Carnival on September 8. Men's teams also played three games at the carnival, but the local newspaper reported that the women offered "the most interesting game of the series, and the most successful one in point of attendance."[50] Onaga returned the favor on September 27 by playing at the Wamego Fall Festival, the community celebration that had prompted the Wamego women to organize their baseball teams nearly three months earlier. Wamego won another close game 4–2.[51] It was a fitting end to the season, and it was the final game for the women's teams of Pottawatomie County. None of the teams reorganized the following year. The final records for the five teams in their intercity games were:

Westmoreland	4–0
Wamego	4–2
Belvue	1–1
Louisville	1–5
Onaga	0–2

In retrospect, what was important about the events of these three months in Pottawatomie County during the summer of 1911 was not the number of innings played or the distances between the bases. It was the fact that these five teams of young women—town teams—enjoyed a season of intercity competition on the ball diamond with the general support of their communities at a time when their peers throughout Kansas generally endured ridicule and were fortunate to play games among the members of their own group.

Although the women's teams in Pottawatomie County did not reorganize after 1911, baseball continued for girls and young women in the state. Baseball games between girls' teams were sometimes part of "field day" activities sponsored by schools near the end of the academic year. Perhaps the most inclusive such event was the Hodgeman County field day in Jetmore in May 1912. The first baseball game featured two girls' teams and "caused even more excitement among old fans than the boys' game which came later"—a boys' game that matched a white team against an African American team.[52] During the First World War, a youth "playground league" in Wichita offered numerous forms of recreation, including boys' and girls' baseball (probably some form of softball), and more than once a girls' team defeated a boys' team.[53]

As with men's teams, some intramural women's teams were organized through their employers. For example, in Topeka, clerks from the Mills' [Department] Store played a game in 1905, with both teams using men as pitchers and catchers.[54] Fourteen years later, another game in Topeka was the featured event at a summer picnic for the women of the local telephone company. The women worked in shifts so that each of them could spend time at the park. Included in the newspaper article were the names of the players and their positions on the two teams, apparently organized according to the women's respective roles as switchboard operators—the Toll Players and the Locals. The score "was kept a secret" because the two men serving as umpire and scorekeeper were biased toward certain players. However, the women took the game seriously. As a result, the "umpire's decisions were frequently reversed after a session with a group of disgruntled players on one side or the other." The newspaper reporter concluded, "the fact is that the two teams showed excellent form [and] played fine baseball in most instances."[55]

Women's baseball teams representing Kansas towns continued to play here and there through the 1920s and 1930s.[56] In Smolan, a small town southwest of Salina, the girls had uniforms and "can play real baseball," even beating the Smolan boys' team in 1921.[57] Although nothing apparently came from it, a call for boys ten to fifteen years old to participate in a Hays baseball league in 1930 even included the following offer of integration—"the call for boys does not mean the girls are to be slighted in the sport for all girls who wish to play are to be given an opportunity."[58]

Barnstorming Bloomer Girls

The most widely known female baseball teams of the late 1800s and early 1900s were the various barnstorming teams originally referred to as "bloomer girls," named for the uniforms worn by early teams. Several women's barnstorming teams traveled through Kansas to play local men's teams, and they perhaps stimulated the organization of some of the local women's teams. The first team known to have toured the eastern part of the state was the Young Ladies Base Ball Club in November 1885. They traveled in their own railcar with a canvas fence and a covered grandstand that reportedly could hold 1,000 spectators. The women would play a local men's team in the afternoon and perform a "grand military drill" indoors during the evening. Newspapers that glowingly promoted the event in advance panned it afterward because of the women's poor baseball skills.[59]

Two more teams of female players toured Kansas in 1892. In July and October, a Denver "Ladies Aggregation" also traveled in a special railcar and was similarly panned in newspapers for their limited baseball skills.[60] In August and September, the New York Champion Ladies Base Ball Club, featuring ten women players accompanied by a female brass band, toured the state.[61] A game played against a Wichita men's team—the Maroons— was attended by an estimated 1,500 spectators. The newspaper account was less than generous and illustrates what female baseball players some-times endured from the press and the fans:

> Instead of seeing that charmingly beautiful model of femininity rep-resented on the lithographs, they saw a lot of little sunburnt women, ranging in ages from 16 to 30 years. It is customary to say all who wear skirts are handsome; but the line ought to be drawn somewhere. They would probably be handsomer under different circumstances, but it is hardly expected that any base ball girl would be handsome after a base ball season. What they lacked in beauty they made up in development and as they appeared on the grounds in abbreviated skirts the church deacon shook his head and wondered what in the mischief the world was coming to. . . . Miss Gorman, the pitcher for the female nine, was actually a good player for a woman, and the girl who stood at third was a good thrower. The catcher could neither catch the cholera or a bad cold, and as for balls she could not catch them with a bushel basket.[62]

The local newspaper reported that the fans actually "went to the grounds for the novelty of the affair. . . . Everyone was in a good humor and from a standpoint of amusement and light spiritedness it was a success."[63]

In the summer of 1898 one of the better-known women's barnstorming teams, the Boston Bloomer Girls, toured Kansas and Oklahoma. The team had spent the winter in Texas and started making plans to come north in February, when the team's manager, W. P. Needham, contacted baseball managers in various towns to ask about possible games that summer.[64] Games in Kansas began in mid-June. The team traveled in their own Pullman Palace Sleeping Car, which was given the popular lucky number 4-11-44.[65] The railcar was attached to various trains and dropped at rail sidings as they traveled from town to town. Like some of their predeces-sors, they carried a canvas fence (twelve feet tall), which could be erected around the ball grounds to limit the audience to paying customers. If the town lacked a grandstand—and many did—the Boston Bloomers could provide one.[66]

However, local communities did not always welcome the team, and some newspapers ridiculed the games. When newspaper accounts were decidedly negative they were usually premeditated tirades about the inability of a women's team to match a men's team in baseball skills.[67] Some newspapers even refused to consider the possibility or appropriateness of women playing baseball. "The Boston Bloomers, a base ball club composed of girls wearing bloomers, are touring Kansas, and thanks to the intelligence and good sense of Kansas people, are meeting with a cold reception everywhere."[68] Contrary to the newspaper's assertion, this sentiment was not universal. Other newspapers expressed positive views for some aspects of the Bloomer games, though the descriptions were sometimes overtly sexist or even rude in the extreme with regard to their descriptions of the women's appearance. One newspaper referred to the women ballplayers as the "flotsam and jetsam aggregation of blonds and brunettes, known to the credulous people of western cities as The Boston Bloomer Girls."[69]

The dichotomy of opinions about the Boston Bloomers specifically and women's baseball teams in general is evident in two Lawrence newspaper reports of the same game in June 1898. The *Lawrence Daily Journal* reported, "Just one street car load of boys went over to Bismarck grove to witness the ball exhibition between the 'Boston Bloomers' and a team of Lawrence boys. There wasn't anything exciting about the game, which was won by the Lawrence players."[70] Conversely, the *Lawrence Daily World* reported,

The game of base ball yesterday between the Boston Bloomers and a local nine was an interesting game. The home boys played the best they knew how but only succeeded in giving the girls practice. . . . Otis Erp did excellent work as pitcher and scored the only run that was made [for Lawrence]. . . . The girls played excellent ball and made scores every time they felt like running. There was a crowd of several hundred present."[71]

The fact that the two accounts differed with regard to attendance and who won the game suggests that one or both reports were obtained secondhand (or worse) from unreliably biased observers.

Like most of the later women's barnstorming teams, the Boston Bloomers who toured Kansas in 1898 (and again in the spring and autumn of 1901) fielded two or three men—toppers—sometimes dressed to match their female counterparts. However, the male catcher for the Boston Bloomers in 1898 wore a traditional baseball uniform.[72] Among the women reported to be on the 1898 Boston Bloomers team touring Kansas was Maud Nelson (spelled as Neilson and listed as Maud Wilson in a Wichita newspaper).[73] She was one of the most renowned female baseball players of the era, noted for her skills as a pitcher. She was born in northern Italy, perhaps in 1881, and christened Clementina Brida.[74] It is unknown why she played under the name Maud Nelson. A person going by that name had played second base on the New York Champion Ladies Base Ball Club in Kansas in September 1892, before Clementina became a well-known player.[75] If not the same Maud Nelson, perhaps she was a mentor or was otherwise known to young Clementina.

Maud Nelson first pitched for the Boston Bloomers in 1897, and she pitched for other teams until her last game on the mound in 1922. She married twice, first to John Olsen and, after his death, to Constante Dellacqua. Alone and in partnership with both husbands, she became a successful owner and manager of female baseball teams into the 1930s, including the Western Bloomer Girls (with John) and the All-Star Ranger Girls (with Constante). Maud died at her home near Chicago's venerable Wrigley Field in 1944.[76]

On the 1898 trip through Kansas, early in Maud's professional career with the Boston Bloomers, a Leavenworth newspaper wrote about her pitching performance and the various attitudes to which she was exposed:

> Maud was announced on the score cards as the pitcher. She showed the locals that she had things up in her sleeve, which they could not hit—a mixture of "drops," "in-shoots" and "out curves," in addition to great speed. Maud did not possess the symmetrical outlines of a Venus and it did not take long for the 33 degree "fans" on hand to yell out: "She's a man, she's a man." Maud was not disconcerted by this clamor, however, and continued to push 'em over the "pan" with accuracy. While she was waiting for the catcher to return the ball after her delivery, she chewed gum with a girlish nonchalance, and as one of the devotees remarked: "She's O.K., whether she's a man or a woman." The local ball players, who tried in vain to connect with her "benderinos," swore that Maud

was a man, but their opinion on the subject was biased, of course, and did not carry much weight.[77]

A Wichita newspaper also complimented the pitching of "Maud Wilson," which was the "feature of the game" as she sent "the leather whizzing by the batsman." Although she surrendered several hits, Maud got her revenge on some of the Wichita hitters "by seeing them swat the ambient atmosphere three times in vain efforts to find the ball."[78]

Kansas also had its own traveling bloomer baseball team. The National Bloomer Girls was a barnstorming team based in Kansas City, Kansas. A game between the National Bloomer Girls and the men's town team in Hays in the autumn of 1906 featured a topper recently recruited from the town team in nearby Ness City—a young Howard "Smoky Joe" Wood. He was soon a pitching sensation in the major leagues with the Boston Red Sox (1908–1915), winning thirty-four games (including ten shutouts) in 1912, tops in the American League that year.[79]

A long list of touring women's baseball teams—the American Bloomer Girls of Boston, Boston Bloomer Girls, Federal Bloomer Girls (Kansas City, Missouri), National Bloomer Girls (Kansas City, Kansas), New York Bloomer Girls, Saint Louis Bloomer Girls (an African American team), Star Bloomer Girls of Chicago, Star Bloomer Girls of Detroit, Western Bloomer Girls, and others—continued to play periodically in Kansas into the 1930s, with a few teams having as many as six or seven men on the field.[80]

Some people viewed the bloomers as con artists simply out to fleece gullible people, and a few teams might have been less than scrupulous. However, some women's barnstorming teams provided legitimate entertainment in communities of all sizes. After an 1898 Boston Bloomers game, a Fort Scott newspaper noted, "The score was—but no matter, no one kept a correct score and it made no difference, as all present simply wanted to see the game and cared not what the result was or in whose favor."[81] In 1901 the Boston Bloomer Girls even participated in a pair of weekend fund-raising games against male players from Arkansas City, in which each team donated 10 percent of their earnings to the family of Larkin "Curley" Herron. Herron, only twenty-one years old, had died a week earlier while pitching for the Arkansas City Grays against a team from Joplin, Missouri. He had recently suffered from typhoid fever and "recovered" only about two weeks prior to his death. Herron was the starting pitcher for the Grays, and while waiting for a foul ball to be retrieved in the eighth inning, with Arkansas City leading 4–1, he rested his hands on his knees, laid down next to the pitcher's box, and rolled over on his back. Two physicians treated him to no avail.[82]

As the novelty of watching teams with female players began to fade, the games received less press coverage, and the term *bloomer* was sometimes used in a derogatory manner when referring to the poor quality of men's teams.[83] Some bloomer teams experienced financial difficulties while touring and disbanded partway through the summer.[84]

Baseball was not a lucrative profession in the early 1900s, and players, as well as teams, sometimes fell on hard times. Such was the case for twenty-four-year-old "Miss Daisy Hoover, said to have been the best professional second baseman among women baseball players in the United States." She played several years for the Boston Bloomers, Saint Louis Stars (in 1908), and American Bloomers (in 1909), living for a time in Kansas City, Kansas. After returning to Kansas City at the close of the season in 1909, she became ill in October and "died destitute in the city hospital" in Kansas City, Missouri, on November 11. Although she had family in Navarre, Ohio, they did not claim her body. Consequently, Daisy was buried in a grave (now lost to development) in the local pauper's cemetery, which at the time was part of Union Cemetery, immediately south of the present upscale Crown Center neighborhood in Kansas City, Missouri.[85]

However, changes were under way for women and for baseball. On August 18, 1920, the Nineteenth Amendment to the US Constitution was ratified, granting women throughout the country the right to vote. During that same summer, the Western Bloomer Girls barnstorming baseball team toured Kansas in a Pullman railcar that carried lights for use during games played in the evening. In a Saturday doubleheader against the team from Parsons, the afternoon game was played with a standard baseball, but the evening game was played with the larger "indoor" ball (softball).[86] The same arrangement had occurred twelve years earlier in 1908 in Junction City, when indoor ball was still an uncommon event in Kansas and played mostly by men's teams indoors. As in Parsons, it was a touring bloomer girls' team that scheduled afternoon baseball games and an evening game to be played under arc lights with a larger indoor ball, which would be easier to see under the dim lights.[87]

As softball became more widespread between 1910 and 1940, determining whether women's baseball teams mentioned in Kansas newspapers were actually baseball teams or softball teams is sometimes difficult, made even more challenging because indoor balls came in multiple sizes. On the one hand, the view that women should not play any variant of baseball was softening, as increasing numbers of schools and churches in Kansas organized ball teams for young girls between 1910 and 1930. But Victorian sexism was not completely abolished, because girls' teams were being forced to switch from baseball to softball—a bias that persists today.[88] Florence Freeman, a young student at Holy Name School in Topeka in 1921, perhaps best expressed the changing circumstances. She wrote in the school column of the city newspaper (sounding a bit disappointed) that her baseball team of seventh- and eighth-grade girls had at first "played with a hard ball but the other schools refused to play us unless we used an indoor ball."[89]

CHAPTER 3

African American Baseball

Until Jackie Robinson became a member of the Brooklyn Dodgers organization in 1946 and 1947 (with the minor league Montreal Royals and the major league Dodgers), racial segregation had prevented African Americans from playing in organized baseball during the twentieth century. The same generally held true for town teams, although there were exceptions. This gave rise to numerous independent African American teams, as well as teams that played in several Negro Leagues established in the early 1900s.[1] Some of these teams also made barnstorming tours, during which they traveled extensively to generate extra income by playing teams of all races.

The Kansas City Monarchs is one of the best-known teams of the Negro Leagues. Robinson played for the Monarchs in 1945 before joining the Dodgers, and several other Monarchs players later joined teams in both the American and National Leagues. The Monarchs made their home across the border in Missouri, but they frequently barnstormed from that base across Kansas (and other states) from 1920 through the 1950s.[2] Viewed with retrospective fondness, people in several towns now proudly recall the games played on their ball fields by the Monarchs or Satchel Paige, their famous pitcher, who also played for other barnstorming teams. Sometimes the Monarchs played a local team, usually composed of white players, but they also played other barnstorming teams and league teams. One of the more unusual barnstorming teams with whom the Monarchs had a strong relationship was the House of David, usually composed of white men.

The House of David religious colony in Benton Harbor, Michigan, was founded in 1903. They engaged in several activities, including barnstorming baseball teams, to raise money and recruit members. The men were noted for the long hair and beards required of members. Although they did not play in Kansas until the late 1920s, the House of David fielded a team in 1914 composed solely of the colony's members. Later, other players, including Paige and former major league pitcher Grover Cleveland Alexander, were hired to play for the team (Alexander also managed the team). In 1934 the Kansas City Monarchs and House of David both played in the prestigious Denver Post Tournament. By a score of 2–1, the Monarchs lost the championship game to the House of David, behind pitcher Satchel Paige. By 1930 the colony had split into two factions that together fielded as many as four barnstorming baseball teams. The House of David stopped fielding a traveling team in 1936, while the City of David continued to do so through 1955, except during the Second World War.[3]

During the Great Depression, a David team sometimes toured alone and sometimes with the Kansas City Monarchs.[4] The professional arrangement benefited both teams financially. At a game in Wichita's new Lawrence Stadium in August 1934, an overflow crowd of 7,500 to 8,100 fans watched the Monarchs defeat the House of David 8–5. A month later they returned to Wichita, and Mildred "Babe" Didrikson pitched a scoreless first inning for the House of David in a game won by the Monarchs 7–6. Attendance at the second game was about 2,000.[5] Large crowds also attended games in smaller cities and towns. In Dodge City, with a population in 1930 of about 10,000 people, an estimated 3,500 spectators attended a game in 1933—said to be the largest crowd to ever attend a baseball game in the city—in which the House of David defeated the Monarchs 11–3.[6]

During the 1930s the Monarchs traveled with portable lights mounted on trucks for night games, a novelty at the time for most towns, and this attracted large numbers of spectators. They leased the lights to the House of David during the first part of the season, before the Monarchs began traveling. When the Monarchs hit the road later in the year, they traveled with their lights and often played against a David team in cities across Kansas and elsewhere.[7]

Kansas Town Teams

Although the Kansas City Monarchs are perhaps the best-known African American team that played on Kansas ball fields, numerous other

African American teams made their homes in Kansas towns, both large and small. They simply reside in the historical shadow of the Monarchs. The first African American baseball teams in the state were organized nearly as early as the first white clubs were established immediately after the US Civil War. In 1868, the Independent Base Ball Club of Leavenworth and the Union Base Ball Club of Lawrence played one game in each city.[8] The following year the African American teams of White Cloud and Highland played a match game.[9] The 1869 contest for the silver ball awarded to the Kansas baseball champion (described in chapter 1) began with the reigning champion Kaw Valley BBC of Lawrence—an all-white team—offering an open invitation to "all base ball organizations of the State" wanting to play for the championship at the State Fair to be held in Lawrence that autumn.[10] The first team to accept the challenge was the Union BBC of Lawrence. As reported in the *Daily Tribune*, "The Union ball club (colored) of this city have been the first to respond to the Kaw Valley club's challenge for a game during the State Fair. They have an undoubted right, under the fifteenth amendment, or civil rights bill, or some other new-fangled radical arrangement, to beat the Kaws, but whether the latter will accept the challenge remains to be seen."[11] The Kaw Valleys apparently did not respond to the challenge from the Unions and played only white teams to retain the trophy. A year later, another white club in Lawrence also declined a challenge from the Unions.[12]

Although early white clubs in Lawrence, the abolitionist city brutally victimized by Quantrill's Southern raiders in 1863, were disinclined to play their African American counterparts, teams in other Kansas towns seemed less troubled by such matches. In March 1870 the Crescent baseball team of Fort Scott, a white team, defeated an unnamed African American team in what was, perhaps, the first interracial baseball game between two town teams in the state. Although baseball championships are typically decided later in the summer or autumn, a second game between the two Fort Scott teams a few days after their March contest was to be played for "a ball and the championship." However, the game was canceled because the boys were "making snow forts" instead.[13] Four years later, in April 1874, the Fort Scott Colored Star Club defeated the white Clippers for the champion's ball.[14]

As the Colored Star Club was earning their local trophy ball, an African American baseball team was organized in Wichita,[15] and in June 1874,

The feathers of the [white] Douglas avenue nine [were] down. They were smoothed out by the club made up of the colored boys of the city, last Thursday, most gracefully and completely, the score standing twenty-eight to thirteen in favor of the subjects of civil rights. We now pit our colored nine against any club of the state, and Eldorado [sic] and Winfield had better put up or shut up.[16]

Instead, the white team from El Dorado played the Douglas Avenue nine in July, and the Wichita team lost again.[17] Also in 1874, the "colored athletes of Topeka . . . organized a base ball club, and as the evening shades approach they hie [hasten] to the practice grounds with sturdy feet and blistered hands, and without a murmur stop red-hot grounders with their swollen palms." The following year, a Topeka "colored club played a white one." The white team won 21–15.[18]

Among the numerous African American baseball teams organized in smaller towns was the long-standing Chanute Black Diamonds in southeastern Kansas.[19] The team's name was a term often used for coal at the time. As in Lawrence, the African American and white teams in Chanute typically did not play each other, but the "color line [was] dissolved" on the afternoon of August 28, 1904, when a white team from Lansing failed to show for a game with their counterparts in Chanute. To provide a baseball game for the already congregated fans (and to avoid losing the $80 in gate receipts), the Chanute Black Diamonds were asked to fill in. The Black Diamonds lost 2–1, probably because "the umpire helped" the white team, according to the white publishers of the local newspapers.[20] In 1911 the Chanute Browns briefly replaced the Black Diamonds, with former Black Diamond players on the roster. The Browns won a well-attended game in Chanute against the Saint Louis Bloomer Girls, an African American barnstorming team of five men and four women.[21] As their predecessors had done seven years earlier, the Chanute Browns also played a game against the Chanute "Whites," but this time the Browns won on a tie-breaking home run in the ninth inning.[22]

In nearby Iola, an African American team was organized in 1908 and christened the Go-Devils. Like the Black Diamonds, they played competitive baseball in the region through 1916, initially against other African American teams. However, in 1911 the Go-Devils played a five-game series with the white town team—the Iola White Sox—for the city

Ballplayers representing African American teams from several southeastern Kansas towns, possibly taken about 1912. The players standing second and fourth from the left are wearing different uniform styles representing the Iola Go-Devils. The player standing on the far right possibly represented the Paola Monarchs. The player sitting third from the left has "Y.C." on his jersey (possibly Yates Center). The only player identified is George Sweatt (standing third from the right), who played for both the Chanute Browns and the Iola Go-Devils. African American teams in Kansas were numerous, yet, as in the photograph, largely anonymous in the news media. Courtesy of the Allen County Historical Society, Iola.

championship. A partition was installed in the grandstand to segregate the fans, just as they were typically segregated in other public facilities. The Go-Devils's pitcher was hit in the head by a pitched ball in the opening game of a doubleheader, but managed to walk off the field. There were no batting helmets in those days, but he recovered sufficiently while the Go-Devils continued to bat in their half inning and was able to pitch the rest of the nine-inning game (earning the victory). He followed this feat by pitching all ten innings of the second game (taking the loss). The White Sox won the fifth and deciding game 1–0. The two evenly matched teams continued to play each other through 1915 (the White Sox became the Boosters in 1914), each enjoying time as the city champion. The relationship between the two teams progressed to the point that players from both teams joined together on an integrated team in October 1914 under team captain George Sweatt, an African American (covered in more detail later in the chapter). Referred to as the "Black-and-Tans," they defeated the Toronto, Kansas, town team. The following year the local newspaper referred to the Go-Devils and Boosters collectively as the "town teams" (plural), a designation usually applied only to the white team. After the First World War, the Go-Devils switched to "armory ball" (softball), but an African American baseball team was organized in the mid-1920s under the name Ramblers. They played several teams, mostly white teams, through the mid-1930s in Iola and nearby towns.[23]

Like the Go-Devils, the Ramblers had their turns as city champions. In October 1927 the Ramblers claimed the Iola city title by defeating the Modern Woodmen of America (MWA). The following year, three teams—the Ramblers, Register Printers (sponsored by the local newspaper), and MWA—met to discuss organizing a twilight league. The result of these discussions was a six-team league, but the Ramblers soon dropped out to continue playing ball on Sundays against a variety of opponents from Iola and elsewhere. In June, the Ramblers' pitcher and catcher even played for the white DeMolay team in the twilight league, helping them defeat the Register team.[24]

Three years later the Ramblers again joined five white teams in the Iola Twilight League for the 1931 season. The league was once again integrated, but the teams still were not. In addition, one of the league's umpires was Lewis "Ax" Grubbs, a former member of the Iola Go-Devils and Chanute Black Diamonds during the first two decades of the century. The Ramblers claimed first place in the second half of the season to earn a spot in the five-game series to determine the overall champion. After losing the first two games against the Register Printers, the Ramblers came back to win the final three games. The same two teams repeated their performance during the regular season in 1932 in a five-team league. However, the Ramblers picked up a sponsor that year, Van's Bakery, and played under that name. The Vans won the first game of the championship series, the Registers won the second game, and the third game was a 0–0 tie called on account of darkness. The Registers won game four, but game five was another scoreless tie. Game six went to the Vans to even the series 2–2 (plus 2 tied games). The Register Printers finally won the deciding game 3–0.[25] As with the Go-Devils and the White Sox/Boosters, the top African

American and white teams played competitive baseball. It would be the Ramblers' last trip to the league's championship series.

The following year, the Ramblers had a new sponsor, playing under the name Iola Theater Stars, with Ax Grubbs serving as their manager. The old-time baseballer also played on the infield. The geographical limit from which players on twilight league teams could be recruited was extended from five to eight miles as measured from the courthouse in Iola. Because that extension would not benefit the African American team, they were allowed to recruit up to three players from Humboldt, which sat just beyond the eight-mile limit. The Theater Stars again played their best baseball in the second half but lost the deciding game of the second-half championship 1–0. Their opponents had scored that run in the bottom of the fourth inning as darkness approached. The Stars tied the game in the top of the fifth inning, but the umpire then called the game on account of darkness, which meant the score reverted to the last full inning completed, leaving the Stars in second place. Not surprisingly, a "heated discussion followed," but the result stood.[26]

In 1934, the African American team was sponsored by Brigham Hardware and became the Brigham Ramblers. Segregated teams were still the rule in league contests. Attendance at the games dwindled in 1934, which was blamed on poor play, poor umpiring, frequent arguments, and unsportsmanlike behavior from the players. The Ramblers struggled to stay viable, but the team reorganized to finish the season. A pair of games between league all-stars chosen by the fans was played after the close of the regular season. Tom England of the Ramblers was chosen as the pitcher for one of the teams, and he was joined by teammate Edgar Flippin, resulting in one team being integrated for this special occasion.[27]

Troubles for the league continued, as they struggled to find sponsors for four teams in 1935, but the Brigham Ramblers returned. In a mid-July game, however, only three of their regular players were on hand at the beginning of a game. People from the stands were called upon to fill the remaining six positions, and the team was down 4–0 after the first inning. Three more regulars and their manager (an undersheriff detained by official duties) arrived in the third inning, and the Ramblers started their comeback. Harold Perkins, a "young Brigham fan taken from the sidelines as a replacement" at the start of the game, came to bat in the fifth inning with the bases loaded and Brigham down 4–3. Under the circumstances, no pinch hitter was available, which turned out to be fortunate for the Ramblers. Perkins sent a drive over the center fielder, who nearly caught it. Yet the ball continued its flight and "hid under a box car" while Perkins and his three teammates circled the bases. Brigham held on to win the game 7–5. Perkins continued to play occasionally for the Ramblers, but the team folded at the end of July, dropping the league to only three teams. The Iola Twilight League's run came to an end, and in 1937 the city joined the Southeastern Division of the Kansas Ban Johnson League (described in chapter 8).[28]

African American baseball teams were also organized in rural areas of western Kansas. Among these towns, Nicodemus was unique—and is now the home of the Nicodemus National Historic Site administered by the National Park Service. The town was founded in 1877 by former slaves and their families from Kentucky as part of the initial emigration from the South that expanded in what was known as the Kansas Exodus (or Exoduster movement) beginning in 1879. Kansas was an early destination of homesteaders in this exodus because it was strongly associated with John Brown and abolition in the years leading to the US Civil War. In 1886–1888, the community experienced a boom in anticipation of the railroad laying tracks and establishing a station in Nicodemus, which increased the numbers of both African American and white residents. During this boom, an integrated town team was organized in 1887 and named the Western Cyclone Baseball Club, after the local African American newspaper. Neither the baseball team nor the town's attempt to lure the railroad was particularly successful (the railroad ran a few miles to the south). Without the railroad, the population of Nicodemus quickly declined. The town persisted, however, and baseball teams composed of African American residents were organized periodically through the 1940s. They traveled extensively throughout northwestern Kansas and sometimes hosted teams from farther afield, such as the Kansas City Monarchs. In addition to the Cyclones, names for the town team included the Nicodemus Blues and Nicodemus Old Hickorys.[29] In recent years, the Nicodemus Blues II have played a vintage baseball game during the annual Homecoming-Emancipation Celebration, held on a weekend in late July or early August.

After the US Civil War, African American communities in Kansas towns of all sizes celebrated Emancipation Day, a commemoration that predated Abraham Lincoln's Emancipation Proclamation of January 1, 1863. Emancipation Day celebrations in the United States were initially held on August 1 to coincide with the anniversary of the abolition of

Nicodemus Blues baseball team in 1907. Nicodemus was founded in 1877 by former slaves and their families from Kentucky. Nicodemus played several teams in the region, which were often composed of white players. They also hosted the Kansas City Monarchs and other teams at their Emancipation Day celebrations on August 1. The celebration was first held in 1878 and continues as the annual Homecoming–Emancipation Celebration. The town is now home to the Nicodemus National Historic Site, administered by the National Park Service. Courtesy of the Graham County Historical Society, Hill City, and the Kansas Historical Society, Topeka.

slavery in the British West Indies in 1834. After the Civil War, some towns changed the date of Emancipation Day to coincide with the preliminary announcement of Lincoln's Emancipation Proclamation on September 22, 1862, following the Union victory on the bloody battlefield at Antietam Creek near Sharpsburg, Maryland.[30] These celebrations featured a variety of activities—parades, picnics, speeches, music, dancing, and sports, including baseball.[31] Although African American teams typically played in the baseball games at these festivities, this was not always the case. A 1921 Emancipation Day celebration in Garden City's Finnup Park featured a morning baseball game between a pair of African American teams—the Garden City Giants and Dodge City Bear Cats—followed by an afternoon game between the Giants and "Garden City's first white nine."[32] In 1931 the Kansas City Monarchs traveled to Nicodemus to play the hometown Blues as part of the annual Emancipation Day festivities.[33] Emancipation Day continues as a weekend celebration in Nicodemus (held since 1878 on a weekend near the original August 1 holiday) and in Hutchinson (held since 1889 on a weekend close to the September 22 holiday).

Topeka Jack Johnson and the Giants

One of the more compelling people associated with African American baseball in Kansas during the early 1900s was John Thomas "Topeka Jack" Johnson. He had long careers as a baseball player and a heavyweight boxer, and took the moniker of Topeka Jack to distinguish himself from a heavyweight champion also of the early 1900s named Jack Johnson, with whom he sometimes sparred.[34] Topeka Jack Johnson became widely known in the state and the region.

Topeka Jack Johnson fit all of his sporting accomplishments into a life of not quite fifty-seven years. He was born in Topeka or nearby on April 25, 1883, and he died in Topeka on January 26, 1940.[35] He briefly attended Washburn Academy, a prep school (later Washburn Rural High School), but he played on the integrated baseball team at Washburn College (now Washburn University). Johnson's professional baseball career began in 1901 with the Chicago Union Giants, successor to the Chicago Unions (1896–1900).[36] He returned to Kansas in 1906, where he reorganized and managed the Topeka Giants, an African American team captained in 1905 by Gaitha Page. The Chicago Union Giants had traveled to Kansas and played Page's Giants. The Topeka Giants played games at home when the Topeka White Sox of the Western Association (Class C) were out of town, and the Giants would travel elsewhere in Kansas and other states on barnstorming tours. Combining his two sports, Johnson boxed at the ballpark the night before playing shortstop in the Giants' first game of the 1906 season. He won the bout in the ninth round on a foul when his white opponent bit him on the shoulder. The Giants also won their first game against a white minor league team from Iola, and Johnson's wounded shoulder did not seem to bother him.[37]

After a successful season managing and playing in Topeka, Johnson returned to the Chicago Union Giants in 1907 and then moved again in 1908 to play for the Minneapolis Keystones. The Topeka Giants continued to play without him and featured several of the players from the 1906 team, such as first baseman Dudley "Tullie" McAdoo, a Topeka native whose baseball career extended through the 1924 season in the Negro National League. In 1908 McAdoo joined an infielder from Troy, Kansas, named Bert Wakefield on the original Kansas City Monarchs, a team unrelated to the one that would be organized in 1920. In Johnson's absence, the Topeka Giants received little mention in the local press, which was sometimes limited to items such as announcements of games at Emancipation Day celebrations. However, the Topeka Giants played in Kansas City against the Kansas City (Kansas) Giants (KCK Giants) in June 1909 and the Kansas City (Missouri) Royal Giants in May 1910. It has been reported erroneously in some histories that the Topeka Giants moved east to become the KCK Giants in 1909, but both teams existed before then—the teams were founded in 1905 and 1907, respectively. In fact, the KCK Giants were scheduled to play the original Kansas City Monarchs for the "amateur championship of the two Kansas Citys" in 1908.[38] Players often signed with different teams each year, and the name Giants was simply popular among baseball teams at the time.

The two Kansas City Giants teams are noteworthy in the story of Topeka Jack Johnson, because he had relocated once again in 1909, this time to Kansas City, where he became manager and infielder for the KCK Giants. The team played its home games at Riverside Park at the "foot" of Franklin Avenue at Second Street (the ball diamond is no longer there). It was an excellent team: in 1909 they claimed a record of 128 wins and 19 losses, including a winning streak of 54 consecutive games. Their on-field success and fan support were cited in editorials calling for Kansas City, Kansas, to sponsor its own white minor league team.[39]

In 1910 Johnson and a few of the players with the KCK Giants crossed the state line to join the newly organized Kansas City Royal Giants. George W. Walden was the Missouri club's secretary, but the team was sometimes referred to in local newspapers as "Jack Johnson's Royal Giants" after its manager. The Royal Giants played their home games at Shelley Park at Independence Avenue and Oak Street (the area is now an Interstate Highway 70 interchange). Johnson's departure and his efforts to promote his new team created tension with the owner of the KCK Giants. Despite the friction, the Royal Giants' opponents in 1910 included both the Topeka Giants and the KCK Giants. Johnson's stay with the Royal Giants lasted one year; he returned to the KCK Giants in 1911. The KCK

Giants bested the Royal Giants and followed that accomplishment in October with three games against the postseason barnstorming version of the minor league Kansas City Blues of the American Association (Class A) "for the championship of Kansas City." In a doubleheader, the Blues won the first game 3–2 in ten innings, and the second game ended in a 0–0 tie after seven innings. After playing two close games, the KCK Giants lost the final game 8–2.[40] In 1912 Johnson was back with the Royal Giants in what was reported as a consolidation of the Royal Giants and the KCK Giants. But a new KCK Giants team was organized that same spring.[41] The contest for supremacy in African American baseball in the Kansas City metropolitan area was not settled until Wilkinson's long-standing Kansas City (Missouri) Monarchs were organized in 1920, although other African American teams continued to play in the two cities.

Meanwhile, the Topeka Giants played occasionally during 1913, but Johnson was absent from the baseball scene while he trained a white heavyweight boxer from Oklahoma. In 1914 he was back in Topeka managing the Giants, although the team did not generate the same high level of press coverage as the 1906 team. When they visited other towns, the team introduced "joke plays" and "baseball comedy" into the games to entertain the crowds, if local organizers thought fans would be receptive. In 1915 the Giants were denied admittance to the city league in Topeka, with the other managers "deciding to draw the color line." However, that same year, Johnson was appointed to the Topeka police force by the mayor, and he joined the Topeka Fire Department at the end of the year. The Giants—sometimes referred to as Johnson's Giants—played most years into the 1920s. Press coverage for the 1917 team was second only to that of the 1906 team. In late September 1917 the white Knights of Columbus team agreed to play the Topeka Giants for the "real" city championship, and arrangements were made for an umpire from the nearby Mayetta Indians baseball team. The Knights of Columbus imported a former Western League (Class A minor league) pitcher and defeated the Giants 8–1. The Giants were not organized during the next two years, as America's military expanded during the First World War, and Sergeant Johnson served in the Kansas State Guard in 1918. The following year he was again employed at Fire Station Number 3 in Topeka. The Topeka Giants were reorganized in 1920, and they joined the Colored Western League in 1922. Topeka Jack Johnson was chosen as president of the league.[42] But it was a Wichita team that enjoyed the most success in that league.

The Colored Western League and the Wichita Monrovians

Topeka and other larger cities in Kansas often supported more than one African American team each year, though one team tended to dominate. During the 1920s two "fast" Wichita teams attracted notice from local white newspapers, though it was less coverage than was received by the numerous white teams, and box scores were rare. Announcements of upcoming games between the African American teams appeared in white newspapers more frequently than the results of their games. In addition, players on a white team would sometimes be listed while their African American opponents were not, which probably reflected the source of the information submitted to the newspaper.[43]

In 1920 and 1921 the top African American team in Wichita was the ABCs, who defeated the Wichita Gray Sox in a July 1920 game to claim the "colored baseball title of the city."[44] The ABCs also played amateur white teams. A newspaper announcement promoting a pair of games between the ABCs and the white Dunaway All-Stars noted that the "clubs appeared well matched and the race rivalry which always comes up in games of this kind is bound to make the double header exciting."[45] In May 1921 the ABCs scheduled road trips to cities in Oklahoma and then to Nebraska, Iowa, Missouri, and Kansas.[46]

In 1921 the Black Wonders were the up-and-coming African American baseball team in the city, and they supplanted the ABCs as the top team in 1922. The Black Wonders also played other African American teams and white teams in Wichita and neighboring towns, including the ABCs.[47] As with the Topeka Giants in 1915, the Black Wonders were mentioned as possible members of the eight-team City League otherwise composed of teams with only white players in 1921. Their bid to join the league was likewise unsuccessful, but they continued to play independently and became a professional team, which made them ineligible to join the city's amateur leagues.[48] Still, other amateur African American teams also continued to be excluded from local leagues. The first team to break the ethnic barrier in a Wichita league was a Mexican American baseball team—the Aztecs—in the Commercial League in 1932, even though African American baseball had a much longer history in the city, including exhibition games with white teams from the earliest years of the sport.[49] Of course, Mexican and Mexican American baseball teams were also victims of racism.[50]

COOLECROWS.	AB	R	H	P	A	E
Graves, cf	4	1	0	0	0	0
Cole, lf	4	2	2	4	1	0
Downs, 2b	5	2	1	0	5	0
Cooley, 1b	4	0	1	17	0	1
Shafft, rf	4	0	1	0	0	1
Wample, 3b	5	0	1	2	3	0
Reagan, ss	3	1	0	2	3	0
Morgan, c	4	2	2	2	3	0
McInnis, p	3	1	2	0	4	0
Totals	36	9	10	27	19	2

GIANTS.	AB	R	H	P	A	E
Marthel, cf	4	1	2	4	0	0
Orendorff, 3b	4	0	0	2	4	2
Richardson, 2b	4	0	0	1	2	0
Johnson, ss	3	0	0	1	1	0
Robinson, lf	2	1	0	3	0	0
McAdoo, 1b	4	0	0	10	0	0
Harris, rf	4	0	1	1	0	0
Struthers, c	3	0	0	2	1	0
Smith, p	3	1	1	0	2	1
Anderson, p	0	0	0	0	0	0
Totals	31	3	4	24	10	4

Score by innings:
Cooleycrows ....1 0 0 2 0 0 3 3 *—9
Giants ....0 0 1 0 0 0 1 1 0—3
Summary: Two base hits—McInnis, Marthel (2), Smith. Home run—Downs. Double play—Cole to Reagan. Stolen bases—Cole, Reagan, Robinson, Struthers. Struck out—By McInnis, 4; by Smith, 1; by Anderson, 1. Bases on balls—Off McInnis, 1; off Smith, 4; off Anderson, 1. Passed balls—Struthers (2). Attendance—1,200. Umpire—Meyer.

MONRAVIANS	AB	R	H	PO	A	E
Nubbie ss	4	1	0	0	3	3
Russel 1b	4	0	1	7	3	0
Young, c	4	0	1	9	0	1
Coleman lf	4	0	1	1	0	0
Butler, cf	4	1	1	0	0	0
Dean 2b	4	0	1	3	1	2
Hamilton 4b	4	0	1	4	2	0
Ragsby, rf	4	0	1	4	2	0
Farmer p	4	0	1	0	3	1
Totals	36	2	8	24	13	7

WICHITA	AB	R	H	PO	A	E
Smith cf. p. ss	4	2	2	4	1	0
Griffin, lf	5	1	1	1	0	0
Washburn 2b. c	5	0	2	1	6	0
East, rf	5	1	2	1	0	0
McDowell, ss. p	2	0	0	1	2	0
McMullan, 1b	4	2	2	2	1	0
Griffith, c. 1b	4	1	1	8	0	0
McDonnell, 1b	3	1	2	7	0	1
Gregory p cf	4	1	2	2	2	0
Totals	36	9	14	27	12	1

Score by innings:
Monrovians .... 000 010 010—2
Wichita .... 003 231 00x—9
Summary:
Two base hits—Smith, Griffith, Dean, McDonnell; Three base hits—Hamilton. Home run—East; Stolen bases—Griffin Washburn. McMillan; Double plays—Farmer Hamilton Dean; Struck out—by Farmer 4, Gregory 6, Smith 2; Bases on balls Smith 1; Hit by pitcher—McDowell (2). Time of game 1:30.

A. A 1906 box score for the Topeka (Colored) Giants, featuring "Topeka Jack" Johnson at shortstop along with Dudley "Tullie" McAdoo at first base. Their opponents were the Cooleycrows (the nickname of the Topeka White Sox) of the Western Association (Class C), featuring Dick Cooley, who had played in the major leagues in 1893–1905. Source: Topeka Daily Capital, 30 April 1906.

B. A 1922 box score for the Wichita Monrovians, who played in the Colored Western League that year. Their catcher was Thomas Jefferson "T. J." Young, who subsequently caught for the Kansas City Monarchs. This box score summarizes a benefit game against the Wichita Izzies (officially the Witches) of the Western League (Class A). Source: Wichita Daily Eagle, 26 September 1922.

Newspaper box scores for games involving African American teams were rare in Kansas. These two examples are for prominent teams of the early twentieth century for games against local minor league (white) teams.

Most African American teams played their games at ballparks used by white ball teams when the white teams were not using them, although the KCK Giants and Kansas City Royal Giants were exceptions. In the spring of 1922 a park association in Wichita oversaw the construction of a ball diamond at the Monrovia Amusement Park—usually referred to simply as Monrovia Park—at 12th and Mosley Streets (the park and ball diamond are no longer there). The manager of the Black Wonders was the secretary of the group building the ballpark, and arrangements were soon made for the team to use it as their home field. Over the next few weeks the team's name was changed to the Monrovians, matching the name of their ballpark, and the team was sold to the Monrovia Amusement Park Corporation.[51]

These changes coincided with the team joining the newly organized Western League of Professional Baseball Teams. In newspaper accounts the league was typically referred to as the Colored Western League, and occasionally as the Western Colored League, the Western League of Colored Baseball Clubs, or the Southwestern Colored League. In what little press coverage the league received, these names added the word *colored* to familiar names of white minor leagues—the Western League (Class A), which included a team in Wichita, and the Southwestern League (Class C), which included teams in Coffeyville, Hutchinson, Independence, Salina, and Topeka. Some of these towns would also have teams in the Colored Western League.

The 1922 Colored Western League was not the first baseball league to include Kansas teams under this general name. An attempt was made on June 6, 1910, to organize the Western Colored Baseball League in Saint Louis, Missouri. The league reportedly would include teams from Chicago, Kansas City (Kansas), Kansas City (Missouri), Peoria (Illinois), Saint Joseph (Missouri), Saint Louis, Springfield (Illinois), and Topeka.[52] Eleven days later, the organization of the Colored Central Western Baseball League was announced in Topeka. The cities hosting teams in this league reportedly included Chicago, Kansas City (Kansas), Omaha, Saint Joseph, Saint Louis, and Topeka.[53] Neither of these leagues apparently came to be.

In 1916 a Colored Western League in the Kansas City area reportedly included teams from Fort Leavenworth (Army Service Schools Colored Detachment Number 2); Independence, Missouri; and Kansas City (Giants and Royal Giants). However, there is little evidence of league organization or league games.[54] In 1920 the Negro National League, which included the Kansas City Monarchs, was referred to as the Western Colored League in a few newspapers.[55] A year later, the New Colored Western League was organized at a meeting in Kansas City, Kansas. Charles Pennell of Lawrence was elected president. The league included the Lawrence Kaw Valleys, Topeka Cubs, and apparently two teams in Kansas City—the

Armour Helmets and the Allies. Records are scant, but a Lawrence newspaper reported that the Kansas City Armour Helmets were league champions. On the other hand, this might have been unsubstantiated hype to encourage attendance at an upcoming nonleague game on October 2, after the baseball season had all but ended.[56]

The most ambitious attempt to establish a league of African American teams in Kansas and neighboring states began in the spring of 1922, but there was confusion regarding the nature of this league at the time, and much confusion remains because documentation is sparse. In early April, Wichita Red Sox manager Charley Coleman claimed that a Western Colored League had been formed, with teams from Des Moines, Muskogee (Oklahoma), Oklahoma City, Omaha, Saint Joseph, Tulsa, and Wichita. Later in the month, Dallas and Fort Worth had replaced Des Moines and Muskogee on the list.[57] Ultimately, though, none of these four cities had teams that played in the league.

Despite the April pronouncements, the first organizational meeting of the nascent league was actually held on May 2 at the Water Street YMCA in Wichita. The purpose of the meeting was to elect officers, establish league rules, and adopt a schedule. The officers elected were President Topeka Jack Johnson of Topeka, Vice President Ed Mason of Oklahoma City, Secretary Charles Bettis of Wichita, and Treasurer Charles Phelps of Saint Joseph. Johnson had been an advocate for African American baseball leagues for some time, including an attempt in 1914 to organize a league with six teams, mostly from Kansas—Atchison, Leavenworth, Kansas City (Kansas), Kansas City (Missouri), Saint Joseph, and Topeka. The 1922 Colored Western League initially consisted of eight franchises in the cities of Independence (Kansas), Kansas City (Kansas), Oklahoma City, Omaha, Saint Joseph, Topeka, Tulsa, and Wichita. The season was to open on May 10 in Wichita and run through September 15.[58]

Plans for a new league developed at a meeting of optimistic "baseball magnates" were oftentimes difficult to implement, and problems apparently arose for the Colored Western League during May. On June 2, a meeting to reorganize the league was held at the law office of J. M. Booker. Among the issues was concern that President Johnson was unable "to give time to the work of the league on account of his connection with the Topeka Fire Department." There was speculation that Charles Prince Edwards of Wichita would replace him at the June meeting, but Johnson retained the presidency.[59]

Changes were made in the league's teams, however. The Wichita Monrovians replaced the Wichita Red Sox as that city's representative. The Red Sox had "failed to meet the requirements" of the association, although the Wichita newspaper story on the subject did not specify what the requirements were. An Oklahoma newspaper reported that the Red Sox were expelled for not traveling to games.[60] It is possible the recently organized Red Sox were not financially strong enough to participate in the league. The Monrovians, on the other hand, were in their third year and were still owned by the Monrovia Amusement Park Corporation.[61] In addition to the replacement of the Wichita team, there was a question as to whether the Kansas City Monarchs of the Negro National League would consent to another African American team in an organized league within their territorial "limit zone."[62]

Kansas City (Kansas), Omaha, and Saint Joseph are often listed in recent accounts of the league because they were awarded franchises in early May. They were also included in the early league standings published by a Wichita newspaper on June 20, and a list of scores was published on June 21 for games featuring Oklahoma City vs. Wichita, Tulsa vs. Topeka, Independence vs. Saint Joseph, and Kansas City vs. Coffeyville. No other mention has been discovered in Kansas and Oklahoma newspapers of any league games played by teams from Kansas City, Omaha, or Saint Joseph following the reorganization. The absence of these cities from the reorganized league is further supported by the agenda for the midyear meeting of the league on August 2–3 in Coffeyville. Discussion about "putting the league on a larger basis" through "admittance of Omaha and Kansas City with St. Joseph" was planned for the meeting.[63] These cities apparently had been replaced by two other Kansas towns in June, when the league was reorganized. The African American team in El Dorado moved to Coffeyville in anticipation of joining the league, and the long-standing Chanute Black Diamonds also joined the reorganized league.[64] Adding to the general confusion, a June 3 newspaper in Tulsa listed the league's teams as Bristow (Oklahoma), Coffeyville, Independence, Kansas City, Oklahoma City, Omaha, Saint Joseph, Topeka, Tulsa, and Wichita.[65]

A more accurate list of teams was provided by a Topeka newspaper that otherwise provided virtually no coverage of the league, which is surprising given that Topeka Jack Johnson was the league president. The newspaper reported in early July that the Topeka Giants had recently "returned from a swing around the Western league circuit," in which they played games in Oklahoma City, Tulsa, Wichita, Independence, Coffeyville, and Chanute. Thus, from June through the end of the season in September, there were seven teams in the league, five in Kansas and two in Oklahoma—the Chanute Black Diamonds, Coffeyville Hot Shots, Independence Red Sox, Oklahoma City Black Indians, Topeka Giants, Tulsa Black Oilers, and Wichita Monrovians.[66]

With the limited information available, the final records of each team are unknown for their league games (most also played nonleague games, which might have been included in newspaper reports of wins and losses for some teams). The Tulsa Black Oilers billed themselves as the winners of the "colored Western Association."[67] However, Oklahoma City and Wichita apparently played for the league title in their final four games. According to a Wichita newspaper, Oklahoma City had a one-game lead going into the series at Monrovia Park, but Wichita swept the series and claimed the league championship.[68]

Unfortunately, the Colored Western League experienced disagreements regarding its management during the course of the season. In the understated words of one newspaper report, the affairs of the league were "becoming very much complicated." Accusations against the league included inadequate returns on money invested by the teams and inadequate efforts by league officials to promote the teams' interests. In addition, President Johnson was accused of unjustly deposing Secretary Bettis and not providing a proper accounting of the league funds he held. Consequently, the league survived only a single year.[69]

The Monrovians also played exhibition games against other teams during 1922 when they had openings in their league schedule. This was a common practice to improve a team's income. In September they played a benefit game against the city's white minor league team—the Wichita Izzies (Witches) of the Western League. The game was for the benefit of one of the Izzies' players, Jimmy Blakesley, to help defray the expenses resulting from his young wife's medical treatments and funeral. The Izzies defeated the Monrovians, and the game netted Blakesley about $400 (equivalent to about $5,600 in 2016).[70]

After the Colored Western League folded, the Monrovians continued to play other teams in the area, both black and white, and they barnstormed into the 1930s. They also competed in the state semipro tournament in Wichita during the 1930s.[71] The Monrovian catcher sometimes sat in a rocking chair while he caught during the team's barnstorming tours.[72]

Traveling from town to town presented unique challenges to African American teams, whose players were often prohibited from sleeping or eating in white establishments. Arriving a day early for a 1937 game in Emporia, the Monrovians spent the night in the grandstand at the ballpark, using whatever articles of clothing and other items they had to fashion beds on the bench seats.[73] In June 1925 the Monrovians even played a game against a team from Klan Number 6 of the Wichita Ku Klux Klan. A local newspaper reported that "strangle holds, razors, horsewhips and other violent implements of argument will be barred." Two white Catholics were suggested as umpires, presumably because they would be neutral. The Monrovians won the game 10–8.[74] Today the team is better known for the novelty of this one game than for its championship year in the Colored Western League or its long history.

Integrated Professional Baseball

The Colored Western League and other African American leagues arose from the prohibition against African Americans playing in the major or minor leagues after 1900. However, integrated town teams, such as the 1887 team in Nicodemus, did exist, although they were rare in Kansas and elsewhere. For example, an integrated team in Atchison was organized in 1883, and a local newspaper noted an eclectic mix of the team's players—"three negroes, two Germans, two Swedes, one American, and one Irishman."[75] Prior to the First World War, the Evans All-Nations Team, a barnstorming team based in northeastern Kansas at Horton, publicized its integrated roster of "Indians, Mexicans, white and colored ball players." One of those white players in 1917 was Virgil "Zeke" Barnes of Circleville. Barnes actually pitched more games that year for another integrated team, the World's All-Nations Team of Kansas City, Missouri (sometimes referred to as Schmelzer's All-Nations Team), organized by J. L. Wilkinson, who later founded the Kansas City Monarchs. Barnes's season was cut short by military service during the First World War. After he returned from France, he pitched for the New York Giants in 1919–1920 and 1922–1928, closing his final major league season with the Boston Braves (now the Atlanta Braves).[76]

One of the better-known instances of integration on the baseball diamond in Kansas occurred in Topeka in 1886. Topeka played in the Western League, an independent minor league, along with teams from

JOHN McCULLOUGH, PRESIDENT
E. PERRY, MANAGER

MONROVIA AMUSEMENT COMPANY
OWNERS OF MONROVIA PARK ALL NEW

THE MONROVIANS
Southwest's Premier Base Ball Club
A GALAXY OF FAST, CLEAN, GENTLEMANLY, BIG LEAGUE STARS
MEMBER OF
WESTERN COLORED LEAGUE
A FEW OPEN DATES FOR FAST CLUBS THAT WANT A BIG BOX OFFICE ATTRACTION
C. S. BETTIS, DIRECTOR OF TOUR AND PUBLICITY

Wichita, Kansas June 22nd _____ 192 3

R.E. Kirke

Mgr. American Legion
Base Ball Club.

Dear Sir;

Your received the 22nd inst,and endeed very glad to here from You,at this time
I will except of Your date July the 8th, and You may book the Monrovians there
on that date. I will also send You some advertisement to help You to bill Your
City in plenty of time, such as a Cut of the Club to Run in Your City Paper,
andn a few Picture of the Club to stick around on the window of the business
places. I am also filling out a contract as to Your agreement and mailing with
this letter.

Sencerely Yours for a Clean Gentlemanly brand of base ball

F. C. Jamison

Business Agent for the Monrovians B.B.Club.

519 1/2 N. Main ST.
Phone Market 2649
·· ··   6574
·· ··   6674J

Here hopeing that the Weather will be favorable to Us on that date for a
Game to the Public.

F.C. Jamison.

*If the Contract is O.K. Fill and
Keep one and Mail one Back*

Letter dated June 22, 1923, sent by F. C. Jamison, business agent for the Wichita Monrovians Base
Ball Club, to R. E. Kirke of the Newton American Legion baseball team to arrange a game on July 8.
In 1922 the Monrovians had played in the Colored Western League, officially named the Western
League of Professional Baseball Teams. The Monrovians won the championship in the league's only
year of existence. They continued to play local teams and barnstorm for several years. Courtesy of the
Kansas Historical Society, Topeka.

Leavenworth, Denver, Leadville (Colorado), Saint Joseph, and Lincoln (Nebraska). The Topeka players were white except for an African American
second baseman who went by the name of Bud Fowler. His real name
was John Jackson, and it is unknown why he changed it. Born in 1858,
Fowler grew up and learned to play baseball in Cooperstown, New York.
He is generally acknowledged to be the first professional African American baseball player (1878); he played in the minor leagues into the 1890s,

before men with dark skin were fully excluded. Fowler had trouble sticking with a minor league team more than one season, sometimes playing on as many as four teams in a year. Often this was because teammates and opponents resented playing with an African American, but sometimes black players on white teams were simply convenient scapegoats for other problems with the team. Fowler reportedly wore wooden slats on his shins to protect them from the spikes of sliding baserunners intent on hurting him. He continued to find teams who would hire him, however, because he was an excellent ballplayer, offensively and defensively. Fowler played mostly in the Midwest and the Northeast, but he also played for Pueblo in the Colorado League (1885), Santa Fe in the New Mexico League (1888), and for a Lincoln team in the Nebraska State League that moved to Kearney before disbanding in July (1892). And he played in Kansas for Topeka in 1886.[77]

In their opening exhibition game against the professional team from Kansas City, Missouri, Topeka lost 13–1, but Fowler's skills were highlighted in the newspaper accounts, as were his race and the issue of an integrated team.

> Every man on the grounds was heartily in sympathy with the fifteenth amendment when Fowler (colored) made a brilliant running catch from second base into center field. . . . Fowler's two-base hit saved the day and Topeka from being shut out. He is a decided brunette, but can play ball. Fowler is certainly the dark horse of the team, and enough like him is all that is needed.[78]

Fowler had numerous extra-base hits that summer. In fact, he led the Western League in triples, and his speed allowed him to steal bases regularly. He was also a savvy player. In a game against Leadville, "Fowler knocked the ball to the right field fence, making a clean three base hit. The visitors immediately raised a quibble about Fowler's base running and while they were attempting to bulldoze the umpire, Fowler quietly crossed home plate, scoring the first run for Topeka." Fowler also displayed guile while fielding his position. Two Topeka newspapers provided different details of one event illustrating this, but they match in the essential points: A runner for Saint Joseph reached second base, but the Topeka players argued the point after calling time (something the team from Leadville had neglected to do). Following the argument, Fowler kept the ball in his glove. His teammates moved toward their positions as if getting ready to resume play, and the Saint Joseph player took his lead from second base, at which point Fowler tagged him out, executing the hidden-ball trick. Fowler played so well that there was speculation in June 1886 that he would sign elsewhere for more money, but he remained with the Topeka league team until September, once again short of a full season. He was reported as "disabled" on September 3 but closed the month playing a few games for amateur teams in Lawrence and Topeka. In 1887 Fowler was back in upstate New York and continued playing as long as he could while the color line throughout organized baseball was being drawn ever more completely.[79]

Through the 1890s a few other African Americans played on professional teams in Kansas, which was one of the last states in the country to give up integrated professional baseball. Between 1895 and 1899 no other state reportedly fielded more integrated professional teams than Kansas.[80] For example, the integrated Nebraska State League was unable to complete a full season in 1892 for a variety of reasons, including objections from ardent segregationists.[81] However, the numbers of integrated teams and their African American players in Kansas were still shamefully low. Although much of the segregation in Kansas was related to individual actions rather than codified in league rules, it was during this period, in 1896, that the US Supreme Court handed down its decision in the case of *Plessy v. Ferguson*, which upheld state laws imposing racial segregation in the context of "separate but equal."[82]

The last of the integrated professional baseball teams in the state featured four African American men from Kansas, whose baseball skills were so strong that they were briefly allowed to cross the color line on the ball diamond.[83] Monroe Ingram was a deaf player from Coffeyville, who graduated from the Kansas Deaf and Dumb Institute (now the Kansas School for the Deaf) in Olathe in 1889. Consequently, he was given the common but inappropriate nickname of Dummy. In August 1889 he became an instructor at the Missouri School for the Deaf. When school was not in session, his "services as a pitcher [were] in demand," and he returned to his parents' farm near Deering to play baseball during the summers. He pitched for Independence until July 1896, when the team joined the Kansas State League (an independent minor league). However, the "well known colored scholar and ball player" was soon pitching for the league team in Emporia (1896–1897). He pitched briefly for Emporia again in 1899, but he played mostly for various teams around Coffeyville.

He later left his job in Missouri for a similar position in Oklahoma. In 1897 the Independence newspaper lamented that if their former pitcher "was a white man he would be pitching in the big league."[84]

Bert Wakefield was a good student at Troy High School. In 1889 he became a "Tonsorial Artist" (barber), and in 1893 he owned a barbershop in Troy with the only public baths (both hot and cold) in Doniphan County. He played second base and pitched for Troy and other teams around the county. The local newspaper declared that it was "only his color that keeps him out of the League. He's a hard hitter and is mighty handy getting in front of batted balls as a baseman." In 1894 Wakefield also "gave satisfaction as umpire" in a game between white teams from Troy and Denton— clear evidence of the respect he received on the baseball diamond and in the community. Wakefield finally got his chance to play in the Kansas State League, beginning with Emporia in 1895. However, the barbershop suffered during his absence, so he returned to Troy in late August and played for his hometown team, which had also joined the league that year, finishing in first place. Troy did not join the Kansas State League in subsequent years, so Wakefield played for professional teams in Hiawatha (1896), Atchison (1896), Abilene (1897–1898), and Salina (1898), which was a member of the Kansas State League. Salina released Wakefield, and he had to sue the manager for $25 in back pay. In 1899 he played for the Chicago Unions, an African American team, and he was a member of the earlier Kansas City Monarchs in 1908. Wakefield later returned to Troy and was "still in the game" in 1915, managing the Troy Trojans, a local African American team.[85]

Bert Jones was a left-handed pitcher whose baseball career began in his hometown of Hiawatha (about twenty-five miles west of Troy). In newspaper accounts he was given the nicknames of Yellow, Yellow Kid, Walkin' Windmill, or some variation of these names. Jones left Hiawatha in 1896–1898 to pitch for Atchison, which was a member of the Kansas State League in 1897–1898. Near the end of the 1898 season Jones left Atchison for Chicago, where he played for the Chicago Unions and was joined a year later by Wakefield.[86]

Gaitha Page graduated from Topeka High School in 1897, where he was one of only two African American students to graduate that year. In the autumn, he enrolled at the State Normal School in Emporia (now Emporia State University), and two years later he was one of the first two

African American graduates of the college, where he also played shortstop during the springs of 1898 and 1899. After graduating, he was selected for a teaching position in Topeka, but he stayed in Emporia that summer to play for the city's professional team. In August 1899 Page left Emporia to play for the white team in Arkansas City before returning to Topeka to assume his teaching duties. He continued to play baseball for African American teams in his hometown, serving as captain of the 1905 Topeka Giants. Page was also selected to play on Dick Cooley's integrated picked nine from Topeka in a game against Connie Mack's barnstorming All-American Stars in 1900, but he was replaced before the game, without comment in the newspaper as to the reason. As Wakefield had done a decade earlier, Page umpired an exhibition game in 1905 between the white Topeka White Sox of the Western Association (Class C) and Washburn College, which had admitted women and minorities since its founding as Lincoln College in 1865. He also umpired a game between Washburn and the State Agricultural College (now Kansas State University) and had previously umpired for African American teams. However, in 1906 the University of Kansas baseball team refused to take the field in Topeka to play Washburn if Page were allowed to umpire as scheduled. He was replaced by a white umpire chosen "on the strength of the report that he had once been a baseball writer on a newspaper."[87]

The end of integrated professional leagues in Kansas experienced by these four players at the close of the nineteenth century was perhaps associated, at least in part, with the increasing practice of importing players from other states, some of whom judged people they did not know on the basis of their skin color. This, in turn, might have brought local elements of racism more into the open.[88] Little was written about Bert Jones in local newspapers other than his baseball activities, but Monroe Ingram, Bert Wakefield, and Gaitha Page were respected members of their communities on and off the diamond. Wakefield ran his own business, and Ingram and Page had earned college educations and become teachers. The underlying causes of segregation in professional baseball occurring in the late nineteenth century are unquestionably complex, and *Plessy v. Ferguson* certainly played a role by making racial segregation legally acceptable. Yet if the segregation of professional teams in Kansas was in some degree associated with a shift away from relying primarily on players living in the local area and familiar with its culture, this might partially explain why

African American men continued to play for otherwise all-white amateur and semiprofessional teams still drawn from the local talent pool during the late 1800s and early 1900s.

Pomp Reagor and George Sweatt

Of course, African American players on local teams in subsequent years still had to deal with racism. When Kansas newspapers owned by white publishers wrote about African American teams or players, any praise was often tainted with condescension and racial epithets, and these published views reflected public opinion, some of which would have been even harsher than what was printed. Relationships between white and African American players on and off the baseball diamond sometimes resulted in violence.[89] For example, the white Garnett town team played an African American team from Osawatomie at an Emancipation Day celebration in August 1895. As often happened regardless of who was playing, there was an argument about a call during the game. John Jones, whose two sons were playing on the Osawatomie team, entered the argument and "was apparently getting a revolver ready for action, [when] he received a blow on the head from a ball bat in the hands of [Garnett's] Charlie Sargent, from the effect of which he died a few hours later." A coroner's inquest resulted in Sargent's arrest on a charge of malicious assault, but the county attorney dropped that charge and pursued a charge of murder in the first degree, which was changed to manslaughter in the second degree. The trial was conducted in October, and "after a very short deliberation the jury returned a verdict of not guilty."[90]

Into this social climate came the career of Albert Reagor, a now largely unknown baseball player who lived in the small town of Humboldt in southeastern Kansas. In newspapers and census records his last name was variously misspelled as Rager, Reager, Raeger, or as some variation of Sweatt, his mother's name after she remarried. However, he usually went by the nickname of Pomp, short for Pompey. Sometimes the local newspapers even omitted his last name. Unlike Fowler, Ingram, Wakefield, Jones, and Page, Albert Reagor never played in the minor leagues, but when it came to baseball in southeastern Kansas, everyone knew who Pomp was. His experiences living under Jim Crow were not unique to him, but they are more evident because Pomp was a local baseball legend.

Pomp Reagor was born in Waxahachie, Texas, on July 14, 1872. Sometime in the 1880s he moved to Humboldt, Kansas, where he lived most of his life in a home owned by his widowed mother, Rachel Sweatt, who had been born a slave in the Deep South and moved to Texas with her "master and mistress" when she was eight years old.[91] The first newspaper mention of Pomp in a baseball game was in May 1888, when Humboldt secured five "pick ups" to play against the team from nearby Iola "for the fun there was in it." Pomp served as the "back stop" (catcher).[92] He was two months shy of his sixteenth birthday. Pomp began to play on a regular basis in 1895, when he became the "boss pitcher" for the Humboldt Maroons, the local town team composed mostly of white players, although Pomp's nephew, William "Shotts" Turner, sometimes played second base.[93] Pomp also played first base and elsewhere on occasion, mostly later in his career.[94]

Pomp continued to pitch regularly through 1908 for several teams in the region. In the late 1800s and early 1900s it was not uncommon for a few players, especially pitchers, to be hired by teams for a particular game or even for several weeks.[95] In addition to his hometown team, Pomp (and sometimes Shotts) played for white teams in several towns, including Buffalo, Burlington, Chanute, Erie, Fredonia, Iola, Moran, Neosho Falls, and Yates Center.[96] He also played for African American teams—primarily the Chanute Black Diamonds and Iola Go-Devils—especially later in his career.[97] Money earned playing baseball was not enough to support a person through the entire year, so during the offseason Pomp worked various jobs, including "helping Mr. Milliken take care of horses at Salina," working in a hotel in Cherryvale, and working on streets in Humboldt.[98] Yet playing baseball was the one constant during those years, and Pomp had a reputation as a winning pitcher.

Perhaps Pomp's most noteworthy pitching performance came in 1901. On October 9, after having won the championship of the Western League, the minor league Kansas City Blues traveled to southeastern Kansas to play the Fredonia Reds, a white town team that included Pomp on its roster. The Blues won the first game 7–2, scoring six of their runs in the first inning. Pomp played right field. The following day, the two teams played again, this time with Pomp on the mound. The Reds scored one run in the first inning, and the Blues tied the score in the sixth. The score remained tied as both teams scored a run in the eleventh inning. The contest was finally settled in the twelfth inning, when Fredonia scored a run for a 3–2 victory, with Pomp earning a complete game victory. "The defeat of the

Blues by the Reds was unexpected and will give the Reds and steady Pomp Reagor a great reputation as manipulators of the horsehide."[99]

Because Pomp was a local baseball legend, his actions off the field were also widely reported in newspapers.[100] For example, in 1894 he was sentenced to ninety days in jail for disturbing the peace and striking a police officer.[101] During a fight in 1896, he was shot behind his ear, with the bullet lodging in his neck, "and at last accounts had not been found." Yet Pomp "was reported as not seriously hurt."[102] Probably the low point for Pomp came during the offseason in December 1908, when he and another man pleaded guilty to petty larceny. They were sentenced to six months in the county jail in Erie and ordered to pay court costs. "The trouble which will cause them to be residents of Erie for half a year came out of a game of dice, which the defendants, who are negroes, engaged in with a white stranger early in the week. The stranger had money and there came to be $5 in the pot, all at one time . . . so they just grabbed the coin and fled."[103] Pomp was paroled the following summer.[104]

By this time his playing days were winding down, but not long after being released from jail Pomp crossed one more racial barrier, as Bert Wakefield and Gaitha Page had done a few years earlier. He umpired a baseball game between two white teams in Humboldt on July 11, 1909. The town paper reported, "One new and novel feature of the game was a colored man as umpire. Pomp Reager, the old time colored pitcher, was chosen as umpire and gave splendid satisfaction."[105]

It was not only Pomp's baseball exploits and troubles with the law that were deemed newsworthy. In the spring of 1899 "the house of Geo. Hettinger, of Humboldt, caught fire from a gasoline stove on Thursday and would have burned but for the timely arrival of Pomp Rager who discovered the flames."[106] A more dramatic event occurred two years later, during Pomp's tenure as a pitcher for Fredonia: "A runaway team [of horses] came down through the streets Sunday with two ladies in the buggy. The horses were running and kicking and matters looked serious for the passengers. 'Pomp' Reager was on hand and seems to have 'juned quite a hickory' down the road, and caught the team before any damage was done."[107]

Despite accolades for his actions on and off the baseball diamond, Pomp was still subjected to the well-entrenched bigotry of the time. Although pitching for several white teams gave him the opportunity to play against most white teams in the region, he was not welcomed everywhere. In 1902 the Humboldt Maroons lost two games at Weir City, where "they wouldn't let Pomp pitch . . . because the miners objected to colored people taking part in the game."[108] Lines could be crossed but they could not yet be erased. A year earlier, Pomp had almost been prevented from pitching for Fredonia against the white team in Augusta:

> Pomp Reager was in the game with all his heart and soul and every time he wiggled his foot and made a few smiling goo goo eyes at the batter, the ball shot through the air as if it had come from a gatling [sic] gun. He was in fine trim and pitched beautifully. The Augusta boys kicked on his color at first and threatened to not play if Pomp was permitted to enter, but they finally yielded to the inevitable. After the exercises were over the Augustans became so attentive and friendly to Pomp that some of the Fredonia boys got uneasy, lest they might steal him. Augusta had heard of him and they were probably more "skeered" than offended by his presence. There is not a fairer and more agreeable ball player anywhere than Pomp Reager.[109]

Even praise in the local newspapers owned by white publishers was often laced with the language and prejudices of the day. Routinely, the race of Pomp and other African Americans was identified to distinguish them from the majority of the people mentioned in newspaper stories—"'Pomp' Rager, a young colored man," "'Pomp' Switt the Humboldt negro," "'Pomp' the dusky twirler," and "'Pomp,' the colored cyclone, pitched a game of ball."[110] A few times the language was even harsher. The story about Pomp stopping the runaway team of horses in Fredonia was reprinted with the opening, "Old base ball fans who remember Pomp Reager, the Humboldt coon who made the Iola players fan the air oft and again, will read with interest of the colored boy's good work in other lines."[111]

Sometimes the aspersions cast on African Americans were less direct but no less demeaning. A 1920 headline announcing an upcoming ballgame between the Chanute Black Diamonds and the Independence Bear Cats, two African American teams, read: "Dark Day in Baseball Tomorrow."[112] Following another game between the Black Diamonds and a team of white players, in which the Black Diamond hitters got on base but had trouble advancing or scoring, the newspaper reported, "By putting watermelons on first, second and third bases Earlton won off the Black Diamonds yesterday by the score of 14 to 9. The Black Diamonds is composed of colored players."[113]

Pomp Reagor died in his home on the evening of July 29, 1928, at only fifty-six years of age, as a result of complications arising from a growth in his throat. He had watched a baseball game that afternoon between two of his former teams, Humboldt and Moran. His death was front-page news in the local newspaper.[114] Pomp shared his hometown with another great pitcher, Walter Johnson, one of the first five players elected to the National Baseball Hall of Fame in 1936.[115] It is possible that, as a young boy, Johnson knew about Pomp, the local pitching legend, but no record of it has come to light. Albert "Pomp" Reagor never garnered attention on a national level or even in the larger cities of the region such as Wichita or Topeka. However, a 1906 article in a local newspaper referred to him as "the colored Christy Mathewson of Kansas."[116] Had he lived a little later, his skills as a pitcher that allowed him to cross Jim Crow's color lines on the rural baseball diamonds of his day might have warranted a comparison as the Satchel Paige of Kansas.

In addition to Pomp Reagor, another African American sometimes played for the Humboldt town team. Humboldt native George Alexander Sweatt, born in 1893, was Pomp's nephew. As Pomp's playing days ended, Sweatt's were just beginning. In 1912 he pitched for three teams—Humboldt High School's integrated baseball team; the Humboldt Grays, the white town team; and the African American Iola Go-Devils. Although integrated teams were still rare at this time, games between local white and black teams were becoming more commonplace. While playing for the Go-Devils, Sweatt pitched a no-hitter against the Moran town team, and he had a game-winning home run against the Iola White Sox when he "lost the ball in the corn field." The cornfield was a regular outfield hazard at Electric Park in Iola, and Sweatt planted several baseballs there. In a 1913 game between the Go-Devils and the White Sox, Sweatt again "put one out into the right field corn patch [and] Wade got tangled up with corn tassels and chinch bugs," giving Sweatt a double. He then stole third base and was attempting to steal home when the batter swung and missed for strike three and the third out.[117]

Not used solely as a pitcher by local teams, Sweatt also served as catcher, shortstop, and third baseman. In addition to playing baseball, the eighteen-year-old Sweatt passed an exam in 1912 that entitled him to a teaching certificate in his home county, but teaching positions were hard to come by. Thus, he found other employment, such as working at a local cement plant and an automobile repair shop.[118] In June 1918 Sweatt was living in Peoria, Illinois, when he was drafted into military service, and he returned to Kansas to report for duty. He served in the 816th Pioneer Infantry, a segregated African American unit organized at Camp Funston near Junction City in September 1918. The unit arrived in France in October 1918, shortly before the armistice of November 11. They returned to the United States in August 1919.[119]

In 1920 the Humboldt Grays—white players, with the exception of George Sweatt—played the Chanute Black Diamonds four times, each team winning two games. A fifth game was rained out. The crowd in Humboldt at the second game of the series was estimated to be more than 1,000 people, and the grandstand held only 500, so these were widely popular events. However, there were still occasions when African American players had to display the level of forbearance associated with Jackie Robinson when he joined the Brooklyn Dodgers in 1947. In a 1920 game between the white teams from Humboldt and Chanute, Sweatt was serving as Humboldt's catcher. In the ninth inning, Sweatt dropped the third strike and tagged the Chanute batter. Already angry with himself, the batter was enraged by Sweatt tagging him. The batter "'cussed' Sweatt and drew back his bat with the intention of hitting him." Two or three Humboldt players stepped in to prevent any violence, while Sweatt, "one of the cleanest and most popular ball players in this part of the country . . . played the part of a gentleman." Sweatt was a regular in the Grays lineup in 1920, leading the team with a .358 batting average and tying for the team lead in runs.[120]

In the spring of 1921 Sweatt, who had recently married, was working on his teaching degree at the State Manual Training Normal School at Pittsburg, Kansas (now Pittsburg State University), where he lettered in football, basketball, and track and field (not baseball). This degree would allow him to teach statewide, and the academic year would leave his summers largely open for playing baseball. Beginning in 1922, he moved up to the Negro National League. He spent four seasons with the Kansas City Monarchs and two seasons with the Chicago American Giants. As a result, he is one of only two players to have played in the first four Negro World Series—1924 and 1925 with Kansas City and 1926 and 1927 with Chicago. All of his teams except the 1925 Monarchs won the series.[121]

During the school year, Sweatt was a coach and supervisor of athletics at Cleveland School, the African American public school in Coffeyville. Sweatt was called to testify in the 1924 case of *Thurman-Watts v. Board of Education of the City of Coffeyville* regarding the school district's segregation of students based on race. At the time, segregation was allowed only in grade schools in Kansas cities, not in high schools (except in Kansas City). Ninth-grade classrooms were in Coffeyville's segregated junior high school buildings, and the African American student at the heart of the case wanted to enroll in the ninth grade at the nearby white junior high school. The Kansas Supreme Court ruled that ninth grade is a component of a high school program, regardless of the building arrangement, and it could not be segregated by race under Kansas law. Following his testimony, Sweatt lost his job in Coffeyville. Traded by the Monarchs to Chicago in 1926, he retired from Negro League baseball in 1928 and subsequently worked for the US Postal Service until 1957. The folks back in Kansas remembered him, though, and September 21, 1930, was declared George Sweatt Day in Iola. The feature event of the day was a baseball game between the Iola Ramblers, with the addition of a couple of former Go-Devils players, and the white Iola Hustlers. Sweatt returned from Illinois for the event and suited up for the game. He began the game at shortstop but took over as pitcher for the Ramblers and contributed substantially to their 10–7 victory. Sweatt had three hits in five at bats (including two doubles), and he struck out five opposing batters while allowing only one walk. Sweatt later moved from Illinois to Los Angeles, California, where he passed away in 1983, just short of his ninetieth birthday.[122]

Other African Americans with Kansas connections who are not mentioned elsewhere in this book enjoyed success on the segregated baseball diamond during the early 1900s, playing mostly for the Kansas City Monarchs or other African American teams based outside Kansas. Some were born in the state, such as pitcher Chet Brewer (Leavenworth),[123] second baseman Elwood "Bingo" DeMoss (Topeka), first baseman George Giles (Junction City), catcher and outfielder Oscar "Heavy" Johnson (Atchison),[124] utility player Carroll "Dink" Mothell (Topeka), and pitcher Frank Wickware (Girard).[125]

Others lived in Kansas, such as pitcher Wilber "Bullet" Rogan (Kansas City)[126] and catcher Thomas Jefferson "T. J." Young (Wichita), both born in Oklahoma. Rogan was inducted into the National Baseball Hall of Fame in 1998, three decades after his death. T. J. Young also played briefly for the Wichita Monrovians and was their catcher during the 1922 season in the Colored Western League before he moved on to the Monarchs, catching for Chet Brewer. In 1933 Young spent time back in Wichita, where he sought to help an African American team enter a city league. While his effort to integrate a city league was unsuccessful, he did play part of that summer for an otherwise all-white team from the nearby town of Mulvane in the local Oil Belt League. Although the city leagues remained segregated, the Wichita Colored Devils were invited to participate in the 1932 state semipro tournament in Wichita organized by Raymond "Hap" Dumont.[127] Three years later, the racially integrated Bismarck Churchills of North Dakota, featuring pitcher Satchel Paige, won Wichita's first National Baseball Congress (NBC) tournament, organized by Dumont, which also included thirty-one segregated teams of white, African American, American Indian, and Japanese American players from twenty-five states.[128]

Although the racial divide was sometimes crossed on the baseball field—by individual players or entire teams—racial relations in baseball generally reflected those off the diamond at the turn of the century, and players experienced harsh, sometimes violent racism. In spite of a self-perpetuated reputation as the "free state," earned in the years leading up to the US Civil War, Kansas was no stranger to segregation or even lynchings, riots, and other forms of racist violence against African Americans for decades afterward.[129] Yet men from two generations of one African American family in rural southeastern Kansas had routinely crossed the color lines on the ball ground to play for white semipro teams during the early twentieth century, when the same opportunity was denied to African Americans in the major and minor leagues. In addition, African American teams such as the Kansas City Monarchs and Wichita Monrovians made popular barnstorming tours during the 1920s and 1930s, in which they played local white teams across much of Kansas. And Hap Dumont's state and national semipro tournaments of the 1930s were not racially exclusive. The racial segregation of Jim Crow in Kansas was oppressive and widespread but not absolute, on the ball field or in the communities, as a number of courageous citizens and officials demonstrated by their actions.[130] While the baseball diamond is now racially integrated, the broader effort to eliminate racial bias is ongoing.

CHAPTER 4

American Indian Baseball

On May 21, 1877, in what was perhaps the first baseball game played by a team of American Indians in Kansas, a team organized by soldiers at Fort Hays in western Kansas defeated a picked team of the famed Pawnee Scouts, who had served with Major Frank North in the wars with the Cheyenne and Lakota. The score was close, 18–16. The Pawnee had been mustered out of service with the US Army in Nebraska and were bivouacked at the fort while traveling south to the Indian Territory (Oklahoma).[1]

While white and African American settlers were first organizing baseball teams in Kansas, American Indians on reservations in the northeastern part of the state still played their own centuries-old game involving a stick and ball. In 1879 a game of "Indian Base Ball"—lacrosse—between the Potawatomi and the Sac and Fox was played at the Potawatomi reserve near Holton. Points were scored by hitting the assigned pole ("base") with the ball.

> The game was played by twenty Indians on either side, the club used being a hickory stick, bent cup-fashion at the end, with buckskin strings tied across for [the] bottom. The bases are hickory saplings, about 12 feet high and set 500 feet apart. The game was started by a blind Indian tossing up the ball near the center pole, when the scrambling party rushed for it, pell-mell, helter-skelter, and a scene most exciting followed. The Pottawattomies [*sic*] were assigned the north pole and the Socs [*sic*] and Foxes the South. Either side were extremely anxious, it would seem from the manner in which they played, to strike the particular pole which had been assigned to it. The game was four straight innings, which was won by the Pottawattomies, together with horses,

jewelry, blankets, clothing, etc., bet on the game. . . . The game was played in all friendliness—no one getting mad, though some got battered and bruised badly. . . . The game lasted for two hours.[2]

The newspaper account of the lacrosse match led a few weeks later to an invitation for the Potawatomi to play an exhibition match of lacrosse at the county fair. The match was to be "five innings (best three in five)" for a $50 purse to the winning team.[3] In subsequent years, the tribes in Kansas continued to play lacrosse but also formed baseball teams that sometimes played each other and sometimes played white or African American teams. In 1897 a game of lacrosse was played by a barnstorming group of Choctaw on an open field in Pittsburg, while other American Indian teams began to play baseball throughout the state.[4]

Indian Schools and Reservation Teams

Until 1854, when the Kansas-Nebraska Act established the Kansas Territory, land that now constitutes Kansas, Nebraska, and portions of other states was part of the Western [Indian] Territory set aside for the forced resettlement of American Indians from the eastern part of the country. While most of the relocated tribes living in eastern Kansas—such as the Delaware, Shawnee, and Wyandot—were again relocated to what remained of the reduced Indian Territory, four tribes—the Iowa Tribe of Kansas and Nebraska, the Kickapoo Tribe in Kansas, the Prairie Band Potawatomi Nation, and the Sac and Fox Nation of Missouri in Kansas and Nebraska—remained on reservations in northeastern Kansas.[5] The Wyandot also maintained a presence in Kansas centered on the Wyandot National Burying Ground (Huron Indian Cemetery) in Kansas City. In the late 1800s two boarding schools were established in northeastern Kansas with the goal of assimilating these and other American Indians into European American culture. As part of this assimilation, both schools organized teams to participate in the national pastime.

From 1877 through 1917, the Kickapoo Training School (usually referred to locally as the Kickapoo Indian School) was operated west of Horton in northeastern Kansas. Kansas congressman Charles Curtis, a member of the Kaw Nation who later served as vice president of the United States under President Herbert Hoover, secured funding in 1898 for a new building at the school. In 1897 the school's first dormitory had been reported as "a mere wreck of a building, really unfit for occupation for any purpose." It had been constructed in about 1860 for a stage line. Among the activities at the school, a baseball team was organized. Usually referred to as the Kickapoo Indian team, its players actually came from various tribes in the region. It was "one of the crack teams in Brown county," playing against white and African American teams in Kansas and elsewhere during the 1890s and early 1900s. The 1897 team seems to have been particularly successful. In his annual report that year, the school superintendent reported that although he was "not much of an admirer of baseball playing, I am forced to admit that the successful career of the Kickapoo nine in defeating all the crack clubs of this section of Kansas speaks well for their industry and sobriety." In 1904 the team "received invitations from distant towns in other states for matched games."[6]

In Lawrence, about seventy miles south of the Kickapoo Training School, the United States Indian Industrial Training School was established in 1884.[7] Its name was changed to Haskell Institute in 1887, after Congressman Dudley Haskell, a charter member of the Kaw Valley Base Ball Club of Lawrence in 1867. The name was changed again in 1993 to Haskell Indian Nations University. By March 1890 Haskell had a baseball team that "defeated every club that has met it," initially other nearby schools, including the State University in Lawrence (now the University of Kansas).[8] A Haskell baseball team traveled around Kansas during the summer of 1896 and through northern Kansas and southern Nebraska in 1901. The team continued to play in Kansas and elsewhere into the early 1900s. They competed in as many as sixty-six games during the summer, sometimes with hired players, earning enough profit to supplement the budget of the school's athletic program.[9] Their games were often major events in other cities. In 1902 they played a game against the team from Bethany College in Lindsborg that was preceded by a "grand concert" in the afternoon and followed by an evening performance of the Messiah. In 1908 they participated in a tournament in Lucas that featured western Kansas teams, including white teams and the African American team from Nicodemus.[10] Later, most of Haskell's games were again limited to nearby teams, which reduced travel expenses. Baseball was one of several programs eliminated in 1980 as a result of federal budget cuts.[11]

Haskell Institute was one of the first five Indian boarding schools established by the US Congress. One of the other four schools was the Chilocco Indian Agricultural School, founded in 1884 at a site north of Ponca

Photograph of the 1917 baseball team from Haskell Institute in Lawrence, Kansas (now Haskell Indian Nations University). Both Haskell and the Kickapoo Training School (referred to locally as the Kickapoo Indian School) west of Horton fielded baseball teams that played teams usually composed of white or African American players. The team from Haskell also barnstormed during the summer in some years, earning enough money to supplement the school's athletic budget. Courtesy of the Kansas Historical Society, Topeka.

City in what is now Oklahoma, near the Kansas border.[12] Chilocco fielded as many as three baseball teams that played teams in several Kansas towns beginning in the 1890s. Initially, they played in Oklahoma and nearby Kansas, including the cities of Arkansas City and Winfield, but the Chilocco team occasionally traveled farther afield into the early twentieth century.[13] Baseball teams from Chilocco and Haskell also played each other.[14] Budget cuts that ended the baseball program at Haskell in 1980 also led to the closing of the school at Chilocco the same year.[15]

In addition to the Kickapoo and Haskell teams in Kansas, the Potawatomi fielded baseball teams at least as early as 1900. In 1906 a sporting goods business in Topeka sold baseball equipment to the Indian baseball team from Mayetta, who played town teams in northeastern Kansas. The town of Mayetta was just outside the eastern boundary of the Potawatomi Reservation. In 1906 and 1908 the Mayetta Indians baseball team was a member of the Shawnee County Amateur Baseball League, even though Mayetta is in Jackson County, on the northern border of Shawnee County. They continued playing summer baseball into the 1920s, mostly as an independent team.[16]

The Mayetta team also played baseball at several of the early Potawatomi Indian Fairs held each autumn, beginning in 1915. Likewise, the Kickapoo Indians played in baseball games at the Kickapoo Indian Fair, cohosted with the Iowa and the Sac and Fox. In addition to baseball, the festivities included traditional lacrosse matches. In 1920 A. R. Snyder became superintendent of all four reservations in northeastern Kansas, and he combined the Indian fairs into a single event on the fairgrounds two and a half miles west of Mayetta. The scheduled baseball games that year featured the Mayetta Indians, the Potawatomi Indians, and the Kickapoo Indians. However, in 1922 baseball was replaced by the rodeo as the principal attraction at the fair.[17]

On a Sunday afternoon in June 1921, the Mayetta Indians participated in a ballgame hosted by the white town team from Valley Falls that ended with more than the usual complaining about an umpire's calls. In fact, the dispute ultimately made its way into court. With Mayetta leading 5–4 in the ninth inning, a Valley Falls runner was called out at the plate. Snyder, the Indian agent, claimed that the Valley Falls players "ganged Mitchell, an Indian umpire [from Nebraska], and escorted him from the park." He further claimed that Valley Falls refused to pay the Mayetta Indians their share of the gate receipts, which were to be split, 60 percent for the winning team and 40 percent for the losers, a common practice at the time. The minimum payment to Mayetta was alleged to be $35, but gate receipts came to $300, for a split of $180 and $120. Lou Hauck, manager of the Valley Falls team, denied that they interfered with the umpire, who had replaced the first umpire because Mayetta complained that he was partial to Valley Falls. Hauck also said that Mayetta walked off the field (with Valley Falls claiming victory on a forfeit), and no one from Mayetta ever came to collect their money. Yet there was also no offer to send the money to the Indians, so the Mayetta manager, Charles Cooney, filed a lawsuit against Hauck in an effort to claim a share of the receipts. In November the judge in the case ruled that the game violated the state's Sunday labor laws because it involved a contract between the two teams. Thus, the contract was unenforceable. In the judge's opinion, the contract was also illegal because the unequal sixty-forty split was a form of gambling. The case was appealed to the Kansas Supreme Court. In January 1923 the court ruled that if a team did not receive its share of a sixty-forty split from a baseball game, it could make no claim to it in Kansas courts because such an arrangement was considered to be gambling. Given that gambling was illegal in the state, the courts could not be a party in helping Mayetta collect any money. However, no mention was made of the Sunday labor laws and the legal standing of Sunday baseball games where admission was charged and teams were compensated.[18]

Barnstorming Teams

As with some teams of women and African Americans, there were strictly barnstorming teams of American Indians, in addition to teams from the Indian schools that barnstormed during the summer. The Nebraska Indians were a professional barnstorming team established in 1897 by Guy Wilder Green. Although the team was not associated with an Indian school, most of the players were American Indians initially recruited from the Indian schools and reservations in Nebraska, South Dakota, and Kansas. These players were supplemented by a few white players, often pitchers. The team also traveled with its own umpire, who would co-officiate with the umpire supplied by the host team, providing a counterpoint to any possible biases displayed by the local umpire. The team toured Nebraska, Kansas, and elsewhere, playing about 150 games each year, typically winning more than 70 percent. During their first year, the team traveled by wagon, an exhausting experience, but they eventually purchased their own Pullman railcar as used by other barnstorming teams. Instead of sleeping in hotels, the players typically slept in the Pullman railcar or camped in an "Indian village" of tents at the ball ground. Camping saved them money, generated publicity, and, according to Green, made his players more comfortable than the confining spaces of a hotel, assuming the local hotel was even open to Indian guests. Exploiting the stereotype, the players also paraded to the ballpark in buckskins and feathered headdresses to stimulate interest among local fans. Through the years, the Nebraska Indians played numerous town teams, along with a few college teams, minor league teams, and African American teams. After 1910 the success of the team began to decline, but they continued to play under new owners from 1912 to 1917.[19]

Other American Indian barnstorming teams tried to copy the success of the Nebraska Indians and likewise included a few white players. In the early 1900s, Kansas was visited by Sioux from Spokane (Washington) and by Cherokee, Ponca, and Cheyenne from the Indian and Oklahoma Territories, which collectively became the state of Oklahoma in 1907. In 1910 the Cherokee team toured not only with a portable grandstand and canvas fence but also with a set of fifty acetylene gaslights, producing a reported total of 50,000 candlepower for use at games in the evenings.[20]

Given his success with the Nebraska Indians, Green was inspired to seek even more financial gains with other novelty baseball teams. This led him to organize a barnstorming Japanese team, the Mikado Club, in 1906, advertised as "the most marvelous team of genuine Japanese ball players on earth, and [the] only one in America." Green hired Tozan T. Masko, a ballplayer in Saint Louis, to organize the team and serve as the player-manager. The team scheduled at least one game in Kansas, against a team from Fort Riley. After 1906 Masko took the team out on his own for several seasons, including games in Kansas.[21]

What the barnstorming American Indian teams and the Mikado Club had in common was that white communities viewed their games as a novelty, although not in the same way they viewed the games against women's or African American teams. The American Indian and Japanese teams were an exotic novelty, and good attendance at their games was driven by the curiosity of townspeople to see men of an ethnic group not represented in the local population play baseball against a local white team. In many instances, that curiosity was similarly tainted with racial bigotry. In Fort Scott, the stereotype "that the Japs are a stunted and runty class of people" was only partially debunked by "the muscular proportions of one or two of the Japs here yesterday with the Mikado baseball outfit. . . . One of the Japs was almost as large as Jim Jeffries. . . . However a majority of them were small men." A Garden City newspaper ran the headline "Yellow Peril Threatens the Arkansas Valley—Jap Ball Team."[22]

In 1908, advertisements in Kansas newspapers for "Jap silk," "Jap tea," and "Jap Rose Soap" shared space with stories of possible war between the United States and Japan. Interspersed among these items were newspaper reports of games played by the Mikado Club against local Kansas teams in April and May. They traveled from west to east through several Kansas cities, including Garden City, Dodge City, Larned, Great Bend, Ellinwood, Newton, Fort Scott, Olathe, and Kansas City. And the Mikado Club played well against them.[23] A Fort Scott newspaper claimed that the Japanese team had two white players (catcher and third base) and two American Indian players (pitcher and second base). A Garden City newspaper listed only last names and positions of the players, but made no reference to ethnicity (only one name on the 1908 roster matched the 1906 roster).[24] Despite the political tensions of the day, some newspaper accounts remarked favorably on the team's baseball skills, although the language could be tarnished with bigotry; for example, "The home team says the Japs were clean players and have nothing but good words for the little brown men who are endeavoring to break into the national game."[25] An Emporia newspaper even went so far as to suggest that "the fact that Japs are playing base ball in Kansas should silence at once the foolish war talk that fills the public print."[26] The Mikado Club continued to play into the 1920s, and university baseball teams from Japan also toured the United States, including Kansas.[27]

Players Named "Chief" and Other Stereotypes

As with the Japanese, African Americans, and other minorities, American Indians who played baseball were subjected to racial stereotypes by fans and newspapers. The principal difference is that they were not banned from organized baseball, as African American players were. In game write-ups, references to scalping were common, bats became "war clubs," and Indian players were often referred to as "redskin" or "Chief." The similarity among racial stereotypes is evident in a newspaper story from southeastern Kansas reporting that the local team was being augmented "with the well known Redskins, Kahdot at short[stop] and 'Nig' Dodson at the keystone stop" (second base). Barnstorming teams often catered to some of the racial stereotypes by dressing the players in buckskin and headdresses to promote their games, helping to draw large, paying crowds.[28] The Kickapoo and Haskell teams did not cater to the stereotypes, but their players were still subjected to the same racially insensitive language: "The Kickapoo Indians scalped the Horton club 13 to 5,"[29] according to one account, while another explained, "No, Willie, the Haskell Indians do not carry tomahawks and scalping knives, but they are terrors when it comes to playing base ball."[30] As noted by Jeffrey Powers-Beck, the Nebraska Indians (and I would add American Indian teams in Kansas) consistently played well against their white opponents on the field and triumphed even more consistently against commonplace racially offensive heckling from the grandstands.

The newspaper coverage in Hays for a pair of games played by the Haskell Institute baseball team in 1905 illustrates the dichotomy of praise and racial stereotype experienced by American Indian teams. They were scheduled to play the Western Branch of the State Normal School team (now Fort Hays State University) on Monday and the town team on Friday. On the front page of the edition prior to the arrival of the Haskell team, the weekly newspaper stated, "The young students from the Haskell Institute are a nice lot of young fellows and well educated, and as they come here to see the town and historic fort, . . . we hope all our citizens having carriages will come to the hotel early on Monday morning and take them out for a ride."

What the members of the Haskell baseball team thought of their tour of a fort that played a prominent role in the removal of American Indians from the area was not reported. However, the baseball game was certainly popular with local residents. Stores were to close during the game, "from 1 to 3:30, so all can attend," and the paid adult admissions were 1,391 spectators—approximately equal to the population of Hays at the time. An admission of 25¢ was charged to cover the cost of the visitors' hotel and rail travel expenses.[31]

On another page in the same newspaper, there appeared a caricature of "Uncle Hank," a white-bearded man wearing a top hat and carrying a carpetbag. It was accompanied by his instructions to his wife:

Come Jane, get ready all nine of the children (for Mr Mathew says all children under 12 go in to the Base ball game FREE) and we will go have a picnic on the creek and see the Normals beat the Haskel [sic] Indians in the Ball game Monday. Them Ingins may defeat our boys, but by Golly, they shant [sic] scalp any of them like they did father.[32]

Haskell defeated the Normal School 1–0, and the game summary in the following week's newspaper was a mix of praise and racial stereotype:

The Haskell Indians . . . showed a crowd of 2000 the best game ever seen in Hays, and their many good plays were greeted with wild applause, especially the one hand, high jumping catch that saved the game. . . . A special feature of the game was the remarkable pitching of Houser [for Haskell] in the 8th and 9th innings. Bases were full, the Normals and their friends yelled like wild men when his Indian blood rose and he pitched for blood, while the war whoop sounded and every Indian "held the field for life or death." It was a wild scene of players and the vast audience worth seeing.[33]

On the following Friday, Haskell lost to the Hays town team (9–7) in front of about 800 fans. After a week in Hays, playing two games on a diamond built on land that was formerly part of the Fort Hays military reservation, the "Haskell Institute boys expressed themselves as much elated over their fine treatment while here and the manager will bring his famous foot ball team here this fall."[34]

Unlike African American ballplayers, several men of American Indian heritage played in the major leagues in the early 1900s, and a few gained notoriety. Jim Thorpe was a Sac and Fox born in Oklahoma. He spent two years at Haskell Institute in Lawrence but apparently did not play for the baseball team. Better known as a football player and Olympic athlete, Thorpe played baseball for the New York Giants in 1913–1915 and 1917–1919, as well as the Cincinnati Reds in 1917 and Boston Braves in 1919. In 1913 he joined major league players touring the world to play a series of exhibition games promoting baseball, including a game in Blue Rapids.[35]

There are other, less well-known players of American Indian heritage that have stronger baseball connections to Kansas. Among them was a prominent pitcher who played for several years in the state and had one of the briefest major league careers—Emmett Jerome "Chief" Bowles, a Potawatomi born in Wanette, Oklahoma, in 1898. From 1919 to 1923 he pitched most frequently for teams in Larned and Great Bend, although he picked up additional games with other teams, which was a common practice for good pitchers. At the semiprofessional level, Bowles was a dominant pitcher, usually striking out more than ten batters per game. While playing in Kansas, he threw at least two no-hitters and initiated two triple plays in one game. Based on this success, Bowles was invited to spring training with the Chicago White Sox in 1922, but he experienced arm problems and was sent to the minor leagues in Arkansas and Missouri. Not content with this assignment, he returned to Great Bend in March and was chosen as the manager of the Benders that May at age twenty-three. Shortly after accepting this position, however, he was picked up by the Hutchinson Wheat Shockers of the Southwestern League (Class C), but the team released him a week later. Playing and managing again in Great Bend, Bowles was told at the end of July to report to the White Sox. He played in Iowa during the following week and returned to Great Bend for a Sunday game before going to Chicago in mid-August. Bowles's career in the major leagues consisted of pitching one inning for the White Sox on September 12, 1922. He faced six batters and gave up three runs. By the beginning of October, Bowles was back in Great Bend, where he pitched a game in his White Sox uniform. On October 27, Bowles pitched for the Belpre town team against the Pratt American Legion team of ex-servicemen. The game featured two New York Yankees outfielders—"Babe" Ruth at first base for Pratt and Bob Meusel at shortstop for Belpre. Belpre and Bowles won 13–2.[36]

In 1923 Bowles returned to Larned, where he pitched for the town team. The following year he played well for the Independence Producers of the Southwestern League (Class D), but the team disbanded in July, and he was picked up by the Topeka Senators of the Western Association (Class C). His stint with Topeka was unsuccessful and consequently brief. By the end of the month he was back in the Southwestern League pitching for the Eureka Oilers. In 1925 Bowles tried to catch on with the reorganized Independence Producers of the Western Association (Class C), but the team released him in May. Bowles returned to semiprofessional baseball and during the late 1920s and most of the 1930s spent time as the star pitcher for the Madrid Miners, a coal company team in the Central New Mexico League. He died on a trip to Flagstaff, Arizona, in 1959 and was buried in Albuquerque, New Mexico.[37]

Bowles was not the only Potawatomi from Oklahoma to have a successful baseball career in Kansas. Isaac Leonard "Ike" Kahdot was born in 1899 (sometimes reported as 1901) in Georgetown, Oklahoma (near Konawa). He attended high school at Haskell Institute from the autumn of 1915 to the spring of 1919, and he played third base for the school baseball team. In his second season on the team in the spring of 1917, the Lawrence newspaper reported, "With Kahdot at third the fans are always assured of some thrilling fielding about this sack." After Kahdot had moved on, the newspaper reminisced, "Ike Kahdot was a performer who won the admiration of all who have ever seen him play. He is a player of the type who believes there is always a chance to field a ball until it touches the ground no matter how far away its [sic] going to light." After graduating from Haskell, Kahdot played for the Iola Oilers, the Independence (Kansas) town team, the Sinclair Refiners team of Coffeyville, and the Empire Oil and Gas Company team in Bartlesville, Oklahoma, in 1919 and 1920 before moving on to the minor leagues.[38]

As with Bowles, Kahdot was referred to by the nickname of "Chief" during his long minor league career, which began in 1921 with the Pittsburg (Kansas) Manuals of the Southwestern League (Class D). Short biographies introducing the players were published in the local newspaper that April. Under the heading "'Chief' Kahdot," the biography opens with, "[It's all] the name he's got; it's been so long since he heard his first name, he's forgotten it." However, as his career progressed, many Kansas newspapers that referred to Kahdot by more than just his last name identified him as Ike Kahdot, omitting the nickname Chief, although they frequently mentioned that he was an Indian. In 1922 he played for the Coffeyville Refiners of the Southwestern League (which had advanced to Class C). Kahdot's shot at the major leagues came at the close of the 1922 minor league season, when he made a brief visit to the Cleveland Indians in September, the same month Bowles played for the White Sox. Kahdot played five innings in four games and had two at bats but did not reach base. In his three chances as third baseman, he had one putout and two assists, including a double play. As he was a promising young player, Cleveland wanted him to play for a team in Grand Rapids, Michigan, in 1923, but Kahdot arranged to return to the Coffeyville Refiners and be closer to home. He became a good friend and hunting partner of future Hall of Fame pitcher Walter Johnson, a Kansas native who made his off-season home in Coffeyville for a time.[39]

From 1924 to 1931, Kahdot primarily played shortstop for various teams in the Western League (Class A), Texas League (Class A), Western Association (Class C), South Atlantic League (Class B), and Piedmont League (Class C). Late in 1931 he returned to Kansas, joining the Independence Producers of the Western Association (Class C). The following year, Kahdot and the team started the season in Independence but both moved to Joplin and Hutchinson as the summer progressed. In 1933 he remained in Hutchinson to play for the Wheatshockers, a Detroit Tigers farm team in the Western League (Class A). Yet again, his team moved while the season was in progress, becoming the Bartlesville Broncos. Kahdot closed his minor league baseball career with the Bartlesville Reds, a Cincinnati

Reds farm team in the Western Association (Class C) in 1934 and 1935. He continued to play on semiprofessional teams until 1941 and worked in the Oklahoma oil fields. Ike Kahdot passed away in 1999 in Oklahoma City and was buried next to his first wife (who died in 1958) in the cemetery at Altoona in southeastern Kansas.[40]

Another native Kansan tagged with the same racial stereotypes who eventually played in the major leagues was Elon "Chief" Hogsett, a left-handed submarine pitcher who was greeted by "war whoops" from the home crowd when he entered a game to pitch.[41] Hogsett, who continued to go by the nickname Chief after his retirement from baseball, was born in 1903 on a western Kansas farm near the small town of Brownell, southwest of Hays. He once claimed distant Cherokee ancestry ($^{1}/_{32}$) on his mother's side of the family, although this has been questioned. But this debate over his heritage misses the bigger point. Whether or not he truly had American Indian heritage, his experience illustrates how easily players were racially profiled based on their appearance. Adrian Burgos has thoroughly described how baseball variously accepted or excluded players since the 1860s based on the color of their skin, especially those of American Indian and Latino heritage. These players were often promoted as "curiosities" to attract more fans to games. While pitching for the minor league Montreal Royals in 1929 (seventeen years before Jackie Robinson played for the team), local Iroquois adopted Hogsett in a ceremony at home plate and gave him the name Ranantasse, translated as "strong arm." He kept a photograph of the event on a wall in his home during his retirement in Hays.[42]

As Kahdot's minor league career was winding down, Hogsett played for the Detroit Tigers from late 1929 to early 1936, appearing in the 1934 and 1935 World Series (the Tigers were victorious in 1935). He also played for the Saint Louis Browns (1936–1937, now the Baltimore Orioles) and the Washington Senators (1938, now the Minnesota Twins). After 1931 he was used primarily as a relief pitcher in Detroit, before that specialty was highly prized, and he ranked second or third in saves in the American League during 1932, 1933, and 1935. In 1936 and 1937 he returned to the role of starting pitcher.[43] His lifetime record in the major leagues was 63 wins and 87 losses, and his earned run average (ERA) was 5.02 (the league ERA was 4.73 during the same time).[44] Today he likely would be used solely as a reliever (his ERA was 3.88 in 1932–1935, when he started only 17 of his 158 games).[45]

Hogsett kept it all in perspective and wrote at age eighty-seven, "I never was a star—but I played with and against a lot of them. I am not in the Hall of Fame either but being a pitcher, perhaps I helped get some of them there."[46] He closed his professional career in the minor leagues with the Indianapolis Indians and Minneapolis Millers (both Class AA) from 1939 through 1944, with a brief return to the Detroit Tigers for three games in 1944 during the period of depleted rosters as the Second World War continued.[47] Like Kahdot, Hogsett also lived for nearly a century, dying in Hays in 2001, just short of his ninety-eighth birthday. He was buried in the Brownell cemetery.[48]

The racial barrier around baseball's major and minor leagues was not absolute with regard to American Indians, and several players managed to cross that line during the late 1800s and the early decades of the 1900s. Although exclusion of American Indians was not official policy in organized baseball, players in the major and minor leagues, as well as those on barnstorming teams, had to endure the challenges of widespread racial harassment and stereotyping to play a sport they loved. Grateful for the opportunity to play professional baseball, especially during the Great Depression, Ike Kahdot reminisced about his career on the diamond when he was in his nineties, reflecting, "Baseball's been good to me."[49]

CHAPTER 5

Mexican and Mexican American Baseball and Softball

The history of Mexican and Mexican American baseball teams in Kansas is not as long or as well documented in contemporary sources as that of white, African American, or American Indian teams. This history began early in the 1900s as men from Mexico came north to work on the railroads and in occupations in agriculture (especially sugar beets), meatpacking plants, salt mines, and factories.[1] These immigrants began arriving at the same time that Kansas veterans of the US–Mexican War (1846–1848) were holding the last of their reunions.[2] That war had added California, Nevada, Utah, Arizona, New Mexico, and parts of other modern states—including territory in what became southwestern Kansas—to the United States, along with their native populations of Mexicans and American Indians.

Most Mexican immigrants in the early 1900s came from the states north of Mexico City, an agricultural region where they had lived in poverty, some tied by debt to the landowners, while others lived in the region's cities. They all had little time for baseball. Many of these people spent time in northern Mexico or Texas before coming to Kansas. Expansion of the railroads in Mexico and the southwestern United States in the late nineteenth century provided the means for them to travel from central Mexico to the international border and from there to the central United States. The railroads were also major employers. Other events also contributed to this emigration from Mexico. Beginning in 1910, the decade-long Mexican Revolution and its aftermath upset political and economic stability in the country, providing a workforce seeking employment opportunities elsewhere. A Kansas newspaper lamented in 1916 that spring rain showers were making dates for baseball games "as provisional as a Mexican administration." Meanwhile, there was economic expansion in the United States, including labor-intensive railroad construction and maintenance, as well as agricultural jobs in the sparsely populated Great Plains and elsewhere in the West. Much of this work was unappealing to American workers because it was seasonal and paid low wages. In addition, the First World War reduced immigration from Eastern Europe, as did subsequent laws and policies in the United States that excluded or substantially limited European immigration. The immigration of Chinese laborers, noted for their contributions to construction of the transcontinental railroad, had ended similarly in the 1880s with the Chinese Exclusion Act.[3]

At first, the majority of immigrants from Mexico were men. Because much of the early work on the railroad and in agriculture was seasonal, many of them returned to Mexico during the winter and came back north to work again the following year. Slowly, communities of Mexican immigrants began to form when men working on the railroads were assigned to longer-term jobs that required less travel, such as section gangs maintaining a local stretch of track or men working in railroad roundhouses and shops. Mexican communities also developed in towns with salt mines, sugar beet–processing facilities, meatpacking plants, or similar industries that allowed them to live with their families. Women and children could also work in agricultural fields or other jobs, and often did so to supplement the incomes earned by their husbands and fathers. As the number of Mexican families increased during the First World War and into the mid-1920s, the number of Kansas-born Mexican Americans increased, further transforming these communities throughout much of Kansas. Yet they remained relatively isolated because of differences in language and culture and because of racial bias. This isolation, along with the need for entire families to work, also limited educational opportunities for the children. Through this combination of factors, Mexican immigrants retained much of their culture. In addition, large portions of the early immigrant populations in each of the cities of Kansas came from the same states in Mexico, which contributed to their sense of community. It was this strong sense of community that helped many of these families survive during difficult economic times, such as the Great Depression.[4]

This process was evident even in Chanute, a small town compared to Kansas City, Wichita, or Topeka. The first group of sixty-two Mexicans—forty-six male laborers with sixteen of their wives—arrived in 1905 after traveling in three boxcars. Soon after, another group of ten Mexican laborers with two of their wives arrived, this time in two passenger coaches. Although many of these men returned to Mexico periodically, others remained in Kansas, and their numbers slowly increased. Initially, they labored with immigrants from countries such as Greece and Italy, and general complaints about hiring cheap foreign laborers led to reports in the spring of 1907 that "white, educated laborers" would replace them. However, a few months later, the Santa Fe Railroad reduced the workday for section gangs to nine hours, with a corresponding reduction in wages from $1.50 to $1.15 per day, making the physically demanding work even less attractive to people with employment alternatives.[5] That same year, construction began on two cement plants in Chanute, which also employed numerous Mexican laborers.[6] By 1920 Chanute, with a population of about 10,000 people at the time, had developed two Mexican communities, one on the northern edge of the city associated with the cement plant and one on the southern edge of town associated with the Santa Fe Railroad.[7] This sort of segregation among Mexican communities based on employment occurred in other Kansas towns as well.[8]

Living conditions for the laborers and their families were typically poor. In the early years, railroad laborers often lived in old wooden boxcars in the rail yards or at their temporary worksites away from towns.[9] As part of an effort to retain employees in the years preceding the entry of the United States into the First World War, the Santa Fe Railroad began constructing houses in the Mexican communities on its properties, with relatively nicer houses built in conspicuous locations along the main line and lower-quality houses elsewhere. For example, in Newton, the railroad replaced the boxcar homes used for "four or five years" with whitewashed "shanties." By the 1920s and 1930s, brick homes were constructed for workers and their families, and some families were able to rent or buy houses on the periphery of the Mexican communities.[10]

It was against this backdrop of isolation and poverty that the Mexican communities retained elements of their culture, such as establishing churches that offered services in Spanish and celebrating holidays as they had done in Mexico. Some of these activities integrated elements of the Mexican and US communities. For example, a front-page story in a Garden City newspaper reported that the city's "Little Mexico" celebrated Mexican independence in September 1925. The festivities extended over three days and included concerts, dances, speeches, plays, and food. At a sunrise concert, the first two songs played were the Mexican and US national anthems, and both flags were flown. The *Garden City Herald* reported that "Americanos and colored people" were among those enjoying the festival.[11] It was in this climate that some members of the Mexican community began to organize baseball teams, just as the white railroad employees were doing. However, the general isolation of the Mexican communities in space and language contributed to the limited number of early reports on baseball as a recreational activity among the immigrants.

Baseball had been played in northern Mexico since the 1880s. Several Kansas newspapers reprinted stories in 1904 and for several years afterward about baseball games in Mexico City between teams of players from the United States and Mexico.[12] There was even a story about a baseball game in Vera Cruz, Mexico, in May 1914 between men from the Fourth US Infantry and an "all-star Mexican team." In addition to US Navy and Army personnel, the spectators included "hundreds of cheering natives. The Mexicans in the grandstand proved themselves thorough baseball fans by their vigorous rooting in Spanish and broken English."[13] This game was noteworthy because tensions were high after the United States had forcibly seized the Mexican port in late April during the ongoing Mexican Revolution (the occupation ended in November 1914). Eventually, cultural divides were also crossed on the baseball diamond in Kansas.

Baseball in Kansas

For immigrant communities, baseball was a means of social interaction for the large groups of men who did not live with their families. In Topeka, men organized the El Diamante Club in 1920, which provided instruction in English, Spanish, and arithmetic, as well as opportunities to participate in dances and various sports, including a baseball team—the Mexican Nine. The club folded in 1924, however, because work became scarce, causing many of the members to move away.[14] Yet baseball persisted as a culturally important activity that allowed all family members to come together to socialize and discuss social issues, strengthening community unity. Sunday afternoon games were especially festive affairs.[15]

There were Mexican baseball teams in Topeka at least as early as 1916, and the number of teams organized in various Kansas cities increased in subsequent years.[16] As the Mexican community in Kansas City known as Argentine transitioned from a camp for migratory laborers to a stable community, a baseball team including three white players was established in 1919 to play a team from the barrio on the Missouri side of the border.[17] However, these early Mexican teams typically did not play on the ball diamonds in city parks or other fields used by the white teams.[18] African American teams could share the use of these parks with the white teams, but they spoke English. The Mexican laborers and their families were outsiders, who lived in areas often referred to as "colonies" or "settlements."[19] As a result, early Mexican baseball teams cleared their own baseball fields and played most of their games against other Mexican teams.[20] Nonetheless, some of the earliest teams occasionally played interracial games. For example, in 1917 the white Linwood team of Wichita defeated the "North End Mexican team" 19–6. The site of the game was not mentioned, but the Linwoods took their name from their home ball ground in Linwood Park. The battery for the Mexican team was even reported in the Wichita newspaper (pitchers and catchers were often the only players mentioned, if any were mentioned at all, for amateur and semiprofessional teams).[21]

Kansas newspapers typically offered meager and sporadic reports about baseball teams of women, African Americans, and American Indians. Initially, they provided even less coverage of Mexican baseball teams due in part to differences in language. However, a few game summaries were reported in English-language newspapers with the assistance of interpreters. For example, a Mexican team from Olathe lost to a Mexican team from Kansas City in a game played "at the diamonds near the stockyards" in 1922. Adrian Huertavo, who pitched for Olathe (and occasionally for Gardner), was the losing pitcher against the team from Kansas City. Players sometimes did not report the results of their team's losses in games played outside organized leagues to their local newspapers, even if there was no language barrier, but Huertavo reported his team's loss to the Olathe newspaper through a grocer who served as interpreter.[22]

Newspaper reports of interracial games involving Mexican teams increased during the 1920s. In 1921 the Chanute Black Diamonds, an African American team, was unable to play a game in Neosho Falls because of a storm there, so they played a game against a Mexican team from the local cement plant on its field.[23] The following April, an Olathe African American baseball team defeated the local Mexican team twice "at the Stock yards ground" in Olathe.[24] Later that month, two Johnson County teams, the Sons of Rest and the Zarah Blues, were scheduled to play a Sunday morning game in Zarah, with the winner playing the Mexican team from nearby Craig in the afternoon.[25] In 1927, J. A. "Jack" Keena,

Newton baseball players wearing street clothes and posing with their equipment in 1919. Formal teams, sometimes representing social clubs, also were organized during and after the First World War. Courtesy of Raymond Olais, Newton.

owner of a Hutchinson radiator shop (and Democratic candidate for Reno County sheriff in 1926), sponsored a Mexican team that lost to a white team representing organized labor at the Labor Day celebration sponsored by the union. The game was played at the city's principal baseball ground in Carey Park. A Mexican team from Hutchinson also played a team from the Reno County courthouse in July.[26] In Emporia, the Black Sox, a local African American team, even played a Mexican team from El Paso, Texas, at Soden's Grove in 1928. During the late 1920s the white and Mexican workers for the Rock Island Railroad in Horton fielded two baseball teams. Although they shared the same employer, they did not share a ball ground. The Mexican Nine played both Mexican and non-Mexican teams from other cities on their ballpark west of town referred to as Tweentracks.[27]

During the Great Depression, pressure was applied to railroad companies, agricultural businesses, and others to stop hiring Mexican and Mexican American workers and give those jobs to unemployed white laborers. The effort met with some success, and many Mexican families were forced to leave. Those who stayed continued to seek support within their communities and sought distraction through social activities, including baseball.[28] In fact, opportunities for Mexican American baseball teams to compete with a variety of teams began to increase, and after 1930, summaries of games involving Mexican American teams were reported more frequently in newspapers printed by white publishers.

As before, some of these games were played against other Mexican American teams.[29] In addition, games were played against African American teams or against various opponents at Emancipation Day celebrations. For example, in 1934, the Chanute Ramblers, an African American team, played a local Mexican team, just as their predecessors, the Black Diamonds, had done in 1921.[30] Increasingly, however, games were played against white teams at the home parks of the white teams, as well as on the diamonds of the Mexican American teams.[31] The first team to break the ethnic barrier in a Wichita city league was a Mexican American baseball team—the Aztecs—in the Commercial League in 1932.[32]

Barnstorming teams from Mexico also played in Kansas. In 1935 a visiting baseball team from Mexico known as Las Juntas—the "Champions of Old Mexico"—played Emporia's white Santa Fe Railroad team. In 1936 it was the Emporia town team that played the Aztecas, a team of professional players from Mexico.[33] The local Mexican team was also active. Through a notice in the English-language newspaper, the Emporia Morelos solicited games with any other teams to be played on the Santa Fe Railroad ball diamond.[34]

Teams were also organized in the Mexican communities for young players who were taking an interest in baseball. One of the saddest incidents during this period was the reported death of a fourteen-year-old boy hit in the temple by a baseball and killed while he watched his companions play.[35] Nonetheless, youth baseball increased. In 1920 the Hutchinson YMCA helped organize two teams of Mexican boys:

The "Mexican league" is the latest in back lot base ball in Hutchinson. Two ball teams were organized among the Mexican boys in the Santa

Fe colony yesterday afternoon by L. R. Mark, director of boys' work in the Y. M. C. A. The Mexican lads formed their own teams, selecting their own captains. There will be organized play every Thursday at 4:15 in this colony, under the direction of Mr. Mark, cooperating with the Americanization committee.[36]

As with the assimilation of American Indian youths at boarding schools, the goal of groups such as the "Americanization committee" was to help the Mexican "colony" conform to the prevailing culture of the United States. However, the goal was not integration, and a sense of cultural identity within the Mexican community was retained.

Although these youth teams initially played against other Mexican American teams, they later played against teams of African American or white players, and some Mexican American teams became members of youth leagues composed primarily of white teams.[37] For example, in 1932 Saint Catherine's Mission in Emporia sponsored a team of Mexican American youths who played in the city's American Legion Junior League against teams sponsored by the Kiwanis, Lions, and Rotary Clubs and by local businesses. The teams played among themselves during April, May, and early June. One of the Saint Catherine's players was pitcher Jacinto "Spider" Zabala (also spelled *Sabala*, *Savala*, and *Zabola* in the local newspaper). Zabala was a good young pitcher, throwing a no-hitter against the Lions team in May. Given his pitching skill, he became a member of the Junior League's all-star team that played teams from other cities beginning in June. At the end of the season in early August, Emporia lost a three-game series against Salina for the state championship. The following year Zabala was again pitching in the Junior League for Saint Catherine's Mission. On May 28, the Junior All-Stars of Lyon and Greenwood Counties, consisting of twelve boys aged seventeen to twenty-one years old, departed on a barnstorming trip through Missouri. An eighteen-year-old Spider Zabala and another Mexican American player named Hidalgo constituted two-thirds of the team's pitching staff.

In 1935 Zabala jumped from the local Mexican American team to the Imps of the Emporia City League. He even pitched against his former team at the "Old Santa Fe ball diamond" on South Avenue.[38] Yet segregation still dominated in the broader community. For example, at Emporia's public wading pool in 1940, the schedule was: children seven years old and younger at 1:00–2:00, girls from eight to twelve years old at 2:00–3:00, boys eight to twelve years old at 3:00–4:00, and "Mexican and colored children" at 4:00–5:00 (with no distinction as to age or sex).[39]

Into the Major Leagues

As with American Indians, men of Latino heritage occasionally crossed the color line in professional baseball. However, most of these early players came from Cuba or California. The first Mexican American to play in the major leagues was Vincente "Sandy" Nava from San Francisco. While playing in the Pacific Base Ball League and the California League in 1878–1881, he used his stepfather's surname of Irwin. Nava joined the major leagues as a backup catcher for the Providence Grays of the National League in 1882–1884, working behind the plate for pitchers such as John Montgomery Ward and Hoss Radbourn. Nava was released by Providence before the end of the 1884 season, but he had brief stints with the Baltimore Orioles of the American Association (not related to the current team) in 1885 and 1886.[40] Mexican Americans from Kansas also had occasional opportunities to enter the major leagues prior to the Second World War. For example, Ramon Apolonio Martinez was born in Copeland to parents who came to southwestern Kansas from Jalisco, Mexico. His father worked for the Santa Fe Railroad, eventually becoming an American citizen. In 1938 Ramon joined a semiprofessional team in Liberal. The following year, the Brooklyn Dodgers offered him a contract for $90 per month plus room and board, but he turned them down because he made more money in Liberal, where the team also arranged for him to have a part-time job.[41]

Perhaps the best-known major league player to come from the Mexican American community in Kansas, albeit after the Second World War, was Mike Torrez from Topeka. His family's history in Kansas is rooted in the immigration story of Mexican laborers during the early 1900s. His paternal grandfather, Mariano Torrez, came to Kansas in 1911 to work for the railroad near Topeka. In 1917, at the urging of his supervisor with the Santa Fe Railroad, Mariano brought his wife and children to Kansas. When Mike's father, Juan, was old enough, he left high school and also worked for the railroad. Mike's maternal grandparents came to Kansas in 1922. Mike was born in 1946, and faced the same discrimination that had existed before the Second World War. However, he was able to compete on integrated baseball teams in Topeka, including the American Legion team, as Spider Zabala had done. His performance as a pitcher in Legion baseball led to his signing with the Saint Louis Cardinals in 1964. His major league debut was in the autumn of 1967, after the close of the minor league season. Traded several times, Torrez pitched for the Saint Louis Cardinals, Montreal Expos (now the Washington Nationals), Baltimore Orioles, Oakland Athletics, New York Yankees, Boston Red Sox, and New York Mets between 1967 and 1984. Pitching for the Yankees in 1977, he was 0–1 as a starter against the Kansas City Royals in the American League Championship Series, but he had two complete-game victories in the World Series, including the sixth and deciding game against the Los Angeles Dodgers. During his successful baseball career, Torrez remained a prominent member of his local community, especially his Topeka barrio.[42]

Fast-Pitch Softball

Although baseball was relatively new for the early Mexican immigrants in Kansas, the sport had been played in the centuries-old Hispanic communities of the New Mexico and Arizona Territories since the late 1800s. After statehood was granted to New Mexico in January 1912, baseball continued to be an important component of community identity and unity into the 1960s, with both men's and women's teams participating. This aspect of the sport then faded as town team baseball declined in the region.[43]

In Kansas, the importance to the Mexican American community first held by baseball shifted to softball after the Second World War, although some baseball teams continued to play.[44] Softball offered a few advantages over baseball; for example, the shorter base paths and distances in the outfield meant less space was needed for a softball field. But more important, softball allowed people with a broader range of physical abilities and ages to play, which expanded participation within the community beyond what was possible in baseball. And just as there had been baseball teams of Mexican American women in some Kansas towns, including Newton and Emporia, women also played on softball teams. All of this meant that softball could include active participation by multiple generations of families. Thus, softball was incorporated into the culture of the Mexican American communities and remained important to community identity and unity.[45]

Newton Cuauhtemoc baseball team in 1932, posing on the front porch of one of the brick ranchito units that housed the families of railroad employees after the First World War. Courtesy of Raymond Olais, Newton.

Mexican Catholics softball team, which was first organized in 1939. In 1946 they started the first fast-pitch softball tournament during the July 4 holiday in Newton, which continues today. Festivities also included food and dances, with proceeds from the early tournaments going to the building fund for Our Lady of Guadalupe Catholic Church. Teams from Hutchinson, Newton, Topeka, and Wichita competed in the first tournament, which was won by Newton. In subsequent years, teams from other states also participated. Courtesy of Raymond Olais, Newton.

Perhaps the best-known and the longest-running softball tournament for Mexican American teams is held in Newton. As in other Mexican American communities in Kansas, baseball had been played in Newton since the 1910s. During the 1930s the Cuauhtemocs were one of the best teams in the region, and Anderson's Sporting Goods extended the team credit to purchase uniforms, costing a total of $27 (equivalent to about $467 in 2016). They were named after Cuauhtémoc, the last of the Aztec rulers, who was defeated in 1521 by Hernán Cortés and his Indian allies at Tenochtitlán (now Mexico City). While baseball teams continued to play in Newton, a men's softball team named the Mexican Catholics was organized in 1939. Following the end of the Second World War, they organized the first Newton fast-pitch softball tournament held at Athletic Park on the Fourth of July. Four teams competed in the 1946 tournament. Newton defeated Hutchinson, Topeka defeated Wichita, and Newton defeated Topeka to claim the first championship. In 1947 three women's softball teams from Newton, Lyons, and Wichita also competed among themselves to provide breaks between the men's games. More than just softball, the festivities also included food and dances, with proceeds going to the building fund for Our Lady of Guadalupe Catholic Church. In 1963 Guadalupe Park was established at the church and became the site of the ballgames and other activities for more than thirty years. The games then returned to Athletic Park, supplemented by other diamonds in the city. During that time, the tournament expanded to include teams from several states in addition to Kansas, including Colorado, Missouri, Nebraska, Oklahoma, and Texas.[46] The tournament continues today, with players representing the most recent generations participating and maintaining a sense of community with the early immigrants.

CHAPTER 6

Minor Leagues and the Establishment of Night Baseball

As Kansas towns competed for status with their peers, one early expression of this competition took the form of amateur baseball teams composed of local players. This competitive drive soon led to a few players from outside the community being paid to play in a particular game or for an entire season. At first it was a pitcher, then a catcher who could handle a good pitcher, and perhaps a few position players. The competition escalated when several towns hired professional teams, but paying players substantially increased the cost to the community supporting the team representing them.[1] Few Kansas towns could sustain this expense, although many tried.

Just as amateur and semiprofessional town teams flourished during the late 1800s and early 1900s, professional baseball teams in the state participating in what are now referred to as the minor leagues also had an early start. In 1886 Topeka and Leavenworth fielded teams in the Western League, along with Denver, Leadville (Colorado), Saint Joseph (Missouri), and Lincoln (Nebraska). Topeka had an integrated team in 1886, with African American Bud Fowler playing second base. One of the prominent players in the league was Jake Beckley, a native of Hannibal, Missouri, who played several positions but settled at first base for Leavenworth in 1886 and the early part of 1887. A strong hitter, he enjoyed a good career in the major leagues after joining the Pittsburgh Alleghenies (now the Pittsburgh Pirates) in 1888. He had 2,934 hits and a batting average of .308 in the major leagues. The number of games Beckley played at first base (2,380) is second only to Eddie Murray's, but Beckley's 23,731 putouts at that position is still a major league record. He retired from the major leagues in 1907, and in 1910 he returned to the Western League, playing briefly for Topeka. The Veterans Committee elected him to the National Baseball Hall of Fame in 1971.[2]

In 1887, Leadville dropped out of the Western League before the season began, but teams from Kansas City (Missouri), Hastings (Nebraska), and Omaha were added. However, the league continued to have problems retaining teams. Leavenworth folded in July and was replaced by a team from Wichita. (Jake Beckley was picked up by the team in Lincoln.) Saint Joseph soon followed Leavenworth out of the league and was replaced by a team from Emporia. Unfortunately, Emporia and Wichita did not fare any better than their predecessors, and both teams folded in September, several weeks before the scheduled end of the season. Because of their short runs, the league did not include any games played against Emporia and Wichita in the final standings of the remaining teams. The bright spot for Kansas teams that year was the first-place finish by the Topeka Golden Giants, also known as Goldsby's Golden Giants after their manager, Walt Goldsby. Their record was 73–23 (.760), eleven and a half games ahead of second-place Lincoln. For years afterward, the glory days of Goldsby's Golden Giants were remembered fondly in Topeka. Despite the problems of the previous year, the 1888 season began with five teams. Kansas City and Omaha departed to join the newly organized Western Association, but Leavenworth rejoined the Western League, along with new teams from Hutchinson and Newton. The returning teams from Denver and Lincoln rounded out the league. Departures from the league began in early June, however, when Lincoln folded, followed a few days later by Newton. With only three teams remaining, the league was dissolved on June 21.[3]

The early years of the Western League typified professional baseball during its infancy. Teams and leagues were frequently founded, folded, moved, or resurrected. From 1877 through 1901, what are now referred to as minor league teams and their leagues were independent, local businesses established with the intention of immediate gains, which resulted in the variable quality of play and the uneven persistence of both the teams and the leagues. The organizational effort of some early minor leagues was so minimal that at least one league with Kansas teams made a contest of setting the season's schedule, in which a prize of $100 was offered to the individual who presented what was judged to be the best arrangement of games.[4] Yet minor league baseball persisted in Kansas.

Organization of the Minor Leagues

Just which league was the first minor league (also referred to at first as a minor association) is open to debate, but the contenders were active between 1877 and 1885. Prior to 1902 minor leagues that were party to the National Agreement would be assigned to Classes A through F. These classifications did not necessarily reflect the quality of play, because they were based on how much they paid in dues. Instead, the classes were more of an aid in recruiting and retaining players, who could be drafted by other teams. Class A leagues paid the highest dues and received the highest level of protection; Class F was the lowest. Even so, Class F leagues were sometimes the strongest, and therefore had little trouble recruiting and retaining players, so they paid the lowest dues. The structure we now recognize as the minor leagues began to take shape in the autumn of 1901. With two major leagues in place after the American League joined the National League at the top, most of the professional baseball teams below the major league level were organized into minor leagues through the National Association of Professional Baseball Leagues. The name Minor League Baseball was not formally adopted until 1999.[5] In this book, classes are noted only for leagues after 1901.

After 1901, the minor leagues were divided into several skill levels or classes. The organizational system has changed through the decades, which can be a bit confusing (table 2). The original four classes were A, B, C, and D, with A being the highest level, closest to the major leagues. Periodically into the 1960s, additional levels were added, eventually expanding the number of classes to seven. In 1963 the trend of expansion was briefly reversed, and the number of classes was reduced from seven to four. The consolidation did not last, however, as Class A was twice divided to create Advanced A (in 1990), A, and Short Season A (in 1966), essentially re-creating the A, B, and C classifications of 1936–1962. There are also various short season rookie leagues in the United States and elsewhere.[6]

Most minor league teams in Kansas were Class C or D (table 3). However, early Class A professional baseball came to Kansas in 1909, when teams in Wichita and Topeka joined Denver, Des Moines, Sioux City, Saint Joseph, Lincoln, and Omaha in the resurrected Western League. In 1910 the number of minor league teams in Kansas peaked at twenty-four teams

Table 2. Principal minor league classifications used since 1902. The highest class (closest to the major leagues) is listed first for each period. (Source: Cronin 2013.)

Years			Classes				
1902–1911	A	B	C	D			
1912–1935	AA	A	B	C	D		
1936–1937	AA	A1	A	B	C	D	
1938–1945	AA	A1	A	B	C	D	E
1946–1962	AAA	AA	A	B	C	D	E
1963–1965	AAA	AA	A	Rookie			
1966–1989	AAA	AA	A	Short Season A	Rookie		
1990–	AAA	AA	Advanced A	A	Short Season A	Rookie	

spread among the Western League (two teams, Class A), Central Kansas League (eight teams, Class D), Eastern Kansas League (six teams, Class D), and Kansas State League (eight teams, Class D), with schedules ranging from 99 to 164 games. The surge quickly subsided, though, and by 1915 the number of minor league teams in the state had dwindled to only two—Topeka and Wichita in the Western League. Topeka left the league in 1916, but returned in 1929–1931 and 1933–1934. Wichita was a member through 1933. During this time, the Western League remained in Class A, which dropped from the top tier of the minor leagues to the second tier in 1912.

A few other Kansas teams played sporadically in various minor leagues through 1942, but a brief resurgence in team numbers occurred after the Second World War. From 1946 through 1952, towns in southeastern Kansas had two to four teams in the Kansas-Oklahoma-Missouri League (KOM League, Class D), and there were two to four Kansas teams in the revived Western Association (Class C) from 1946 through 1954. In addition, Wichita again had a team in the Western League (Class A, now the third tier) from 1950 through 1955 and was replaced by Topeka in 1956–1958, when Wichita picked up the AAA affiliate of the Milwaukee Braves (now the Atlanta Braves) for three years. But minor league baseball was once again absent from Kansas during 1959–1969, and since then, only Wichita has had a AAA (1970–1984) or AA (1987–2007) minor league team. The AAA team was the Wichita Aeros, affiliated with the Cleveland Indians (1970–1971), Chicago Cubs (1972–1980), Texas Rangers (1981), Montreal Expos (1982–1983; now the Washington Nationals), and

Table 3. Alphabetical list of minor leagues, classes, and the years in which they included teams in Kansas from 1886 through 2016. Prior to 1902, minor leagues were either unclassified or classified under a system represented by letters unrelated to the current system, as described in the text. (Sources: "Leagues" 2016; Kansas Baseball History Project.)

Minor League	Class	Years
American Association	AAA	1956–1958, 1970–1984
	Independent	2008–present
Central Kansas League	D	1908–1912
Eastern Kansas League	D	1910
Kansas-Oklahoma-Missouri (KOM) League	D	1946–1952
Kansas State League		1887, 1895–1898
	D	1905–1906, 1909–1911, 1913–1914
Missouri-Iowa-Nebraska-Kansas (MINK) League	D	1912
Missouri-Kansas League	1898	
Missouri Valley League	D	1902–1903
	C	1904
	Independent	1905
Nebraska State League	D	1929–1930
Northern League	Independent	2003–2010
Oklahoma-Arkansas-Kansas (OAK) League	D	1907
Oklahoma-Kansas League	D	1908
Pecos League	Independent	2015–present
Southwestern League	D	1921, 1924–1926
	C	1922–1923
Southwest League	1891	
Texas League	AA	1987–2007
Three-I League	B	1959–1961
Western Association	1893	
	C	1905–1909, 1924–1925, 1927–1932, 1934–1942, 1946–1954
	D	1911
Western League	1886–1888	
	A	1909–1934, 1950–1958

Cincinnati Reds (1984). The AA teams were the Wichita Pilots, affiliated with the San Diego Padres (1987–1988), and the Wichita Wranglers, affiliated with the San Diego Padres (1989–1994) and Kansas City Royals (1995–2007). In 2008, the Royals' AA team moved to Springdale, Arkansas, and became the Northwest Arkansas Naturals.[7]

Minor league baseball continues elsewhere in Kansas through independent teams not affiliated with Major League Baseball. The Kansas City T-Bones played in the Northern League from 2003 to 2010 and became part of the American Association in 2011. The T-Bones were first organized in 1993 as the Duluth-Superior Dukes (Duluth is in northeastern Minnesota; Superior, Wisconsin, is just across the border). The Wichita Wingnuts joined the American Association in 2008 and play at Lawrence-Dumont Stadium, one of the nine historical baseball parks in Kansas discussed in this book. This version of the American Association (officially the American Association of Independent Professional Baseball Leagues) was established as an independent minor league in October 2005 through the merger of the Northern and Central Leagues. The new league has teams in central North America from Manitoba to Texas, and it is one of four independent leagues established since 1993 affiliated with the Independent Professional Baseball Federation.[8]

In addition to the American Association, the independent Pecos League moved to Kansas in 2015, when the Garden City Wind opened its first season. The Pecos League was organized in 2011 in the southwestern United States, with most of its teams based in New Mexico. Since then, the league has featured teams in Arizona, Colorado, Kansas, New Mexico, and Texas, primarily in smaller cities than those of the Independent Professional Baseball Federation. The Wind's home ballpark is Clint Lightner Field, another of the nine historical Kansas ballparks. In 2016 additional Pecos League teams came to Kansas when the Las Vegas Train Robbers moved from New Mexico to Topeka and new teams were established in Great Bend (Boom) and Salina (Stockade).[9] Minor league baseball is still somewhat volatile, and teams are periodically organized and folded. Yet Kansas has benefited recently from the rise of independent baseball since the early 1990s. The six Kansas minor league teams in 2016 were the most in the state during a single year since the 1950s, but the number continues to fluctuate.

Kansas and the Early Minor Leagues

From 1886 through 2016, there have been fifty-five towns in Kansas represented by a team in at least one of nineteen minor leagues.[10] To celebrate the 100th anniversary of Minor League Baseball in 2001, Bill Weiss and Marshall Wright compiled a list of the top 100 minor league teams, and the 1907 Wichita Jobbers were ranked number forty-one on that list. Playing in the Western Association (Class C), the Jobbers posted a record of 98–35 (.737), the third-best record among minor league teams during the twentieth century. The team had four of the top five hitters in the league among players with at least 300 at bats—Beals Becker (.310), Jack Holland (.306), Clyde Milan (.304), and Dick Bayless (.297). (Red Davies of the Topeka White Sox batted .308.) Center fielder Clyde "Deerfoot" Milan was purchased by the Washington Senators (now the Minnesota Twins) later that summer, and he joined the team the same month as pitcher Walter Johnson, who was born near Humboldt, Kansas. The two men were roommates for ten years. Noted for his base-stealing skills, Milan briefly dethroned Ty Cobb as the American League leader in stolen bases in 1912 and 1913. He ended his major league career with 481 stolen bases (third best during the deadball era) and a batting average of .285. After his playing days ended, Milan coached periodically for the Senators, as well as a few minor league teams.[11]

Prior to the Second World War, several Kansas natives played at the uppermost minor league level available in the state (the Class A Western League) with teams in Topeka or Wichita and also spent time in the major leagues. Some of these players barely got to sip their "cup of coffee," an idiom applied to players with brief stints in the major leagues, in some instances limited to a single game. However, many of them enjoyed minor league careers for several years. For example, Jimmy Whelan, a utility player and occasional pitcher born in Kansas City, Kansas, started his minor league career with Junction City in the Central Kansas League (Class D) in 1909–1910, although he resisted coming back the second year. He reached the major leagues in 1913 with the Saint Louis Cardinals and had a single plate appearance as a pinch hitter (hitting into an out). In 1914 Whelan was back in the minor leagues and was sold to the Topeka Kaws midway through the season. He played three additional years for other minor league teams and passed away in Ohio in 1929 at only thirty-nine years of age.[12]

Life in the major leagues lasted a little longer for Les Barnhart, a Hoxie native. In 1928 he played most of the year just north of the border in McCook, Nebraska (Nebraska State League, Class D), but he also pitched two games for the Cleveland Indians, posting a record of 0–1. In 1930 he returned to the Indians and pitched in only one game. However, he earned the victory to even his career record at 1–1. As noted by a newspaper at the time, Barnhart and Babe Ruth were the only American League pitchers that year with a winning percentage of 1.000 (Ruth was also 1–0). His major league career over, Barnhart later spent parts of the 1933 and 1934 seasons with the Topeka Senators at the end of his six-year minor league career.[13]

Other minor league standouts on the Western League teams in Topeka and Wichita enjoyed longer stays in the major leagues. Some were on their way up, while others had fallen from the pinnacle. Addison "Ad" Brennan (whose abbreviated name was sometimes spelled "Add") was born in La Harpe (near Iola) in July 1887. At the time of his death, it was reported that he did not start playing baseball until he volunteered to fill in as the right fielder for a team with only eight players when he was nineteen years old. It makes a nice story, but he actually played first base for Coffeyville in the Kansas State League (Class D) in 1906, several months before his nineteenth birthday. However, the eighteen-year-old was released at the beginning of June. In late June 1907, the then nineteen-year-old Brennan did fill in for an injured player on Iola's team (their second baseman), but he was already an established ballplayer in southeastern Kansas by then. During 1907 he played for Petrolia, Gas City, La Harpe, Altoona, and other area teams. Brennan's position on the field was rarely mentioned except when he was pitching, and he developed a strong reputation as a pitcher that summer, which partly explains why he was invited to play for so many teams. In 1908 he signed with the Iola team in the Oklahoma-Kansas League (Class D) as a first baseman and pitcher. The Iola team folded in early July, and several of the players, including Brennan, joined the Springfield, Missouri, team in the Western Association (Class C), where his record as a pitcher was 8–8. In October 1908 Brennan was drafted by the Kansas City Blues (American Association, Class A), who sold him to the Wichita Jobbers in 1909, where he compiled a record of 18–16. He moved up to the major leagues with the Philadelphia Phillies in 1910–1913, but he jumped to the Chicago team in the Federal League, a short-lived major league, during 1914–1915. After two more years in the minor leagues in Atlanta, Brennan returned to the major leagues briefly in 1918 with the Washington Senators (two games) and Cleveland Indians (one game), closing out an eleven-year career. His overall record in the major leagues, as in Springfield and Wichita, was nearly even (37–36), although his earned run average (ERA) was only 3.11.[14]

A catcher for the Wichita Jobbers when Ad Brennan was pitching for the team was Art Weaver, a Wichita native. In Weaver's case, his time with Wichita in 1909 followed his years playing with the Saint Louis Cardinals (1902–1903), Pittsburgh Pirates (1903), Saint Louis Browns (1905; now the Baltimore Orioles), and Chicago White Sox (1908). In his four major league seasons, he played in only 86 games (270 plate appearances), compiling a lowly batting average of .183. His strength rested in his defensive skills behind the plate, where he threw out 46 percent of the runners attempting to steal a base. He also had an unusual superstition on the baseball diamond. During a game between Weaver's Wichita Jobbers and the Joplin (Missouri) Miners, competing superstitions led the umpire behind the plate to assume the role of Solomon, with only partial success.

> Perhaps there is no more peculiar superstition possessed than the one which haunts [Arthur] Buck Weaver [who was catching for the Jobbers]. Buck has an idea that his team cannot play winning ball on the home grounds if the broom, with which the umpire amuses himself between innings, is kept on the home team's side of the plate. Whenever anyone, by design or otherwise, places that awful broom on the Jabber [sic] side of the line Buck will stop the game long enough to hurl the sweeper back where it belongs.
>
> "Dutch" Perch, the [M]iners' crack left fielder, is troubled in the same way as Weaver is. He cannot bat when the broom is on his side of the plate. Thus it was that every time Perch would come up to bat he would throw the broom over to Wichita's side of the line. Weaver would promptly throw it back, but would no sooner turn away than Perch would repeat his part of the performance. It kept going this way for several rounds till at last the umpire took the broom and carefully placed it on a direct line with the home plate so that half of it would be on each team's ground. That seemed to be satisfactory to everyone and the game progressed in the usual manner.

However, a Joplin player walking by to get a drink kicked the broom back onto the Wichita side of the field. Alerted to this transgression by a fan,

Weaver stopped play and kicked the broom back toward the Joplin bench with such determination that it remained there for the rest of the game.[15]

Weaver had played two years earlier for the standout Wichita team in 1907 that won nearly 74 percent of its games. Compared to his stints with other teams, his batting averages during both years in his hometown were a relatively high .280. Playing in Wichita might have agreed with Weaver as a hitter, but he suffered from severe asthma, which began to limit his ability to play. He and his family moved to Denver, where his respiratory ailments abated, and the popular player periodically filled in as catcher for Denver minor league teams, mostly when they played at home. Attempts to play elsewhere were usually thwarted by his asthma. Sadly, Weaver developed peritonitis following surgery to remove his appendix in 1917, and he died at only thirty-seven years old.[16]

As with Weaver and the Jobbers a decade earlier, Hiawatha native Joe Wilhoit's tenure with the Wichita Witches during 1919 came after his time in the major leagues. Wilhoit played with the Boston Braves (1916–1917; now the Atlanta Braves), Pittsburgh Pirates (1917), and New York Giants (1917–1918; now the San Francisco Giants). He also played in six games for the Boston Red Sox at the close of the 1919 season. In Wilhoit's four seasons in the major leagues, his batting average was only .257, yet he is best known for an incredible hitting feat accomplished while playing for Wichita. Mired in a batting slump in New York, Wilhoit had been sent to the Class AA team in Seattle, where he hit only .164 in 17 games. He was then traded to Class A Wichita, where he hit only .198 in his first 25 games. However, Wichita had no alternatives in the outfield—and Wilhoit was a good outfielder—so he continued to play. Then it happened. Wilhoit got at least one hit in the next 69 games, establishing the longest hitting streak in organized baseball. Joe DiMaggio's major league record hitting streak is 56 games, accomplished in 1941, and he hit safely in 61 consecutive games in the minor leagues in 1933, good for second best. Wilhoit ended his season with Wichita batting .422 in 128 games. During four more years in the minor leagues playing for Class AA teams (the highest level at the time), he never hit below .300. Wichita cured his batting slump, but his major league career had ended.[17]

Sometimes the Kansas boys came in bunches. In 1916 the Topeka Savages (named for team owner John Savage) had four Kansas-born players on their roster who also spent time in the major leagues—a catcher and three pitchers. Catcher Nick Allen, from Norton, began his minor league career in Newton in 1910 (Kansas State League, Class D) before moving on to Iowa and Minnesota. His entry into the major leagues came in 1914–1915, when he joined the Federal League team in Buffalo, New York, where he played in 116 games. After playing in five games with the Chicago Cubs at the beginning of the 1916 season, Allen landed in Topeka. The following year, he was picked up by the Cincinnati Reds and spent 1917 in the minors before joining the Reds during 1918–1920, although he played in a total of only ninety-five games. The Reds defeated the Chicago White Sox in a 1919 World Series marred by a gambling scandal. Allen returned to the minor leagues through 1924, and became a minor league manager in 1924–1930, 1934, and 1936.[18] Another Topeka player in 1916 who moved up to the major leagues was pitcher Roy Lee Sanders, from Pittsburg. His career in organized baseball ran from 1914 to 1930 and included six games for the New York Yankees in 1918 (with a record of 0–2), plus eight games for the Saint Louis Browns in 1920 (1–1). He is not to be confused with his contemporary, Roy Garvin Sanders, from Stafford, who pitched for the Kansas City Blues in 1915–1917, the Cincinnati Reds in 1917 (two games), and the Pittsburgh Pirates in 1918 (twenty-eight games).[19]

A second Kansas pitcher for the 1916 Topeka Savages had his major league career sidetracked by the First World War. Otis Lambeth was born in Berlin, Kansas, which was not marked on early maps of Bourbon County. He lived in nearby Moran (sixteen miles west in Allen County), which was usually given as his hometown in newspapers at the time. Lambeth tried out for the Wichita Jobbers in 1911 but ended up playing for Fort Scott and other towns near his home before joining Emporia in the Kansas State League (Class D) in 1914. Preparing for the 1915 season, Ira Bidwell, owner of the Emporia team, resigned "Big Otis" in January and predicted that "Lambeth would be in the major leagues before another season." He was almost right. In May 1915 the Emporia team moved to Fort Dodge, Iowa, and Lambeth was among the players to move with them. In 1916 he returned to Kansas, where he started the season with Topeka. After compiling a record of 9–7 in 20 games (including a no-hitter against Saint Joseph) and an ERA of 2.50, Lambeth was sold to the Cleveland Indians in July, and he played for the team until April 1918. His combined record in Cleveland was 11–10 in 43 games, with an ERA of 3.18. His 1918 season was cut short by induction into the US Army during the First World War, during which Sergeant Lambeth served in France. In midsummer 1919 he was released by both the army and the Indians. He played two more years in the minor leagues, but was released by the Kansas City Blues (American Association, Class AA) in 1921 because his arm had given out, one report stating that he had rheumatism. However, he continued to play and umpire games in Moran and Iola for several more years.[20]

The most successful of the three Topeka pitchers in 1916 in terms of a baseball career was Bill Burwell, who was born in Jarbalo, an unincorporated town in northeastern Kansas. He pitched for only one year in Topeka, going 6–8, with an ERA of 2.82. The following year he played in Iowa and Missouri. Like Lambeth, he missed a year of baseball in 1918 while serving in France during the First World War, but he got his opportunity to play in the major leagues when he came home. Returning to the Western League team in Joplin to finish the season in 1919, Burwell joined the Saint Louis Browns the following year, primarily serving as a relief pitcher in 1920–1921 (thirty-three games each year). He also had a brief four-game tour with the Pittsburgh Pirates in 1928. Yet his playing career spanned twenty-two seasons (twenty in the minors) between 1915 and 1938, with a combined minor league record of 239–206 in 601 games. Burwell was also a manager for fourteen seasons between 1934 and 1955, mostly in the minor leagues, but he also piloted the Pittsburgh Pirates in 1947—for one game as the interim manager at the end of the season. From 1947 through 1962 he served the Pirates as a well-respected manager and coach. His final position with the major league club before retiring was as the pitching coach in 1958–1962, including the team's dramatic 1960 World Series victory in seven games over the New York Yankees. Even in retirement, he remained involved with the organization.[21]

Night Baseball and the Role of Kansas Minor League Teams

Thousands of minor league games have been played in Kansas in the more than 130 years since the first minor league teams were organized in Leavenworth and Topeka. Yet one of the most important events in Kansas minor league history was also important at the national level. On April 28, 1930, the first season of official night games in organized baseball played under permanent lights began at Riverside Park in Independence, Kansas, and it helped usher in the now commonplace practice of night baseball.

To provide context for this important event, the brief history of several firsts for baseball under the lights, with their respective caveats, begins in 1880. The earliest games were played under temporary lights, usually for the novelty of the event or to promote the use of outdoor lighting. However, the illumination provided by early lights was typically inadequate for practical use at baseball games. Two types of outdoor lights were used at early ballgames—gaslights and arc lights. Gaslights were powered by flammable gases derived from coal or other sources, with acetylene or other compounds sometimes added to make the them brighter. Arc lights provided illumination when an electric arc passed through the air between two rods of carbon or other material. Both types of lights were used during the late 1800s and early 1900s, and some newspaper accounts apparently confused them, so the names used in newspaper stories are sometimes incorrect.

The first game of baseball under the lights was apparently on September 2, 1880, at Nantasket Beach, Hull, Massachusetts, between teams representing local department stores. The first night game between a pair of professional teams was probably an exhibition game on July 23, 1890, at the Ward Street Grounds in Hartford, Connecticut, between the Hartford Nutmeggers and the Baltimore Orioles (not related to the current major league team) of the Atlantic Association. Numerous other exhibitions were held under the lights after 1880 and into the early 1900s.[22]

Exhibition games aside, the first official night game under artificial lights in organized baseball might have occurred in Oswego, New York, on July 6, 1905. The Oswego Starchmakers of the Empire State League (Class D) hosted the Oneida Indians in a doubleheader, with an afternoon game followed by an evening game in which the diamond was illuminated by only four sets of lights. Oneida won the night game 7–3. Another league game was held in Michigan on July 7, 1909. The host team from Grand Rapids defeated their counterparts from Zanesville, Ohio, 11–10 in seven innings. Both teams were members of the Central League (Class B). The light at this game was provided by a portable system of thirty arc lamps around the grandstand and diamond, while ten searchlights "swept the sky and carried to the outfield." The lighting was reportedly "much better for the batters than the fielders," although three fly balls to the outfield were caught. It was later determined that the game could not be counted in the official standings because a league rule stated that games must begin at least two hours before sunset. In 1927 an exhibition game that might have been included in the official records was played in Lynn, Massachusetts, between the teams from Lynn and Salem in the New England League (Class B). The seventy-two lights were mounted on poles only fifty feet high, so an additional twenty-five stationary lights (not searchlights) were used to shoot light upward and raise the illuminated canopy. Salem defeated their hosts 7–2 in seven innings.[23] All of these games were isolated events rather than regular use of permanent lights. Nonetheless, it was these minor league teams that led the way to regular night baseball in 1930.

The major leagues were slower than the minor leagues to adopt night baseball. The first official night game in Major League Baseball was played on May 24, 1935, at Crosley Field in Cincinnati, Ohio, between the Cincinnati Reds and Philadelphia Phillies. Pitcher Joe Bowman of the Phillies (born in Kansas City, Kansas) started—and lost—that inaugural contest. The first night game in the World Series was not until October 13, 1971 (game four), at Three Rivers Stadium in Pittsburgh, Pennsylvania, as the Pittsburgh Pirates hosted the Baltimore Orioles. The last major league ballpark to use lights for a night game was Wrigley Field in Chicago, Illinois, in August 1988.[24]

Ballgames played under portable lights in Kansas began at least as early as 1905. That summer, the Haskell Indians from the government boarding school in Lawrence defeated the host team from Concordia in an outdoor version of "indoor ball" (softball) played under gaslights. Only the infield was illuminated, which concentrated all the fielders in a much smaller area. The owner of the lights, J. L. Murray, even "stopped the game in the third inning to dig a hole and plant a light in the center of the diamond."[25] The larger indoor ball used in several of the early night games was easier to see in the dim lighting and did not travel as far when hit, which reduced the size of the playing field that had to be illuminated. Of course, limiting the players to the infield, even during a softball game, was not practical beyond the novelty of the first night ballgame. On July 2, 1910, the Kansas City (Kansas) Giants, an African American team, scheduled a game under electric lights at Riverside Park, their home field, against the original Kansas City (Missouri) Monarchs, but no record of the game actually being played has been found.[26]

Lights were occasionally part of the equipment provided by barnstorming teams, along with portable grandstands and canvas fences. The novelty of ballgames played after dark attracted more paying spectators. Sometimes barnstorming teams scheduled multiple games, playing a traditional baseball game in the afternoon and a game of "indoor ball" under the lights in the evening. For example, in 1908, a touring bloomer girls' team scheduled two afternoon baseball games and an evening game played with an indoor ball in Junction City.[27] In 1910 a Cherokee team from Oklahoma also toured Kansas with a portable grandstand, canvas fence, and a set of fifty acetylene gaslights.[28] A decade later the Western Bloomer Girls barnstorming baseball team toured the state with lights for evening games in which they switched to an indoor ball.[29] In 1930, however, baseball—not softball—played under the lights became widespread, and Kansas was in the vanguard in more ways than one.[30]

Although the first minor league game under the newly installed lights at the Independence ballpark occurred in 1930, the town's history in minor league baseball started in 1896. As in many Kansas towns, baseball in Independence began with teams playing at the local fairgrounds and various other sites during the late 1880s. From 1890 to 1896 the primary baseball ground in the city was Washburn Park, southwest of the intersection of Sycamore and 12th Streets. The ballpark fell into disuse after 1896, when Independence opted not to retain its professional team, even though they finished first in their only year as a member of the Kansas State League.[31]

Minor league baseball returned to Independence in 1906, when the Coyotes joined a new version of the Kansas State League (Class D). Like their predecessors, they finished first in the league. Consequently, the team's name was changed to the Independence Champions for 1907. In a sport rife with superstition, some people might believe the name change jinxed the team, because they finished third in the Oklahoma-Arkansas-Kansas League (OAK League, Class D). The team's new ballpark, constructed in 1906, was southwest of the intersection of Pennsylvania Avenue and Birch Street (formerly L.T. Street) and was sometimes referred to as Sylvania Park. The Elks Club donated lumber from their grandstand to construct a portion of the grandstand at the new ballpark, which even had a telephone to communicate scores. In 1907 the grandstand was disassembled and rebuilt at the northern end of the ballpark. Following the team's fall to third place in 1907, their name was changed again in 1908 to the Independence Jewelers, and they became part of the more geographically constrained Oklahoma-Kansas League (Class D). It did not improve their standing, as the team repeated its third-place finish.[32]

A severe windstorm in January 1909 blew down the fence and tore off the grandstand roof at Sylvania Park. Both were restored that spring, but minor league baseball was not. A city league replaced the minor league team as the main tenant of the ballpark in 1909, and a semiprofessional team was organized in 1910. In 1911 the minor league Independence Packers fixed up the ballpark and joined the Western Association (Class D), but the team folded in June. That was the beginning of another ten-year absence for minor league baseball in Independence. In the spring of 1912 the lumber in the grandstand and fence was offered for sale, although the field continued to be used by various teams.[33] The following year, another city league was organized, and a baseball ground was constructed west of 10th and Pecan Streets. The ballpark was also used by an Independence team playing in a trolley league of teams in nearby towns.[34] However, a more substantial ballpark was on the horizon, as was the return of minor league baseball.

In 1913 the city of Independence established Riverside Park on the east side of town at what had been the proposed location of a health resort at the close of the nineteenth century. While the "park [was] still in embryo," boys established a baseball diamond "in the open space at the crest of the hill." At a picnic that June "the young men and the ladies" of the Methodist Church Epworth League played each other in a leisurely baseball game, and additional games were played in the park by various teams in subsequent years. However, the seating at the diamond in 1915 accommodated only 200 spectators—hardly enough for an exhibition game that autumn between a team from Independence and the Kansas City Packers of the Federal League, a short-lived major league.[35] A more substantial baseball grandstand was needed. Enter A. W. Shulthis.

Albert W. Shulthis was born in Quincy, Illinois, in 1863 and moved to Independence with his family in 1876. He worked his way up through the bank hierarchy to become the president of Citizens National Bank, but he also served as president of several other commercial ventures in Independence, including the Western States Portland Cement Company and the Southwestern Oil, Gas, and Coal Company.[36] He was also a philanthropist. Though he initially remained anonymous, the community eventually learned that Shulthis had donated a concrete-and-brick grandstand in Riverside Park to the city. The reinforced concrete structure designed to seat 1,200 spectators was constructed between mid-1918 and early 1919. A wooden fence installed in 1920 was paid for by local merchants and featured advertisements for contributing businesses. Also that year, a temporary, wooden roof was placed over the grandstand to provide shade for spectators in the days before night baseball.[37]

In 1921 Independence welcomed its first minor league team in ten years—the Independence Producers. A roof of galvanized metal supported by "a web of welded pipe in various sizes" replaced the wooden roof and was installed with the help of "Southwestern Gas company welders." In addition to the metal canopy, twenty-four spectator boxes with four chairs each were installed in front of the grandstand, and a bleacher section for 800 spectators extended from the west end. Twelve automobile stalls were placed between the grandstand and the bleacher, and twenty additional stalls were placed along the east side. During games, a canvas sheet was stretched across the open space between the grandstand and the bleacher to block the view of those who chose to avoid paying admission and watch from the high ground in the adjacent cemetery. With the stadium finally completed, a "baby tornado" in August 1921 knocked down much of the fence, and a "considerable hole was blown in the top of the new grandstand" roof.[38]

In early 1922 a new outfield fence was built thirty to sixty feet farther back than the original. Given the damage done the previous August, "the fence posts [were] set in concrete and doubly braced." New dugouts and other improvements and repairs were also made at the ballpark that spring.[39] After four years of construction and repairs, Independence had the most substantial baseball stadium in Kansas at the time, built of concrete and brick rather than wood, and with a metal roof. This coincided with the elevation of the Independence Producers from a Class D minor league team to the city's first Class C team. Sadly, A. W. Shulthis—the man who made the ballpark possible through his donation of the first concrete baseball grandstand built in Kansas (among numerous other acts of local philanthropy)—passed away unexpectedly after suffering a heart attack on December 29, 1922.[40] Through its early years, the baseball field was known by a series of names—League Park, Producers Park, and Western Association Ballpark—but the name was changed a final time in June 1937 to Shulthis Stadium in honor of its primary benefactor.[41]

Between the World Wars, the stadium served as the home field for the Independence Producers from 1921 through 1925 and again from 1928 to 1932. The team played as a member of the Southwestern League through 1924 (Class D in 1921 and 1924) and the Western Association (Class C) afterward. In Weiss and Wright's list of the top 100 teams during the

Exterior of the Shulthis Stadium grandstand in Riverside Park, Independence, Kansas. Albert W. Shulthis donated the grandstand to the city. It was constructed of reinforced concrete and enclosed with red brick between mid-1918 and early 1919. The baseball field was known by a series of names—League Park, Producers Park, and Western Association Ballpark—but the name was changed in June 1937 to Shulthis Stadium in honor of its primary benefactor. At the time of its demolition in 2015 it was one of the ten oldest baseball grandstands in the country. Courtesy of the Independence Historical Museum and Art Center, Independence, Kansas.

first century of organized minor league baseball, the 1921 Independence Producers were number seventy-seven, and they were the only Kansas team to make the list other than the 1907 Wichita Jobbers. The Producers claimed first place with a record of 103–38 (.730). The 1930 Producers also finished in first place with a less spectacular but still respectable record of 76–56 (.576). Despite these successes, the 1932 team was transferred first to Joplin, back to Independence, and finally to Hutchinson during the season, leaving Independence without a minor league team for the duration of the Great Depression and Second World War. Following the war, Independence became a member of the Kansas-Oklahoma-Missouri League (KOM League, Class D), and Shulthis Stadium was home to the New York Yankees' minor league team from 1947 through 1950 and the Saint Louis Browns' farm club in 1952.[42] Mickey Mantle played his rookie season as shortstop for the Independence Yankees in 1949, helping the team to a first-place finish (71–53, .573), the town's fifth league championship in twenty years of minor league baseball.[43]

Baseball under artificial lights had begun as a novelty, but it became a necessity during the 1930s. Following the First World War, a few minor league teams were established in Kansas, but their numbers began to decline at the end of the 1920s, as they did elsewhere in the nation. The reasons were likely complex but may have included the expanded recreational opportunities offered by the mobility of motor vehicles and an increasing interest in other sports, such as tennis and golf.[44] The limited daylight available for leisure activities outside traditional work hours, six days per week, concentrated the competition among outdoor leisure activities into limited periods during the evenings and on Sunday afternoons, assuming there was no local ban on Sunday baseball. As support for professional teams weakened, they were replaced in several Kansas towns by less costly amateur or semipro teams or teams in the Kansas Ban Johnson League.[45] The economic depression of the 1930s exacerbated the difficulties experienced by towns trying to support minor league teams. As a result, professional baseball teams needed new options for attracting enough fans to remain financially viable.

One solution to this challenge was to move the ballgames to evening hours, illuminated by artificial lights, which would allow more fans to attend games after work. The Kansas City Monarchs were among the pioneers of night baseball in the central United States during the 1930s. They traveled with a portable system of lights on telescoping poles mounted to trucks and powered by a portable generator.[46] The Monarchs' lighting system was an improvement on the earlier portable systems used by barnstorming teams, and this allowed games to be played with a baseball on a full-sized field. An opportunity to play their first game with the new lights on April 26, 1930, in Arkansas City, Kansas, was canceled due to rain. Two nights later the Monarchs played an exhibition game under their portable lighting system against the team from Philips University in Enid, Oklahoma.[47] April 28, 1930, turned out to be a busy day in the history of night baseball.

Leading the move to install lights at the Independence ballpark were Mayor Charles H. Kerr and Marvin L. Truby, a leading businessman and longtime president of the Independence Base Ball Association (and a former player). Truby advanced the funds needed to purchase the lights for the ballpark from the Giant Manufacturing Company in Council Bluffs, Iowa, and they arrived in mid-March. Metal pipes used in the local oil and gas fields were welded together to fashion poles sixty feet tall for the lights. Five poles were erected down the foul lines and around the outfield, while additional lights were mounted above the grandstand. Together, they provided 90,000 watts of electrical lighting. Lights were also installed in the parking lot, where men were stationed "to prevent the borrowing of automobiles" during night ballgames. On April 17, only a month after the light fixtures had arrived from Iowa and work had begun on the poles, the Independence Producers defeated the House of David barnstorming team 9–1 in an exhibition game that inaugurated the new lighting system.[48]

The first night game against a league opponent—the Muskogee (Oklahoma) Chiefs—that would count toward the Producers' standings in the Western Association was scheduled for Saturday, April 26, but rain forced a delay, just as it had done for the Kansas City Monarchs under their new portable lights in Arkansas City.[49] The game in Independence was rescheduled for Monday, April 28. Muskogee won the game 13–3 in front of about 1,000 spectators (about 8 percent of the 1930 population of Independence). Despite the inauspicious opening to the 1930 season, the Producers captured first place in the Western Association with a record of 76–56.[50]

The first night game in Independence was followed four days later, on May 2, by an official night game under permanent lights between two other minor league teams, this time in Iowa. Coincidentally, Kansas had a role in that game as well. The Des Moines Demons and Wichita Aviators of the Western League (Class A, not the Class C Western Association to which the Independence Producers belonged) played the game at Western League Park in Des Moines in front of about 12,000 fans (about 8 percent of the 1930 population of Des Moines). Again, the Kansas team lost (13–6), but the Aviators went on to take first place in the Western League with a record of 89–56. The Demons had opened their season on the road, which allowed Independence to host the first official game in organized baseball under permanent lights despite the challenging weather. The game in Des Moines received more attention at the time because the owner of the Demons, E. Lee Keyser, had done such an effective job of promoting the idea of night baseball. The National Broadcasting Company (NBC) even broadcast the game live on the radio after the fourth inning.[51]

The similarities between these two night games are a conspiracy theorist's dream. The Kansas team lost in both games after surrendering thirteen runs in front of equal proportions of the local populations, yet each Kansas team went on to win their respective leagues, losing fifty-six games. Coincidences aside, there is a tangible connection between the

Night game at the ballpark in Independence, Kansas. The first game in which the lights were used during the regular season, on April 28, 1930, marked the beginning of official night games in organized baseball (major and minor leagues) played under permanent lights. Soon Des Moines, Iowa, and other minor league teams were playing under lights after people got off work, which helped the teams to survive financially during the Great Depression. Courtesy of the Independence Historical Museum and Art Center, Independence, Kansas.

night games played by teams in these similarly named leagues—Western Association and Western League. Dale Gear of Topeka served as president of both leagues, and he was a strong proponent of night baseball.[52] The race between Independence and Des Moines to play an official game under the lights was just the beginning. In 1930 lights were installed at the ballparks of thirty-eight teams in fourteen minor leagues. The three minor league teams not affiliated with major league teams in the Western Association (Independence, Joplin, and Muskogee) expected to break even financially thanks to the higher attendance for the night baseball games at their parks, while the three affiliated minor league teams without lights (Fort Smith, Shawnee, and Springfield) faced deficits.[53] This financial disparity was no coincidence. Night baseball had arrived.

As noted in their advertisements, the Giant Manufacturing Company installed floodlights at ballparks in several other cities across the country in 1930, including Topeka and Muskogee. They also built the portable lighting system used by the Kansas City Monarchs. Continued reports that the lights in Independence were temporary and that the game in Des Moines was the first game in organized baseball under permanent lights are incorrect. Some historical accounts even refer incorrectly to the lights being a loan of the portable system used by the Monarchs. In all, the Producers scheduled more than fifty night games at home in 1930, with evening games starting at seven forty-five or eight o'clock.[54] The lighting system in Independence was improved the following year with the addition of more light fixtures to the existing set.[55]

The unfortunate end of the historic grandstand at Shulthis Stadium came in July 2015, when the concrete structure was torn down just four years short of the 100th anniversary. It was one of the ten oldest baseball grandstands in North America, representing the era when Rickwood Field (Birmingham, Alabama, 1910), Fenway Park (Boston, Massachusetts, 1912), Wrigley Field (Chicago, Illinois, 1914), and Bosse Field (Evansville, Indiana, 1915) were constructed. Although football games and track meets had been held at the stadium since its early years, recent renovations to the athletic field at Shulthis Stadium were devoted entirely to football and track, leaving the baseball grandstand standing as a forlorn relic in the southwestern corner of the field, minus its roof. Efforts to save the historic structure were unsuccessful, and the only tangible reminders of that important sporting event in 1930 (or Mantle's rookie season) are housed at the Independence Historical Museum and Art Center, which displays one of the original lights and photographs of early night games at the stadium. Sadly, the oldest baseball grandstand in Kansas is gone, but nine others that are at least seventy-five years old are still preserved and used by their communities.

Major League Exhibition Games and Tours

Although no city in Kansas has ever fielded a Major League Baseball team, the state can claim its share of major league players by birth or residence. Several are the subjects of biographies—full-length books and entries in the Society for American Baseball Research (SABR) Baseball Biography Project. These and other players are also included in a 1988 article by Thomas Busch in the journal *Kansas History* and a 2014 book by Tony Hall (both included in the reference list near the end of this book). Given that the focus here is on local baseball in Kansas, only a few of these players are mentioned in chapters throughout this book.

Several of these early major league players were born in the state. Most prominent among them is Walter Johnson, who was born on a farm near Humboldt and lived for a time during the offseason in Coffeyville. He pitched for the Washington Senators in 1907–1927, compiling a record of 417–279, the second most career wins behind Cy Young's 511 (Christy Mathewson and Nebraska's Grover Cleveland Alexander are tied for third place with 373 wins). Johnson also completed 531 games (fifth all-time), with a major league record 110 shutouts (Alexander is second with 90). Johnson's 3,509 strikeouts are ninth all-time. It is little wonder he was among the first five players elected to the National Baseball Hall of Fame in 1936, alongside Ty Cobb, Babe Ruth, Honus Wagner, and Christy Mathewson (Cy Young was elected in 1937 and Grover Cleveland Alexander in 1938). Johnson is the subject of a thorough 1995 biography by his grandson, Henry Thomas.[1]

Other players born in Kansas mentioned elsewhere in this book include Beals Becker (born in El Dorado; major league outfielder, 1908–1915), Joe Bowman (Kansas City; pitcher, 1932, 1934–1941, 1944–1945),[2] Duff Cooley (Leavenworth; outfielder and first baseman, 1893–1905), Elon Hogsett

(Brownell; pitcher, 1929–1938, 1944),[3] Luther Taylor (Oskaloosa; pitcher, 1900–1908),[4] and Claude Willoughby (Buffalo; pitcher, 1925–1931). Also mentioned elsewhere is Jesse Barnes (pitcher, 1915–1927), who was born in Oklahoma. A year later his parents returned to northeastern Kansas, where his younger brother Virgil "Zeke" Barnes (pitcher, 1919–1920, 1922–1928) was born near Ontario. The town of Ontario is now gone, and nearby Circleville is usually given as their hometown.[5]

One early major leaguer who chose to move to Kansas as a young adult was William "Buck" ("Farmer") Weaver (outfielder, 1888–1894). He was born in West Virginia in 1865 and moved to Kansas in the mid-1880s. Before entering the major leagues, William Weaver played for minor league teams in Topeka, Wellington, and Wichita, and after his major league career ended he played in Larned and elsewhere in Kansas during 1907–1910. He is no relation to George "Buck" Weaver, who was one of the eight players implicated in the 1919 "Black Sox" gambling scandal. Nor is he related to Arthur "Buck" Weaver, who was an excellent defensive catcher born in Wichita. Another immigrant to Kansas was Howard "Smoky Joe" Wood, who pitched for the Boston Red Sox in 1908–1915, compiling a record of 117–57. He suffered an injury to his shoulder and, after sitting out the 1916 season, played mostly in the outfield for the Cleveland Indians in 1917–1922, where he batted .297. He was born in Kansas City, Missouri, but his family lived for a time in Ness City. Wood's path toward the major leagues included playing for the Ness City town team and the National Bloomer Girls of Kansas City, Kansas, in 1906. He is the subject of a 2013 biography by Gerald Wood.[6]

In addition to the players mentioned elsewhere in this book, four major leaguers with ties to Kansas are noted here—two for their alleged association with the darker side of baseball and two inducted into the National Baseball Hall of Fame. First up is Claude Hendrix, who was born in Olathe in 1889. In 1908 he pitched at Fairmount College (now Wichita State University) before moving on to the Lincoln (Nebraska) Railsplitters (Western League, Class A) at the end of the season. The following year he returned to Kansas and pitched for Salina in a lower-level minor league (Central Kansas League, Class D), and then pitched for an independent team in Cheyenne, Wyoming, in 1910. Hendrix reversed his trajectory in 1911, jumping to the major leagues with the Pittsburgh Pirates. After three years with the Pirates he spent two years with the Chicago Whales in the Federal League (a short-lived major league) and five years with the

Chicago Cubs. He closed his ten-year major league career (including the Federal League) with a record of 144–116 and an earned run average (ERA) of 2.65. Near the end of the 1920 season, Hendrix was accused of betting against the Cubs in a game against the Philadelphia Phillies and was replaced as the starting pitcher prior to the game. A grand jury was empaneled that September to examine that accusation and other reported instances of gambling in baseball. The accusations against Hendrix were never resolved, but the Cubs released him, ending his major league career. He continued to play for independent teams in Kansas City and in Allentown, Pennsylvania, where he passed away in 1944.[7]

The Kansas connection with gambling scandals after the First World War goes a little deeper in the person of Fred McMullin. He was born in Scammon in 1891, but in 1905 his family moved to southern California, where Fred played baseball in high school and for a variety of teams around Los Angeles, as well as in Seattle and Tacoma, Washington. Late in 1914 the infielder moved from the Tacoma Tigers (Northwestern League, Class B) to the Detroit Tigers, where he had one plate appearance (a strikeout). The following year McMullin returned to California and played for the Los Angeles Angels (Pacific Coast League, Class AA). At the end of the year he was picked up by the Chicago White Sox, where he played mostly at third base from 1916 through 1920. The team was competitive, and in 1917 they defeated the New York Giants in the World Series. The following year the White Sox dropped to sixth place, due in part to injuries and players lost to service during the First World War, but the team returned to the World Series in 1919. Sadly, McMullin and seven other White Sox players reportedly took payoffs to throw the nine-game series, which the Reds won five games to three. Although McMullin's involvement in the scandal is generally acknowledged, the extent to which he was involved is unclear. His contribution on the field was certainly limited. He had only two plate appearances, hitting a single in the first game and grounding out in game two. Talk of the fix persisted through 1920, and the accusations against Claude Hendrix, along with other concerns about gambling, led to the Chicago grand jury empaneled in 1920. The result was indictments but no convictions of the eight White Sox players. Nonetheless, newly appointed Commissioner of Baseball Kenesaw Mountain Landis banned all eight men from organized baseball. Back home in California, McMullin held a variety of jobs through the next two decades, but ended his professional life as a deputy marshal for Los Angeles County from 1941 until his death in 1952.[8]

Two other Kansas players from the early days of Major League Baseball were elected to the National Baseball Hall of Fame—one a state native and the other an immigrant. Fred Clarke was born near Winterset, Iowa, in 1872 but spent part of his early childhood near Winfield, Kansas, before the family returned to Iowa. As an adult, his memories of Cowley County led him back to Kansas, where he remained through his retirement. After playing for amateur and semipro teams in Iowa, his professional career began in the minor leagues with Hastings in the Nebraska State League in 1892. The following year Clarke started in Saint Joseph, Missouri (Western Association), but continued in Montgomery, Alabama (Southern Association). His 1894 season began in Savannah, Georgia (Southern Association). Each of these teams disbanded—or stopped playing because of a yellow fever outbreak in Alabama. After the Savannah team disbanded in late June, Clarke's luck changed, and he was invited to join the Louisville Colonels of the National League. He played in the outfield for Louisville for five more years and became the player-manager of the team in 1897, at the age of only twenty-four. As the Colonels were on the verge of folding at the end of the century, Clarke was among a group of players, including Honus Wagner, who were traded to the Pittsburgh Pirates for the 1900 season. He played and managed the Pirates through 1911 and served solely as manager in 1912. In his final three years as manager he played in only a dozen games during 1913–1915. Clarke ended his major league career with a lifetime batting average of .316, and his record in nineteen years as a major league manager was 1,619–1,205. Under his guidance, the Pirates defeated the Detroit Tigers four games to three in the 1909 World Series. The Pirates had lost the first World Series in 1903 to the Boston Americans (now the Boston Red Sox), featuring pitcher Cy Young, five games to three. Clarke returned to Pittsburgh partway through the 1925 season as a personal assistant to the team owner, head of scouting, and assistant to the manager, the latter role placing him back in the dugout. The Pirates again won the World Series four games to three, against the Washington Senators (now the Minnesota Twins) and Walter Johnson. Clarke returned to the Pirates in 1926, but disagreements led him to part ways with the team and return to his home (Little Pirate Ranch) near Winfield. The Veterans Committee elected him to the National Baseball

Hall of Fame in 1945. He remained active in the community during his retirement from major league baseball, including work with the National Baseball Congress in Wichita.[9] Clarke passed away in Winfield in 1960.[10]

Native son Joe Tinker was born at Muscotah (north of Topeka) in 1880. Two years later his family moved to Kansas City, where he played for semi-pro teams at the close of the century, followed by stints with teams in Parsons and Coffeyville in southeastern Kansas. In 1900 Tinker played briefly for the Denver Grizzlies (Western League)—as did William Weaver—before moving on to Great Falls and Helena in the Montana State League. He moved farther west in 1901, playing third base for the Portland Webfoots (Pacific Northwest League). As a member of the Chicago Cubs for the next eleven years, Tinker was the shortstop in what became one of baseball's storied infield defenses—Tinker to Evers to Chance—with second baseman Johnny Evers and first baseman Frank Chance. In 1913 Tinker was traded to the Cincinnati Reds, but in 1914 he jumped to the Chicago Whales of the Federal League during its only two years of existence. When the Federal League folded after the 1915 season, the Whales' owner bought the Cubs, bringing Tinker back to the original major league team for his final season. Tinker was elected to the National Baseball Hall of Fame in 1946, two years before his death in Orlando, Florida.[11]

Exhibition Games: Spring Training and Postseason Tours

While these players participated in baseball's premier level of competition outside Kansas, several towns in the state have hosted major league teams traveling around the country from the earliest days of professional baseball. The National League was established in 1876, but the first prominent baseball team to visit Kansas was the Forest City Base Ball Club of Rockford, Illinois, in 1870 and 1871. The Forest City club progressed from amateur to semiprofessional to professional status between 1865 and 1871. Beginning with their first year as an amateur team, the Forest Citys played their home games at the fairgrounds of the Winnebago County Agricultural Society, which is now Fairgrounds Park, a city park in Rockford.[12] Although there is no ball diamond on the site, this is perhaps the oldest baseball ground in the country where baseball could be played in a public park.[13]

In 1870 one of Rockford's star players was pitcher Albert G. Spalding, who later founded the sporting goods company that still bears his name (now a subsidiary of the Russell Brands Corporation).[14] In April 1870 the Forest Citys offered to visit Kansas and play the Lawrence Kaw Valleys, Leavenworth Frontiers, Topeka Shawnees, and a "nine selected from the State at large." Each club would help pay the expenses for the Forest Citys, estimated at $100–$150 apiece.[15] There was also word that the Cincinnati Red Stockings were coming to Kansas, but that trip was never made.[16] In the end, only two games were played by the Forest Citys at the fairgrounds in Topeka, one with the Kaw Valleys on May 11, and one with a picked nine of local players the following day. A special train ran from Lawrence to Topeka, with tickets selling for $1.90. In addition to hometown supporters from Lawrence, "admirers of the National game from all parts of the State will attend, and the affair promises to be one of the most important of the kind that has ever taken place in Kansas." The games were reportedly attended by large crowds, who watched Spalding pitch the Forest Citys to victories in the first game (41–6) and the second game (97–12), which was called after only seven innings. Newspapers carried detailed, inning-by-inning descriptions.[17]

In 1871 the Forest City BBC became a professional team in the National Association of Professional Base Ball Players and returned to Kansas in June to play the Kaw Valleys, this time on their home field in Lawrence. The Lawrence game followed one against a picked nine in Kansas City a day earlier. The 1871 Forest Citys featured a nineteen-year-old third baseman named Adrian Anson (later to be nicknamed "Cap"), who was an excellent hitter but unfortunately also a racist who contributed to the segregation of professional baseball. Spalding was no longer with the team, having moved on to pitch in Boston.[18] The contest with the Forest Citys was such a big event that the district court in Lawrence closed for the game. The amphitheater at the Kaw Valleys' ballpark was reserved for ladies, but admission to the game in Lawrence was still higher than usual, at 50¢ per person, with an additional charge of 25¢ for a saddle horse or a horse and buggy (50¢ for a two-horse vehicle). What the horses in attendance thought of the big game was not reported, but the Forest Citys once again had little trouble defeating the Kaw Valleys 67–11. However, the picked nine in Kansas City had been defeated even more decisively, 70–0.[19] Despite their successes in Kansas City and Lawrence, the Forest Citys did not fare as well against the other teams in the National Association, finishing in last place among the nine teams, with a record of four wins and twenty-one losses. The team folded at the end of the season.[20]

Spalding and Anson were later united on the Chicago White Stockings of the National League (present-day Chicago Cubs). In 1888–1889 Spalding took the White Stockings, with Anson at the helm, on a tour around the world, accompanied by a team of National League all-stars as their opponents. The two teams played each other in sixteen games in twelve cities on their trip from Chicago to California. The closest game to Kansas was in Hastings, Nebraska, on October 26, during a break in the team's journey by train from Omaha to Denver. Hastings had grown rapidly between 1880 and 1890, jumping in population from 2,817 to 13,584. The town also boasted a professional team—the Reds—from 1885 through 1887. During their final year the team was a member of the Western League. However, by 1888 the economic boom had collapsed and taken professional baseball with it. Town baseball did not return to Hastings until 1891, and the city placed a team in the Nebraska State League in 1892, although that early edition of the league folded on July 4.[21] Thus, the game played by major leaguers on their 1888–1889 world tour filled a baseball void in Hastings during the interim. The major league teams were guaranteed $500, but the game in Hastings attracted over 2,000 spectators, resulting in gate receipts of $1,300. One section of the grandstand collapsed just prior to the game, sending about a hundred people tumbling to the ground, but no one was seriously hurt. Chicago won the game 8–4 in eight innings. Originally planning to travel only as far as Australia, the tour was initially referred to as the Australian Base Ball Tour or some variation of this name in newspapers, but the trip was quickly expanded into a world tour. After leaving the West Coast, the teams circled the globe to play games in New Zealand, Australia, Ceylon (Sri Lanka), Egypt, and Europe.[22]

The first major league team to visit a Kansas ball diamond was the short-lived Saint Louis Maroons. The Maroons played in the National League for only two years in Saint Louis (1885–1886) and three years as the Indianapolis Hoosiers (1887–1889). In April 1886, prior to the start of the regular season, the Maroons played one game in Emporia, two in Topeka, and two in Leavenworth. The Maroons won all five games, but the scores were not as lopsided as in the earlier games with the Forest Citys. The Emporia Blues lost their game against the Maroons 24–3. The Topeka team was a member of the Western League and featured African American second baseman Bud Fowler. Topeka lost its two games by scores of 13–3 and 12–4. Another member of the Western League, the Leavenworth

Reds, lost their first game to the Maroons 19–2, but Leavenworth pitcher Robert Lee "Billy" Hart threw a no-hitter in their second game, the first no-hitter by a pitcher on a minor league team in Kansas. Unfortunately for Hart, the Maroons scored three unearned runs, handing him a 3–0 loss. On the following day, Leavenworth played an exhibition game with the Chicago White Stockings (the current Chicago Cubs), led by first baseman and manager Cap Anson. The White Sox defeated the Reds 38–2.[23]

In early November 1889 the Saint Louis Browns (now the Cardinals) of the American Association, a major league at the time, also traveled through Kansas after the close of their season. Their trip to Denver was to include games in Kansas City (Missouri), Fort Scott, Wichita, Hutchinson, and Pueblo (Colorado). The game in Fort Scott was announced as an exhibition game between the Kansas City Cowboys and the Saint Louis Browns, captained by Charles Comiskey. That summer, Kansas City had finished seventh among the eight teams in the American Association, while Saint Louis had finished second. Kansas City did not make the trip to Fort Scott, so the Saint Louis Browns played the Fort Scott Browns, supplemented by players from the nearby Weir City Browns. Apparently, brown was a popular uniform color that year. "Although the sun shone forth . . . in all its beauty and splendor, the atmosphere in the neighborhood of the ball grounds was quite chilly" in Fort Scott. The game ended after seven innings with the score 20–3 in favor of Saint Louis. The game against the Wichita Clippers also ended after seven innings because of darkness, with Saint Louis leading 11–3. The game between Saint Louis and a picked nine from Hutchinson and nearby towns was postponed for two days due to rain, as the Browns delayed their trip to Colorado. In front of a crowd of 600–800 fans, Saint Louis won 12–1, with light effort on their part.[24]

In 1897 the Baltimore Orioles were a successful team in the National League, but they were dumped from the league two years later, when the number of teams was reduced from twelve to eight at the end of the 1899 season. Thus, the team is not directly related to the current Baltimore Orioles of the American League. Before their departure from the league, the 1897 Orioles barnstormed their way west to California in October, with stops in Topeka and Emporia. Rather than local teams, their opponent was a team of major leaguers playing as the All-Americas. The All-Americas defeated the Orioles in Topeka 6–1 in front of 1,273 fans, which generated receipts of $749. The Orioles earned a split of their two games in Kansas with an 18–6 victory in Emporia three days later. The Topeka game featured Duff "Dick" Cooley in left field for the All-Americas, although he was not a regular member of the team during the tour. Cooley was born in Leavenworth, but he got his start in intercity baseball with Topeka teams in the late 1880s. In July 1893 he was offered $175 per month to play third base and catch for the Saint Louis Browns. During the offseason, he would return to Topeka. At the time of the 1897 game in Topeka, Cooley was a member of the Philadelphia Phillies. During his fifteen-year career in the major leagues (1893–1905), he had 1,579 hits and a batting average of .294. Late in his career, Cooley suffered from alcoholism, and in August of his final year with the Detroit Tigers he broke his leg. Cooley's baseball career was ending anyway, but his absence in the outfield was filled a few days later by a rookie named Ty Cobb.[25]

In 1901, as the new century arrived, the American League became a major league. It was derived from the Western League, not the earlier major league known as the American Association. In October 1902, with two major leagues in place, a pair of teams named the All-Americans and the All-Nationals—from the respectively named leagues—toured after the season ended. Games in Topeka and Newton were on their schedule. A Topeka newspaper referred to the 15–6 All-Nationals victory as "probably the poorest game of ball ever played on Washburn field. . . . It was the players themselves and not their skill that was on exhibition." Nearing the end of his career, Dick Cooley played for the All-Nationals in Topeka. The paid admissions exceeded 1,000 people, and "several hundred" others "worked" at the ballpark that day. In contrast, the Newton newspaper reported that the fifty-three-minute game on their diamond "was the finest exhibition of ball playing ever seen in Newton." The All-Americans rebounded with a 2–0 victory.[26]

In subsequent years teams from the two major leagues occasionally played exhibition games against minor league teams or other local teams in Kansas as they made their way from spring training sites to their home parks. Sometimes the players on the major league team were the first nine, and other times rookies ("colts") or second-string players ("yannigans"). In April 1903 Charles Comiskey's Chicago White Sox played a pair of games against the Minneapolis Millers, a minor league team in the American Association (Class A, the top minor league level at the time).

The Millers were training in Leavenworth before heading north to Minnesota, and they received extensive coverage in the local newspaper. Almost 1,000 spectators attended their first exhibition game against the Saint Joseph Saints of the Western League (Class A), which the Millers won 17–8. The Chicago White Sox defeated the Millers 18–4 in front of only about 500 fans, but the Millers won 3–2 the following day. The White Sox started five position players who played in more than 100 regular-season games that year.[27]

More than a decade later, the Millers returned to Kansas in 1917 for spring training, but this time they practiced farther south, in Parsons. Minor league teams from Saint Joseph and Joplin, Missouri, traveled to Parsons for games, and the Millers traveled to Wichita and Oklahoma. The Millers also hosted two exhibition games against Saint Louis Cardinals rookies. The Millers won the first game 6–5 on a chilly, breezy afternoon, with 500 to 600 fans braving the weather. The Cardinals won the next day 10–8.[28] The Millers did not return the following year, so the Kansas City Blues, rivals of the Millers in the American Association, moved to Parsons for the spring. They played more exhibition games against major league teams than their predecessors, and these games were against the starters for the Cardinals and White Sox. The Blues won two of three against the Cardinals and one of two against the White Sox. At the time, the ranks of the US military had expanded during the First World War, and both the Cardinals and White Sox played a team of soldiers at Camp Funston on the Fort Riley military reservation near Junction City.[29]

Between 1903 and 1918 several major league teams stopped in Kansas to play spring ballgames, including the Boston Red Sox (1911), Chicago Cubs (1905, 1917–1918), Chicago White Sox (1903, 1906, 1908–1912, 1914, 1916–1918), Detroit Tigers (1909, 1911, 1916–1917), New York Giants (1917; now the San Francisco Giants), Pittsburgh Pirates (1908, 1913–1914), Saint Louis Browns (1910; now the Baltimore Orioles), Saint Louis Cardinals (1917–1918), and Washington Senators (1907–1909; now the Minnesota Twins). Two of the best pitchers at the time who played in exhibition games in Kansas were no strangers to the state. Walter Johnson pitched for the 1909 Washington Senators, and Howard "Smoky Joe" Wood pitched for the 1911 Boston Red Sox. In addition to these spring training visits from American and National League teams, the Kansas City Packers of the Federal League, a third major league in 1914–1915, played exhibition games in Kansas in the autumn of 1915.[30]

World Tours and the Road to Blue Rapids

As popular as some of these games were, none could match the notoriety of the game in Blue Rapids in northeastern Kansas on October 24, 1913, which featured major league players on both teams. The game was part of a 1913–1914 "Round the World" tour similar to Spalding's 1888–1889 tour. Chicago White Sox owner Charles Comiskey and John McGraw of the New York Giants organized the 1913–1914 tour, and it captured national headlines. The 1888–1889 tour led by Albert Spalding with the earlier version of the Chicago White Stockings (now the Chicago Cubs) played few games while traveling west from Chicago. In comparison, the 1913–1914 tour generated more interest across the United States than its predecessor because the teams played more games before leaving the country—thirty-one games in twenty-six cities (plus four rainouts).[31] With Saint Louis being the city farthest west to have a major league team, the 1913–1914 trip was not only important as a world tour, it was also important as a tour across the United States west of the Mississippi River. Some White Sox and Giants players chose not to participate, so players from other teams supplemented their rosters. Blue Rapids successfully bid for a spot on the tour as it crossed the United States from Chicago to the West Coast before heading overseas. During the tour from mid-October 1913 through February 1914, the teams played each other forty-six times. They also played five games against local teams in Japan and Australia. Blue Rapids hosted game number seven. It was the smallest town to host a game and was the only town in Kansas to do so.[32]

The effort to arrange the game in Blue Rapids began in the late summer of 1913. The *Blue Rapids Times* reported that "Manager F. W. Hamilton of our base ball team is endeavoring to secure a game here late in October between the New York Giants and Chicago White Sox. It takes a thousand dollar guarantee to bring them here and an effort is being made to get 40 men to stand for $25 each." A week later, on September 8, the newspaper published the headline: "Big League Players Coming." Comiskey had agreed to play in Blue Rapids, following a game in Sioux City, Iowa, and preceding games in Saint Joseph and Kansas City, Missouri.[33] It was nearly a month later when the date of the game was confirmed, but preparations had already begun in earnest.[34] As one newspaper in central Kansas put it, "Blue Rapids, one of the livest of live towns in Kansas[,] has done another stunt that will bring a big crowd to that city."[35]

There was much to do. A "base ball headquarters" was set up in a building next to the State Bank of Blue Rapids, where organizers maintained correspondence with dozens of people, including bankers in various towns who would sell tickets, as well as railroad officials who would arrange special trains for spectators. Shops, banks, and other businesses agreed to close from one to five o'clock on game day. Local restaurants and cafés prepared to feed a large crowd, and church groups planned to accommodate 200 to 300 hungry fans.[36]

For the "world tourists" to award a game to Blue Rapids, the community had guaranteed the major leaguers a minimum of $1,000, but the teams could claim 80 percent of the gate and grandstand receipts, whichever was greater. To cover this expense and attempt to earn a small profit, ticket prices were set at $1 in advance (equivalent to about $24 in 2016). Tickets purchased the afternoon of the game were $1.50. Children under twelve years old were charged 50¢. The opportunity to watch the game from one of the seats in the bleacher or grandstand would cost the ticket holder an additional 25¢ or 50¢, respectively. The bleacher—expected to hold up to 1,800 fans—was constructed especially for the game. A limited number of automobiles also were allowed to park around the margin of the outfield for 50¢. Additional revenue was obtained by leasing five concessions for the game—popcorn and peanuts, hot candy, hot and cold drinks, cigars and gum, and a lunch stand.[37]

The game was to be advertised in 140 towns in Kansas and Nebraska, which "ought to put Blue Rapids on the map in real large letters." An order was placed for "big paper" to be used for printing posters.[38] With the large number of people expected for the event, policing was the responsibility of local organizers. General Leonard Wood had agreed to send a company of soldiers from Fort Riley to maintain order, unless it interfered with autumn maneuvers. In the end, the soldiers were not needed, and security was strictly a local affair. The city marshal appointed four extra deputies. During the game two deputies were stationed in the depopulated uptown area, while the rest of the officers patrolled outside the ballpark. Members of the local committee policed the area inside the ballpark.[39]

Blue Rapids was a rural community, but the organizers hoped to draw fans from larger cities in the region, so transportation arrangements also needed to be addressed. Two railway companies in the region added special trains to their regular passenger service for fans traveling to the game. The Union Pacific ran a special train round-trip from Manhattan (south of Blue Rapids), and the Missouri Pacific ran another from Atchison (east of Blue Rapids). The train depot in tiny Blue Rapids was a busy place on game day. The scheduled arrivals that morning were:

the special train for the baseball teams at 7:00,
Union Pacific passenger train from the south at 8:45,
Missouri Pacific passenger train from the west at 9:45,
Union Pacific passenger train from the north at 10:35, and
Missouri Pacific passenger train from the east at 11:10.

Fans from as far away as WaKeeney in northwestern Kansas reportedly traveled to the game on eastbound Union Pacific trains passing through Salina on the Denver–Kansas City route. Outbound trains from Blue Rapids departed that evening in each direction except to the west. Because the Missouri Pacific did not grant a request for a special train to Concordia (west of Blue Rapids), fans who wanted to enjoy the festivities to their conclusion risked having to spend the night in Blue Rapids to catch a later train home. Although some of these people did travel by train, a Concordia newspaper reported that "a number of auto owners will make the drive of about 70 miles if the roads are good," as would people "from Cuba, Beloit, Glasco, Delphos and all points in this territory."[40]

They were not alone. Many people from all over northeastern Kansas drove as many as 100 miles to Blue Rapids. This was no small feat given the automobiles available at the time and the roads on which they would travel. Ford had introduced the Model T only five years earlier, and Ford's assembly line mode of manufacturing vehicles to reduce retail prices had just been implemented in 1913. Rural byways in Kansas were dirt or gravel, rather than paved highways with numbers. The numbering system for federal highways was not developed until the 1920s, and cross-country roads were often marked with little more than painted posts or telephone poles. For example, the Red Line Division of the transcontinental Midland Trail generally followed the current route of US Highway 24 across Kansas, from Kansas City to Denver. It was marked by red bands six inches wide painted on telephone poles, usually by volunteers. In early 1915 the Glasco Red Liners barnstorming basketball team traveled along the route painting poles during the day and playing games against local teams in the evenings to earn money to pay their expenses, including the cost of the paint. Later in the spring the cause was taken up by baseball teams, including a team from Plainville that traveled into Colorado, painting and playing. Not only did they perform a community service and bring positive attention to their hometowns, the Glasco and Plainville teams won most of their games.[41]

In 1913 the east–west road through Blue Rapids was known as the White Way. The road north from Manhattan to Marysville that passed through Blue Rapids was known as the Blue Post Road. "C. Chenoworth who makes the drive [of seventy-six miles from Junction City] to Blue Rapids every month, may pilot a crowd. . . . The route from Manhattan is marked by blue poles and the roads are usually in good shape." Some automobile owners advertised in the local newspaper for passengers. Fans from Clay Center, southwest of Blue Rapids, also planned to drive to the game "if the roads and weather are good." A boy even rode to the game from Clay Center on a motorbike with his uncle. There was only one incident among the Clay Center automobiles, and that was on the return trip, when one of the vehicles had to be towed into a town and repaired before completing the trip home late that evening. In a bit of faint praise, drivers from Junction City reported that the road to Blue Rapids "was good with the exception of several places."[42] It would not be long before automobiles replaced trains (and horses) for intercity travel, and the game in Blue Rapids was at the forefront of this cultural change.

As with fishing tales, stories in baseball are often embellished in the telling, and such was the case for a story about the people who traveled to the game in Blue Rapids by automobile:

> Sam Crawford [from Wahoo, Nebraska], the big right fielder of the Detroit Tigers, who is touring the world as a member of the White Sox, now coupled with the New York Giants for the tour, is also acting as a scribe. Writing of a game at Blue Rapids, Kan., Sam told of how the town only has a couple of hundred inhabitants but that nearly 20,000 people came in from the surrounding country to see the game, and the most of them came by motor car. "I always wondered where the Ford cars went to until I reached that town," wrote Sam. "But when the people began to arrive for the game I knew. I'm not kidding when I say that there were literally hundreds of Ford cars around Blue Rapids the day of the game"[43]

The official population for Blue Rapids and the surrounding township in 1913 was actually 2,292 residents (1,832 in the city).[44] More realistic

A few of the many automobiles that brought fans into Blue Rapids from around northeastern Kansas for the world tour baseball game in October 1913. Roads at the time were dirt and gravel, and cross-country roads had names, such as the White Way and the Blue Post Road, rather than the numbers used today. Special trains also transported hundreds of people to Blue Rapids for the festivities and returned them home that evening. Courtesy of the Theo Musil Estate.

estimates of the number of fans ranged from 2,000 to 2,500 at the game, with additional people visiting town for the festivities but not attending the ballgame.[45]

Despite all the long hours of diligent preparation, there was one uncontrollable aspect of the event that could render it all for naught—the weather. However, that autumn day was pleasantly warm and ideal for baseball.[46] How easily it could have been otherwise was evident in three of the next four cities on the tour. The game in Saint Joseph the day after the game in Blue Rapids was played without any incidents, but in Kansas City the following day, rain and snow greeted the teams.[47] John McGraw, manager of the New York Giants, served as a special correspondent for the *New York Times* during the tour and wrote about the playing conditions at Association Park, home of the minor league Kansas City Blues (Class AA,

American Association).[48] "The field was about as bad as a base-ball diamond could be, and there were large puddles behind the home plate and back of second base. To make matters worse, a cold biting wind blew across the field."[49] A muddy field also greeted the world tourists at Joplin in southwestern Missouri the next day.[50] The game in Tulsa, Oklahoma, featured the much-anticipated pitching matchup between Walter Johnson and Christy Mathewson, two pitchers destined for the National Baseball Hall of Fame. The two stars had been scheduled to face each other in Joplin, but the poor field conditions caused Mathewson to sit the game out and Johnson pitched only three innings. Although the tour continued to move south, the autumn weather in Tulsa was again less than ideal. It was a cold afternoon, and snowflakes fell before the game was completed. Reminiscent of events twenty-five years earlier at Hastings in October 1888, the Tulsa game was also marred by the collapse of the right field bleacher, killing one person on the scene and injuring more than three dozen others, some seriously. Rescuing people trapped in the debris at Tulsa became the immediate priority, and the game was delayed about thirty minutes.[51] In light of all this misfortune, it seems that the stars were aligned in Blue Rapids' favor.

McGraw, writing again for the *New York Times*, offered his impression of the reception the teams received at Blue Rapids: "We were agreeably surprised to find a crowd of fully three thousand waiting for us to begin. The people came from all points within a radius of 100 miles to greet the world's tourists, and as the day was ideal for the national game many came in automobiles and other vehicles, while the special trains brought loads of human freight to this country town on the prairies."[52] The *Chicago Tribune* also described the teams' reception:

The special train arrived a little ahead of schedule . . . but the reception committee was not caught unawares. Twenty-five motor cars were at the depot, and all the tourists were driven around the town and out into the country while the natives looked on in admiring wonder. . . . The country folks swarmed into the town early in the morning. They came in automobiles, top buggies, milk wagons, and lumber wagons. It was estimated that 500 automobiles were in the town, and Main street "resembled" State street in Chicago.[53]

Following the automobile tour through the countryside, the teams and fans were treated to a band concert at the park in the public square in the

A parade of players, led by the local band, marching through Blue Rapids to the baseball park in October 1913. Such parades often preceded games featuring prominent barnstorming teams. Courtesy of the Theo Musil Estate.

heart of town. Most town squares in Kansas have the county courthouse at their center, but the town square in Blue Rapids, established in 1874, is unique in featuring a small, shaded park. Following the concert, the band led a parade of uniformed players and others to the ball ground west and north down Sixth, Park, and Fifth Streets, a short walk of less than half a mile. National League umpire Bill Klem called the game at 2:30. As they came to bat, Klem also announced the names of the players. Klem was one of the first two umpires elected to the National Baseball Hall of Fame in 1953, two years after his death.[54]

"The game was fast, less than an hour and a half being required for the nine innings."[55] The White Sox were victorious, 8–5. They hit four home runs, although some of these hits reportedly would not have been home runs if the "auto line [had not] interfered with the fielders." The only real disappointment among the fans was that Christy Mathewson coached first base instead of pitching. Given the length of the tour after a full baseball season, he was limited to pitching on a schedule similar to what would be used during the regular season.[56] However, Mathewson reportedly showed off a bit for spectators by throwing a fastball through a wooden plank one-quarter inch thick while standing at a distance of forty paces.[57]

Action at home plate during the world tour baseball game in Blue Rapids, October 1913, with umpire Bill Klem behind the plate. The grandstand and bleachers were crowded with fans. The "dugouts" consisted of wooden planks in front of the bleachers. Courtesy of the Theo Musil Estate.

In addition to the teams' hometown newspapers in Chicago and New York, newspapers across the country carried reports of the game as they tracked the progress of the world tourists.[58] Most newspapers praised the small Kansas community for its determination to host the game and the success of the organizers' efforts.[59] This was especially noteworthy because larger cities in Kansas, such as Wichita and Topeka, did not arrange a game. Belatedly, on the day of the game in Blue Rapids, Salina attempted to arrange a game on their ball diamond. While some games during the tour were rescheduled—such as one in Fort Smith, Arkansas, that was moved to Muskogee, Oklahoma—no open date was available for Salina.[60]

In addition to the game itself, the event spawned other stories. With Blue Rapids being the smallest town on the tour and the baseball players being accustomed to living in some of the largest cities of the eastern United States, one "base canard" or "little yarn" that was spread after the game centered on a bathtub:

> Some of the players say that after they finished their game at the small Kansas town last week they returned to the hotel and asked the clerk

View of the baseball field in Blue Rapids as seen from the top of the grandstand during the world tour baseball game in October 1913. Owners of the automobiles lining the outfield had to pay an extra fee to park around the ball field. These automobiles also made some home runs possible when the ball passed between them. Courtesy of the Theo Musil Estate.

to direct them to the hotel's bathrooms. The hotel clerk denied having any such articles concealed about the hostelry, according to the story, but went out scouting for a bath tub. He soon returned with the news that he had been successful and piloted the small army of ball players down the street to a preacher's home. The divine proudly showed the ball players to a room upstairs where there was a bathtub. But it had no faucets. The preacher carried a bucket of water up the stairs for each player's bath. . . . We shudder about shouldering the responsibility for [the story], especially when it is read in Blue Rapids.[61]

The world tourists probably expected to claim the $1,000 minimum for the game in this small prairie village, but they chose the option for 80 percent of the gate receipts instead. The final counts were 1,728 advance general admissions at $1.00 each, 328 late general admissions at $1.50 each, 386 grandstand admissions at $1.50 each, and 34 children's tickets at 50¢ each, for a total of $2,366. Thus, the teams claimed $1,892.80, and the local organizing committee received $473.20. The local boosters also received $43.50 charged for the automobiles, the 25¢ for each bleacher ticket, and the concessions leases, putting their total at $800–$900. After expenses, which were expected to be about $300, the local organizers made a profit. One expense that was not incurred was any fees paid to the many banks in the region that sold tickets "without any recompense whatever." The tickets sold represented a paid admission of 2,026 people. With the band, teams, and workers, the total number of people in attendance was likely closer to 2,500. Only a Chautauqua event featuring the well-known orator William Jennings Bryan that August had drawn a larger paying crowd in Blue Rapids.[62]

The players, as much as the game, were the attraction. The *Blue Rapids Times* correctly predicted, "There will undoubtedly be an army of kodakees on the grounds."[63] Local resident George Hewitt took numerous photographs of the players and events that day (four are reprinted here). Interest in the players was even strong in towns not hosting a ballgame. On the Saturday morning following the game in Blue Rapids, "Upwards of 100 persons" went to the Union Pacific depot in Atchison at 7:15 just for a chance to see the professional ballplayers as they passed through on their way to the game in Saint Joseph. The team's train of six special coaches traveled a different route, however, so the fans "returned to their usual vocations somewhat disappointed."[64]

After leaving Kansas and its neighboring states, the world tour traveled through the Southwest and up the West Coast to British Columbia. From there the players sailed to Japan, China, Hong Kong, the Philippines, Australia, Ceylon, Egypt, Italy, France, and England, an itinerary similar to Spalding's 1888–1889 tour.[65] The baseball ground where the game was played in Blue Rapids is still in use, but the wooden grandstand and bleachers (and their wooden replacements) are gone. A marker and black silhouettes of a pitcher, hitter, and catcher commemorate the ballgame. The Blue Rapids Historical Society, on the south side of the Round Town Square, displays photographs and other items from the 1913 event. Of the other ball grounds in the United States to host games during the tour, only those in Bisbee and Douglas in southeastern Arizona, near the US–Mexico border, still host baseball games, although their current grandstands were built after the world tour (1937 and 1948, respectively).

Barnstorming tours by major league teams or individual players began to decline during the 1950s as a result of several changes occurring in baseball, such as the expanded coverage of regular season and postseason games on radio and television. Similarly, exhibition games in Kansas during spring training as teams made their way north and east from sites in Texas and elsewhere in the Southwest declined after the Second World War, when spring training was largely concentrated in California, Florida, and Arizona (and continued to concentrate in the latter two states).[66] In addition, major league teams began to move west of Saint Louis beginning in the 1950s, supplemented by later expansion franchises. Interest in major league baseball in Kansas began to shift to Kansas City, Missouri, when the Athletics moved there from Philadelphia in 1955, followed by the Kansas City Royals expansion team in 1969, after the A's continued their westward emigration to Oakland, California, in 1968. But it is fair to say that no place in Kansas put on a better major league show than tiny Blue Rapids did.

CHAPTER 8

The Game Goes On

Town teams were widespread and dominated the baseball scene across Kansas during the late 1800s and early 1900s. In the first decades after the Second World War, the number of town teams—and their segregated siblings—declined in Kansas and elsewhere. The integration of baseball obviously reduced the number of teams, as towns no longer fielded baseball teams of exclusively African American, Mexican American, or American Indian players. However, this only explains part of the decline in the number of town teams. The reasons are likely numerous and interrelated, but they are difficult to document. Yet historians who comment on this change typically round up a consistent set of the usual suspects. The results of this change, however, vary from one state to another. Town teams still exist in some states, but they are absent in others. In Kansas, the first and second nines evolved into different organizational models.

Second Nines and the Organization of Youth Leagues

In the case of the second nines—usually younger, less experienced players—a transition began between the First and Second World Wars. Boys of all ages in Kansas almost certainly played pickup games of baseball or kindred sports from the beginning. Organized youth teams in the state have been around since at least the 1870s.[1] Between the world wars, baseball expanded in the United States for both adults and youths, and the number of high school baseball teams increased.[2] Initially, Kansas high school teams functioned much as the town teams did, challenging other teams to games. These opponents included not only their peers but also town teams and teams at normal schools, among others. The competition became more focused on peers as high school baseball leagues in the state were organized, at least as early as the 1890s.[3] With the brief baseball season at high schools ending when the school year closed in May, youth summer leagues were sometimes organized, mostly based on the ages of the players. However, in 1922, Coffeyville boasted of having over 500 boys up to twenty-one years of age playing on thirty-six teams in four leagues, some of which were organized by weight. Three of the city's leagues were arranged to include boys up to 110 pounds, boys up to 130 pounds, and the boys over 130 pounds. There were also twenty-six girls' teams.[4] In addition to these local leagues, well-known multistate summer leagues for youngsters were organized in the 1920s, offering competition at another level.

The first major effort to organize interstate summer baseball leagues for teens was sponsored by the American Legion, beginning in 1926. After its founding in 1919, immediately after the First World War, American Legion posts often supported baseball teams of their members. In 1926, Legion posts in fifteen states, including Kansas, began sponsoring teams of teenage boys, and the program expanded rapidly.[5] Initially, Legion teams were open to boys fourteen to sixteen years old. However, in 1928 Margaret Gisolo played second base for the Legion team in Blanford, Indiana. In the county's championship game with Clinton, she drove in what proved to be the winning run in the top of the twelfth inning. After losing, Clinton protested that girls were not allowed to play on Legion teams, but they lost the appeal. The Blanford team went on to win the state championship and play in the national tournament. The following year, the American Legion banned girls from playing on teams they sponsored, and the rule stood until the 1970s.[6] Legion teams are now organized into various levels, with players in their teens up to nineteen years old. The season still concludes with the American Legion Baseball World Series.

At the first national American Legion tournament in 1926, the team from El Dorado was one of the four finalists, along with teams from Pocatello (Idaho), Springfield (Illinois), and Yonkers (New York).[7] It was the best finish for a Kansas team, although Olathe (1990), Kansas City (1991), and Lawrence (2006) have been champions of Region 6 (of eight regions).[8] One of the more unusual events players experienced during an American Legion baseball game in Kansas—or anywhere else—occurred on Decoration Day (Memorial Day) in 1933. The exhibition game was played by Legion teams from Leavenworth and Topeka inside the Kansas

State Penitentiary (now the Lansing Correctional Facility). In the fifth inning of a 2–2 tie, a group of inmates kidnapped the warden and made their way to the baseball diamond. There, more prisoners chose to join them. Using the warden and guards as shields, eleven prisoners made their escape to Oklahoma, where the warden and other hostages were released. A Leavenworth pitcher at the game that day was Murry Dickson, who was drafted by the Saint Louis Cardinals in 1936. He pitched in a single game for the Cardinals each year in 1939 and 1940, but had a 14–5 record during 1942 and 1943. He was drafted again in 1943, this time by the US Army, and he was on a ten-day furlough to the Cardinals when he pitched to the final three hitters in game five of the World Series against the New York Yankees, making him one of only two players on active military duty to appear in a World Series. After serving in Europe during 1944 and 1945, Dickson returned to the Cardinals in 1946 and continued to pitch until 1959 for five teams (the Saint Louis Cardinals, Pittsburgh Pirates, Philadelphia Phillies, Kansas City Athletics, and New York Yankees). He also made two more trips to the World Series, with the Cardinals in 1946 and the Yankees in 1958. Dickson continued to make his home in Leavenworth until his death in 1989.[9]

As a counterpart of the Legion program, Little League Baseball was founded in Williamsport, Pennsylvania, in 1939 to give preteen children an opportunity to play organized baseball. Consequently, the Little League World Series features teams whose players are nine to twelve years old, although teams are now organized into various divisions based on ages ranging from four to eighteen years old. While many communities in Kansas have amateur youth baseball leagues sometimes referred to as little leagues, only a few have actually been members of Little League Baseball, and they are now limited to a few towns in southeastern Kansas. No Kansas team has yet advanced to the Little League World Series.[10]

Additional leagues were established after the Second World War, such as the Babe Ruth League, founded in 1951 as the Little Bigger League in New Jersey for boys thirteen to fifteen years old. In 1954, with the permission of Babe Ruth's widow, Claire Merritt Ruth, the league was renamed in his honor. Within Kansas, there are local Babe Ruth Leagues offering baseball for boys and softball for girls between the ages of four and eighteen.[11] In 1974 the Kansas National Baseball Congress Hap Dumont Youth Baseball program was established for boys twelve and under. As with the other youth leagues, the classifications have expanded through the years, and the program now features several state tournaments for players in various age categories from eight and under (8U) through nineteen and under (19U).[12] Thus, the second nines of the late 1800s have morphed into a variety of leagues organized for youths across a wide range of ages who can compete at the local, state, and national levels.

Decline of the Town Teams (First Nines)

Although the number of town teams—the first nines—has declined in Kansas and elsewhere, this does not mean there are no longer any town teams with rosters filled by local players. For example, Minnesota, perhaps as much as any state, is a baseball state. Baseball has been played in Minnesota since 1857, but the history of "town ball" (sometimes spelled as a single word) is often chronicled from 1924, when the first state tournament was organized, and it has continued into the twenty-first century. The Association of Minnesota Amateur Baseball Leagues was organized in 1925, and by 1940 the number of teams increased to 452 before declining during the Second World War to 162 in 1945. A resurgence occurred after the war, with the number of teams reaching a peak of 799 in 1950, many of which paid players or arranged local employment for them. The number of teams began to decline again during the 1950s, associated with escalating costs, declining revenues, and changes in society, such as the rise of television and the increased mobility provided by automobiles, which facilitated alternate leisure activities away from town.[13]

Nonetheless, there have been about 300 teams assigned to one of three classes of the Minnesota Baseball Association in recent years. Class A includes teams in the Minneapolis–Saint Paul area, Class B includes the better teams outside the Twin Cities (47 teams in 2016), and Class C comprises the majority of teams (216 in 2016). These teams compete in various league, regional, sectional, and state tournaments within each class. The days of professional or semipro teams and imported ringers are gone. Only amateur players may sign contracts with teams, and they must maintain a permanent residence within thirty miles of their team's ballpark beginning no later than March 15, although special rules apply to college players and members of the military. The rules of professional baseball are generally followed, with a few exceptions. For example, wood composite bats may be used in addition to traditional wooden bats, and a designated hitter may be used for any player, not just the pitcher.[14]

Similar to the umbrella organization in Minnesota, the South Dakota Amateur Baseball Association has hosted a state tournament since 1933, now divided into Classes A and B. Interest in baseball in South Dakota also spiked after the Second World War, with 48 amateur leagues and 300 teams in the late 1940s. By 1962 the number of registered teams had dropped to 154, and in 2014 there were 79 teams in 10 leagues. Reasons usually given for the decline are similar to those given elsewhere—television and easy access to recreation outside town, along with declines in the rural population.[15]

Moving still closer to Kansas, the Nebraska Baseball Association was organized in 2006, but struggled.[16] Nonetheless, there are amateur adult leagues in the state, including recreational leagues in Omaha and Lincoln for those who would rather play baseball than softball. In addition, a few smaller towns are represented by traditional town teams—teams that represent the entire town. For example, in 2016 the Dodge County Baseball League, northwest of Omaha, included three teams in the county and five in neighboring counties, some with historical ballparks that were in use prior to the Second World War, contributing to the ambience of old-time, town team baseball. The team rosters include college players returning home for the summer and other local players. The towns in the 2016 Dodge County Baseball League were Arlington (population 1,243), Dodge (612), North Bend (1,177), Schuyler (6,211), Scribner (857), Wahoo (4,508), West Point (3,364), and Wisner (1,170).[17]

As in these nearby states, the number of town teams also declined in Kansas. Some reasons for the decline are clear, but others are more speculative, based primarily on correlating events in time. One obvious reason for the decline in the number of town teams in Kansas is simply that the number of towns has declined in this rural landscape. In the late 1800s farming was much more labor-intensive, and farms were smaller and more numerous. Many small communities (some not large enough to be incorporated) sprang up throughout the state to provide convenient services to these rural residents. It was not unusual, even into the early 1900s, for baseball teams to suspend play in midsummer so the players could help with the wheat harvest. As agriculture became more mechanized, the number of less-profitable farms decreased; fewer people were operating increasingly larger farms, and rural populations declined.[18] The decline in the number of towns has continued into the twenty-first century, as small towns fight to retain their local schools and businesses. The increased mobility provided by automobiles and improved roads means that travel to schools and businesses thirty miles away now takes much less time than it took to travel five miles on foot or in a horse-drawn wagon over rutted, dirt roads. This has allowed the consolidation of these community services in fewer towns, and people move elsewhere in search of careers.

Changes in Ellis County illustrate the decline in the number of towns—towns once represented among their peers by baseball teams. The county is in northwestern Kansas, where minor league and Ban Johnson baseball (discussed later in this chapter) made no inroads prior to the Second World War and the state university abandoned baseball after 1924. Town teams reigned. The early town team in Hays (the county seat and largest town) typically played teams in other towns within the county or in adjacent counties. For example, in 1928 the Two-County Baseball League consisted of teams from Ellis, Hays, Hyacinth, Munjor, Schoenchen, and LaCrosse (in Rush County). In 1940 the Ellis County League included baseball teams of local players from Emmeram, Hyacinth, Munjor, Severin, Toulon, Victoria, Walker, and Gorham (in Russell County), while teams from Hays and Ellis played independently. The towns of Catherine and Pfeifer also supported teams during the early 1900s.[19] Of the twelve towns in Ellis County sponsoring baseball teams during this period, only Ellis (2,042 residents in 1940), Hays (6,385 residents), Schoenchen (259 residents), and Victoria (884 residents) were incorporated cities tallied in the federal census. The villages of Emmeram, Hyacinth, Severin, and Toulon no longer exist, while clusters of homes and historical Catholic churches constructed of native limestone are still present at Catherine, Munjor, Pfeifer, and Walker—easy commutes into Hays for their residents.

Among the other 104 counties, some likely had fewer towns with baseball teams, and some likely had more, but it is not unreasonable to hypothesize that hundreds of Kansas towns fielded town teams between 1865 and 1941. More specific estimates of the total number of towns to field a town team at any point in their histories or during specific years or other periods await documentation, but it is clear that the number of teams has dropped dramatically. For example, 91 of the 105 Kansas counties had no towns represented by an amateur, adult baseball team during 2016 (three of these counties had minor league teams, though).

Thus, other factors besides ghost towns contributed to the decline in the number of town teams. Particularly difficult to quantify is the impact of the increased availability of alternative leisure activities during the summer. As mentioned for other states, blame is sometimes assigned to easier access to activities outside town provided by automobiles (for example, a family camping trip to a lake or a trip to a special event in another town). Another possible competitor for support of a town team is indoor activities, such as those involving electronic devices (video games, home movies, etc.) used in a home that is now likely to be air-conditioned. However, it is difficult to know how many people involved in these activities would support a local baseball team if those alternatives were not available. Certainly, town teams never enjoyed the support of a community's entire population.

Perhaps a bit more likely are changes occurring in baseball that generally coincided with the decline of town teams, such as the increasing number of radio stations broadcasting major league games. In the late 1800s and early 1900s, people sometimes obtained same-day news about games in other towns through telegraph or wire service reports posted on bulletin boards or made available by calling newspaper offices. In 1888, for example, Bradley's billiard hall in Atchison was "base ball headquarters" and "totals of all the base ball games [were] received by telegraph and bulletined on the black board." A Pittsburg, Kansas, newspaper announced plays during the World Series through a megaphone, but this was replaced with an electric scoreboard by 1920. In 1917, reports of baseball games in Oklahoma bypassed the telegraph wires and were relayed north to the newspaper in Parsons "via wireless" radio signals. As happens with changes in technology, the old overlaps the new. Thus, posting sports information received through telegraph lines from across the country continued into the 1930s, even as the "wireless" option began to enter homes. Events in Wellington during the 1923 World Series illustrate the change. During the first game of the series, a "large crowd gathered around the electrical score board . . . as the telegraph instrument began to click and Jack Watson, operator and manager of the board[,] began to call out reports." Meanwhile, "many radio enthusiasts were sitting comfortably at home," listening to radio broadcasts of the game.[20]

A decade later, in September 1936, a newspaper in Chanute ran a front-page advertisement under the banner, "You Need a New Radio for the World's Series." The ad explained that if the reader had owned a radio for "a few years, it is terribly out of date" and should be replaced with a new radio that had an "almost unlimited range of stations." However, there was a bit of a twist on the trend toward staying home to enjoy ballgames on the radio in Chanute during that year's World Series. To entice local fans to attend a game between the Chanute town team and an all-star team from Kansas City, radios were set up at the local diamond to broadcast the World Series game to the spectators gathered in the new stone and concrete grandstand (described in chapter 13), with the local game beginning immediately after the World Series game ended.[21]

Initially, sportscasters on the radio were not even at the ballpark, but instead re-created the game from facts transmitted by the wire services, similar to the megaphone in Pittsburg, if it could have been heard in people's homes. This often resulted in a broadcast that was as much a radio dramatization as it was a play-by-play description. However, radio broadcasts of ballgames by on-site sportscasters soon became more widely available, and radio signals could travel across hundreds of miles to reach listeners in rural areas. For example, some of the fans in Wellington were listening to the 1923 World Series broadcast transmitted by a radio station in Kansas City, 200 miles to the northeast. It was now possible for fans to satisfy their interest in baseball with major league teams as the games were played. In addition, the number of night games in the major leagues slowly increased after 1935, meaning that the audience for radio broadcasts could expand as people listened to games in their own homes after they got off work, eventually enjoying air-conditioned comfort on hot summer evenings. These changes made baseball played at the highest level more accessible to fans and presented town teams with competition for their support.[22]

This might have become even more pronounced in Kansas during the late 1950s, as the westward movement of major league teams made it possible to follow radio broadcasts of a "local" major league team. In 1955 the Athletics moved from Philadelphia to Kansas City, Missouri, replacing the minor league Kansas City Blues. The A's played in Kansas City through 1967, with games carried by a network of radio stations in Iowa, Kansas, Missouri, Nebraska, and Oklahoma.[23] It was also during the 1950s that televised baseball games became more widely available. The first Major

League Baseball game broadcast on television was in August 1939, but it was available to only a limited audience in New York. During the late 1940s and early 1950s, television expanded rapidly, and baseball—the national pastime—became a featured program.[24]

From Town Teams to Collegiate Summer Leagues

Events that contributed to the decline in the number of town teams can be explored further by examining the fates of these teams in Kansas. Unlike the ongoing town teams among our northern neighbors, Kansas town teams (and those in several other states) evolved. A hint of the changes that were to come can be seen in the organization of the Ban Johnson Amateur Baseball League. The league was established in Kansas City, Missouri, in 1927 as the Kansas City Junior Baseball League for players up to twenty-one years old (now twenty-three), with civic groups and businesses sponsoring the teams. The name of the league was changed in 1929 with the permission of Byron Bancroft "Ban" Johnson, who had established the American League in 1901.[25] It was not the intent of the league to replace town teams, and they often coexisted.

In 1933 Harry Suter of Salina was authorized to form the Ban Johnson League of Kansas, which initially included eight teams in Abilene, Beloit, Dodge City, El Dorado, Emporia, Salina, Topeka, and Wichita. Suter ran local youth baseball, including the American Legion program, and his intent was to provide an opportunity for his young players to continue playing baseball after they were no longer eligible for these programs.[26] Some of the small towns with Ban Johnson teams were equally interested in bringing high-quality baseball to their communities with young players who might draw interest from organized baseball.

The number of teams in the Kansas Ban Johnson League varied from year to year, but there were soon enough teams that the league was split into four regional divisions, which shortened the distances teams had to travel. The Western Division comprised towns in southwestern Kansas, the Central Division included towns mostly in north-central Kansas, the Eastern Division was represented by towns in northeastern Kansas, and the Southeastern Division was the most accurately named division in the state. A Northwestern Division was considered in 1938 but was not organized. Occasionally, teams from Nebraska (Fairbury and Beatrice) and Missouri (Carthage, Joplin, and Saint Joseph) were also members. Although Kansas Ban Johnson teams coexisted with town teams in some cities, the league tried to avoid competition with minor league clubs, and a few Ban Johnson teams folded when new minor league teams were established. The winners of the divisions met in a tournament to determine the overall champion.[27]

The Eastern Division of the Kansas Ban Johnson League lasted only a few years and was dissolved after the 1938 season.[28] The other three divisions continued to play until the league was suspended during the Second World War, resuming competition in 1946. In 1947 the Central Division ended its affiliation with the Kansas Ban Johnson League and reorganized as the Amateur Baseball League of America, a rather bold name for a regional Kansas league. A disagreement had arisen over Central Division teams paying their players $3 per week plus room and board. The Central Division had also continued to use an older Ban Johnson contract, which stated that "the club will promote the player for eventual entry into professional baseball." The Ban Johnson contract used in Kansas City no longer included that statement. The smaller, rural towns of the Central Division felt they could not conform to rules that worked in Kansas City, where travel costs were lower and a larger pool of local players made it unnecessary to import good players to provide high-quality baseball that would be supported by fans. Prior to the 1947 season the Ban Johnson League had restricted teams to recruiting players within a radius of seventy-five miles. The Amateur Baseball League of America survived only through the 1950 season, when it was reduced to four teams—Abilene, Clay Center, Junction City, and Manhattan.[29]

With the Central Division gone, the Kansas Ban Johnson League survived another decade with only two divisions. Financial difficulties led the Southeastern Division (sometimes called the Eastern Division) to fold in 1957.[30] The Western Division was still playing in 1959, but it was down to five teams—Dodge City, Garden City, Great Bend, Liberal, and McPherson. The following spring, the teams in Dodge City and Great Bend folded and could not be replaced, bringing the league to an end outside the Kansas City area.[31]

Seventeen years after the Ban Johnson League ended play in western Kansas, various collegiate summer baseball leagues began organizing in Kansas and elsewhere. Teams in these leagues used only amateur players recruited from across the country who retained their eligibility to participate in college sports. These teams are the successors of the old town teams in Kansas. Given the similar ages and experience of the players, teams from collegiate summer leagues sometimes played teams in the Ban Johnson League in the Kansas City area, where it is still active. The similarity between the leagues is also reflected in the name of the Liberal Bee Jays, currently a collegiate summer league team. The name Bee Jay was derived from the initials of Ban Johnson and was retained from the team's original affiliation with the Kansas Ban Johnson League from 1955 through 1959.

As with the early town teams and minor league teams, the number of collegiate summer league baseball teams in Kansas has varied over the years, and teams have sometimes moved to different towns or shifted from one league to another. In 2016 there were three collegiate summer baseball leagues with twenty teams in Kansas—the Jayhawk League (founded in 1976; seven teams in Kansas and one in Oklahoma), Kansas Collegiate League Baseball (formerly the Walter Johnson League, founded in 1976; eight Kansas teams), and the Mid-Plains League (founded in 2014; five teams in Kansas and three in Missouri). Four of these teams play in ballparks with grandstands built prior to the Second World War (El Dorado, Hays, Junction City, and Rossville). A fourth league, the MINK League (Missouri, Iowa, Nebraska, and Kansas), was founded in 1910 as a minor league that lasted through 1913 and was resurrected in 1996 as a collegiate summer baseball league. One Topeka team—the Golden Giants—was a member in 2005–2009, but the league has included no Kansas team since. In 2016 the MINK League consisted of seven teams in Missouri and one in Iowa.[32]

Despite their similarities, the collegiate summer league teams are not direct descendants of the Ban Johnson League. The transition from town teams to collegiate summer league teams can be seen through the history of another Kansas institution—the National Baseball Congress (NBC), which hosts the NBC World Series in Wichita during late July and early August. The story of the NBC World Series begins in 1931, when Wichita businessman Raymond "Hap" Dumont founded the Kansas State Semi-Pro Baseball Tournament. Despite the economically challenging times of the Great Depression, the state tournament was successful and led to the national semipro tournament in 1935.[33]

The NBC tournament was one of several tournaments for amateur or semiprofessional teams during the 1920s and 1930s. Some, such as the regional Denver Post Tournament, were relatively short-lived. Others, including the NBC tournament, have persisted, as has the tournament sponsored by the American Amateur Baseball Congress (AABC), now based in Farmington, New Mexico. The AABC continues to sponsor national tournaments in several age categories.[34] Originally named the American Baseball Congress, it was the amateur counterpart for the early National Semi-Pro Baseball Congress in Wichita.[35] During the Great Depression, these and other tournaments provided money through cash prizes to players on the best semiprofessional teams and expense money for amateur teams. The tournaments also offered spectators a summer distraction from the economic troubles they and the rest of the country experienced.[36]

The founder of the NBC, Hap Dumont, was born in Wichita in December 1904. He grew up to become a consummate promoter who was just a little eccentric. In high school he worked at the *Wichita Eagle*, taking local sports scores on the telephone and posting the scores and other news bulletins on the windows of the newspaper office. Working briefly after graduating in 1923 as class valedictorian, Dumont filled in as the sports editor in Hutchinson and promoted boxing matches in Hutchinson and Topeka. He soon returned to Wichita, working for the *Eagle* in the evenings and setting up a sporting goods store for local businessman Ike Goldsmith. In 1931 he offered to organize a game between circus employees, who were barred from performing on Sundays, and a local team of firemen. The game was played at Island Park Stadium and brought in about $1,600, despite the economic depression. Following that success, Dumont organized a sixteen-team state baseball tournament, won by the Abilene Bakers. The following year, the second chance offered by the tournament's double-elimination format allowed the Southern Kansas Stage Lines team to win the 1932 tournament after losing their first game. In 1933 the Wichita Water Company team, runners-up in 1931, defeated the Arkansas City Colored Beavers for the championship. The state tournament itself had no color line, even if the teams were segregated.[37]

The NBC state tournament suffered a potential setback when the grandstand at Island Park was destroyed by fire at the close of the 1933 season. In addition, Wichita lost its minor league team that year, and the Great Depression continued. However, in 1934 Dumont convinced the city, with assistance from federal work programs, to build a new, concrete baseball park, to be named Lawrence Stadium after an early settler.[38] In return,

Dumont promised to bring a national semipro baseball tournament to Wichita. The Kansas state tournament (expanded to fifty-four teams) was played on the new diamond in 1934, and Dumont began organizing the national tournament for 1935. The expenses of such a tournament and the challenge of drawing teams from across the country had intimidated other cities, and these obstacles would be even more imposing in the midst of the Great Depression. Yet Dumont met the challenge, perhaps driven by the need to stay active following the unexpected death of his first wife in January 1934.[39]

To entice spectators to the first year of what became the NBC World Series, Hap Dumont, ever the promoter and showman, reportedly promised $1,000 to the already well-known African American pitcher Satchel Paige and the racially integrated Bismarck Churchills from North Dakota if they played in the tournament—$1,000 Dumont did not have at the time. Fortunately, the NBC tournament was a financial success, as described in detail by Bob Broeg, Travis Larsen, and Tom Dunkel in articles and books listed among the sources. Long story short, Paige lived up to expectations, striking out sixty batters and winning four games on the way to the series title. The success of Paige and the Churchills, along with coverage of the tournament provided by the *Sporting News*, helped ensure the future of the venture. Hap Dumont died at work in 1971, but his legacy lives on at what is now Lawrence-Dumont Stadium—where a resurrected Gertie the Goose still lays "goose eggs" instead of zeros on the scoreboard when visiting teams fail to score in an inning—and in the NBC World Series that he created.[40]

Initially, most teams at the NBC tournament were semiprofessional barnstorming teams or teams sponsored by towns or local businesses, and some of the players had previously played in the major or minor leagues. During the Second World War, teams associated with industry and the military were prominent in the tournament. In the 1960s, however, a change began to occur as teams of collegiate players entered the tournament and competed well, while semiprofessional teams around the country began to fold. Fairbanks, Alaska, is credited with starting the trend of using college players, who were encouraged by their schools to play amateur baseball during the summer, thus providing them with additional experience. The combined college and summer league seasons were equivalent in duration to a minor league season. Businesses and individuals supported the teams because the players could not be paid to play baseball and remain eligible to play in college. Teams of collegiate players in Colorado, Kansas, and elsewhere soon followed Alaska's lead.[41] Most participants in the NBC World Series are now amateur teams, including some of the teams in the current collegiate leagues in Kansas. However, in 2016 a team sponsored by the Kansas Star Casino south of Wichita, named the Kansas Stars, featured twenty-four former major league players, eight of whom had played in the NBC tournament prior to joining organized baseball. They tied for third place.

The transition from town teams to collegiate summer leagues in Kansas can be illustrated with the Hays Larks, one of the oldest baseball teams in the state. In addition to the factors mentioned earlier as possible contributors to the decline of town teams, softball leagues and youth baseball leagues became regular features in many towns and may have diluted support for town teams. As noted by supporters of adult baseball in Hays during the late 1960s, all of this competition for community interest and financial support presented towns across Kansas with the challenge to "attract the local fans and bring townteam [sic] baseball back to what it used to be." In response to this challenge, the Hays town team recruited a mix of local and outside players who could play competitive games against good teams in other towns in Kansas and elsewhere. Some of the first teams scheduled to play Hays under this new model were from Dodge City, Leavenworth, Liberal, and Topeka, as well as Colorado Springs and Pueblo, Colorado. The process of finding players to supplement the local talent in Hays was aided by the revival of the baseball program at Fort Hays Kansas State College (now Fort Hays State University) in 1966, as some of the college players recruited from across the country stayed in Hays during the summer to play for the Larks.[42] Kansas towns without a college established connections to recruit college players from elsewhere, as did Hays. This transition to college players was essentially complete by 1976, when the first collegiate summer league was organized in Kansas. Hays and Liberal (a Ban Johnson town in the 1950s) are the two original members of this league that are still playing more than forty years later.

The collegiate summer leagues that feature amateur players of college age provide viable alternatives for towns that want to continue intercity competition at their local ballparks. Nonetheless, the hundreds of towns that once had baseball teams of young adults to represent them declined to only twenty towns in Kansas with collegiate summer league teams in 2016. Similarly, only about fifty American Legion teams of high school players have replaced what were sometimes referred to as the towns' second nines. Just as the collegiate summer league teams continue the tradition of town team baseball in Kansas, several of these teams, along with American Legion teams, high school teams, and a few college and minor league teams, play important roles in the preservation and continued use of the few remaining historical ballparks in the state built during the "golden age of town team baseball."[43]

PART II
Historical Baseball Parks in Kansas

When early town teams were organized, their top players made up what was referred to as the "first nine." The nine baseball parks described here have the oldest grandstands in Kansas still in use today. In terms of their ages, they are the state's first nine. They are presented in sequence from oldest to youngest. All were constructed prior to the Second World War, most as federal work projects intended to alleviate unemployment during the Great Depression. These work projects resulted in the construction of many public buildings and other structures, such as swimming pools, schools, courthouses, post offices, bridges, and roads. There were two principal programs associated with the construction of historical baseball parks in Kansas. The Civil Works Administration (CWA) was initiated in November 1933 to employ people as winter approached, but it was phased out from March through May 1934. In April 1935 the Works Progress Administration was established with the same general goal. It was renamed the Work Projects Administration in 1939, retaining the iconic initials WPA. Between 1935 and 1943, the WPA built or improved 3,228 stadiums, grandstands, and bleachers, in addition to 5,551 athletic fields for baseball, football, and other sporting activities across the country.[1]

The earliest baseball grounds were often relatively flat fields that received minimal preparation, but town teams soon employed scrapers and rollers to prepare playing fields that local newspapers would proudly proclaim to be among the finest in the area, the entire state, or perhaps anywhere. Of course, these boasts were not based on empirical data, and many towns made similar claims. Yet, along with the construction of the grandstand and other facilities, the effort put into preparing the playing field was indicative of the importance placed on baseball as representative of the community through an arena that displayed a young town's pride in itself and its team. Thankfully, nine communities have chosen to preserve their historical baseball parks constructed between 1924 and 1940, and they continue to use them for their original purpose.

Why only nine ballparks? Of the hundreds of baseball grounds of various qualities constructed in Kansas between 1865 and 1941, only these nine historical structures remain. Why did these towns choose to build the grandstands while so many other towns with the same access to federal assistance chose not to? And why are they still in use after more than seventy-five years?

Some towns did not build grandstands because they had little or no long-term interest in baseball, and some devoted their matching funds to other projects. For those grandstands that were constructed, one factor was the history of the site. Three of the extant grandstands replaced earlier structures. In Chanute and Kinsley, they were used by spectators at horse races, baseball games, and other sporting events at the local fairgrounds first used in the 1890s. Thus, the grandstands were improvements at athletic fields with well-established histories going back several decades. Both fields are now used solely for baseball. The 1936 grandstand in Garden City also replaced an older structure at a baseball park established sixteen years earlier.

The early wooden grandstands built in all nine cities, as typified by the grandstand in Rossville built in 1924, suffered from weathering and fires, and needed to be replaced periodically. They were not viewed as permanent structures, and permanence was the image towns wanted to project for themselves. The federal work programs offered an opportunity to build structures that could last longer and require less maintenance, projecting community pride and expectations for the future. The new grandstands in Junction City and Kinsley are somewhat transitional in that they have wooden seating areas and wooden roofs, but the space under the seats is enclosed by native stone, giving the structures a look of strength and stability, unlike the unenclosed wooden grandstand in Rossville. The other six grandstands have concrete seating areas, and all except the grandstand in El Dorado are enclosed by stone, concrete, or brick. However, the concrete of the El Dorado grandstand is unique in that it extends onto the roof, while the other roofs are wood or metal (the Chanute, Hays, and Larned grandstands have no roofs).

The grandstands in El Dorado, Hays, Junction City, Larned, Rossville, and Wichita were original constructions at their respective sites, rather than being replacements at longstanding parks. All of these projects clearly enjoyed local support, but four of these new ballparks benefited from strong advocates, who received prominent notice at the time in local newspapers. The efforts of Manuel "Babe" Goff in El Dorado, Alvus Moffet in Larned, Arthur Rathert in Junction City, and Raymond "Hap" Dumont in Wichita are described in subsequent chapters. Three of these stadiums are now named for their benefactors—Moffet, Rathert, and Dumont.

All nine ballparks are now associated with multiuse public parks (if we count the Riverwalk in Wichita). In fact, their association with municipal parks has likely afforded them a level of protection from demolition, as commonly occurred during the late 1800s and early 1900s, when private landowners converted their property to uses more profitable than a stadium. The locations of the ballparks probably also contributed to their longevity. As proud as communities might have been of their ballparks, they often placed them along streams prone to flooding, near railroad tracks, or both. Earlier ballparks in Larned and Wichita were even built on land that transformed into islands during periods of high streamflow. All pride aside, there was no sense in placing the ballpark on property that could be more profitably developed for residences or businesses in growing towns. In addition, many citizens complained that ballgames attracted excessively loud and vulgar elements of society unsuitable to respectable neighborhoods. Thus, ballparks were sometimes forced to move as towns grew. As a consequence of all these factors, early ballparks were typically built on the fringes of towns, but not too far away for people to reach by an easy walk or a ride on streetcars powered by horses or electricity. Several of the historical ballparks survived because they were near creeks or rivers in areas used for public parks, where the growth of the city did not lead to calls for the stadium to be relocated.

The wooden grandstand in Rossville, the oldest in this group, is the only one that was not replaced through the federal work programs of the Great Depression. Instead, it was maintained through repairs and replacement of its wooden components as they wore out or were damaged. The reason why is unknown, but it might be related to the small population of the city (see table 4). Town leaders might not have felt that a larger, more substantial structure was necessary or better than the one built by the community only a few years earlier. The small population also would mean that Rossville would have a correspondingly smaller economic base from which to provide the matching funds required for the federal programs. A new high school and a football field in Rossville, which were constructed as a WPA project in 1936, were probably viewed as higher priorities than a replacement grandstand for one that was still usable, especially when its primary tenants would be the high school baseball team and city softball leagues during the mid-1930s, not a town team.

In part, the quality of the construction of the grandstands explains their continued use. They show their ages but have not worn out beyond repair. In addition, the financial cost of maintaining the old ballparks through the decades in smaller communities was likely preferable to the cost of building new facilities, although a few communities, such as McPherson and Wellington, replaced their wooden grandstands in the 1960s.

Support for maintaining the historical grandstands might be associated with their continued use in some towns by high school teams in the spring and youth leagues during the summer. In addition, collegiate summer league teams used four of the historical ballparks and minor league teams used two others during the summer of 2016. All of these teams are reminiscent of the original first and second nines that represented their towns in the early years of baseball. These historical connections are also reflected in the substantial restorations and renovations undertaken by local communities at several of the ballparks. The long history of these ballparks has become an important part of their value and is now seen as

Table 4. Populations of the nine cities with historical baseball parks in Kansas during the period the ballparks were used and the grandstands were constructed, along with the populations from the most recent federal census.

	Population					
	1900	1910	1920	1930	1940	2010
Chanute	4,208	9,272	10,286	10,277	10,142	9,119
El Dorado	3,466	3,129	10,995	10,311	10,045	13,021
Garden City	1,590	3,171	3,848	6,121	6,285	26,658
Hays	1,136	1,961	3,165	4,618	6,385	20,510
Junction City	4,695	5,598	7,533	7,407	8,507	23,353
Kinsley		1,547	1,986	2,270	2,178	1,457
Larned		2,911	3,139	3,532	3,533	4,054
Rossville		672	664	701	601	1,151
Wichita	24,671	52,450	72,217	111,110	114,966	382,368

an additional reason to continue their maintenance and use. The spirit of community pride in which these historical venues were built decades ago now sustains them.

There are a few other features worth noting during a visit to one of the ballparks that might enhance your understanding of its long history. For example, consider the footprint of the grandstand. Most straight grandstands at baseball fields were formerly used for races or football in addition to baseball (the straight baseball grandstand in Hays is an exception). Curved grandstands behind home plate were built specifically for baseball diamonds, although they were sometimes used by spectators attending events such as speeches, boxing matches, or fireworks displays.

In addition to the grandstands, other features of each ballpark differ. The orientation and overall dimensions of playing fields (other than the diamond) vary among ballparks, making them additional points of discussion among fans regarding their pros and cons. Unlike the aesthetic qualities of ballparks, these two features of the ball ground are quantifiable, and

South Park racetrack in Kinsley in front of the 1904 wooden grandstand. Smaller cities sometimes placed their baseball fields within the oval racetracks to derive the most use from the costly facilities. The photograph was taken from the two-story judge's stand. Courtesy of the Kinsley Public Library.

South Park baseball diamond in Kinsley, with the wooden grandstand from 1904 in the background. A small bleacher provided seating closer to the ball field than the grandstand on the far side of the racetrack. The two-story wooden structure beside the bleacher is the judge's stand used during horse races. Courtesy of the Kinsley Public Library.

yet they still accommodate diverse opinions through the variation allowed by the rules. As a starting point, rule 2.01 of Major League Baseball recommends that ballparks should have minimum distances of 320 feet down each foul line and 400 feet to center field.[2] When visiting one of the historical ballparks in Kansas, you can see how it compares to major league standards and how the builders dealt with the local topography. Some of the historical ballparks in Kansas do not have the outfield distances posted on the fence, so you might have to ask someone what they are. The height of the outfield fence also varies from one ballpark to another and sometimes from left field to right field at a single ballpark.

Rule 2.01 further recommends that the orientation of the baseball diamond should be east-northeast, based on a line from home plate through second base. This keeps the afternoon sun out of the eyes of the batter—though it shines in the eyes of some fielders, who now wear sunglasses. However, other concerns can override the sun factor to some degree when builders design a ballpark. These include topographical features that limit

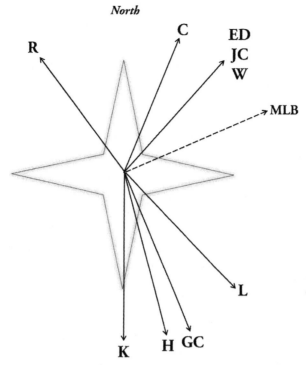

Field orientations from home plate through second base for the nine historical baseball parks in Kansas relative to Major League Baseball's recommendation of east-northeast. Orientations were derived from Earth View in Google Maps. C = Chanute, ED = El Dorado, GC = Garden City, H = Hays, JC = Junction City, K = Kinsley, L = Larned, R = Rossville, and W = Wichita.

the size of the field, the direction of prevailing winds, the aesthetics of the view from the grandstand beyond the outfield fence, and the placement of the grandstand entrance near a preferred access point. Of the nine historical ballparks in Kansas, none face east-northeast; most face generally northeast or southeast. The two exceptions are the ballpark in Kinsley, which faces south, and the stadium in Rossville, which faces northwest to provide the best fit within the space available for the baseball field. While visiting a ballpark, consider why the builders might have oriented the ballpark the way they did.

One final thought before beginning this tour of historical ballparks. I love all of the historical ballparks in Kansas (and elsewhere), but in my mind's eye I have an image of my ideal ballpark, and I encourage you to contemplate your own view. I prefer a small grandstand that holds less than 2,000 spectators and is constructed mostly of wood, built by craftsmen decades ago and lovingly maintained or restored. This grandstand puts you close to the field, protected in front by a net of dark fibers that flutters slightly in the breeze. Overhead, a wooden roof provides protection from the sun and foul balls. The top of the grandstand's outer wall is open below the roof, allowing the breeze to pass through and cool spectators seated in the shade on wooden bleachers or classic folding seats. It is an intimate grandstand that embraces you in the ambience of the game, where the grandstand collects every pop of the ball hitting a leather glove and every crack of the wooden bat, the iconic sounds resonating between the roof and seats. It makes you feel as though you are actually part of the game. No upper deck. No luxury suites. All of the ballparks listed here are great places to enjoy a ballgame and worthy of preservation, even if they lack one or more elements of my ideal ballpark. There are some real baseball gems in Kansas to match those anywhere. Anyone who suggests tearing them down or replacing them with something more modern should be brushed back with an inside fastball.

CHAPTER 9

Joe Campbell Memorial Stadium, Rossville

The first town teams in Rossville were organized during the 1870s, shortly after the town was founded. Events such as ice cream socials were held to raise funds for the team to buy "bats, gloves and other paraphernalia." As elsewhere, the organization of the town team was intermittent through the end of the century. In fact, a town team was sometimes absent for several years during the late 1800s. By 1910, the local newspaper reported, "People are getting more and more enthusiastic over this game every year and we don't believe that the people of Rossville will lie down for one minute and allow a smaller portion of the world to get ahead of them in this respect, for just such things are the life and prosperity of our town." Because it represented a rural community, the town team often took a break for a few weeks during midsummer for harvest. As in other small towns, there was no town team during 1918, while many of the young men served in the military during the First World War. Initially, most games in Rossville were played on Saturdays, and Reverend Ward got two triples for Rossville in a 1916 game. After the war, however, the team switched their game day to Sundays.[1]

In 1920 the Rossville semipro team had a record of 19–2, and the two losses were each by a single run. To congratulate the team, a supporter from Colorado Springs sent them two casks of "Mexican hot," a spiced hard cider, to share with their friends. With strong fan support and all of the team members expected back in 1921, plans were made to build "a new diamond . . . and a real grand stand." Since at least 1900, the baseball diamond had been at the high school on the north side of the city.

Apparently there was no fence, as one ball hit to the outfield in 1917 went "past the school house and the [Topeka Colored] Giant's right fielder lost the ball in the grass," resulting in a home run for Rossville. The proposed site of the new ballpark was on the north side of the school grounds, near the existing ball diamond. In the summer of 1921, "Lizzie Wooster, the cockleburr [sic] in charge of the state educational department" had ordered the school board in Rossville to prohibit the town team from using the baseball ground on Sundays, but the order was apparently ignored. Meanwhile, the proposal for a new ballpark continued to develop.[2]

The issue of establishing a city park with a variety of amenities had been on the minds of local citizens for years. The topic was raised again in January 1922 by the high school economics class, whose members wrote articles for the local newspaper in support of a public park. One of the triggers cited for raising this issue that year came from people who had traveled to Wamego for baseball games the previous summer and admired their fine city park. Two sites were mentioned as leading contenders for the Rossville city park—the earlier site proposed for a new ballpark north of the school and a parcel of land just outside the southern city limits. A vote for an $8,000 bond issue (equivalent to about $113,000 in 2016) to purchase land and develop a public park carried easily in April 1922. The eight-acre property adjacent to the southern city limits was selected as the preferred site.[3]

The park grounds were surveyed in November, but negotiations with the landowner continued through the winter before the bonds were finally issued in March 1923.[4] Work to grade roads and plant trees began in April, when volunteers, especially those "with teams [of horses], wagons, plows[,] shovels and other implements," were asked to bring their dinners and spend the day landscaping the park. Professor W. S. Wiedorn of the State Agricultural College (now Kansas State University) designed the park, and his plans called for the planting of nearly 400 trees, as well as the construction of a bandstand and shelter, an athletic field, a tourist campground, a children's playground, and a picnic area.[5] Although it was usually referred to as the "city park," the proposal to actually incorporate the tract of land within the city limits was not presented until 1931.[6]

Work on the baseball field and grandstand began in the spring of 1924. Originally, the diamond was to have been in the northwestern corner of the field (as illustrated in the local newspaper), but it was moved to the opposite corner to provide a better fit for the outfield. The dimensions of the playing field would be a short 290 feet to right field, while the lengths of left and center fields would be "unlimited."[7] Strong winds during a game in June 1925 pushed several balls into "the cattle yards far beyond the right field limits."[8] "Practically every carpenter in the city" promised to assist with the construction of the grandstand under the supervision of two carpenters who also sat on the city council. It was to seat 500 people, with a central section behind home plate and wings extending down the first and third base lines.[9] In the meantime, baseball games continued at the school diamond.[10]

Finishing touches were put on the diamond and grandstand in early June 1924. In the first game played at the new ballpark on June 8, 1924, Rossville defeated Tecumseh 4–3. The "new grandstand, which seats comfortably six hundred, was filled and late-comers were seated along the fences paralleling the right and left field foul lines. The city band gave a fine concert preceding the game that lasted an hour and a half."[11] Parking was prohibited along the foul lines, because everyone who paid the regular admission would be allowed to use the grandstand at no additional charge (assuming there was room). The city received 10 percent of the gate receipts for use of the park by the local town team.[12] Admission was initially 35¢ for men, 25¢ for ladies, and 10¢ for children, but it dropped a few years later to 25¢ for men, with ladies admitted at no charge.[13]

Exterior of the wooden grandstand, built in 1924, at Joe Campbell Memorial Stadium in Rossville (2014). From the author's personal collection.

Wooden seating in the grandstand, built in 1924, at Joe Campbell Memorial Stadium in Rossville (2014). From the author's personal collection.

It is rare to find detailed accounts of the income and expenses for town teams, but they were published in Rossville newspapers in 1887 and 1924, providing a glimpse into this aspect of early town team baseball.[14] The July 1, 1887, financial summary included income and expenses up to that date. All of the income came from twenty-two businesses and individuals who donated a total of $51.10, with contributions ranging from 50¢ to $5.00. Expenditures to that point totaled $36.50, primarily for upkeep of the ball ground and equipment (table 5). A bat, a ball, and three bases could be purchased in 1887 for $1.00. Apparently, no admission was charged, as no income of that type was reported.

Nearly four decades later, the accounts for 1924 cover the entire season (table 6). Income was again derived from subscriptions (donations), but the total from subscriptions was lower than in 1887. Most of the income in 1924 shifted from subscriptions to gate receipts for home games and "team guarantees" provided by the host teams at away games. A Sunday home game against Hoyt in August had to be played in Silver Lake because "the game had been forbidden . . . on the Rossville grounds upon orders

Table 5. Rossville town team expenses for the 1887 season through June.
(Source: *Carpenter's Kansas Lyre* [Rossville], 1 July 1887.)

Expense	$
rent of the ground	15.00
lumber and nails	3.85
livery (travel) to Maple Hill	3.50
mowing ground	1.00
one bat and scorebook	0.65
hoeing ground and incidentals	2.40
twine, box, rod, and shoemaker's fee	0.60
three bases	0.25
hoeing and mowing ground	3.50
one bat and ball	0.75
balls and bats H & T*	5.00

*David Hartzell and Melvin Tatman owned a local drugstore and donated $5.00 to the baseball team.

from the Attorney General." Two weeks later, another Sunday ballgame in Rossville had to be called off because a "revival" had not yet ended.[15] As can be seen in the report, gate receipts (attendance) declined dramatically late in the season. Yet income ($1,143.48) still exceeded expenditures ($1,013.23) by $135.25 (equivalent to about $1,875 in 2016), even after repaying a deficit of $41.23 carried over from 1923 and purchasing new uniforms. Most expenses listed were for unspecified services, probably for work associated with the ballpark, travel to away games, and perhaps for umpires. In addition, team guarantees of $20–$25 were paid to twelve teams that traveled to Rossville for games at the new ballpark. Comparing the team guarantees to actual gate receipts, it would seem to be much more profitable to play at home, at least until attendance dropped at the end of the season. However, much of the "extra" income was needed to lease and maintain the ballpark. In addition to starting the 1925 season with a positive cash balance, the second year at the new ballpark included some notable events.

At a game on the Fourth of July, 1925, an estimated 1,500 spectators "were packed in the grandstand, temporary bleachers west of the stand[,] and out beyond the left field limits."[16] That summer Rossville was playing well and winning all of their games until they lost in late July to the American Indian team from Mayetta. The Mayetta Indians also won the second game against Rossville in August.[17] Perhaps the most prestigious

Table 6. Rossville town team income and expenses for 1924.

(Source: *Rossville Reporter,* 19 September 1923, 2 April 1925.)

Income	$	Expense	$
subscriptions	35.00	C. R. Kenney, deficit for 1923 supplies	41.23
Holton game	61.90	D. Maupin, services	61.50
additional subscriptions	11.50	F. Tibbs, services	152.15
Lecompton game	69.10	Pete Kovar, services	73.80
Wilson Stars game	60.21	C. R. Kenney, supplies and uniforms	277.65
M.W.A. game	58.50	Chas. Harrison, services	7.00
Tecumseh game	134.34	L. Trahoon, services	13.25
Holton game (at Holton)	25.00	R. A. Shipley, services	3.50
Valley Falls game	112.48	F. Lambotte, services	7.00
Manhattan game	73.33	Tom Oldfield, services	1.00
White Eagle game	151.47	P. Navarre, meals for team	7.40
Paxico game (at Paxico)	25.00	C. E. Cless, services	15.90
Paxico game	64.25	J. Navarre, auto hire	11.00
Hoyt (at Silver Lake)	95.35	Sam Crow, services	3.00
Tecumseh (at Tecumseh)	25.00	Joe Curwick, services	10.00
Topeka All-Star game	34.00	White Eagle Oil Company	3.00
Harley-Davidson game	29.20	Wm. Bush, services	1.00
Emmett game	57.35	Wm. Bixby, services	1.00
Alma game	20.50	W. C. Wells, services	8.00
		C. D. Campbell, services	5.00
		Rossville Band, services	9.00
		H. R. Miller, mask	7.00
		Ira Hopkins, for July 4 celebration	5.00
Team guarantees:			
Alma	25.00		
Emmett	25.00		
Topeka	20.00		
Paxico	25.00		
White Eagle	25.00		
Manhattan	25.00		
Wilson Stars	25.00		
M.W.A.	20.00		
Tecumseh	25.00		
Holton	25.00		
Lecompton	20.00		
Harley-Davidsons	20.00		
J. Thomas and Co., lumberyard supplies	3.85		

opponent hosted by the town team at the new ballpark in 1925 was the Kansas City Monarchs, who were soon to play in their second Negro World Series. The Monarchs played eight games on a brief barnstorming tour through northern Kansas and southern Nebraska during a break in their league schedule, stopping for their final game in Rossville on August 3. Not surprisingly, the Monarchs won, but the score was a respectable 4–1. Rossville's only run was scored "in the second inning when Maupin drove one to right field, ordinarily good for a single, but [Hurley] McNair lost so much time finding the ball in a bunch of weeds Maupin made the circuit." In the Rossville game, Humboldt native George Sweatt played left field and Topeka native Carroll "Dink" Mothell played first base. In 1917 Mothell had traveled to Rossville to catch for the Topeka Giants in a game that ended in a 4–4 tie after eleven innings. Although the Monarchs' pitching staff in 1925 included Hall of Famers Wilber "Bullet" Rogan and José Méndez (nearing the end of his long career), Cliff Bell pitched in Rossville. The Rossville newspaper reported that "in one Nebraska town the fans got personal and the Monarchs got sore and the Nebraska team was beaten 43 to 3. The crowd here acted courteously and we saw a good ball game."[18] Rossville town teams continued to play African American teams from towns in the region.[19]

Electrical wiring for lights and outlets on the grandstand had been installed at the ballpark when it was first constructed,[20] and fire associated with early electrical wiring was a concern in wooden grandstands. However, it was other events at the Fourth of July celebration in 1928 that could have easily ended in disaster at the four-year-old ballpark. Two daylight baseball games were among the many activities in Rossville that year. During the evening display of fireworks, sparks accidentally ignited two skyrockets, which "shot toward the packed grandstand with a roar and a stream of sparks." One skyrocket pierced a one-inch board on the front of the wooden grandstand, and the other went through the netting intended to stop only baseballs. There was a momentary panic, but no one was seriously injured, although one woman was badly bruised when hit by a rocket, and she and another woman had their dresses burned.[21]

Although electricity was installed at the grandstand in 1924, the first floodlights at the city park were not installed until June 1934, at a cost of about $200 from the city, plus funds from subscriptions by local boosters. Intended primarily for use at softball games, the six reflectors, each with a bulb of 1,500 watts, were placed on as many poles set around the outfield by local volunteers.[22] In the mid-1930s, men's and women's softball, rather than town team baseball, was played at the city park diamond.[23] However, by late spring 1938, "softball [was] on its way out as the amusement feature for the communities' [sic] athletic-minded, and the fine base ball plant at the park will come back into its own."[24] In 1939 Rossville organized the Kaw Valley League with the nearby towns of Delia, Harveyville, Hoyt, McFarland, Paxico, Silver Lake, and Willard, but the league lasted only one year.[25]

In November 1936 it was decided to build a new high school and football field through the Works Progress Administration (WPA) adjacent to the eastern end of the city park, allowing the high school team to use the city ball diamond.[26] When games could not be played at the city park, they were moved to the "old school diamond."[27] Two small baseball fields still sit north of the elementary school, which is on the site of the old high school.

Town team baseball continued in Rossville for several years after the Second World War. In the spring of 1954, the city council discussed making some needed repairs to the ballpark grandstand as part of a general community improvement program. Improvements at the city park included work on tennis courts, horseshoe pits, and picnic tables, but not the ballpark.[28] The following year, Rossville High School organized a baseball team for the first time in "several years." During the summer the town team was joined by high school and cookie (youth) baseball teams and by women's and girls' softball teams. Interest in Rossville baseball was increasing, and improvements at the ballpark followed. The Rossville Lions Club worked with the city to install a city water line to the grandstand and to repair the old wooden structure. They also worked with the city and other organizations to install new lights at the baseball park. A "group of young people" interested in art painted the word *Rossville* in letters three feet tall across the front of the grandstand, flanked by "cartoon" images of baseball players.[29]

Dedicated to the memory of Rossville baseball supporter and chair of the recreational park committee Joe Campbell, the stadium features one of the few historical wooden grandstands remaining in the United States and the only historical all-wood grandstand in Kansas. The exterior of the covered grandstand is open, exposing the supporting framework. There is no press box, only a built-in table among the seats behind home plate. The infield is all dirt ("skinned"), and the outfield is grass. The outfield fence is chain-link, mostly six feet tall except in the short right field, where it is twenty-four feet tall, offering some protection to cars parked at the convenience store just beyond the tree-lined street that borders the fence.

In 2014 the city of Rossville (a town of only about 1,150 people) received a Shawnee County Historical Society Preservation Award for its work preserving the historical stadium. In 2015 the ballpark was used for re-created baseball scenes in a documentary on town team baseball in Kansas during the early 1900s titled *Town Teams: Bigger than Baseball*. Currently, the ballpark is the home of the high school team and the Rossville Rattlers (Mid-Plains Collegiate Baseball League).

CHAPTER 10

South Park Field, Kinsley

BASEBALL GROUNDS FIRST USED: 1899

GRANDSTAND BUILT: 1934

Kinsley was founded in 1873, and the town's first baseball team was apparently organized in 1877. Although some early teams in rural Kansas were referred to only by the names of their towns, the Kinsley town team chose a name. "The 'Star' Base Ball Club is the cognomen of the Kinsley club." A July 4 game between the Kinsley Stars and the Offerle Haymakers was played after the horse races at "the race grounds on the south side of town," which were probably on the south side of Coon Creek near Marsh Avenue. Kinsley won the game 38–12. Despite having only one victory, the Kinsley "Base Ball club wears the champion belt, and would like to hear from the boys down at Larned, Great Bend and Hutchinson." As they waited, members of the baseball club presented a minstrel show at the church and raised about $15 to support the team. The Larned Base Ball Club made the trip to Kinsley in August and lost 33–15. The Stars' perfect record remained unblemished in their brief inaugural season.[1]

Perhaps a bit impatient, a local newspaper asked in April 1878, "Where are the nine? The Kinsley base ball club we mean." During the early years, baseball teams in rural areas sometimes did not organize until late June or July, in anticipation of the wheat harvest being completed. Thus, the White Star Base Ball Club of Kinsley received their new caps on June 1, 1878, in preparation for their second season. The Stars played a game that year with the team from Larned on the Fourth of July that was stopped after the fifth inning "on account of the races," with Kinsley claiming victory. The Stars had "their [own] ball ground" at an undetermined site.[2] Being a small town, everyone would know where the ball ground was, so newspapers often did not mention the specific location unless it differed from the regular site.

Players on the 1879 town team included veterans of baseball teams in the Northeast and Midwest who had moved west to Kinsley. Earl and Frank Spencer (pitcher and second baseman) had reportedly played professional baseball in Ithaca, New York, as had Charles Snapp (catcher) in Chicago, Illinois. Other members of the club had apparently played on teams in Ohio, Pennsylvania, and Wisconsin before moving west to Kinsley. Games in the early years were infrequent, so a few of these players sometimes played for the baseball team in Larned when Kinsley was idle.[3] Despite the strong interest in baseball among its members, the limited number of games played by the Stars led a local newspaper to lament in July 1880 that "the game of base ball has passed to the pages of history, as far as this part of the country is concerned."[4]

The absence was brief, however, and in July 1881 a team of new players was organized and initially referred to as the Colonels. Perhaps to make a statement that they planned to represent Kinsley for years to come, they were not content to have only team caps. A local newspaper reported that the Colonels' "new base ball suits . . . are very pretty." By the time they played their first game against Larned on August 2, the team's name had reverted to the earlier name of Stars.[5] Uniforms had a relatively short life, being either damaged or lost, so the early Kinsley teams periodically raised funds through various means, such as selling team subscriptions or holding benefit dances, to purchase "nobby" (chic) new uniforms.[6] In addition to the Stars, Kinsley also supported a second team known as the Red Stockings (usually shortened to Reds) in the early years, along with occasional other teams composed of players of various ages. One such team was the Mercurys, organized by a local newspaper. Only the Reds were mentioned in newspaper accounts during 1889, but the reorganized Kinsley Star Base Ball Club returned in 1890 as the town's first nine.[7]

There was little mention of early African American baseball teams in Kinsley, but a local newspaper reported in December 1878, "Base ball every day in front of our office. No distinction of color shown."[8] A "match game of base ball between the small white and black boys of town" was played in 1879, and there was an integrated boys' team of eight white boys captained by an African American boy.[9] Apparently, the youngsters were playing on Sixth Street in the business district during the evenings. "There will be some costly windows to pay for before this thing is stopped," the newspaper predicted.[10] Adult African American teams in Kinsley were not mentioned in newspapers until 1916, when the Bear Cats were organized.[11]

Beginning in 1886, baseball games were often played at the Edwards County fairgrounds near Kinsley, where plans were made to greatly enlarge the grandstand built the previous year.[12] The fairgrounds had been constructed in the autumn of 1885 for the county fair held that October. The grounds sat east of the city near the bridge across the Arkansas River and were convenient to passenger trains on the railroad from Hutchinson, providing easy access to visitors from other towns.[13] There was no fair in 1889, but the fairgrounds continued to be used for horse, bicycle, and foot races, as well as picnics, Fourth of July celebrations, a state Grand Army of the Republic (GAR) reunion, and baseball games.[14] However, because the fairgrounds were about a mile east of the downtown area, more convenient locations were also used for baseball games, including sites "just north of the Depot Hotel" in 1885, "the commons south of the Santa Fe eating house" in 1889, "near the South Side school building" in 1895, and "just north of Mrs. Read's" in 1903.[15] The last baseball game played at the old fairgrounds was probably in 1895. The property had a new owner that winter.

An 1896 baseball game between Kinsley and Larned was described as being played "at the park."[16] This might have been the city park "on the north side" that was conceived in 1896 and "fronted the old depot" (near the intersection of Sixth Street and Colony Avenue). In 1897 "the ground had all been plowed and partially graded and a thorough track man employed to put it in fine shape." In 1898 the Old Settlers' Picnic, featuring races and baseball games, was held at the "City Park," but it was moved to "south park" the following year. The new park's name reflected its location "just south of Kinsley on the outskirts of the city."[17] It goes by the same name today.

After five years of races, baseball games, and other events in South Park, a wooden grandstand with a roof was built in 1904, in time for the annual Old Settlers' Day on June 15. As in previous years, a baseball game was a featured event of the celebration and carried a $15 prize for the winning team. The contest between the Kinsley Stars and the rival team from nearby Belpre, with a neutral umpire from Garfield, was a "hummer" won by Kinsley 8–7 in ten innings. Some of the other events on the program that afternoon included a baby show (with $5 prizes for the prettiest boy and prettiest girl), several horse races, a foot race, a bicycle race, a "slow mule" race, bronco busting, and at 6:00 p.m., the "usual shower with hail," which failed to arrive as scheduled. Special trains operated by the Santa Fe Railroad carried participants from nearby towns, and the crowd was estimated at 3,500–4,000 people, while the population of Kinsley was only about 1,200 people that year.[18]

The 1904 wooden grandstand was a straight structure, sixty-four feet long, sixteen feet deep, and "convenient for those who wish to see the races or the base ball games."[19] The baseball diamond was inside the oval racetrack immediately across from the grandstand near an octagonal wooden judge's stand. For several years a small wooden bleacher with no roof sat near home plate on the first base side that would put a few spectators closer to the diamond (shown in the photographs in the introduction to part II). In its inaugural event at the Old Settlers Day, "the grand stand was greatly appreciated by visitors and brought to the treasurer of the association $52.35."[20] In 1910 improvements to the baseball ground included a new backstop, fences to control the crowd, new seats, and new gates.[21] In 1914 and 1920 it was reported that the ball diamond still had both a grandstand and a bleacher.[22]

Beginning in 1907 the Kinsley town team was involved in a few attempts to organize regular competition through local baseball leagues. Some of the proposed leagues failed to materialize, and those that were organized usually lasted a single year. The towns varied from year to year, but they tended to be located along the Atchison, Topeka, and Santa Fe Railroad lines, which made it easier for the teams and their fans to travel among the league cities for games. In 1907 Ellinwood, Great Bend, Kinsley, and Larned formed the Wheat Belt League. There were unsuccessful attempts to organize the Wheat and [Sugar] Beet Baseball League in 1908 with Dodge City, Garden City, Larned, and Kinsley (known that year as the Senators) and a league of teams from Dodge City, Kinsley, Lewis, and Spearville in 1910. The advantage of a league was that it provided a regular schedule of games, but even when leagues could not be organized, the teams still played each other whenever games could be arranged. In 1911 Belpre, Dodge City, Kinsley, Lewis, Spearville, and Stafford organized the Santa Fe Baseball League, with Larned replacing Belpre at the beginning of the season. The name of the league referred to the Santa Fe Trail, which had passed through the area. As with the Wheat Belt League, the Santa Fe League lasted only a single year.[23]

Kinsley also had twilight leagues that only scheduled games Monday through Saturday in 1915–1917. The league played a split season, with a midseason break during harvest. Attempts to organize similar twilight or Sunday school leagues in the 1920s met with limited success. These twilight leagues did not inhibit the yearly organization of a town team, which often played on Sunday afternoons until Sunday baseball was banned by the city in 1916. The Kinsley town team still played in other towns on Sundays, and it was allowed to play Sunday games again on its home field after the First World War. In 1915 the Kinsley Travelers (the white town team) hosted a pair of games against a Cheyenne and Arapaho barnstorming team from Oklahoma, which included a mix of American Indian and white players. In 1916, the Kinsley "Bear Cats (colored) defeated the Travelers (uncolored)" 8–4. The following year the Bear Cats challenged the twilight league teams to games "at any time." The league responded by inviting the Bear Cats to join.[24] In addition to the twilight leagues, there was an unsuccessful attempt to organize indoor baseball (softball) for men in Kinsley during the winter of 1921–1922 by W. H. Murray, who had played the sport in Chicago, birthplace of the game. The following winter Kinsley did play indoor baseball and defeated Larned twice, but the winter sport does not seem to have benefited from the town's interest in the traditional version played outdoors during the summer.[25]

During the 1920s the Kinsley town team experienced difficulties faced by other small cities with regard to playing competitive baseball. They struggled with the choice of playing in leagues with larger towns or joining leagues with smaller towns. Fielding a competitive semiprofessional team to play against its larger neighbors could be costly for a small city such as Kinsley, which had a population of only 1,986 in 1920. By comparison, Dodge City had 5,061 people, Great Bend 4,460, Larned 3,139, and Pratt 5,183. At the other end of the scale, nearby towns such as Belpre, Garfield, Lewis, Offerle, and Spearville had between 225 and 629 people. As they endeavored to find the appropriate fit among potential competitors, a local newspaper explained the importance of having the best baseball team possible:

> One of the very best advertisements a town can have is a good base ball team. There will be no questions over that point. We know that Kinsley has paved streets, a great white way [outside lights], good schools, fine

churches, good [railroad] facilities, a good band, . . . and as fine a set of people as can be found anywhere. Why not get the "do it now" habit and organize a base ball team that will put Kinsley on the map?[26]

In 1920 Kinsley fielded an independent team that played towns of various sizes, resulting in a roughly equal mix of victories and defeats. They also played the Kinsley Bear Cats, who continued to play both white and African American teams for a few more years.[27] For the 1921 season, teams in Belpre, Burdette, Ely, Garfield, Kinsley, Lewis, Larned, and Rozel formed the Pawnee and Edwards County (P. & E.) Baseball League. To control costs, teams could hire only one player. At midseason, a June flood along the Arkansas River and Coon Creek inundated Kinsley's South Park. "One of the interesting sights was to stand in the grand stand at the South park and look out across the baseball diamond and race track. It was all just water, looked like a sea." Not surprisingly, the rain and flood caused a few home games to be canceled or moved to their opponents' ballparks. Rain or shine, Kinsley struggled to win games and even advertised in a local newspaper for a pitcher in August. Although there was talk of organizing a similar league in 1922, Kinsley played independently and was more successful.[28]

League play returned in 1923, when Kinsley joined the smaller towns of Lewis, Offerle, and Spearville in the Santa Fe Trail League. It was reorganized as the Santa Fe League the following year, with the departure of Spearville and the addition of Belpre, Greensburg, and Rozel. As in 1921, Kinsley struggled to win consistently in league play with semiprofessional teams from smaller towns in the region. From 1925 to 1927 the Kinsley team again played independently, using no salaried players in 1927. That changed again in 1928, when Kinsley joined the larger towns of Dodge City, Ellinwood, Great Bend, Larned, and Pratt in organizing the Southwest Kansas Baseball League. Because "semi-professional baseball players [were] asking too much money for their services, making the national pastime almost prohibitive in Southwestern Kansas," salaries were capped equally for each team. Again, Kinsley did not fare well in a league with its larger neighbors and opted to organize the Sunflower League in 1929 with the smaller towns of Garfield, Hanston, Offerle, Rozel, and Spearville. In May, Kinsley scheduled an exhibition game against an African American team referred to as a House of David team, although it was not associated with the religious sect. Among the team's players was John Donaldson, a native of Glasgow, Missouri, who was considered one of the best left-handed pitchers in baseball during the 1910s. However, he played center field against Kinsley, as he often did at this late point in his career. Kinsley lost 9–1, and that was the high point of their 1929 baseball season. In July, the team quit in the fourth inning of a home game against Rozel, ending their season prematurely. They had experienced trouble fielding a team of their regular players that summer.[29]

Following the setback in 1929, a town team was organized again in 1930, although fan turnout and press coverage were light for a victory in May against the team from Dodge City. One of Kinsley's games was a softball game against the Wallenstein and Raffman Girls team of Wichita. The Kinsley men had a little trouble getting used to softball, and the game lasted nineteen innings, with Kinsley finally gaining a 3–2 victory. There was no further mention of Kinsley baseball that year.[30]

The ballpark would also suffer a setback. Early wooden grandstands, such as the structure at the Kinsley racetrack and baseball grounds in the "South Side Park" constructed in 1904, must have seemed somewhat less than permanent to the local communities, who were generally concerned about perpetuating their young towns and enhancing the attractiveness of the community's amenities to potential residents and businesses. Sometimes wooden grandstands simply collapsed under the weight of the spectators.[31] Sometimes they were felled by the strong Kansas wind. In April 1904, the year the grandstand at South Park was built, strong winds collapsed the grandstand at the ball grounds in nearby Belpre.[32] The same fate befell the grandstand at the ballpark in Ellinwood in September 1909.[33] However, fire was more often the fear, and for good reason, as the wooden grandstand in Kinsley burned in the spring of 1931. The local fire chief condemned the remnants, which were subsequently torn down. Although the grandstand was gone, the city provided materials for a new backstop at the baseball diamond, and the American Legion provided the labor to construct it under the supervision of local contractors.[34]

Prior to the conflagration that destroyed the grandstand, an independent town team was organized in April 1931 that played into June, the third consecutive year that Kinsley struggled to field a team the entire summer. The following year, however, the Pawnee and Edwards County Baseball League was reorganized by teams from Belpre, Burdett, Garfield, Kinsley, Larned, Lewis, Offerle, and Rozel. A local newspaper began posting box scores and game summaries on the front page, declaring that "base ball is on the come back in Kinsley." Kinsley and Rozel tied for first place in the league, and the top four teams played a single-elimination championship series. Kinsley won their first game against Burdett but lost to Larned in the championship game 14–8. The league reorganized in 1933 with the same eight teams. Kinsley did not have much success this time, and reports of their games all but disappeared from the local newspaper late in the season, replaced on the front page by the results of games in a punkin ball (softball) league.[35]

With economic depression gripping the country, the city did not make arrangements until early 1934 for a replacement grandstand, which was built as a Civil Works Administration (CWA) project.[36] The CWA was a federal work program during the Great Depression similar to the longer-running Works Progress Administration (WPA), but the CWA operated only during the winter of 1933–1934 and was phased out from March through May. The construction of the grandstand and a pavilion was funded with $1,500 from a city levy (equivalent to about $27,000 in 2016) and $800 from the Old Settlers' Association, which continued to sponsor the annual summer picnic in the park. Based on plans prepared by Roy Hatfield, construction began in March, slowly at first, as workers were hired and materials were purchased.[37] The grandstand neared completion with work on the shingled roof in late May, as the CWA was phased out. As in 1904, the new grandstand was ready for its dedication at the Old Settlers' Picnic on June 7–8.[38] The new judge's stand for the races was built on skids this time, allowing it to be moved onto the infield of the oval track during races and moved off the infield for baseball games.[39]

The 1934 grandstand was constructed as a straight structure 112 feet long and 24 feet deep, covered by a roof, and generally similar to its predecessor, although it was larger (48 feet longer and 8 feet deeper). It had an estimated seating capacity of 550 spectators.[40] Having a straight grandstand made it useful for races and football games as well as baseball or softball games. At first, only the concrete supports, roof, and wooden seats were constructed. The outside of the grandstand on its northern side was later enclosed with native stone to better shield spectators from the north wind and provide booth space for various groups (the space was later used for locker rooms). Although the main structural support for the grandstand built in 1934 is concrete enclosed by stone, the seating area is still wood, with metal covers now placed on the front portions of the tiers. The

Exterior of the grandstand of concrete enclosed by stone, built in 1934, at South Park in Kinsley (2014). From the author's personal collection.

grandstand roof is also wood, with the shingles now replaced by metal roofing. The concrete and wood of the grandstand are painted red and white, the high school colors, which match the colors of the two early baseball teams—the White Stars and the Red Stockings.

Following construction of the new grandstand, the diamond at South Park was first used for softball games. Six teams were organized in 1935, and they somewhat apologetically charged 10¢ admission, as the Great Depression showed no signs of easing. The money was used to cover the cost of lighting the field, allowing more games to be played in the evenings, although they stopped playing night games in midsummer. The softball league opened the season with an evening doubleheader during one of the strong dust storms that raged during the severe drought that decade. The Pawnee and Edwards County Baseball League also reorganized in May 1935, with teams in Burdett, Fellsburg, Garfield, Kinsley, Lewis, and Rozel. The schedule included mostly Sunday afternoon games that would complement the evening softball games on weekdays. In contrast to the dust storm plaguing the first softball games of the spring, the opening weekend of the baseball game was rained out. The men's softball and baseball leagues were joined at South Park by girls' punkin ball teams in July, as the men's teams took time off for harvest. The Kinsley baseball team claimed first place in the 1935 P. & E. League.[41]

Wooden seating in the grandstand, built in 1934, at South Park in Kinsley (2014). From the author's personal collection.

Punkin ball continued in Kinsley and received more press coverage in 1936 than the town team, which joined an expanded Hodgeman-Edwards-Pawnee County League (or Hodgeman-Pawnee-Edwards County League), with teams from Belpre, Burdett, Fellsburg, Garfield, Hanston, Kinsley, Offerle, Ray, and Rozel. Ray led the league, with Kinsley a close second. Despite their success in the new leagues, Kinsley apparently played independently in 1937. During 1936 and 1937, Kinsley also played several games "under the floodlights" at South Park, some against town teams and some against the recently organized Ban Johnson League teams from Larned and Dodge City. In 1936 an African American team playing under the name Kansas City Spiders was "headquartering in Kinsley for three weeks" while they played Kinsley and traveled to other towns in the region for games before heading to Wichita for the National Baseball Congress (NBC) semipro tournament. Perhaps the highlight of the 1937 season for Kinsley was a victory over Garfield in a thirteen-inning contest. Kinsley won 5–3 after turning in a triple play to end the game. Garfield had loaded the bases when a fly ball certain to fall for a base hit was caught, and the runners on second and third were thrown out before they could retreat to their bases. Barnstorming baseball teams were numerous prior to the Second World War, but the local softball all-stars also played a barnstorming softball team known as the Los Angeles Red Devils, who won the game.[42]

After playing two years in leagues with smaller towns and another year as an independent team, Kinsley again joined a league that included a few larger towns. The reorganized Southwest Kansas Baseball League included teams from towns such as Dodge City, Garden City, and Larned in 1938 and 1939. (The name Southwest Kansas League was also used for high school teams.) Local merchants in Kinsley ran large newspaper advertisements offering free tickets to league games during both years, saving their customers 25¢ per game. In 1938 Kinsley also hosted the Washington Browns, an African American team from Yakima headed to the NBC tournament in Wichita. The Browns were victorious. In both years, Kinsley placed in the lower half of the league standings, but they avoided last place finishes. They were more competitive in 1939 and occasionally packed the grandstand for league games. Attendance was no doubt enhanced by the free tickets from the merchants, a gesture likely appreciated by fans during the Great Depression.[43]

As the 1939 baseball season was ending, the Second World War broke out in Europe. In the two years before the United States entered the conflict, life on and off the ball field changed. In 1940 Kinsley was again a member of the Southwest Kansas Baseball League, and local merchants now offered tickets for 10¢, while people without those discounted tickets were still charged 25¢. Kinsley's success in the league was comparable to the previous two years, and they were the victims of a perfect game thrown by Paul Mai of the Garden City league team. In addition to league games, they also played games against teams from other towns and the Ban Johnson teams from Dodge City and Larned. The final game of the season was a benefit game against the Larned Ban Johnson team, which picked up a few players to replace those regulars who had already departed. The two teams donated the proceeds ($30) to John Brack of the Kinsley town team, who had been seriously injured during a game earlier in the summer. In 1941 the newspaper in Kinsley, as elsewhere in Kansas, replaced stories about young men playing on the town team with stories about its young men registering or being drafted for military service.[44]

The ballpark in South Park—currently the second-oldest baseball grandstand in Kansas—is now used for high school, American Legion, and other youth ball games during the spring and summer. Ground-level dugouts were added in 2014. Chain-link fencing, rather than nets, protects the seating behind home plate, and a chain-link fence surrounds the playing field. The infield is all dirt ("skinned"), and the outfield is grass. The distance to the outfield fence is 305 feet to all fields. Although the exact placement of the diamond shifted slightly northward (closer to the grandstand) following the removal of the racetrack, this is one of the oldest baseball grounds still used for the sport in Kansas, with 2017 marking the 118th anniversary of the ground's first use for baseball games in 1899.

CHAPTER 11

Lawrence-Dumont Stadium, Wichita

BASEBALL GROUNDS FIRST USED: 1934

GRANDSTAND BUILT: 1934

Wichita was incorporated in 1870, and the "Base Ball fraternity" formed a club in April 1872. The following spring, the Picked Nine and the Arkansas Valley Boys were vying for the "championship of the city" through games "played on the base ball grounds, corner of Main and Second streets." In February 1873 it was also reported that "some of the young ladies of our city have organized a base ball club, and will soon be ready, we understand, to challenge the Arkansas valley for the belt."[1] However, no games played by the women's team were reported in local newspapers.

Baseball competition in Wichita expanded in 1874. Games were played in the same area as in 1873, "on vacant lots on Market street, between First and Second." Initially, teams from different neighborhoods, such as the Main Street Nine and Douglas Avenue Nine, sought games with each other. An African American baseball team—the Wichita Valleys—was also organized and held Saturday practices on grounds "just north of town." In May the Douglas Avenue Nine defeated the Wichita Valleys but lost the rematch a few weeks later. In June the Winfield town team challenged the Douglas Avenue Nine to a series of games, as did the team in El Dorado.[2] With other towns wanting to play a team from Wichita, the "Wichita base ball club" was organized in July 1874, comprising sixty members. From this group, a first nine was selected to represent the city, "who will not hesitate to sacrifice themselves to maintain the honor of the metropolis of the Southwest." It did not go so well. The Douglas Avenue Nine were still active and offered to play the winless Wichita Base Ball Club in August. The Wichita team finally won a game in October, as the reorganized Wichita Red Stockings defeated the Sedgwick City White Stockings.[3]

As might be expected in a city the size of Wichita, there have been numerous amateur, semipro, and professional teams, as well as baseball fields, through the decades.[4] The city's first minor league team played in 1887. A grandstand at the unnamed "base ball park" was built "at Mr. N. A. English's expense." This Wichita team played several games against teams from Arkansas City, Emporia, and Wellington for the championship of the first Kansas State League, an early minor league in the state that would be resurrected three times before the First World War. However, Wichita left the first Kansas State League in late July to join another minor league— the Western League—as did Emporia shortly thereafter, but both teams disbanded in early September, without completing the league's season.[5]

During most of the 1880s and 1890s the principal baseball diamond in Wichita was at Riverside Park near the mouth of the Little Arkansas River. There was also a ballpark to the north, near the 18th Street bridge across the Little Arkansas River, and games were periodically played at the fairgrounds into the next century. Electric trolleys transported fans from the downtown area to a stop near Riverside Park, but it was suggested in 1892 that a better location should be sought directly on the streetcar line to attract more spectators. Efforts to improve attendance (and revenues) that year included a game between the Wichita Maroons and the New York Champion Ladies Base Ball Club in September, attracting an estimated 1,600 people.[6] In October the Maroons also played a local African American team.[7]

In 1898, as Wichita prepared to field its first minor league team since 1887, a new ballpark was to be constructed on Emporia Street, which would require that 14th Street be blocked to accommodate an area large enough for a baseball field. The intended grounds were to be known as Athletic Park, and the park was to be surrounded by a wooden fence and feature a grandstand and bleacher. However, residents in the area objected to a ballpark in their neighborhood, and although work had already begun on the grounds, the new ballpark was moved to a site about two and a half miles south, bounded by Main and Water Streets on the east and west, and by Gilbert and Morris Streets on the north and south. It featured a grandstand that was 120 feet long with ten rows of seats. The newly organized Wichita Eagles were joining Atchison, Salina, and Topeka in the Kansas

State League, which had been resurrected in 1895. The Eagles were to open play at the new ballpark against the Cincinnati Reds as they returned to Ohio from spring training in Texas, but the Reds had to cancel. Instead, the Eagles opened with a pair of games against the minor league Kansas City Blues of the Western League. The Eagles would play only one year, and the fence and grandstand were torn down in September 1898, at the close of the season. The Kansas State League also folded for a second time. By 1900 the diamond was referred to as "the old Athletic park," although the ground was still used for occasional ballgames.[8]

In 1901 Fairmount College (now Wichita State University) built an athletic field at Ash and First Streets, just east of Chisolm Creek (now constrained in concrete by Interstate Highway 135). The ballpark was just off Douglas Avenue, which had streetcar service, and the athletic field was made available to teams other than the college baseball team.[9] That same year, Friends University laid out a baseball diamond with a bleacher holding 500 fans on its campus at Hess Field.[10] These ball grounds for both schools continued to be used through the First World War.

One of the prominent sites used for baseball in Wichita during the early 1900s was Mathewson's Pasture, owned by William "Buffalo Bill" Mathewson from 1869 to 1906. Mathewson was born in New York in 1830 and began work at age nineteen as a trapper and trader for the Northwestern Fur Company in the Rocky Mountains and Great Plains, from Colorado to Montana. In 1853 he moved to Kansas and opened a trading post on the Arkansas River east of present-day Great Bend. His nickname of Buffalo Bill was earned in central Kansas during the winter of 1860–1861 (predating the appellation of William F. Cody), when he provided buffalo meat—without payment—to starving settlers whose crops had failed as the result of a drought the preceding summer.[11]

Mathewson's Pasture was a relatively large tract of land bounded by Central and Douglas Avenues on the north and south, and by Washington and Hydraulic Avenues on the west and east.[12] In May 1900 Cleveland Avenue was extended, bisecting the "homestead" portion of the property from north to south. As Wichita continued to grow, Mathewson's Pasture persisted as a rural oasis in the heart of the city and was used for a variety of activities in addition to grazing cattle and horses. The field regularly hosted circuses into the 1920s and twice served as the site of William "Buffalo Bill" Cody's Wild West Show (the two men resolved the somewhat contentious issue of their shared nickname). Among the pasture's other uses were military encampments and football games in the autumn, ice skating in the winter, and botany class field trips to observe flowers in the spring. However, damage to the pasture by the circuses sometimes prevented soldiers from using the field for their encampments or baseball teams from playing games.[13] Efforts to lease a portion of the land to construct a half-mile track for horse races failed in 1915.[14]

In September 1901, at a site on Mathewson's Pasture near the intersection of Cleveland Avenue and Third Street, the Wichita Owls amateur baseball team played the Boston Bloomer Girls, who traveled with their own bleachers and canvas fence.[15] Portions of the pasture continued to be used for games of baseball and softball (referred to as "indoor baseball" or "playground ball") on multiple diamonds for several years.[16] By 1909 the number of boys using the pasture to play baseball exceeded its capacity and led to complaints from neighbors about damage to their adjoining property. Consequently, a ball diamond was constructed in the southern part of Linwood Park, southeast of Harry and Hydraulic Streets, to provide an alternate site for games. The following year, the Wichita Linwoods amateur baseball team made Linwood Park their home field, and baseball was played there through 1916 and occasionally afterward.[17] There are still three ball diamonds in Linwood Park.

In the summer of 1917, as the United States entered the First World War, Mathewson's Pasture was the site of Camp Wichita, where two companies of the Kansas Infantry encamped. Some of the soldiers had served earlier along the country's southwestern border as the ongoing Mexican Revolution increased tensions in that region, but other men were new recruits in need of training. In addition to musical entertainment provided for the soldiers and local citizens at the camp, the Wichita Owls defeated a team picked from among the soldiers. It was said that the arm of the infantrymen's pitcher "gave out on account of his recent vaccination."[18] Deaths from disease often accounted for a large portion of the fatalities during wartime, as was to occur during the 1918–1919 influenza pandemic.[19]

In 1920 a proposal was made to purchase a portion of Mathewson's Pasture southeast of the intersection of Central and Cleveland Avenues for construction of a baseball park with four diamonds to be used by amateur teams. Local residents petitioned the city commission against the proposal. They were concerned about "the extreme unpleasantness of the crowds who would be continuously encroaching on their rest," the "loafers who hang around a park," and the fear that a public ballpark near a school "would be a detriment to the education of the child." Countering these concerns, it was pointed out that the land was already being used for an athletic field, and city ownership would mean that a supervisor would be stationed at the park to keep order.[20] The status quo of an informal ballpark remained, however, and by 1922 what remained of Mathewson's Pasture was described as a "bare, unsightly field." Yet games continued to be played at the pasture into the 1930s, although no baseball diamonds remain in the area.[21]

Wichita was also one of the few cities in which an African American team had its own ballpark. Among the various African American teams in Wichita during the early twentieth century was a team named the Black Wonders, organized in 1920. Two years later the team was renamed the Monrovians, a reference to the capital of Liberia in West Africa. Although many African American teams had to play their games at ballparks used by white ball teams when the white teams were out of town, the Monrovians had their own ballpark at 12th and Mosley Streets (nothing now remains of it). The Monrovians played in the Colored Western League in 1922, its only year of existence (as discussed in chapter 3). They also played other teams when they could be scheduled.[22] The well-funded Monrovia Park Corporation, "one of the first colored corporations in the West to own and maintain a baseball park and regular ball team," received a state charter in early August 1922 and planned to purchase the ballpark, which it held under lease. In addition to baseball, the park was used for boxing matches, high school football games, and political rallies. The Monrovia Park Corporation also supported social organizations and services in Wichita, including the Phyllis Wheatley Children's Home, an orphanage for African American children.[23]

After 1900 the city of Wichita had a series of three principal baseball parks used by minor league teams. In 1905 Wichita returned to the ranks of minor league baseball for a third time and would field teams under various names through 1933, and again after the Second World War.[24] The first of these three ballparks was called Association Park, because the Wichita Jobbers (referred to as the Jabbers in one Wichita newspaper) were members of the Western Association (Class C) through 1908 (they joined the Class A Western League the following year). Originally, Association Park was to have been in the northeastern corner of the fairgrounds along the east side of the Arkansas River in southern Wichita, but a site nearby was purchased "about three blocks south of Harry street," with access to the all-important streetcar line. The covered grandstand at the southern end of the park was flanked by bleachers and parking spaces for carriages and automobiles.[25]

Association Park was opened with an exhibition game between the Jobbers and the team from Fairmount College. During the opening league series against the team from Topeka, several local businessmen offered prizes for various feats accomplished by a Wichita player, including $5 in gold for the most runs in the first game, $20 in gold for the first player with a home run over the north fence, and a bottle of "horse liniment" for the first player hit by a pitch. The mayor issued a proclamation declaring a holiday for the Monday afternoon of the first league game in Wichita and asking merchants to close their businesses at three o'clock. The bleachers were lengthened before the first game, and the grandstand was expanded in June, increasing the estimated seating capacity from about 1,200–1,500 to about 2,500 spectators. College and town teams also used Association Park occasionally because it could accommodate the large crowds that attended some of their games, particularly those between the Fairmount College Wheat Shockers and Friends University Quakers.[26]

At the end of the baseball season, Association Park was used for football games, and lights were installed in 1905 so that the Fairmount College football team could play their games at night, when more fans would be able to attend (the workweek included Saturday). Electric lights could not be procured, so "pressure gasolene [sic] lamps" were placed along the sidelines—one every ten yards on each side of the field and two in each end zone. The ball was painted white so it would be visible when punted high in the air. In the first night football game, played on October 6, Fairmount College defeated Cooper College of Sterling (now Sterling College). However, the center of the field was considered too dark, and the dream of evening football games was abandoned. The remaining games that season were played during the afternoon. That same autumn, Association Park was also used for greyhound races ("coursing"). At the first meet, the live rabbits chased by the dogs did not use the escapes, and some were caught by the dogs. The management stated that work would commence immediately to install new escapes and that the rabbits would be trained to use them to avoid being caught.[27]

During 1908 and 1909 the Wichita Baseball Association, owners of the Jobbers and Association Park, considered operating two ballparks. A new ballpark in the heart of the city might improve attendance and revenues for weekday games, while Association Park would be used for Sunday games, because it sat outside the city limits, beyond a municipal ban on Sunday baseball. The plan did not come to pass, but a new ballpark located downtown was only three years away.[28]

With revenues falling well short of expenses, the Wichita Jobbers of the Western League (Class A) moved to Pueblo, Colorado, in May 1911. Shortly thereafter, the Kansas State League team (Class D) in Wellington moved to Association Park to complete its season. In the interim, the old ballpark was used late in the evening as a "'beer garden' for motor car parties," which drew the ire of residents living north of the park. Other local teams used the grounds for baseball throughout the summer, but work to remove the fences at Association Park began in July 1911 to make way for new cottages. Nonetheless, occasional baseball games were played at the site through September, as were Fairmount College football games into the winter, with new bleachers erected on both sides of the field after the old baseball bleachers and part of the grandstand had been torn down. However, with the construction of concrete sidewalks around a portion of the park, a new site was needed for a league ballpark, preferably closer to downtown Wichita.[29]

That new site was on Ackerman Island, which sat between the Douglas Avenue bridge and the confluence of the Arkansas and Little Arkansas Rivers. It had been used for recreation since the 1890s, and Wonderland Park—an amusement park—was built on the northern end of the island in 1905. The park included a carousel from Coney Island, New York, and a figure-eight roller coaster painted white, with eight red cars. Known as the Giant Thriller, the roller coaster was destroyed by a windstorm in January 1917. Wonderland Park closed for the season in August 1917 and did not reopen. The closing was blamed on enforcement of a municipal ban on Sunday recreation. The land was sold in March 1918 to the Palestinian Film Company, which planned to produce "religious and educational films," but in September Company B of the Kansas National Guard was encamped at the former amusement park. In 1920 the remaining park buildings were removed, and the interurban railway used the northern end of the island for its shops.[30]

Separate from Wonderland Park, a ballpark known as Island Park was opened in 1912 near Douglas Avenue at the southern end of Ackerman Island. The reborn Wichita Jobbers played the first game at Island Park against the Chicago White Sox, although the diamond was not quite ready for games because inclement weather slowed construction. The City League and other teams also used the ballpark when the Jobbers were not on the field. The plans for Island Park called for "a first class grandstand, superior in every way to the old grandstand at Association park." The three sections of the grandstand totaled 264 feet in length. During its first two years, temporary awnings were installed to shield people in the premium box seats from the sun, and permanent awnings were installed in 1914. The seating capacity was expanded in 1921 to better accommodate the large number of fans—approaching seven thousand people—who were attending the renamed Wichita Witches' minor league ball games.[31]

As with earlier athletic fields, Island Park was also used for football games and other events, including infantry drills on the field during the First World War. At an evening wrestling bout in 1919, Wichita's Coleman Lamp Company agreed to install lights over the ring set up at home plate.[32] The following year, two African American teams played an exhibition game at Island Park. The Wichita ABCs men's team was defeated by the Alabama Bloomers women's team, 14–10.[33] While Island Park was the primary ballpark in Wichita, the Cudahy Packing Company in Wichita also built a recreational park for its employees, in 1919. Having the only other grandstand in Wichita, the ballpark would serve as the home field for the company's white baseball teams (the company also supported an African American team known as the Cudahy Cubs).[34]

One of the people associated with Wichita baseball during the era that Association Park and Island Park were in use by minor league teams was William Frank "Izzy" Isbell. Born in New York in 1875, he started his professional baseball career in 1896 with the Western League team in Saint Paul, Minnesota, owned by Charles Comiskey. When Comiskey moved the Saints to Chicago and joined the new American League, Isbell initially played first base for the White Sox but became a utility player who played all nine positions during his nine years with the team. In 1910–1911 Isbell was one of the owners and the manager of the Wichita Jobbers, until he transferred the team to Pueblo in May 1911. After spending the next five years with a baseball team in Des Moines, Iowa, he returned as president of the Wichita minor league team from 1917 until retiring from the team at the end of the 1926 season. The Western League (Class A) team was variously known as the Jobbers, Wolves, and Witches, but it was commonly called the Wichita Izzies during Isbell's tenure. After he left, the team played as the Larks and Aviators through 1933 (minor league base-ball would not return to Wichita until 1950). Following his time as a free-lance scout and president of the Western League team in Topeka, Isbell returned to Wichita, where he died in 1941.[35]

The Kansas City Monarchs set up their portable lighting system for a night game at Island Park in 1930. The first permanent lights at the ballpark were installed in 1932, making it the last team in the Western League to have them. That same year, racial integration of baseball in the city improved when the first Mexican American baseball team—the Az-tecs—entered the city's Commercial League, and the first African Ameri-can team—the Wichita Colored Blue Devils—entered the state semipro baseball tournament. The lights at Island Park shone for only two seasons, however, because the grandstand fell victim to fire after the close of the 1933 season. The following year, Ackerman Island was connected to the mainland when the shallow, western river channel was filled as part of a federal work relief project.[36] Exploration Place—the Sedgwick County Sci-ence and Discovery Center—now sits on what was Ackerman Island along the right bank of the Arkansas River.

In addition to the minor league teams, one of the tenants of Island Park was Raymond "Hap" Dumont, who established the National Semi-Pro Baseball Congress in 1931 (later shortened to the National Baseball Congress or NBC, described in chapter 8). Through the NBC, Dumont organized a Kansas state tournament held in Wichita for semipro teams. Games were played at Island Park the first three years, but after the fire and subsequent demolition of the grandstand in 1933, a new baseball park was needed. Dumont successfully lobbied for a ballpark at the corner of Sycamore and Maple Streets, just south of Island Park, on property known as Payne's Pasture. The new ballpark was built of concrete rather than wood, through federal work projects, beginning with the Civil Works Ad-ministration (CWA) in March 1934 and later expanded with funds from the Federal Emergency Relief Administration (FERA). Photographs of the grandstand during construction were published in the Wichita newspa-pers in March and July.[37]

The "unofficial" opening of the stadium was a game on August 1 be-tween the South Side Business Men's Association and the Sunday School All-Stars for possible entry into the thirty-two-team state semipro tour-nament. The formal dedication of Lawrence Stadium was on August 3, as the state tournament officially began. Former major league first base-

Exterior of the concrete grandstand, built in 1934, at Lawrence-Dumont Stadium in Wichita (2014). From the author's personal collection.

man George Sisler spoke at the ceremonies (he was inducted into the National Baseball Hall of Fame in 1939). The stadium was named for Robert E. Lawrence, an early settler in that section of Wichita. The ten "money teams" at the 1934 tournament included three African American teams (Kansas City Colts, Topeka Dodgers, and Wichita Elks), John Levi's Indian team, and the Wichita Martin-Jackson Generals (the local Ban Johnson League team). Prior to the semifinal contests, an exhibition game was played between the "Goddard girls" and the "Harper girls."[38] Other than a Mexican American team, virtually the entire range of diversity in early Kansas baseball was represented at that first NBC tournament in the new stadium. Additional concrete sections in the grandstand were completed that autumn to expand the seating capacity from about 3,600 during the state tournament to about 5,700 in September, with 1,500 bleacher seats installed that winter in front of the tall grandstand to increase the seating capacity even further. The FERA funds approved in November also included money to construct additional sections of the roof, placing about 4,000 grandstand seats under cover.[39] The state and national tournaments (initiated in 1935) continued at the stadium during subsequent decades, though only the national tournament is still played there.

Lawrence Stadium was renamed Lawrence-Dumont Stadium to honor

View of the baseball field from the grandstand, built in 1934, at Lawrence-Dumont Stadium in Wichita (2014). From the author's personal collection.

the legacy of Hap Dumont after he passed away in 1971. Although the essential structure of the 1934 grandstand remains, the ballpark has been renovated in recent decades in keeping with its use as a minor league stadium. For example, the area under the seats has been enclosed and is now occupied by several vendors, restrooms, and other facilities. Synthetic turf was installed on the infield in 2001 and over the entire field (except the pitcher's mound) in 2011, along with additional renovations to the seats, dugouts, outfield fence, lights, and other features of the park. The stadium was home to minor league teams during 1950–1958, 1970–1984, and 1987–2007.[40] Since 2008, Lawrence-Dumont Stadium has been the summer home of the Wichita Wingnuts (American Association, independent minor league), who take an extended road trip in late July and early August while the ballpark continues to host the NBC World Series.

CHAPTER 12

Clint Lightner Field, Garden City

Garden City was founded in 1878; early concerns for the young town included a bridge across the Arkansas River, whose broad bed of loose sand made fording the stream with wagons a dangerous challenge. High tolls for use of a private bridge finally led to community support for a "free bridge" in 1886. Later that summer, a streetcar line was in operation, the "first in western Kansas." While these issues were addressed, a call went out for those interested in baseball to discuss a stock company funded for $1,000 at $10 per share, but there was no further mention of a town team.[1]

In 1887 Garden City worked toward a public water system and electric lights, while covered wagons of immigrants with all their belongings still passed by town on their westward journey from the Midwest. In June the local driving (horse racing) association purchased property near the Arkansas River. They enclosed the park with a fence eight feet tall and constructed an "amphitheater" for spectators at the races, baseball games, and other activities. That same summer Garden City's first nine ordered uniforms and obtained a pitcher and catcher from Kansas City to "supply the long felt want." In July the team made a ten-day trip east to play teams in cities along the Santa Fe Railroad, such as Kinsley and Larned. Upon returning, they hosted teams from towns in southwestern Kansas at the new Lakeside Driving Park (also referred to as Riverside Driving Park). Various muffin games were also played at the park, such as the ubiquitous fats versus leans contests, whose game that year was a benefit for the baseball association. A local newspaper reported that their game was to be attended by "two undertakers and four physicians." Although the temperature that afternoon was 108 degrees Fahrenheit, only minor physical injuries to a few of the players were reported. "Judge C. J. Gavin, who was clothed in deep thought, a wide rimmed straw hat and a good deal of perspiration, to say nothing of an enormous six shooter which hung in the vicinity of his hip pocket, was chosen umpire." The two games the town team won against Scott City on August 15 and 16 were the baseball highlights of the season. Following the second game, local baseball enthusiasts treated both teams to a banquet at Café Freak, where C. J. "Buffalo" Jones presented each of the members of the victorious Garden City nine with a silver dollar.[2]

Buffalo Jones was one of the founders of Garden City, but he became widely known for his efforts to conserve the American bison. He brought bison from various parts of North America to his ranch near Garden City, where he raised them during the late 1880s as he lobbied for the protection of the last remaining wild herds. His reputation as a conservationist (by the definition of the time) led to his becoming the first game warden at Yellowstone National Park during the administration of President Theodore Roosevelt. He served in that capacity from 1902 through 1905.[3]

In May 1888, a local newspaper wondered why no baseball team had been organized. It was not until late June that a "scrub nine" referring to themselves as the Remnants—partly composed of players from the 1887 team—entertained visiting teams at the driving park. In July they defeated the team from Lakin with the help of a trio of ringers: "Three professionals en route to New Mexico assisted the Garden City boys." In 1889 teams on the west and east sides of town occasionally played at the driving park, as did other pickup teams, especially in July and August, after the harvest was completed. One game featured thirteen players on each team. At the end of July the West Side Base Ball Club was reorganized as the Garden City Base Ball Club, and they played a few games with teams from other towns. A town team continued to play occasional games into the 1890s with varying levels of success. After they won a game in Pierceville 21–20 in July 1893, a local newspaper was displeased by how close the score was. "The score is a rank outrage, and we would like to know how long Garden City is to suffer with such ball clubs." By September, after the team had defeated Dodge City, the newspaper was more supportive, remarking that "the Garden City team presented a very nice appearance in their new uniforms."[4]

Beginning in 1895 the town team was known as the Garden City Reds. After defeating Dodge City at the driving park on the Fourth of July in 1899 and winning a $75 purse, the Reds embarked on a weeklong trip west along the Santa Fe railroad into Colorado. They defeated teams in Syracuse, Kansas, and Lamar, Las Animas, La Junta, and Rocky Ford, Colorado, but they lost to Pueblo, Colorado. In a tournament at the Garden City fair in September, Dodge City revenged their loss in July by defeating the Reds and claiming the prize money.[5]

The Garden City town team apparently continued to play as the new century began, but they received little attention in the newspaper.[6] In 1907, "baseball fever [was] finally on the boom in Garden City. . . . The diamond will be put in shape . . . and we will buy new uniforms." Baseball games were being played at the fairgrounds south of Maple Street, with the team sometimes providing seats for spectators. Before the summer was over the town had five nines—three white teams and two African American teams. The African American first nine even scheduled a game against the white second nine. At the Emancipation Day celebration in August, the game between the two African American men's teams was followed by a pickup game between the "young men" and their challengers, "the girls who were at the picnic." Concerns expressed by some citizens about ballgames being played on Sundays led to debate about whether the fairgrounds were actually within the city limits. The Sunday games continued, but gambling at the games was strictly forbidden.[7]

The baseball team remained active in subsequent years, with home games at the fairgrounds. In 1908 Garden City played a barnstorming team of Japanese players—the Mikado Club. In the summer of 1909 there was even talk of organizing a "leisurely trip" by rail to Seattle for the Alaska-Yukon-Pacific Exposition, with the baseball team playing games along the way to help pay expenses, but nothing came of these plans. The following year the team was often referred to as a "picked" team, which played a few games against teams from nearby towns, as well as a team from Wichita and the Boston Bloomer Girls. A "new" ball team was organized in 1911. They scheduled a game with another Japanese team at the "new grounds, just north of the mill." However, baseball continued to be played at the fairgrounds until the entry of the United States into the First World War, although coverage in local newspapers was irregular at best. Games were sometimes played against picked teams of "Navahoe Indians" who were in Kansas to work in the sugar beet fields. The old team name of Reds was resurrected in 1912, but the 1914 team was called the Sluggers, and a local newspaper proclaimed them the best city team "in years." The following week, however, "old time Garden City ball players" defeated the Sluggers 16–1, and when the Sluggers subsequently lost to Dodge City, the newspaper refused to print the score. A doubleheader in August was postponed because Mrs. Frederick Finnup had passed away, four months after the death of her husband, a prominent early business-man in Garden City.[8] A new baseball field in a public park to be named in honor of Frederick Finnup was on the horizon.

As elsewhere, there was a break in town team baseball during the First World War, but plans to restart intercity baseball took shape in 1919, when the local soldiers returned. Land set aside as Frederick Finnup Park—east of the fairgrounds—was transferred to the city in May 1919 by George W. Finnup to honor his father. The city intended to "proceed at the earliest moment to establish the roads and walks, plant trees and establish the lake, build tennis courts and ball grounds and provide a camping ground for tourists passing over the Santa Fe Trail" (highways were just beginning to be paved with concrete, and highway numbers were not yet used). By August 1919 plans were made for the baseball diamond. It was decided that "the permanent base ball grounds for the city will be established in the northeast corner of the Finnup Park, and the work of improving it will commence shortly. It is proposed to erect grandstands and other neces-sary buildings and get it in shape for both base and foot ball games." How-ever, a "new athletic field at the north edge of the city" was used for football beginning in 1922. On July 31, 1919, about 7,000 people attended a cel-ebration to welcome home the city's returning servicemen (the population of Garden City in 1920 was only 3,848). The daylong festivities included a parade to Finnup Park, free barbecue lunch, concert, dance, and various sporting competitions, including a baseball game between the Soldiers and the Civilians. The Soldiers won 8–7 in ten innings.[9]

The idea of organizing teams of soldiers and civilians carried over to the following year. In May 1920 the "ball grounds in Finnup Park" were "being put in shape" by two baseball teams, one a general town team and the other consisting of members of the American Legion, which had been chartered by the US Congress in 1919. The teams obtained money to buy uniforms and still "hoped eventually to build a grand stand on the grounds."[10] A scoreboard was installed in time for a July 4 baseball game "at the fine new ball park, which is beginning to take on the appearance of a real ball diamond." A local business offered $5 to any player who hit the new scoreboard with a batted ball during a game.[11] The two teams played each other as well as teams from other towns. The pitcher for the town team was Ralph Clark, who had been pitching since 1896, including three years in the minor leagues. Clark could still rack up the strikeouts against teams in southwestern Kansas, and he now got to play with his son, also a member of the town team. Funds from a game in August 1920 between the town team and the Legion team were designated for additional improvements at the baseball ground.[12] The town team, with Clark often on the mound, continued to play the next two years, but they still received inconsistent notice in the local newspapers.[13]

In July 1923 the Garden City Elks organized a team known simply as the Elks Ball Team and took charge of the ballpark. They did not play their first game of the season until July, but games continued through September. After enjoying Sunday afternoon games in midsummer, fans were encouraged to enjoy a swim at the nearby municipal pool. Christened the Big Pool, it was constructed in Finnup Park adjacent to the baseball field in 1922. To encourage the Elks during their games, various incentives were offered to players, including a "meal ticket" from the Stone Hotel for any Elks player who hit a home run, $5 from George Finnup for a home run, and "one dollars [sic] worth of fountain drinks" from Baugh's Drug Store—operated by a former player—for the Elks player with the highest batting average during a specified game. In September the baseball team took a six-day tour (including five scheduled games) with other community members representing the Elks Lodge, Chamber of Commerce, and Fair Association to advertise the Garden City Fair and other features of the community. The long history of using baseball teams to promote Kansas towns continued.[14]

In May 1924 the independent Garden City Baseball Team was organized. Players attending the first tryout were asked to bring their uniforms, which would be cleaned, repaired, and "put in shape for use at no charge" by local tailor L. M. Finn. The team won about half their games and had particular difficulty with a Dodge City pitcher who used an underhand delivery, as was used in the early days of baseball.[15] Garden City had picked up a new third baseman that year, Clint Lightner, who would later switch to the outfield and play for the team into the 1930s. Lightner was a Garden City native who worked for AT&T after serving in the army during the First World War. In 1923 Lightner had been working for the Pawnee

Light Company of Larned, but he returned to Garden City in time to join the baseball team in 1924.[16] The Garden City Giants, an African American team, also was active in the 1920s. At the Emancipation Day Celebration in August 1924, the Garden City Giants lost to the Larned Giants 3–2 in a pitchers' duel at Finnup Park.[17]

The American Legion again sponsored a team to represent the city beginning in 1925. They arranged home-and-home series with several towns in southwestern Kansas and adjacent Colorado. Among these games in 1925 was a victory in Holly, Colorado, despite the condition of the diamond. As reported, "Holly's diamond is situated in a plowed field, which accounts for most of [Garden City's eight] errors. A batted ball would not hop at all, and the ground was so loose that the fielders could not get around to play their positions as they should." However, in a subsequent victory over Holly at Finnup Park, Garden City again committed eight errors on their own unplowed field. Garden City played better than .500 ball and began receiving much more coverage from local newspapers. A twilight league with teams sometimes sponsored by local churches—and referred to as the Sunday School Twilight League—also was organized and continued to play a few more years.[18]

In 1926 the Legion town team included Clint Lightner and, for a time, Sheriff Oll Brown among its members. Lightner won the team batting title with a .333 average and was given a "silver baseball cupped in three silver bats." Perhaps his hitting benefited from a batting cage at "Finnup park diamond" completed prior to the second spring workout of the Legion team, during which "a good crowd of spectators looked on from the sidelines." By this time a serious rivalry had developed between Garden City and Dodge City. Before one of their games a local newspaper predicted, "Ball fans will be on hand to see the usual scrap after the heavy end of the score." Their "Little World Series" was tied at three games apiece, so they agreed to play not one but three more games. Cold weather in October began to interfere with these plans, and the series was tied at four games apiece, with no mention of the ninth game in the Garden City newspaper. Garden City's record that year was 22–9. The team also played an exhibition game against the Kansas City Monarchs, who won 8–0. Because it was played on a Thursday, stores were asked to close during the game. A muffin game at that year's Fourth of July celebration featured teams of Republicans and Democrats. A special rule for the game stipulated that the "bats will be used for striking the balls only."[19]

At some point during the early 1920s wooden seating was apparently constructed at the ballpark, but in the spring of 1927 the American Legion town team "put in a new grandstand with lots of shade." The specific mention of "lots of shade" suggests that the original seating might have been a bleacher with no roof. The Legion town team played independently and won most of their games. Cimarron was the first team to defeat them, but when they played again at Finnup Park in July, Garden City pitcher Harry Hibbs threw a no-hit shutout. Sublette was the second team to defeat Garden City, but in the return game at Finnup Park that August, Hibbs threw a one-hit shutout. Apparently, losing a game was a powerful inducement for Hibbs to pitch at his highest level to avenge the earlier loss. The Kansas City Monarchs were scheduled for another visit to Garden City but had to cancel due to the illness of several players. For at least this one season, the local African American team also went by the name Monarchs, but they later returned to the name Giants. The town team's final home game of the season in late September was canceled because the visiting team feared there was an infantile paralysis (polio) outbreak in Garden City. Dr. J. B. Edwards, the county health officer, had closed the elementary and junior high schools for two weeks when a pair of mild polio cases were reported, one in an infant and one in a six-year-old boy.[20]

At the end of the decade the Garden City American Legion decided to sponsor a junior baseball league in addition to the town team. Although the town team played independently to begin the season, in late August 1928 Garden City and Dodge City joined the Short Grass League, which included Copeland, Ensign, Fowler, Ingalls, Meade, and Plains. They replaced Cimarron and Sublette, who had dropped out. In a game against Dodge City, Oll Brown was back in the lineup, and after his performance it was said that they "won't call Oll Brown 'Grandpa' anymore." He hit for the cycle—a single, double, triple, and home run that was "the longest hit ever made at Finnup park." Garden City also hosted the minor league Kansas City Blues of the American Association (Class AA) in October 1928 while they were on a barnstorming tour after the close of their season. The Blues won 10–2.[21]

The American Legion continued to sponsor the town team, and there were several special events on the ball diamond in Finnup Park during 1930. Garden City hosted a Junior Legion District tournament, and the Legion town team played several barnstorming teams, including the Broadway Clowns, Marty's Southern California Indians, Michigan Wolverines (an African American team), Milwaukee Colored Giants, and Kansas City Monarchs. The Monarchs won again, 10–2, under their portable lights in the city's first night baseball game.[22] Garden City's only victory among these games was against the Michigan Wolverines. In fact, as the decade progressed, Garden City struggled to defeat other town teams in southwestern Kansas. The rivalry with Dodge City continued with a series of several games, but Garden City was doing well to win one or two games each year. The losses became routine, and in 1935 the local newspaper noted that the Dodge City jinx was holding. The Legion town team also occasionally played the Garden City Giants and a team from the junior college, which extended its season through the summer. Then, in 1935, these teams were joined by a team in the Kansas Ban Johnson League.[23] They got off to a rough start, defeating Copeland in their first game but losing the next eight. However, the team improved and even earned a 3–4 record against the rival Ban Johnson team from Dodge City.[24]

As the Ban Johnson team inaugurated their long run in Garden City (except during the Second World War), plans for improvements in Finnup Park were submitted to the Kansas Emergency Relief Committee (KERC) in June 1935. Improvements were envisioned at the zoo, swimming pool, and baseball field, including a concrete grandstand on the west side of the diamond to complement the existing wooden grandstand. In 1936, under the auspices of the Works Progress Administration (WPA), a concrete grandstand was constructed behind home plate, with a wooden shingled roof supported by metal posts (the roof is now metal). The section of the concrete grandstand sitting immediately behind home plate was dedicated on May 3, 1936, at a game between the Garden City and Dighton town teams (Garden City won 2–1). Temporary backstops were set up for the game, and the new grandstand was "flanked on either side by sections of the old wooden stand." The foundation for the second section of the concrete grandstand along the first base line was poured in August 1936, and the last of the concrete for the seating was poured in October. All that remained to be done was construction of the roof and the connecting link between the two sections (with entryways). The area under the grandstand was enclosed by coarse bricks covered with stucco.[25]

The town team (named the Gophers in 1937) and the Ban Johnson team shared the upgraded ballpark in Finnup Park, one team playing in town each Sunday. The Garden City Giants only played occasionally. Softball and the lights from the former softball field were moved to the base-

The concrete grandstand (enclosed in stucco-covered bricks), built in 1936, and the concrete extension without a roof, built in 1956, at Clint Lightner Field in Garden City (2014). From the author's personal collection.

ball park in 1937. Although the lights were not sufficient for baseball, they were used for evening softball games, which included intercity games during the week. Clint Lightner no longer played for the town team, but he became the manager of the Garden City Bans. In the years leading up to the entry of the United States in the Second World War, a good year for the Ban Johnson team meant third place, with Dodge City and Larned usually battling for first place in the division. The Western Division of the league dropped to only four teams in 1938—Dodge City, Garden City, Great Bend, and Larned, with Pratt replacing Great Bend in 1939. Meanwhile, the Garden City Gophers joined the Southwest Kansas Baseball League in 1938 with teams from Dodge City, Kinsley, Leoti, Meade, and Protection. During the 1939 season the Gophers became the Elks and continued to compete in the league for two more years. However, the Elks forfeited their last game of 1939 to Protection because they could not gather enough players. Nonetheless, they finished in fourth place among the six teams. The highlight for the Elks in league play during 1940 was the perfect game thrown by Paul Mai against Kinsley. The Elks played well that year, and by August 5 they were 10–3, with all three losses (and one

Seating in the grandstand, built in 1936, at Clint Lightner Field in Garden City (2014). From the author's personal collection.

victory) coming at the hands of their old nemesis, Dodge City. As in other communities, town team baseball faded from the headlines in 1941 as preparations to expand the military were under way.[26]

After the war, baseball resumed in Garden City. By the 1950s the seating available with the concrete grandstand in Finnup Park was considered insufficient at some ballgames, including a crowd of 710 paying fans at the final game of the year for the local Ban Johnson team in 1955.[27] During 1955 and early 1956, plans to add seating for about 300 people were discussed by the city and the Jaycees (the local Ban Johnson team), who would share the construction costs.[28] The options discussed were adding a section made of either concrete or steel on the third base side.[29] Howard Blanchard, who had worked on the design of the existing grandstand built by the WPA, consulted on the design of the new seating. Ultimately, a concrete section was constructed that matched the existing grandstand. It was separated from the 1936 grandstand by an open entryway.[30] Although the new section lacks a roof, it has concrete supports for a roof along the back wall that match those on the main grandstand. The area under this new section was enclosed with concrete blocks rather than bricks.

The seating constructed in 1956 was built shortly after the ballpark received its current name—Clint Lightner Field. In addition to his work as the business manager of the local Ban Johnson team, Clint Lightner had worked as the superintendent of public utilities in Garden City. Given his job with the city, he was involved with installation of the first lights for baseball games at the Finnup Park Diamond in 1948.[31] In 1951 Lightner died unexpectedly of a heart attack at the age of fifty-five.[32]

By the end of the 1959 season both the junior American Legion team and the Ban Johnson team had folded. To fill the void, a town team— the Pioneers—was organized in 1960 that played in a six-team Kansas-Colorado League with teams from Lakin and Syracuse in Kansas and Lamar, Las Animas, and Walsh in Colorado.[33] The Pioneers played well but lasted only a single year. Youth teams sponsored by civic groups in Garden City—such as the Rotary, Kiwanis, and Lions Clubs—also played on Clint Lightner Field in the 1960s.[34] However, the absence of intercity competition led to discussions in early 1962 about converting the ballpark from baseball to softball. That same spring, however, a junior American Legion baseball team was reorganized and played its games at Clint Lightner Field. Along with its use by other youth teams, including the high school and the community college, the field remained in use for baseball (the community college now has its own diamond).[35]

In 2014 the Garden City Recreation Commission and Garden City Unified School District (USD 457) partnered for improvements at Clint Lightner Field. The improvements included installing new lights and laying a synthetic turf infield (including on the pitcher's mound), which gives balls truer bounces for the young players to field, requires less daily maintenance, and conserves water. The outfield is still grass. Enhancements to the seating (now metal benches rather than wood), backstop, locker rooms, parking, and other features of the park also were part of the renovation.[36] In 2015 the Pecos League, an independent minor league, reorganized, dropping three teams in New Mexico and Arizona and placing a new team in Garden City known as the Garden City Wind, who are summer tenants of Clint Lightner Field.

CHAPTER 13

Katy Stadium, Chanute

BASEBALL GROUNDS FIRST USED: 1895

GRANDSTAND BUILT: 1936

As in most Kansas towns during the late 1800s, the Chanute town team was organized irregularly, and the team played only a few games when it did organize. By 1887 the local baseball team played on a field "next to the North school house." The following year a formal baseball team was organized to play "any club in the world." In July they rented land belonging to the railroad on the "vacant square north of the Christian church" for the ball ground. A grandstand and fence were to be constructed in time for games that August at what would be called Railroad Ball Park. The Chanute team lost their first game on the new grounds to Yates Center, 6–0. They rebounded two weeks later to defeat the Osage Mission team, prompting Chanute to claim the championship of southeastern Kansas. The baseball season got off to a late start in 1889. It was not until a game between local doctors and lawyers in August 1889 that preliminary arrangements were made to organize a town team.[1] Yet interest in baseball ran high the following year at a game between Chanute and Earlton on July 4, 1890, won by Chanute 30–10. "The base ball grounds [were] lined by hundreds of wagons and carriages, and by thousands of spectators. Trees and house tops were full of eager watchers, and every foot of sitting and standing room adjacent to the grounds was occupied. Even a train of freight cars that stood upon the track was covered from one end to the other with men and boys intent upon seeing the game."[2] Chanute continued to have a town team during the early 1890s.[3]

In 1896 Chanute hired a team from Saint Louis. Initially, this Chanute Base Ball Club was to be paid $175 plus all gate receipts. The arrangement was later changed to all gate receipts, $75 for uniforms, and about $150 for transportation to Chanute, plus one week's board. Along with a lease for the ball diamond, the total estimated cost would be about $300. However, the team was unable to compete successfully against other teams in southeastern Kansas and quickly folded, with some of its players joining other area teams in June.[4] Unwilling to concede the season, Chanute replaced their first professional team in July with a professional team from Springfield, Missouri, which played in the Southern Kansas State League against teams from Coffeyville, Independence, and Parsons. The Chanute team was in last place when the team disbanded on August 28.[5] As a consequence of these two failed attempts to have a successful professional team, the Chanute baseball association was in debt, and they relied on dances and benefit games played by local businessmen to reduce their losses.[6]

Because of the expenses incurred in 1896, a plan was proposed the following year to organize a professional baseball team—the Southern Kansas Base Ball Club—that would be collectively funded by the towns of Chanute, Coffeyville, Independence, and Parsons.[7] The idea did not come to fruition, and a move to organize a town team of "seven or eight professionals and . . . three or four Chanute boys" likewise met with little success.[8] In 1898, after two years of trying to establish some form of professional baseball in Chanute, a move was made to establish a league of teams in southeastern Kansas that consisted solely of local players, but only the Chanute high school boys organized a team playing intercity games that summer.[9]

In June 1899 a picked team from Chanute was scheduled to play a team from Humboldt at the "Fair Park." The Chanute team continued to play during the summer, although they often used a player or two from other towns.[10] They even ordered uniforms in late July.[11] However, subsequent interest in a baseball team seemed to wane, and attempts to organize a town team in 1900 and 1901 got off to late starts.[12] Even a game played at the Chanute fairground in October 1900 between the Kansas City Blues, a top-level minor league team, and the baseball team from Pittsburg, Kansas, attracted only a small crowd.[13] A request was made in August 1901 for the return of all the baseball uniforms that had been ordered for the 1899 season.[14]

Baseball in Chanute took an upswing in 1902, as the town again fielded a professional baseball team when the financially troubled Coffeyville minor league team in the Missouri Valley League (Class D) was moved to Chanute. The process was not a smooth one, and Chanute considered forming a league with other nearby towns instead.[15] When Chanute finally joined the Missouri Valley League, they wore new, gray uniforms with maroon trim and blue letters spelling "Oil City" across the front of the jerseys.[16] Starting in last place in the league, the team improved after moving to Chanute, where they finished sixth among the eight teams.[17] However, as in 1896, the cost of having a professional team was high, so Chanute opted not to retain its place in the league in 1903.[18]

In subsequent years, Chanute fielded town teams under various names. L. J. Galbreath, the manager of the 1902 Chanute team, attempted again in 1904 to organize a league of teams in southeastern Kansas and northeastern Oklahoma, including Chanute, as did the Parsons Elks Lodge, both without success.[19] In May of that year Galbreath brought the Kansas City Spaldings, "a quasi-professional organization," to Chanute to play teams from other local towns for a few days, but the city finally organized its own team, which included a few professional players.[20] In 1906 Chanute joined the Kansas State League (Class D), finishing sixth in the league—which had been reduced from eight teams to only six in July.[21] Chanute thought it had a minor league team in the Oklahoma-Arkansas-Kansas (O.A.K.) League (Class D) in 1907, but it was transferred to Muskogee, Oklahoma, at the close of the preseason exhibition schedule.[22] The O.A.K. League floundered through the summer, so Chanute was better served by its amateur Chanute Eagles, which were reorganized as the Chanute Blue Legs in late August as part of a four-team Trolley League consisting of Chanute, Humboldt, Iola, and Park.[23] This was the end of minor league baseball in Chanute until after the Second World War.

The white Chanute teams shared use of the baseball diamonds with an African American team named the Chanute Black Diamonds during most years from the 1890s through the 1930s.[24] In addition to playing other African American teams in the region, the Black Diamonds occasionally played white town teams during the early twentieth century.[25] As with other teams, during the First World War the Black Diamonds played fewer games, some of which were fund-raisers for the "benefit of the soldiers" and the Red Cross. There was also a postwar celebration "in honor of the colored soldiers of Southeastern Kansas," some of whom had recently returned from France. For that third game, players formerly with the Chanute Black Diamonds and Iola Go-Devils made up an "All Star" team that defeated the Bear Cats, an African American team from Independence, 1–0.[26] The Black Diamonds also played in the short-lived Colored Western League in 1922, although local newspapers published little information about the games or the league.[27]

Beginning in 1895 most baseball games in Chanute were played in what is now called Katy Park. The park was named for the Katy Railroad, the name by which the Missouri, Kansas, and Texas (M-K-T) Railroad was commonly known. The railroad occasionally ran excursion trains in the summers from Chanute to Kansas City, touting professional baseball games as one of the enticements for potential travelers. The professional team was the minor league Kansas City Blues of the American Association (Class A).[28] Katy Park had its beginning as the local fairground constructed in 1895.

The Chanute Fair Association was "fully organized" in 1894.[29] Its first fairground, which had a wooden grandstand, was used primarily for horse racing.[30] It was some distance outside town, so on the afternoons of August 7–9, 1894, the Katy Railroad ran special trains departing from their depot in town to the fairgrounds every twenty minutes during the three days of the horse races (round-trip fare was 25¢).[31] Bicycle races were also held at the fairground that autumn, but no baseball games.[32]

Dissension arose among members of the fair association. Citing the distance from town, the lack of water and shade, and the dusty conditions at the 1894 fair, plans were made that winter to establish a new fair association and "purchase the ground in the east bottom south of Fourth street" and west of the M-K-T railroad tracks. The grounds were to include a baseball diamond, football field, pond, half-mile racetrack, and fair buildings. Within the racetrack "directly in front of each end of the grand stand will be located a base ball diamond and a foot ball ground."[33]

Baseball games at the new fairground were scheduled as early as June 1895, although the grandstand was not completed until just before the fair in August. The grandstand faced east and was 100 feet long, 45 feet deep, and about 16 feet high, with an estimated seating capacity of 1,200 spectators. In addition to horse races, the track also hosted two days of bicycle races in September 1895, with baseball games as side events.[34] However, the separation of the grandstand from the baseball diamond sometimes created problems, because people who chose to stand at the games would crowd around the field on the track and block the view of people sitting in the grandstand.[35]

In May 1897 the baseball diamond at the fairgrounds was renovated, and several changes were planned "to accommodate spectators more conveniently."[36] Baseball games were usually played at the fairgrounds until 1906, when the Chanute team in the Kansas State League used a diamond and grandstand at Athletic Park, a fenced baseball and football field.[37] This ballpark was also referred to as the "West Main street ball park," because it sat northwest of the corner of West Main Street and Allen Avenue, the current site of Lincoln School.[38] In 1904 the Chanute team had played most of their games at the fairgrounds, but they also played a game in the "pasture west of the city," which might be the same site developed as Athletic Park two years later.[39] Athletic Park continued to be used for baseball games through at least 1916.[40] In the meantime, by July 1911 the diamond at the fairground "had been fixed up" and was again used occasionally for baseball.[41]

In late 1911 and early 1912 the city arranged to purchase the fairground for use as a city park, and Katy Park was dedicated on July 4, 1912, with various horse races but no baseball games.[42] The original grandstand had become unsafe and was initially slated to be replaced in 1912, but the decision was made to repair it to save money for construction of a Four-County Fair building. However, the grandstand was apparently replaced that summer.[43] Like the 1895 grandstand, it was probably a straight wooden structure suitable for viewing horse races and a variety of other events. In May 1913 a new city baseball diamond (with backstops) was constructed within the racetrack in front of the grandstand.[44] The interest in putting a diamond at the Katy Park grandstand arose in part because fences had been removed at Athletic Park in anticipation of the area's development as the city expanded.[45] The Katy Park diamond was once again the city's principal baseball ground through 1920.[46]

In 1921 the Chanute town team leased "a tract of land east of the city and north of the road to the river bridge" ("east of the Katy tracks") for a new ballpark. The Katy Park diamond was still available, but the city had banned Sunday baseball in 1915. With the new ballpark just beyond the city limits, the team could again play games on Sundays.[47] The new East Park (later referred to as Ingraham Park) had a grandstand and a scoreboard in center field ($10 was offered to anyone who could hit it with a batted ball during a game). However, there was no outfield fence to stop a ball hit "into the alfalfa between deep center and right" as a batter "romped around the bases for all he was worth."[48] The ballpark opened with a pair of games on consecutive Sundays in May between the white Boosters and the Black Diamonds, each winning one game (the Black Diamonds won a third game on July 4, and a fourth game was rained out).[49] The Black Diamonds of 1921 featured Humboldt native George Sweatt at third base, who was finishing his training to be a teacher while attending the State Manual Training Normal School at Pittsburg (now Pittsburg State University).[50]

In 1922, a week after major flooding struck the area, strong winds during the third Easter storm in as many years lifted the grandstand at East Park and tossed it onto the road, taking out the power lines to the city water pumps. The damage and inclement weather throughout the spring delayed the baseball season, but the grandstand was replaced and reroofed by early June.[51] Later in the year the Black Diamonds used the ballpark as members of the short-lived Colored Western League.[52]

The Chanute town team replaced Neodesha in the newly organized Oil Belt League in 1923, joining teams from Eureka, Garnett, and Iola. However, the league quickly collapsed, so the town team played independently. A Chanute Sunday School League was organized in 1922 and continued through 1925. They played at Katy Park (referred to as City Park) their first year but moved to Ingraham Park in 1923. The town team, Black Diamonds, and Sunday School League played at Ingraham Park through 1925. This included games with the Kansas City Monarchs. Because games with the Monarchs were often on weekdays, local businesses pledged to close their stores during the game, and an estimated 1,500 fans watched the Monarchs defeat the town team in 1923. In 1926 a twilight league replaced the Sunday School League and opened a new ballpark on West Main Street. An amalgamation of twilight league players usually represented Chanute against white teams from other towns that year.[53]

The twilight league continued into the 1930s, and even included the Black Diamonds in 1935. In addition to the twilight league, a Chanute team joined the Southeastern Kansas League in 1927 with Humboldt, Iola, and Moran, using West Main Street Park as their home field. However, in July, the team moved to Buffalo, once again leaving twilight league players and the Black Diamonds to represent Chanute into the mid-1930s. In 1929 Chanute players represented Cottage Grove in the Verdigris Valley Minor League, using a diamond on K.T. Hill north of Chanute as their home field. That same year, Chanute Junior League players were chosen to represent the city as the American Legion team. The West Main Street

Park (also known as Twilight League Park) continued in use until 1934, when teams returned to Katy Park.[54]

In 1935 Chanute joined the Eastern Kansas League with teams from Burlington, Fredonia, Garnett, Humboldt, Iola, Neodesha, and Waverly (Humboldt withdrew in July). The season consisted of only fourteen games for each team, and frequent rain postponed several games. A typical characteristic of local leagues throughout the state was a split of the season into two halves, with the champions from each half playing a series of games to determine the overall champion. In 1935 Garnett was the first-half champion, but Chanute played better in the second half to earn a spot in the championship series. Chanute claimed the league championship by winning the first two games in the best-of-three series.[55] Their success might have contributed to a renewed interest in town team baseball that coincided with plans for a rejuvenated city ballpark.

On November 19, 1935, voters approved the city's share of funds needed to construct a new grandstand in Katy Park as a Works Progress Administration (WPA) project. Work was scheduled to begin the following Monday. This involved tearing down the existing wooden grandstand and quarrying rock for its replacement, which was to be constructed of longer-lasting concrete and stone. The new grandstand would be almost 182 feet long and 60 feet deep, with eighteen rows of seats. The seating capacity was estimated to be about 2,000 people. A roof was listed as an option for some later date but never built. The estimated cost of the project was $17,510 (equivalent to about $303,000 in 2016), with $13,283 provided through the WPA and $4,227 from the city. The project was delayed several weeks during severe weather that winter, but work resumed at the end of February 1936.[56]

The first game played at the new grandstand was Chanute's 1–0 loss to Fort Scott on June 21. A "big crowd" attended the game, but there was little fanfare for the inaugural event because the stadium was not quite finished. The spectators had to sit directly on the concrete tiers because the wooden planks to be used for seats were not added until early August. Eight poles were installed for floodlights to illuminate the field for night baseball games. The poles were seventy feet tall and held seventy-five lights of 1,500 watts each. The lighting system cost $3,000. With these finishing touches, the formal dedication of the new grandstand was held at a night baseball game on August 20. Following a concert by the local band, the Chanute town team defeated the Lawrence Ban Johnson team

Front view of concrete grandstand faced with stone, built in 1936, at Katy Stadium in Chanute (2014). From the author's personal collection.

4–1 in front of about 1,000 spectators. The local Kiwanis Club organized the ceremonies. On August 27, the Chanute town team played its second game under the new lights in front of more than 1,000 spectators, defeating an African American team from Illinois that was participating in the National Baseball Congress tournament for semipro teams in Wichita. The game also marked the first use of a new electric scoreboard.[57]

Among the final games of the 1936 baseball season were two under the lights against strong opponents. An estimated 2,600 fans watched a game on September 15, in which the Kansas City Blues of the American Association (now Class AA) defeated Chanute 7–0. The Blues became a top minor league affiliate of the New York Yankees in 1937. Two weeks later Chanute lost a game to the Kansas City Monarchs 5–2. The Monarchs were strictly a barnstorming team during most of the 1930s, traveling with their own portable lighting system for night games. As more and more towns, such as Chanute, installed permanent lights at their ballparks, the need for the Monarchs to travel with their portable lights was diminished. They continued to barnstorm, but they became charter members of the

Negro American League in 1937 and sold their light fixtures to the city of Hays in 1940.[58]

As with the previous wooden grandstands, the straight grandstand that now sits along the third base line of the ball diamond was initially used for activities other than baseball, including horse races, motorcycle races, boxing matches, and aerial stunts performed in the sky to the east. Now used solely for baseball, the grandstand is not entirely adjacent to the third base line—home plate is closest to a point near the center of the grandstand, which extends well beyond home plate and the backstop. The infield and outfield are still grass.

The Chanute town team continued to play independently at the new ballpark. They generally did well against local semipro teams, but they played several teams from larger cities, such as Wichita and Kansas City. In addition, Chanute played numerous games with barnstorming teams such as the House of David, Kansas City Monarchs, Kansas City Blues, Satchel Paige's Negro All-Stars, and others. The Monarchs also played against other Negro League teams in Chanute. Although the town team was unable to defeat the Monarchs or the Blues, they defeated teams such as the Wichita Monrovians, the Texas Black Spiders, and the Carta Blanca team from Monterrey, Mexico. In a game on a rainy day in May 1938, the Chanute town team defeated a David team. Both teams agreed to a special ground rule, which a local newspaper more appropriately referred to as a "river rule." Floodwater from the Neosho River covered part of the outfield, so the teams agreed that any ball landing in the water was a single. The Chanute right fielder wore boots, while the David right fielder removed his socks.[59]

From 1936 to 1940 the town team also played in the state baseball tournament in Wichita and finished well enough to claim a share of the prize money each year. After finishing second in the 1937 state tournament, Chanute was invited to the national tournament for the first time. They managed to place seventh, which was expected to pay about $300 (there was a $5,000 guarantee for first place). By comparison, their second-place share at the state tournament in 1939 was $1,000. From 1937 to 1939 the town team was joined at Katy Park by a team in the newly organized Southeast (SEK) Division of the Kansas Ban Johnson League. The Ban Johnson team ordered new blue-and-gold uniforms, but they failed to arrive in time for the first game, so the manager scrounged a variety of uniforms in town before the first game. Teams entered and departed

View from the seats in the grandstand, built in 1936, at Katy Stadium in Chanute (2014). The playing field was named for native son Paul Lindblad, who pitched in the major leagues from 1965 to 1978. From the author's personal collection.

the division, and the Chanute Bans played in the league only three years, struggling to play .500 ball. They also played in the Chanute Industrial League on days they did not have a Ban Johnson League game.[60]

In 1938 and 1939 Claude Willoughby, a native of the nearby town of Buffalo, pitched for the Chanute town team. He had pitched previously for the Philadelphia Phillies (1925–1930) and the Pittsburgh Pirates (1931). Although not a particularly successful pitcher in the major leagues (38 wins, 58 losses, 175 strikeouts, 406 walks, ERA 5.84), Willoughby was selected as the best pitcher in the 1938 Kansas semipro tournament. With Chanute dropping out of the Ban Johnson League after the 1939 season, Willoughby became the manager of the successful Ban Johnson League team in Independence, Kansas, where his son was a pitcher, during 1940 and 1941.[61]

The Sioux City Canaries held spring training in Chanute in 1939, playing three games against the town team, who defeated their guests in all three games. The only complaint the Sioux City manager had was the number of baseballs they had to use because the infield was not sodded, which scuffed the balls. In July 1939 Chanute made the first known triple play at Katy Park diamond. Willoughby was brought in to pitch for Chanute against the Wichita Solomon Kandy Kids with no outs in the ninth inning and the bases loaded. Chanute already trailed by two runs. A ground ball to the third baseman led to force outs at second and first, followed by a throw home to catch the runner coming down from third. Emotions run high for both teams after such events, and Chanute scored three runs in the bottom of the ninth to win the game.[62]

Chanute went forty years without a minor league team, but during 1946–1950 Katy Park was the home field of minor league teams in the Kansas-Oklahoma-Missouri (KOM) League (Class D) during the expansion of minor league baseball after the Second World War. Willoughby became the manager of the team in Bartlesville, Oklahoma, sponsored by his former club, the Pittsburgh Pirates. Some of the other teams in the league were affiliated with major league teams, but the 1946 Chanute Owls were associated with the minor league Topeka Owls (Western Association, Class C), and the 1947 Chanute Athletics were independent. The 1948 Chanute Giants were affiliated with the New York Giants (now the San Francisco Giants), but the arrangement lasted only one year, and the independent Chanute Athletics returned for two years in 1949. The Korean War began in 1950, and the low-level minor league circuit dropped from eight teams to six when the teams in Chanute and Independence folded after that year's season. The entire league folded after the 1952 season.[63]

Currently, the high school and American Legion teams use Katy Stadium. The field at the ballpark was dedicated to Chanute native Paul Lindblad after his death in 2006. He played most of his major league career with the Kansas City Athletics and Oakland A's as a relief pitcher from 1965 to 1978.[64] Although the placement of the diamond has changed somewhat during its history, Katy Park is one of the oldest baseball sites to be used for the sport in Kansas.

CHAPTER 14

Moffet Field Stadium, Larned

Four years after Larned was founded in 1873, the Centennial Base Ball Club and Larned Strikers Croquet Club represented the young town. In March 1878 the "Boys in Blue" at nearby Fort Larned defeated the Larned City Club in a game played at the post, but the town team evened the score at a return game in Larned. The following year the Larned Base Ball Club played a picked team from the Nineteenth US Infantry at Fort Dodge (Fort Larned had been closed). The Larned town team also played teams from nearby cities through the 1880s and 1890s, although interest waxed and waned from year to year, as it did elsewhere.[1] In 1882–1883 the town team was organized as the Henry Booth Base Ball Club. During the US Civil War, Henry Booth had initially served as a sergeant in the Eleventh Kansas Infantry. He became a captain in 1863, when the unit was mounted as the Eleventh Kansas Cavalry, commanded by Colonel Thomas Moonlight, who played for the Frontier Base Ball Club in Leavenworth, the first baseball club in the state. Booth was US Postmaster at Fort Larned in 1873 when he became one of the founders of the city of Larned.[2]

In 1885 the city boasted six white baseball nines plus one African American team, "and nearly all the clubs are uniformed."[3] A reorganized town team in 1887 established its ball ground "near Bright's grove," which was on the north side of the Arkansas River, immediately downstream from the mouth of the Pawnee River. Into the twentieth century, Larned continued to support a town team. Among their games were exhibitions against barnstorming bloomer girl teams in 1898 and 1903. Also in 1903, newspapers around the state published a reported disagreement over the outcome of a seventeen-inning game and $60 side bet in Kingman ending with a confrontation. Five players on the Larned team hailing from Larned and Ellinwood reportedly used baseball bats to fight their way through an angry group of players and supporters of the Kingman team as they made their way from the hotel to the train depot. A few days later, the story was exposed as a complete fabrication.[4] However, the fact that the story could be given credence in newspapers says something about the perceived nature of early baseball.

In 1905 the Pennsylvania Settlers' Association held its annual picnic at Frizell's Fort Ranch (old Fort Larned, now Fort Larned National Historic Site). Among the contests was a ballgame between Larned and Riverside for a $25 prize. The relative value of baseball equipment at the time is evident in prizes for the footrace open to boys under fourteen years old. The first-place finisher received a five-pound tub of creamery butter, while the boy in second place received a ball and bat. The prize for third place was a buggy whip. At a similar event two years later, the relative stature of baseball had improved. The prizes awarded at the footrace for boys twelve and under were a baseball and a catcher's glove for first place and an air rifle for second place.[5]

In 1907 Ellinwood, Great Bend, Kinsley, and Larned organized the Wheat Belt League. Each team was scheduled to play six games against each of the other teams.[6] The following year Larned was part of an unsuccessful attempt to form a Wheat and [Sugar] Beet Base Ball League with Dodge City, Garden City, and Kinsley.[7] The team still played various opponents, including wins in a pair of exhibition games against the Mikado Club, a traveling team of Japanese players.[8] A town team was again organized in 1909, but midway through the summer Strong City's professional team in the Kansas State League (Class D) moved to Larned, and it remained through 1911 under the name Larned Wheat Kings. The team never finished better than sixth place. The league folded in July 1911, and Larned never hosted another minor league club.[9]

In late summer 1907 former major leaguer William "Buck" Weaver joined the Larned town team as its catcher and became a fan favorite. In 1889, William Weaver and his wife, Dora, bought a farm near Lakin, about 120 miles west of Larned, which became his offseason home. In 1886–1887 Weaver played for minor league teams in Topeka, Wellington, and Wichita. He spent most of 1888 playing in Texas before signing in September with the Louisville Colonels of the American Association, a major league at the time. He stayed with the Colonels until his release in 1894. In subsequent years, he played for several minor league and independent teams.[10]

Following his initial season in Larned, Weaver returned in 1908, and his name was used as a drawing card for upcoming games—for example, "Base ball, Sunday, May 17, Kinsley vs. Larned, at City Park. Buck Weaver will catch." Weaver did not return in 1909 until July, when Larned inherited the minor league team in the Kansas State League. He played in only eighteen games at first base, but the local fans welcomed him back just the same. In 1910 he took over as manager of Larned's league team and played mostly in left field. The team performed poorly, however, and Weaver left in June. He closed the season playing for Kansas State League teams in Wellington and Lyons.[11]

Weaver's life crashed around him in Larned during the winter of 1911–1912. Buck and Dora had separated in 1904. She lived in Idaho, and he lived in Kansas with their adopted daughter. Buck had physically abused Dora, and she was granted a divorce in 1910 on the grounds of extreme cruelty. In late 1911, Buck's adopted daughter accused him of fathering her child. She was underage at the time. The Pawnee County sheriff arrested Buck, but he posted bond and fled to Mexico. He was recaptured a month later and returned to Larned. Weaver pleaded guilty and was incarcerated at the Kansas State Penitentiary in Lansing. After arriving in March 1912, he became involved in the prison baseball program and managed one of the intramural prison baseball teams. In 1914, at the age of forty-nine, Weaver played on an integrated state prison team that defeated the top team at the US penitentiary in nearby Leavenworth. Late in 1914 the new Kansas governor, a former teammate of Buck's in the 1880s, paroled him. After his release, Weaver moved to Illinois and then to Ohio, where he died alone in 1943.[12]

Baseball games in Larned in the early 1900s were played at "Moffet's park on the hill" near the "standpipe" (cylindrical water tower) at the site of the current water tower. In 1906 efforts were under way to develop a city park on the "island south of town," which was actually a wedge of land upstream from the confluence of the Pawnee and Arkansas Rivers. In 1907 a baseball field was constructed in City Park, also known as Island Park, and fund-raisers were held to finance construction of seating. However, in late 1909 the decision was made to move the municipal park to another site that had been donated to the city, and the island was leased to the baseball team in the Kansas State League at the time. The team spent about $1,500 on the ballpark, altering the direction of the diamond and building a grandstand that faced northeast. The grandstand was estimated to hold 500 fans under its roof while another 300 fans could sit on an open bleacher. Because the ballpark sometimes flooded, baseball games were still played occasionally at Moffet's park on the hill.[13]

Island Park was used for baseball games until June 1912, a year after the minor league team folded. At that time the grandstand was purchased by the fair association and moved to the fairgrounds in Edwards Park on the northeastern side of town. The land for Edwards Park had been donated to the city and the Pawnee County Agricultural Association by J. G. Edwards in October 1909 for use as a public park and fairground.[14] Some people preferred to retain Island Park, and those feelings apparently lingered. In 1917 Larned resident Peter Schnack passed away and bequeathed a portion of his estate for the maintenance of a city park to bear his name, but he expressly forbade use of the money at Edwards Park. He had favored the Island Park site, but that property was abandoned as a park in 1929 because of flood concerns. Meanwhile, F. D. Lowrey, a local banker, passed away in 1918, and land he had owned on the south side of town was donated to the city for use as a public park. With Island Park abandoned, a site adjacent to Lowrey Park was finally developed as Schnack Park.[15] Of these city parks, Edwards Park became a primary location of the town team's baseball diamond from 1912 through the 1930s.

There was little town team baseball in Larned during the years leading up to the First World War. In 1914 the team apparently suffered from limited support from businesses and fans. Rather than playing at the fairgrounds, they played on a field at 14th and State Streets, several blocks west of Edwards Park. Town team baseball returned to the fairgrounds in 1919, as local soldiers returned from service during the First World War. The team played most of its games at home, and the first game was attended by about 500 fans, "most of whom came out in automobiles." The Kansas secretary of state noted later in the year that Pawnee County had more automobiles (or at least more automobile licenses) per capita than any other county in the state. As sometimes happened at sites used for both baseball and horse races, a ballgame in June was called after six innings—with Larned leading Rozel 6–0—so the horse races could begin. However, fans swarmed the field and convinced the umpire to continue the game to its normal conclusion, with Larned winning 8–3. The town being an agricultural community, the baseball season in the early years was usually halted for a few weeks during late June and early July while the wheat harvest was under way.[16] Baseball could delay horse races but not the harvest.

In 1920 tragedy came to the fairgrounds diamond, when an occasional substitute player for Larned, Harold Sanborn, was struck in the temple by a pitch during the second inning of a game against Burdett. He was stunned but not knocked unconscious, and he took his position in the field the following half inning. However, he was seen facing away from the diamond, appearing to be still stunned as he stood in the outfield. Sanborn was replaced and taken home, where he died a short time later. His body was returned to Burr Oak in north-central Kansas for burial. The Larned baseball team paid for the funeral expenses, and the entire Burdett team attended the funeral.[17]

During the 1920s Larned had an African American baseball team that joined the white town team in hosting games at the fairgrounds. The Larned Giants played other African American teams in the area, as well as teams of white players. The Giants occasionally ran large, two-column ads in the newspaper announcing their games. A 1922 ad included the names and positions of their "strengthened" lineup. They also ran smaller ads for their games through the summer, unlike the town team. The two teams played each other for the city championship in September, won by the "Larned white team" 7–0.[18]

In 1921 the Larned town team joined Belpre, Burdett, Ely, Garfield, Kinsley, Lewis, and Rozel in the Pawnee and Edwards County Base Ball League. Each team was allowed only one professional player in league games. The ambitious league schedule called for games to begin May 1 and run through November 6. When the Larned town team was playing elsewhere, the fairgrounds ball diamond was open for the Larned Giants to host games, and Larned High School also organized its first baseball team that year. The local newspaper began publishing regular box scores for the Larned team and occasionally for other teams, a practice that continued through the 1930s. In 1921, however, as the long league schedule wound down in the autumn, only the scores were published. By the end of the season newspaper coverage had faded almost completely, as Belpre dominated the league.[19]

In addition to its league games in 1921, Larned defeated the Western Bloomer Girls 7–3 in a "good, clean game." The bloomers fielded four men and five women. The women playing pitcher and first base were praised for their skills by the local newspaper. The pitcher for Larned was Emmett "Chief" Bowles, a Potawatomi from Oklahoma, who would pitch one inning for the Chicago White Sox in 1922.[20] On October 19 teams of players from the American and National Leagues played a game at the Larned fairgrounds, with Bowles serving as umpire. The Americans defeated the Nationals 13–8. However, the initial excitement for the game was not sustained—the "preponderance of opinion is . . . that it was rotten entertainment . . . about as exciting as croquet." One spectator lamented, "It's going to take me a long time to convalesce." The local organizers lost money.[21]

In April 1922 a "hurriedly assembled team representing Larned" lost by one run to the semipro team in Great Bend, where Bowles was now pitching. Larned continued to play baseball independently the rest of the year and into 1923. They began the 1923 season in April at the fairgrounds, but a new ballpark—referred to simply as New Ball Park—was donated by Fred Lowrey on land that was, at the time, north of town, "two blocks west of Broadway on Sixteenth." Bowles once again donned a Larned uniform. Various civic club or muffin teams also played at the New Ball Park, as did the Larned Giants.[22]

In 1924, Larned baseball returned to the fairgrounds, which they shared with the Giants and a four-team City League. The town team again defeated the Giants.[23] Larned hosted the Wichita Monrovians the following year, a few days after the black Monrovians defeated the Ku Klux Klan baseball team in Wichita. Larned won 13–2 in front of about 700 fans, the largest crowd for a Larned baseball game in several years. A week later the Ku Klux Klan provided a fireworks display and other events during Larned's Fourth of July celebration, but they were soon unwelcome in town.[24]

The real excitement on the baseball diamond in 1925, however, was the rivalry with Great Bend. A seven-game series between the two teams was tied 2–2. In game five, Great Bend added a few ringers, which helped them secure the victory. Larned did the same in game six to even the series again at 3–3. Clearly, some ground rules were needed before the seventh and deciding game. Larned won a coin toss and chose to host the final game. The two teams also agreed on the number of professional players they could add for the final game. Among the hired players, pitchers would be the key acquisitions. Great Bend added Joe Bloomer from nearby

Claflin. Bloomer went on to pitch for Class A and AA minor league teams from 1926 through 1934 (Class AA was the top level at the time). Larned countered with Stafford native Roy Garvin Sanders, who had pitched for the Kansas City Blues (Class AA) in 1915–1917 and briefly in the major leagues in 1917 and 1918. In the end, it was not the close pitching duel that had been anticipated. Larned defeated Great Bend 12–5 in front of an estimated 3,500 fans, reportedly the largest baseball event in the city's history to that time (the population of Larned did not reach 3,500 until 1930). A few of the hired players stayed to play in a pair of games between Belpre and Larned to close out the season. Larned won both games behind the pitching of Joe Bloomer. Thomas Blodgett, who had pitched for Class A and AA minor league teams in 1915–1917, pitched for Belpre.[25]

Semipro baseball continued in Larned in 1926. The success of the 1925 season left the team with about $400 in the treasury. Some of that was used for new uniforms, and the manager estimated that $125 per game would be spent on salaries in 1926. However, attendance at the games—and the corresponding revenue—was low, so local businesses stepped in to help fund the team. At a game with the Lincoln, Nebraska, team in the Western League (Class A), only about 500 fans attended, resulting in gate receipts of $338. Of that total, $200 was owed to Lincoln. Even games against rival Great Bend failed to draw the expected numbers of fans. The rivalry remained strong but reasonably civilized. In a disputed play during one of their games, a Great Bend player was called out at third base. A heated exchange occurred that was eventually settled with a coin flip, won by the runner from Great Bend, who was declared safe.[26]

In a final attempt to attract fans, Larned scheduled three big games on August 15, 17, and 22. The opponents were Great Bend for game seven of a series tied at 3–3, the Western League team from Omaha, and the Kansas City Monarchs. The games were advertised regionally through an auto tour of boosters, players, and the band. In addition, a novel advertising method was employed to attract potential spectators: bundles of handbills were dropped from "Merle Johnson's aeroplane" at an altitude of 200 to 300 feet over towns between Dodge City in the west and Ellinwood in the east. As part of the promotional flights, a pilot took the team's manager on his first ride in an airplane. Because of the extra weight from the paper flyers, less fuel could be carried on the plane, so frequent stops to refuel were necessary, including one at a farmhouse. In the first game Larned defeated rival Great Bend 4–2. In the second, Larned defeated Omaha 5–4, scoring four runs in the ninth inning and the winning run in the tenth. Yet the crowds at both games were unimpressive. That changed when the Monarchs came to town. Wilber "Bullet" Rogan pitched the Monarchs to a 16–0 win over Larned. Despite the loss, the game was wildly popular with local fans. Paid admissions totaled 3,150 (at 75¢ apiece), with children admitted at no charge, resulting in an estimated attendance of about 3,500 spectators. Of the $2,360 in gate receipts (equivalent to about $32,000 in 2016), $1,720 was paid to the Monarchs and $640 to the Larned town team, which included $50 deducted from the Monarchs's share to cover advertising. To close the season, Larned agreed to play two more games against Great Bend. Larned lost game eight, tying the series again at 4–4. The ninth game was canceled because Great Bend wanted more money than was usually paid for one of their games.[27]

With the financial challenges experienced through most of 1926, the Larned town team in 1927 essentially became a team of local players, and attendance at the games continued to be poor. "It is getting to be a question of good support or no games." Even a game against the Cuban Stars of the Negro National League attracted only 400 to 500 fans. The listless play of the Stars in their 6–2 victory was blamed on the low gate receipts and their correspondingly low payment as a percentage of those receipts. During the summer, local businesses organized a junior baseball league for boys ten to thirteen years old. Boys were chosen for each of the four teams through ballots cut from the local newspaper or picked up at the sponsoring businesses. The junior league continued in subsequent years, and the American Legion assumed sponsorship in 1929.[28]

Struggling to survive as an independent team, Larned joined Dodge City, Ellinwood, Great Bend, Kinsley, and Pratt in organizing the Southwestern Baseball League in 1928. Limits on team salaries were set in order to reduce the financial risk in the smaller towns, and ringers brought in for specific games were prohibited. Larned did not fare well, placing fifth, only half a game ahead of Kinsley. Knowing that they would finish poorly, Larned used Pawnee County native Durward Kelly Swenson as a pitcher in two of their last games, even though he was ineligible to play under league rules. The Larned management reasoned that at least the fans would see a better class of game with him playing. Swenson had recently pitched for Topeka in the Western Association (Class C). Other than the creation of the Southwestern League, the news of the 1928 season in Larned was the organization of a baseball team by the Business and Professional Women's Club in May. They practiced regularly through August, when they played a pickup team of businessmen. The Larned town team refused to play them. The BPWC fielded a team of seven women, with their manager—one of the town team's pitchers—on the mound and another man catching. They defeated the men's team 11–10.[29]

In subsequent years Larned continued to be represented by a semipro town team at Edwards Park, while the African American team changed its name from the Giants to the Monarchs. In 1929 the Kansas City Monarchs defeated the Larned town team 22–0. The following week, Larned defeated the Wallenstein and Raffman girls' team of Wichita 2–0 in a game of softball. The girls' team had men as pitcher, catcher, and shortstop, and all nine players wore traditional baseball uniforms. About 1,800 people watched the Monarchs game and about 500 saw the softball game, netting the Larned town team $306 (of $1,224) and $102 (of $202), respectively. In 1930 and 1931 the town team wore uniforms provided by the Midland Life Insurance Company, so they played under the name Midland Bearcats in 1930 and Midland Life in 1931. Several noteworthy events occurred during 1930. The ceremonial first pitch of the season was made with a fifty-year-old baseball cut from a bootleg and stitched with home-tanned squirrel skin around a rubber core wrapped in twine and yarn. The story was later featured in *Ripley's Believe It or Not*, prompting a letter to Ed Casey, the ball's owner, from Babe Ruth asking, "Can you prove it, and what's the price?" In July the Bearcats piled into six automobiles for a trip west to enter the Denver Post Tournament, where they were eliminated in two games. In September the Kansas City Monarchs defeated the Bearcats 12–5 and 12–4 on Thursday and Sunday evenings under the Monarchs' portable lighting system. The Great Depression was setting in, however, so total gate receipts were only about $250 and $315, substantially less than in 1926 and 1929, despite the novelty of night baseball. A second nine (the Larned Wildcats), a twilight league, the high school, and a junior summer league also played at this time, with most games held on an athletic field in Lowrey Park.[30]

The 1931 season ended in August because low attendance had left the team with insufficient funds to continue. The following year the town team dropped the Midland name and featured more local players. They also rejoined the Pawnee and Edwards County League, with teams from smaller cities rather than towns such as Great Bend and Dodge City, their big rivals in previous years. Larned won the playoff for the 1932 P. & E.

League championship by defeating Kinsley. In 1933 Larned lost the league championship game to Burdett. Toward the end of 1933, there were rumors that the Ban Johnson team from Dodge City would move to Larned, where they hoped to have more support from the fans.[31] They played a few games in Larned against other Ban Johnson teams, but they did not officially leave Dodge City. In 1934 the Larned town team again scheduled games against towns such as Dodge City, Garden City, and Great Bend, while a second nine, the Larned Boosters, took their place in the P. & E. League.[32] At the end of the season, plans were discussed to provide a better baseball park in the city. One possible site was land offered to the city by Alvus H. Moffet.

A. H. Moffet moved to Kansas in the 1880s and established a bank in Garfield (about fifteen miles southwest of Larned). He moved the Moffet Brothers Bank to Larned in 1896, where it became the First National Bank in 1922. It successfully weathered the financial panics of 1893 and 1907, as well as the Great Depression of the 1930s, and Moffet became a leading citizen in Larned and Pawnee County. During the summer of 1903 there was a local shortage of harvest hands, who were paid about $2 per day. Moffet traveled to Wichita and attempted to arrange special train fares for laborers. He was unsuccessful but persisted in his efforts on behalf of local farmers. He recruited about a hundred men and "paid the larger part of their fares" to Larned, where they were met at the depot by local farmers. There was still a shortage of harvest hands, so Moffet again traveled east to continue recruiting. In late 1934, Moffet and E. E. Frizell offered to donate the land west of Carroll Avenue between Second and Fourth Streets to the city of Larned if the site were to be developed as an athletic field with a grandstand. The southern end of the site had once been a miniature golf course, but the northern end was a channel, with slopes rising to the east and west. The property was close to the field near the standpipe referred to earlier as Moffet's Park, which had been developed as a residential area beginning in 1910. The parcel of land on the slope below the standpipe would need to be leveled, but it would be contiguous with the existing Schnack and Lowrey Parks to the south (now merged as Schnack-Lowrey Park). Schnack Park was the site of the city swimming pool, and Lowrey Park had an existing athletic field used by the twilight league and other teams.[33]

Initially, plans were presented to the city in September 1934 for a "permanent and ornamental" grandstand to seat 630 fans in Lowrey Park.

The proposal was for a structure 180 feet long, 19½ feet deep, and 12 feet high constructed of cement faced with native stone. There would be seven rows of seats, with dressing rooms below. County engineer Leroy Harris was in charge of drawing the plans to be submitted for federal funding as a work relief project. Local donors, such as the Rotary Club, offered to assist financially, if necessary. The estimated cost was $3,000 (equivalent to about $54,000 in 2016). At the same time, twenty-four floodlights were installed for use at punkin ball (softball) games on the Lowrey Park diamond. In October, Raymond Rugge was appointed city engineer and assumed responsibility for the design of the new athletic field. The mayor asked a landscaping service in McPherson for advice regarding the best location and type of grandstand to be built in Lowrey Park, because the "improvement is to be a permanent one."[34]

In early December 1934 the city council adopted a resolution to construct the new athletic field through the Kansas Emergency Relief Committee (KERC) on the land to be donated by Moffet and Frizell. On January 31, 1935, the city also requested that Rugge draw plans and estimate costs for a new stadium at the existing site of the athletic field in Lowrey Park. On March 4 the city council voted to approve two plans to be submitted for consideration by KERC—one for Lowrey Park and one for the new site. Consultation with the KERC engineer indicated that the Lowrey Park plan was not likely to be approved, and it had become less attractive to the city because it would cost more money, requiring the city to issue bonds, which it was unwilling to do. The plans Rugge drew up for the new site included a grandstand of concrete with outside walls of "rubble stone" rather than a "modernistic design." It would face the center of an athletic field used for baseball, football, and track. This plan called for a grandstand 100 feet long and 36 feet deep that would seat about 700 people. The hill on the west side of the property provided a slope that could support the tiered seating of the grandstand, reducing the cost compared to a freestanding structure at Lowrey Park. The small rise on the eastern side of the new property would be cut and used to fill the ditch in the center of the field. Plans for the new athletic field were approved in March 1935, and the plans for leveling the field were forwarded to KERC. As these arrangements were made, it was proposed that the name of the site should be Moffet Field to honor the principal donor.[35] Of course, even the best-laid plans often undergo changes as they are implemented.

As work moved forward for a new athletic stadium in 1935, Larned was invited to join a new division in the Kansas Ban Johnson League with teams from Copeland, Dodge City, Garden City, Hays, and Pratt, although Hays and Pratt chose not to field teams. The start of the season was delayed about a month because of dust storms, as the infamous Dust Bowl dragged on, but heavy rains in late May soon sent a flood down the Pawnee River through parts of Larned. The Larned Ban Johnson team lost its first game to Dodge City on June 2, but won their home opener against Copeland a week later at Edwards Park. Larned later clinched the division title, but they lost to Beloit in the divisional playoffs, two games to one. In addition to the new Ban Johnson team, the Larned town team and the punkin league were active during the summer of 1935, as was a junior baseball league playing at Lowrey Park. The Ban Johnson and high school baseball teams shared Edwards Park with the town team. With all this activity, a new ballpark probably seemed like a good investment.[36]

Work to cut the east hill and fill the ditch began on May 3 through KERC, but work was suspended at the end of August. The KERC program was ending and projects not yet completed had to be reauthorized through the Works Progress Administration (WPA), which approved the plans in late November 1935.[37] During this period of transition in the project, A. H. Moffet died at age sixty-eight, so he did not see the completed stadium named in his honor.[38]

The plans in late 1935 called for a grandstand that was larger than in the earlier design. The new dimensions were 108 feet long and 44 feet deep, with twelve rows of seats, yet the estimated seating capacity dropped to 600 people. The floodlights at Lowrey Park would be moved to the new field. The plans changed yet again in early 1936. The Larned board of education agreed to contribute $1,750 to the municipal project so that locker rooms, showers, and toilets could be added under the grandstand. To accommodate these facilities, Rugge redesigned the structure by adding ten more rows of seats to the top of the grandstand, which would cover the locker rooms. This increased the estimated seating capacity from 600 to 1,050 spectators. The decision was also made to build the structure entirely from reinforced concrete, omitting the use of stone. In addition to the funds provided by the school board, the city would contribute $1,500–$2,000 toward the added costs, with additional labor funded by the WPA.[39]

Construction during the summer of 1936 was interrupted from late June through early August, when the WPA workers were given private employment helping with the wheat harvest. Delays also occurred that autumn when cold weather prevented the pouring of concrete. The final plans approved in late summer included a "cantilever truss type roof," although its installation was a low priority due to the construction delays. Concrete footings for the columns and the foundation of the grandstand were completed in early October, as was the grading of the playing field, where Bermuda grass had been planted. By the end of November the northern and southern sections of the grandstand had been poured, with coke and gas heaters used to keep the fresh concrete from getting too cold. The center section was completed in late December. The relatively warm weather that facilitated the concrete work delayed plans to flood the northern end of the field for use by ice skaters. The floodlights were used to illuminate the area so that people could skate after the early winter sunset. Work on the locker rooms was completed in February 1937, as plans were made to install a new water tower west of the athletic field as part of a separate WPA project.[40]

After all the design changes, the completed grandstand was 102 feet long and 65 feet deep, with twenty-two rows of seats. The original wooden planks used for seats have been replaced with aluminum benches. Ornate touches in the concrete include American Indian head reliefs above the windows, which represent the Larned High School Pawnee Indians. Concrete sidewalks around the perimeter of the field and steps down to the grandstand from the parking area were installed in 1938. Forms from a recent bridge project were reused for the concrete barriers around the field and along the steps. Games were played both during the afternoon and in the evening, although the summer heat of the 1930s apparently decreased attendance at Sunday afternoon games. A canopy of "reinforcing steel and galvanized iron" expected to cost about $2,500–$3,000 was placed in the city budget in 1938 and again in 1939, but other needs took precedence as the Great Depression continued. The final cost of the stadium was $21,000 (equivalent to about $350,000 in 2016), with about 55 percent of the total provided through the WPA. Installing the lights cost another $3,500.[41]

The first game for the Ban Johnson team at the new diamond was May 2, 1937. The following month Governor Walter Huxman dedicated Moffet Field Stadium—with musical help from the bands of Larned, Pawnee Rock, Pratt, and Saint John—and the event was broadcast by a new Great Bend radio station. Some of the estimated 2,500 people in attendance

Entrance to the concrete grandstand, built in 1937, at Moffet Field Stadium in Larned (2014). From the author's personal collection.

watched the proceedings from their cars while listening to the governor's speech on their car radios. At the close of the ceremony, the Larned Ban Johnson team hosted the Bazine town team, with Bazine winning 4–3. The newspaper correctly predicted, "The stadium, of modernistic concrete design, has ample seating capacity for crowds attending athletic contests for many years to come."[42]

As the decade came to a close, the new stadium was well used. Larned still hosted Ban Johnson and town teams, both of which remained competitive. The Larned town team competed in the semipro tournament in Wichita organized by Hap Dumont described in chapter 8. The Bee Jays regularly competed with Dodge City for the Ban Johnson division championship, and they also played well against area town teams. In the final regular season game of the 1939 season at Moffet Field Stadium, the Larned Bee Jays defeated Dodge City 3–2 in front of 1,200 fans. An argument broke out on the field, in which the catcher for Dodge City was ejected from the game for arguing with the umpire. The local sheriff, a deputy, and the night marshal had to "assist in quelling the disturbance."

Seating in the grandstand, built in 1937, at Moffet Field Stadium in Larned (2014). Building the grandstand on the slope reduced the construction costs. From the author's personal collection.

In May 1940 Larned's last two Civil War veterans were featured in the local newspaper prior to the Memorial Day observance.[43] It would have been interesting to ask their views on all that had transpired during their lives. Transportation had progressed from horses to automobiles, and the Larned Bee Jays were going to travel more easily in 1940 thanks to a donation by two local men of an old bus refitted with the engine from a former hearse.[44] If fans sensitive to baseball's superstitions worried about the success of a team being transported with the aid of a hearse engine, it was not mentioned in the local newspapers.

In addition to sports events at Moffet Field Stadium, the Larned band gave concerts there.[45] The football field was later moved to the high school, and tennis courts now occupy what was the northern end zone. With use of the stadium now restricted to baseball, a chain-link fence encloses the playing field, which still has natural grass on the infield and outfield. The ballpark is used by the high school and American Legion baseball teams.

Rathert Stadium, Junction City

Junction City's first baseball club was organized in 1867, making it one of the first in the state. Teams picked from among the club's members played the first game. As elsewhere, however, it took the sport a few years to become reasonably well established. In 1870, a local newspaper reported, "We hear it whispered that efforts are being made to organize a base ball club in town. Lord deliver us." In contrast to most Kansas newspapers at the time, the Junction City newspaper was not interested in supporting baseball in the young town. In 1882 it referred to baseball as "a species of bummerism. It tends to loaferism. These two sentences are sufficient to indicate our private opinion." Five years later, it referred to baseball as "that miserable nuisance." This sentiment persisted until a new publisher took over in 1888. Despite the lack of support from the local press, the Junction City Base Ball Club reorganized in April 1871. They were defeated (33–8) by the Government Stockings Base Ball Club from nearby Fort Riley in a game played "for a bet . . . and a Base ball," probably a common arrangement on early Kansas baseball fields. The umpire was a member of the Graham Base Ball Club, also from Fort Riley. Teams from the fort often played the town team, and in some years the Junction City team included players from Fort Riley.[1] The city and the fort were close enough to each other that the Junction City players used four railroad handcars to travel from the city to the fort to play a game in 1877.[2]

The Junction City team continued to play periodically through the late 1800s, with various nicknames, such as the Frontiers, Stars, Coronados, Red Stockings, and Rackets. During most of this period, the city had no purpose-built baseball park, and games were played at several sites. In July 1875 the Junction City Frontiers and the team from Wakefield were to play a game "in [the] rear of Callen's field." The unspecified types of seats were free, even the reserved seats. The 1877 Junction City Stars practiced "on the vacant lots north of Kiehl's livery stable," where they had their baseball ground "between Kiehl's stable and Tom Burn's residence." In July 1885 Junction City hosted the team from Abilene on a field "near the depot" (near 10th Street).[3]

New fairgrounds were constructed at the western end of 8th Street in 1879. Beginning in the 1880s, baseball was frequently played on a diamond inside the oval racetrack, where fans could sit in the grandstand to watch the game. A new diamond was constructed inside the racetrack in 1889. That same year, two games were also played "on the bottom near the railroad," perhaps while the new diamond at the fairground was being prepared.[4]

The city got a purpose-built ballpark in 1895, when the Junction City town team—the Invincibles—leased Callen's field, which had been used as a baseball ground two decades earlier.[5] In May 1895 a game between the town team and a Fort Riley team was played "at the Junction City grounds" to entertain the last four stationed companies of the Seventh US Cavalry as they prepared to leave the post. The game "was attended by many from Fort Riley and almost the entire city. All business houses were closed from 2 to 5. The attendance was fully 2000 people." That same month, the Junction City team also played a game on the "Y." The name referred to the configuration of railroad tracks on the east side of town that branched to the northwest, northeast, and south.[6]

By June 1895 a fence was erected to enclose the ball grounds at Callen's field, and the grandstand was in place for a pair of games on the Fourth of July.[7]

> The Junction City Base Ball association has given Junction City a magnificent park, something we have never had. The grounds cover an entire block in the Callen field, between Tenth and Eleventh, and from Adams to Madison. It is enclosed by an eight-foot board fence, built substantially and in every way in a permanent manner. On the northwest corner, behind the catcher, is a semicircular grandstand sixty-four feet long, with nine rows of seats. The structure is covered, and the front is protected by wire netting.[8]

There was also an uncovered bleacher. In August, additional fencing was added on the western side of the ballpark, which was given the rather generic name of Athletic Park, because it was also used for football.[9]

In 1896, the one-year-old grandstand was moved to the southwestern corner, near the park entrance, and expanded to hold 800 spectators. Its larger size compensated for the absence of the bleacher, which was not rebuilt.[10] The name of the team also changed to the Imperials, and they hosted the first game of the Kansas State League, which also included Emporia, Independence, and Parsons. In July the league was expanded and split into two independent leagues. It was proposed that the top team in each league play its counterpart for the championship at the end of the season. Junction City was in the Northern Kansas State League with Emporia, Minneapolis, and Topeka. The Southern Kansas State League included Chanute, Coffeyville, Independence, and Parsons. Lack of fan support led to an early close of the season for the northern league in mid-August 1896, which ended plans for a championship series. Similarly, the "magnificent" Athletic Park would survive only two more years.[11]

Financial troubles experienced by many towns attempting to support professional teams had also hampered the Junction City Athletic Association from its inception. In 1897 they intentionally waited until late in the summer to field a professional team, hoping that a shorter season would prove more successful. It was not. However, the team had a good pitcher by the name of Luther Taylor from Oskaloosa, Kansas. Because he was born deaf, Taylor was given the demeaning nickname "Dummy," which was widely applied to deaf players at the time. He later claimed the nickname made him stronger. Taylor joined the Junction City team as it organized in late June, but he left at the beginning of August to rest a sore knee. Three years later Taylor joined the New York Giants pitching staff, headlined by Christy Mathewson. Taylor pitched for the Giants from 1900 through 1908 (plus four games at the beginning of the 1902 season for the Cleveland Bronchos in the recently organized American League). In his nine years with the Giants, he won 53 percent of his decisions and had an earned run average (ERA) of 2.77. He was always a popular player, and his coaches and teammates learned sign language to communicate with him on and off the field. Taylor left the Giants because of a weakened arm, but he played in the minor leagues a few more years. After he retired from baseball in 1915 (at age forty), he worked at the Kansas School for the Deaf, the Iowa School for the Deaf (beginning in 1923), and the Illinois School for the Deaf (beginning in 1933), mostly as a successful coach, until he retired in 1949.[12]

With Junction City choosing not to field another professional team in 1898, teams from other cities occasionally played their games at Athletic Park, including teams from Salina and Topeka. There was an unsuccessful plan to move the Salina team to Junction City in August. The proposed move was intended to boost attendance by allowing the team to play Sunday ballgames, which were permitted in Junction City but not in Salina. In the absence of a town team, the Athletic Park's fence, gate, grandstand, and field scraper were sold at auction in October 1898 for $211.20.[13] The site is now a residential block just east of Fegan Field (more on Fegan Field later). Minor league baseball would not return to Junction City until 1909.

Junction City joined the ban on Sunday "base ball, scrub or kindred ball games" in 1899 as the town team reorganized.[14] African American teams were also organized into the early 1900s.[15] With Athletic Park gone, games were frequently played on a ball ground at the railroad Y near the Union Pacific roundhouse (railroad shops) at the eastern end of 16th Street. The roundhouse was tucked into the northern angle of the Y. In a 1907 game on the Y between teams representing the Rockwell and Parrish Brothers stores, Rockwell's second baseman, Arthur Rathert, had three ribs broken when a baserunner accidentally ran into him. He continued to play and only learned of the broken ribs when he later visited a doctor.[16]

In 1909, during a widespread resurgence of minor league teams in Kansas, Junction City fielded a team in the Central Kansas League (Class D). The team's new ballpark was within the Y, "half way between the city and Fort Riley, being directly east of the street car spur." The streetcar line ran east on 18th Street from Washington Street to a point near the railroad tracks, which the streetcar line then paralleled to the northeast (along Grant Avenue north of the roundhouse).[17] After the ground was scraped and rolled, the ballpark was improved with the addition of a roofed grandstand, bleachers, and fence. The grandstand sat on the southern side of the ball ground and consisted of three sections. The center section was estimated to seat 350 spectators, with room for 150 more fans in each wing. The seats were arranged in seventeen tiers and had seatbacks. Bleachers extending from each end of the grandstand provided additional seating.[18] Some fans avoided paying admission at the first baseball game by climbing onto the tall wooden fence, prompting the newspaper to suggest that "a large and burly individual be provided with a hook" to pull the offenders down onto the soft dirt outside the fence.[19]

The first games at the new ballpark were hosted by the "crack Fort Riley team" of players from all the units at the post. Their first opponents were college baseball teams.[20] The location of the ballpark near the electric railway made it convenient for use by both the Junction City and the Fort Riley teams. The proximity to the railway also saved the new grandstand. Late one evening in 1910, a crew on one of the streetcars noticed a fire at one end of the grandstand and contacted authorities. The fire was quickly extinguished, aided by the wind blowing away from the center of the structure.[21]

Junction City fielded a minor league team for five years and was a member of the Central Kansas League (Class D) from 1909 to 1912. During the first two years the league consisted of eight teams in north-central Kansas, and Junction City finished in seventh and fifth places, respectively. In 1911 Junction City placed first among four teams during a short season, closing at the end of July. However, Concordia claimed the pennant after Junction City failed to play a deciding game in a seven-game series. The league reorganized in 1912, and Junction City finished fourth among six teams. As minor league baseball in Kansas began to fade in 1913, the Central Kansas League became the new Kansas State League (Class D). The resurrected name was less geographically restricted, and it was hoped that this would add prestige to the league and its players. The team salary cap in 1909 had been $800 but increased to $900 in 1912 and $1,000 in 1913. However, in early July 1913 the teams in Junction City and Manhattan folded, leaving only four teams to complete the season. Junction City failed to organize a minor league team in 1914, which again left only four teams in the Kansas State League. It was the last year for a minor league of that name.[22]

With no more minor league baseball in Junction City after the 1913 season, the grandstand, fences, and other wooden structures at the League Ball Park in the Y were torn down in early 1915.[23] A new ballpark was constructed in 1916, east of the Union Pacific Depot at the eastern end of 10th Street, a few blocks south of the Y. When the town team was organized in 1917, Arthur Rathert became the team's secretary and treasurer. The following year he became Sergeant Rathert, serving at nearby Camp Funston, where he worked in the waterworks plant. In February 1919 he was appointed to fill his late father's unexpired term as the superintendent of the Junction City waterworks. That same month, the grandstand, fence, and stables of the "ball park or driving park [racetrack] just across from the union station" were auctioned, but the new owners left them standing, allowing the ballpark to be used through 1922.[24]

In late 1922 plans were made to move the city's ballpark back north to the Y near Grant Avenue, which would provide good access for streetcars and automobiles. A fund drive was held in the spring of 1923 to raise $1,400 (equivalent to about $19,500 in 2016) to pay for the new ballpark, including the costs of building the grandstand, bleacher, and fence. The new Y ballpark (also known as the Grant Avenue or Union Pacific Ballpark) was opened with a game in May 1923 between the "Junction City Regulars" and the railway's "Shop team." The ballpark continued to be used into the 1930s. It also hosted other events, including a rodeo, which left the playing field in need of rehabilitation. In 1929, members of the Union Pacific Athletic Club planted new grass on the infield, repaired and repainted the grandstand, and built new fences.[25] Two years later, on August 7, the Union Pacific shop team entertained the Kansas City Monarchs, who defeated their hosts 16–1.[26]

While the new Y Ballpark was in use, the local board of education developed another athletic field in 1925 "northwest of the Tenth Street school house" on property purchased in 1924 from J. B. Callen. It was to include a quarter-mile track, football field, baseball diamond in the northwestern corner, and three tennis courts. A strip of ground thirty feet deep on the southern side of the field along 10th Street was reserved for a "future grandstand and bleachers." The field, named Fegan Field, still sits between 11th and 10th Streets on the north and south, and between Jackson and Madison Streets on the west and east. It is one block west of the Athletic Park on Callen's field, Junction City's first purpose-built baseball park in use during 1895–1898.[27]

The Y Ballpark was entering its fourteenth year in 1936, when 175 of 300 shares of stock in the Junction City Ban Johnson Association were sold at $5 per share to fund the new team. After paying all the expenses for the field and equipment, the association held about $200 in reserve. The Junction City team replaced Abilene in the Central Division of the Kansas Ban Johnson League, which also included Beloit, Concordia, Manhattan, and Wichita that year. The new Y Ballpark underwent repairs to the playing field, grandstand, and fence to get them ready for their first Ban

Johnson season. The opening game at home versus Manhattan on April 19 was promoted in a full-page newspaper ad. Junction City won the game 12–6 in front of 486 paying fans.[28]

As the Junction City Ban Johnson team participated in their first year of league play, plans were made in the summer of 1936 to build a new athletic field with the assistance of the Works Progress Administration (WPA). It would be modeled on the recently constructed Griffith Field in Manhattan. (Only the stone perimeter wall remains at Griffith Field, surrounding an athletic field that includes two small ball diamonds.) The lighted stadium in Junction City was intended to host baseball, football, track, and other events. The first site proposed was the old polo field in the southwestern part of town. Later that summer, the M-K-T (Katy) Railroad offered to sell 5.8 acres "directly north and east of the Tyco Mills" for $1,000. In the end, a 6.6-acre site at the western ends of 13th and 14th Streets was selected. Known as Langvardt Field, after its owners, it was a flat piece of ground sometimes used to land airplanes—an ideal site for a level athletic field. Subscriptions from private donors provided $1,200 (equivalent to about $20,500 in 2016) to purchase the property.[29]

Plans for the stadium were completed in September 1936 and submitted to the WPA, which quickly approved the project. As outlined in the plans, a wooden grandstand that could seat 1,400 spectators under its roof was constructed in the southwestern corner of the property. Native limestone on the exterior of the building came from the nearby Stettgast quarry. In addition, a permanent bleacher for 750 spectators directly north of the grandstand (along the third base line) was to be built, primarily for use at football games. However, this was omitted to focus on other work during construction.[30] The infield was a mixture of clay and sand, while the outfield was seeded to grass. A wooden fence of boards eight feet tall and painted dark green enclosed the playing field. Outfield distances were 337 feet in left, 393 feet in center, and 287 feet in right. Signs six feet high and twenty feet long on the fence advertised local businesses and generated income for the stadium operating fund. The initial lighting system included lights on top of the grandstand, plus light poles behind first and third base and four poles spaced around the outfield. Also included in the plans were a ticket booth near the stadium entrance and a parking lot of crushed rock for 350 automobiles. Coca-Cola provided the first scoreboard, twenty feet tall and twenty-two feet long, with sixteen-inch painted numbers. The projected cost of the project was just over $53,000 (equivalent to about $904,000 in 2016). To help fund the city's share of the construction costs, a fund drive was held to sell 3,000 sacks of cement for 75¢ apiece, providing $2,250.[31]

Work on the stadium began in October 1936 and continued through the winter and into the following summer. As work on the project neared completion in July 1937, the city commission voted to name the stadium for Arthur Rathert, who was then serving as the city engineer. He had devoted much of his own time promoting the project to WPA officials and working on the design and construction of the park. Rathert Stadium was dedicated on July 18, 1937, at a Ban Johnson League game, in which Concordia defeated the JCs 6–3.[32] The Kansas City Monarchs played at Rathert Stadium several times, including a game in September 1937 against the minor league Kansas City Blues All-Stars, a team that included a few players picked up from other teams. The Monarchs won the game 5–4 in ten innings. A portion of the proceeds from the game went to the Junction City Ban Johnson team.[33]

Since the Second World War, Rathert Stadium has been used by town

Exterior of the limestone grandstand, built in 1937, at Rathert Stadium in Junction City (2014). The small building is the ticket booth. From the author's personal collection.

Wooden seating in the grandstand, built in 1937, at Rathert Stadium in Junction City (2014). A modern bleacher extends down the third base line; a wooden deck sits along the first base line. From the author's personal collection.

teams (the city left the Ban Johnson League in 1948), military teams (during the war and shortly afterward), American Legion teams, and high school teams. The Junction City Generals independent summer collegiate team played at Rathert Stadium in 2006–2010. The Junction City Brigade, a collegiate summer league team, began playing at the stadium in 2013. They are members of the Mid-Plains Collegiate Baseball League, which also includes a team that plays in the 1924 ballpark in nearby Rossville.

Rathert Stadium's wonderful grandstand, faced with local limestone and forming an arc behind home plate, looks much as it did when it was completed in 1937. It still has a wooden seating area and wooden roof (with metal supports). The infield and outfield are grass. The outfield fence consists of traditional wooden planks painted green. As called for in the original plans, a bleacher (metal rather than wood) extends from the grandstand down the third base line. An uncovered porch with tables (the "beer garden") was not part of the original design but now extends from the grandstand down the first base line. The freestanding limestone ticket booth still sits just outside the stadium entrance. The latest restoration of the ballpark was completed in 2005, and it is unquestionably one of the nation's finest historical baseball stadiums.

CHAPTER 16

McDonald Stadium, El Dorado

El Dorado was incorporated in 1868, and town teams were organized at least as early as 1871. In May, a newspaper report that "our town is blessed with a Base Ball Club" followed a notice that "the Railroad is within thirty miles of us" and preceded a notice that "quite a number of our boys have gone on a buffalo hunt." These were early days indeed. The initial competition in baseball was among El Dorado, Augusta, and Towanda. An unusual box score that listed runs by inning for each player was published for an 1872 game between El Dorado and Towanda (El Dorado lost 21–6).[1]

El Dorado town teams were organized periodically through the end of the century. Teams of younger boys and muffin games among local groups of players based on their professions were also organized. The town team did not join any leagues, and the local newspaper was disappointed that they were not in the Kansas State League in 1887. In 1890 one resident speculated as to why professional teams of outside players were not popular: "In small towns people don't care for ball much unless some of the home people play," with maybe a professional pitcher and catcher. Thus, the El Dorado Blue Stockings first organized in the early 1880s continued to represent the town into the late 1890s. Early games were played at the fairgrounds, but in 1895 arrangements were made to develop an athletic field on property south of Hazlett Park, owned by prominent businessman Robert H. Hazlett. The athletic field included a cinder bicycle track, with a baseball diamond inside the oval. That August, a ballgame was followed by a ten-mile race pitting a horse against a bicycle. At nine and a half miles the horse bolted from the track, allowing the bicyclist to coast victoriously across the finish line. In 1899 permission was sought to again place a ball field inside the racetrack at the fairgrounds, which sat east of Vine Street, immediately north of the railroad tracks (immediately north of the current ballpark).[2]

Town teams continued to be organized into the 1900s. An effort was made in 1906 to organize "a stock company" baseball club, with a new baseball ground, but games continued to be played at the fairgrounds.[3] Town team baseball seemed to fade during the final years of the century's opening decade, but in 1911 El Dorado hosted its only minor league team. The Arkansas City franchise in the Kansas State League was purchased for $300 in November 1910, but it did not turn out well. The Crushers joined teams from Great Bend, Hutchinson, Larned, Lyons, McPherson, Newton, and Wellington. The season was originally scheduled to run until September, but it was shortened to August as teams struggled financially. Efforts to hold the league together were unsuccessful. The Wellington team moved briefly to Wichita but received even less fan support and consequently returned to Wellington, where it soon folded. The El Dorado team also struggled, and it, too, folded in early July. Then the entire league collapsed. The problem was not unique to the Kansas State League. Several other leagues and teams in the region experienced struggles that year. As the El Dorado team disbanded, several players departed, but a few remained in town and played independently on a team aptly named the Orphans.[4]

El Dorado businessmen opted against supporting another professional team in 1912. However, Ed "Smiles" Kellar, who played for the league team in 1911, organized and managed an independent semipro team. The Athletics played well, winning nearly all of their games, including those against several semipro teams from Wichita. Augusta finally managed to defeat the Athletics 4–0 at the end of the season. Despite their success on the diamond, the Athletics twice were compelled to plead for additional support through donations and attendance at their ballgames. Perhaps not surprisingly, mention of El Dorado town teams all but disappeared from the local newspaper in 1913 and 1914, although the high school fielded its first team in "several years" in 1913. The "boys and girls" of Butler County's normal school also organized teams. There was talk of a Southern Kansas Baseball League in April, but nothing came from these conversations. The 1914 town team did not start organizing until late June.[5]

A notable player from this era was David Beals Becker, who was born in El Dorado in 1886. He played on several outstanding professional teams, three of which went to the World Series, and two others were ranked among the best teams of the first 100 years of the organized minor leagues. Becker played on four minor league teams during 1904–1908, including two years (1906–1907) with the Wichita Jobbers of the Western Association (Class C), where he pitched and played in the outfield. Becker hit .308 during his first year in Wichita and .310 the following year, tops in the league. As a left-handed pitcher for the Jobbers, he was 25–15 in 1906 and 5–5 in 1907. The 1907 Jobbers were ranked number forty-one on the list of the top 100 minor league teams of the twentieth century, compiling a record of 98–35 (.737). Advancing to the major leagues in 1908–1915, Becker played in the outfield for the Pittsburgh Pirates, Boston Doves (now the Atlanta Braves), New York Giants (now the San Francisco Giants), Cincinnati Reds, and Philadelphia Phillies. During his eight major league seasons, he had a lifetime batting average of .276 (763 hits). He played in two World Series with the Giants (1911 and 1912) and one with the Phillies (1915), but all three teams lost. After leaving the major leagues, Becker played for the Kansas City Blues of the American Association (Class AA) during 1916–1919 and 1922–1924, where he batted over .300 every year but one. The 1923 Blues were ranked number eighteen among the 100 best minor league teams, posting a record of 112–54 (.675). Every player in the starting lineup batted over .300 for the season (Becker hit .301). Becker closed his baseball career in the Pacific Coast League (Class AA) with teams in Sacramento, Seattle, and Vernon in 1924–1925. He died in Huntington Park, California, in 1943 at only fifty-seven years of age.[6]

As the First World War entered its second year in 1915, with the United States still officially neutral, El Dorado businessmen organized a twilight league. During its first year the league featured six teams of local amateur players that played seven-inning games at the fairgrounds. Initially, each team was to play the other five teams twice, with a single game scheduled every Monday and Friday evening at 6:15, as the business day came to a close. In late May, shortly after the season had begun, the schedule was expanded with the addition of games on Wednesday evenings. Each team would now play the other teams three times through August. A 10¢ admission was charged, with 40 percent of the gate receipts going to the fairgrounds and 60 percent to the local band fund, minus the costs of balls and bats. The teams were named for various trades represented by their supporters—grocers (Can Chasers), soda fountain employees (Squirts), clothiers (Sheenies), courthouse officials (Grafters), printers (Spreaders), and miscellaneous professions not represented by the other team names (Orphans). Because the players were "business men, or men who hold responsible positions" playing for the benefit of the exercise and the city band, it was suggested that the spiking of a fielder by someone sliding into base be prohibited. The local newspaper applauded the league, offering the opinion that El Dorado was not "big enough to support a salaried team." The Orphans ultimately won the league championship and were to be awarded sterling silver watch fobs bearing the inscription "1915—El Dorado Twilight League." The fob was attached to a miniature baseball inscribed with the winning team's name. Nearly 6,500 fans attended league games through the summer.[7]

A popular anecdote within the story of the twilight league and its support of the local musicians involved Charley Clover, the league's official scorer, who provided detailed game summaries and box scores to the newspaper. At the end of the season, he compiled a complete summary of the batting, pitching, and fielding statistics for every player, which were also published in the newspaper (seventy-six players were registered at the opening of the season, and others joined later). Thanks to Clover, league officials, and the local newspaper, the El Dorado Twilight League was perhaps the best-organized and best-documented city league in Kansas during this period.[8] In 1897, when Charley was a boy, he lost both legs above the knees "to the cruel wheels of a Missouri Pacific train," yet he always "maintained a jovial, cheery disposition toward the world." He was also considered one of the best checker players in town. Showing their support for the league's dutiful scorekeeper and statistician, two picked teams played a benefit game in which all of the gate receipts were donated to a fund to help Charley buy a new pair of prosthetic legs, estimated to cost $250–$300 (equivalent to about $5,900–$7,000 in 2016). All of the gate receipts could be donated to the fund because the use of the fairgrounds was offered at no charge to the league. In addition, the owner of the Gem Theater, where Charley played piano in the days of silent movies, donated the entire receipts from one evening of entertainment to the fund, with members of the baseball league and others volunteering to fill positions such as ticket takers and ushers. The baseball game netted $57.60, suggesting a crowd of nearly 600 people (at 10¢ apiece). Proceeds from the standing-room-only crowd at the Gem Theater added $86.60. Though still short of the total amount necessary, the officers of the twilight league ordered the new legs for Charley, confident that the community would donate the remainder of the necessary funds. One of those subsequent donations came from engineers of the Missouri Pacific Railroad. A final benefit baseball game scheduled for early October between a team of league players and high school students was scheduled to raise the last $10 needed to complete the fund, and any extra money would be donated to the school. By then, Charley had already worn his new legs home from Kansas City, where he had traveled for a final fitting in August. The *Walnut Valley Times* reported,

> "I want to say something—to let the boys know how I appreciate what they are doing and how much it means to me—but I just can't find the words," Charley said Thursday. "Somehow or other it just makes me fill up when I think of it—my heart is so full I just can't talk." But the boys understand—and they're even happier than Charley over the way things have worked out. The folks who have boosted the game along have found in the work a pleasure even greater than Charley will feel when he walks on those new "pins."[9]

After the twilight league season ended that autumn, the Northwest Butler County Baseball League was organized. It included town teams from El Dorado, Potwin, Towanda, and Whitewater that were scheduled to play each other twice between September 17 and October 22. Informal teams of twilight league players had represented El Dorado as early as the July 4 weekend, when they played as part of the festivities at Latham. League all-stars also played against teams from Eureka, Florence, and Toronto during the summer. Despite the limited support for the 1912 semipro team and the subsequent success of the 1915 amateur twilight league, interest in intercity competition was still evident in El Dorado.[10]

In January 1916 the twilight league was reorganized with only four teams that played on Tuesdays and Saturdays from April to August. The four teams were the Orphans (later renamed the Champs), Giants (formerly the Spreaders), Tigers (Can Chasers), and Braves (Squirts). Missing was Charley Clover as scorekeeper. In January 1916 he accepted a job as the piano player for the Strand Theater in Arkansas City, and he moved there with his wife and in-laws. The league organizers sought a new site for a ballpark and arranged to lease land from William E. Stone on the south side of Central Avenue, one and a half blocks from Main Street.

The ballpark—referred to as Stone Park—was enclosed by a wooden fence eight feet tall and had a small grandstand (fifty feet long and twenty-five feet deep) facing to the south that could accommodate 350 fans. While arrangements were being made for the new ballpark in February, controversy was brewing as to how players should be assigned to the four teams. One manager attempted to sign the best players early, while others argued for competitive balance to enhance the success of the league—a familiar debate in sports even today. Balance among teams in any league was a problem that faced the always tenuous leagues across the state. As that argument faded, the league also forcefully rejected a proposal for El Dorado to field a team in a Sunday league with other towns.[11]

Support for the twilight league faded during the summer of 1916, and players began to miss games. Teams resorted to seeking substitute players from the grandstand to fill their rosters at the beginnings of games. At the same time, a new town team was organized. A major oil discovery in the autumn of 1915 led to an oil boom around El Dorado, so the new town team was named the Oilers. They played their home games at the fairgrounds on Sunday afternoons, when the teams of the twilight league were idle. One of the Oilers's first games was a Friday evening victory over a picked team of players from the twilight league at Stone Park. The Oilers played several games through October, drawing as many as 800 fans. In January 1917 the twilight league's run at Stone Park came to an end as they announced the sale of the grandstand and fence at the ballpark, with the materials to be removed from the property by late February.[12]

As the First World War loomed on the horizon for the United States in 1917, the El Dorado Oilers were again organized, with the fairgrounds serving as their home ballpark. They played intercity games through August. Baseball continued occasionally during 1918, although the Oilers played only a few games in May, and even these attempts to play were hampered by rain and a carnival that left the field in rough condition. Through the summer, recreational games were played among local teams. Some, such as the Empire and Gypsy teams, were associated with companies active in the local oil fields, which provided a substantial portion of the nation's oil production during the war. Benefit games for the Red Cross were also part of the summer fare. In September a composite team of players from the Empire teams in El Dorado and Bartlesville, Oklahoma, played against a team from Coffeyville that featured major leaguer Walter Johnson as the pitcher.[13]

After the war, intracity baseball returned to El Dorado in the form of a Civic League with teams sponsored by the Elks, Kiwanis, Lions, and Rotary Clubs, along with a Sunday School League sponsored by various churches. An American Legion team of ex-servicemen was also organized, and African American teams were active, occasionally playing white teams in the region. The principal baseball ground in El Dorado was at Wonderland Park on Fourth Avenue east of Vine Street, at the site of the old fairgrounds.[14] However, it was the company teams that dominated baseball in El Dorado and the surrounding oil fields through the 1930s. Kansas Gas and Electric Company, Gypsy Oil Company, Midland Refining Company, Phillips Petroleum Company, Demo-Collins Produce Company, and the Empire Gas and Fuel Company (in the company towns of Oil Hill and Midian) were some of the employers who supported teams that played among themselves and against teams from other cities, including Wichita. Ballgames in El Dorado were often played at Wonderland Park, while the oil field teams near El Dorado had their own ballparks. The Oil Hill team often played two games on weekday evenings and one game on Sunday afternoons. Company support meant it was possible to welcome fans to weekday games at no charge. Most of the competition was friendly, and players occasionally played for other local teams when their team was idle. However, the competition in 1919 between Oil Hill and Midian was serious.[15]

The communities of Oil Hill and Midian were built to provide housing and other services for workers in the booming oil fields around El Dorado. Both are now gone, but they once were small towns of a few thousand people each. The employer of these workers and the owner of these towns, Empire Gas and Fuel Company, sponsored baseball teams and even recruited quality baseball players to work in the oil field (when they were not busy playing baseball). In 1919 all but three of the players on the team from Oil Hill reportedly had experience in the major or minor leagues, and Midian had an equally strong team. The Oil Hill team even split two games that summer with the Western League team (Class A) from Wichita, each team winning a close game on their home field. As a consequence, the two company towns dominated the local baseball circuit and developed a strong rivalry. By late July Oil Hill and Midian had compiled records of 36–3 and 33–5, respectively, including a few games against each other during June. To settle the question as to who was the top team—and to claim a $500 prize—they agreed to play a best-of-seven series, with games scattered from late July through early September. Between their games, they continued to play other teams. There was almost certainly substantial betting by their respective supporters.[16]

Midian won the first contest 5–4 at its home field on July 27, but Oil Hill evened the series on August 1 with a 9–1 victory on their home ground. "Considerable rag-chewing marred the pastime," and it would only increase. Midian came back with a 2–1 victory on August 3 in a third game at Oil Hill. The two teams took a short break from their series, during which Oil Hill split a pair of games with the Empire team in Bartlesville, Oklahoma. Midian filled the break by defeating a company team from Wichita. The series resumed on August 14, as Midian again traveled to Oil Hill and won decisively, 10–2, for a commanding 3–1 series lead. However, Oil Hill came back on August 17 with an 11–4 victory at home that was "full of disputed plays." A week later, Oil Hill again won 7–1 to force a game seven. As the competition increased, Oil Hill had "followed the example that Midian set by importing" pitcher J. Frank "Lefty" Graham, who had played that year for the Kansas City Blues and the Louisville Colonels in the American Association (Class AA).[17]

Another short break in the series was filled with a victory by Midian over the visiting Empire team from Bartlesville and a set of three games between Oil Hill and Bartlesville. Oil Hill won all three games, but the third game was marred by a fight between Oil Hill's center fielder and a substitute catcher for Bartlesville borrowed from Midian. Then came the seventh and deciding game in the Oil Hill–Midian series on September 7. For this game, Midian imported right fielder Casey Stengel, a native of Kansas City, Missouri, who played in the major leagues from 1912 through 1925. He would later be inducted into the National Baseball Hall of Fame as a manager, having served in that role in the major leagues for twenty-five years, including seven World Series championships with the New York Yankees from 1949 through 1960. In 1919 Stengel was available to play for Midian because in August he had chosen not to report to the Philadelphia Phillies after being traded by the Pittsburgh Pirates. As befitting a contest between two closely matched rivals, Midian won the seventh game 1–0 on a disputed play. Oil Hill protested the call at the plate that accounted for the only run of the game, claiming that the Midian player missed the plate when he slid to avoid the tag and then went back to touch it—an admission of guilt, in their view. The score stood, however. The extensive game summary in an El Dorado newspaper spilled from page one to a second page. The conclusion of the series was the sporting event of the season, yet Oil Hill did not consider the series to be concluded. They filed a formal protest concerning the disputed call at the plate, asking for another game, but it was to no avail. Even that did not end the wrangling between the two teams, though. At the end of September Midian sued Oil Hill, claiming that they did not receive their share of a fifty-fifty split of gate receipts from the five games played at Oil Hill promised as part of a verbal agreement.[18]

The rivalry between Oil Hill and Midian continued in 1920, but this time Oil Hill won the fifth game of a five-game series to claim the oil field championship. The following year a City Baseball League was proposed, which would include teams sponsored by the American Legion, Carter Oil Company, Midian Refining Company, and Oil Hill Baseball Club, but nothing came of this effort. The teams did play each other through the summer, however, and Oil Hill again claimed the oil field championship after defeating Carter Oil Company. Wonderland Park was still in use periodically by teams such as the American Legion and Carter Oil. During that decade there was a rising team sponsored by the Skelly Oil Company refinery in El Dorado that would eventually offer competition for Oil Hill and the other company teams. Baseball in this competitive environment was more lucrative than in most small cities. In 1921 pitcher Clifford Jackson was lured to Butler County to play for Oil Hill. He also played for Midian and Skelly Oil through the early 1930s and turned down an offer to pitch in the Pittsburgh Pirates organization because he could earn more money playing for the company teams around El Dorado. Sunday school, civic, and twilight leagues were also organized periodically during the 1920s and 1930s.[19]

While these local leagues continued to play among themselves, other teams looked further afield for competition. In 1926 Oil Hill joined the newly organized Independent Baseball League with teams from Augusta, McPherson, Newton, Wellington, and Wichita. Oil Hill played reasonably well in the league but was not a dominant team. Meanwhile, the Skelly Oilers played in the El Dorado Twilight League, supplementing their schedule with several games against teams outside the league, including Oil Hill. Skelly won the vast majority of their games, but they lost to the Kansas City Monarchs 8–1 at Wonderland Park in front of more than 1,300 spectators. Also in 1926, an El Dorado team of high-school-age players won the first Kansas State Tournament sponsored by American Legion

Baseball. The Legion Post 81 Wildcats were an all-star team picked from teams playing in the local junior summer league, which included teams in El Dorado, Leon, Midian, Oil Hill, Rosalia, and Towanda. Games in El Dorado were played at Wonderland Park, where the Wildcats defeated Independence twice in the state's southern regional championship and defeated Hays twice to claim the state championship. Traveling to the Western Sectional tournament in Sioux Falls, South Dakota, they defeated Crosby, Minnesota, and Beresford, South Dakota, to advance to the Legion World Series held at Shibe Park, home of the Philadelphia Athletics. The other three teams in the tournament were Pocatello (Idaho), Springfield (Illinois), and Yonkers (New York). The Wildcats' streak came to an end, as they lost their only two games to Pocatello and Yonkers.[20]

Oil Hill returned to the Independent Baseball League in 1927 and 1928, where they were joined by Skelly Oil. The core of the league included teams from Augusta, El Dorado (Skelly Oil), Newton, Oil Hill, and Wichita, with Winfield participating in 1927 and Arkansas City in 1928. Newton withdrew from the league in August 1928. During that second year Wichita won the first half of the season and Skelly Oil the second half, but Wichita took the first two games of the three-game championship series to claim the title. Meanwhile, Midian played in the Butler County Baseball League. In addition to playing baseball, the Oil Hill baseball team defeated the Wichita Sunflower Girls (with a male battery) 10–3 in a softball game in 1929.[21]

Oil Hill, Midian, and Skelly Oil continued to play into the 1930s. These three teams and others from El Dorado occasionally entered the state semipro tournament in Wichita. In addition, Skelly Oil and Oil Hill were back in the Kansas Independent League in 1932, this time with teams from Arkansas City, Augusta, Florence, and Winfield, plus two teams from Wichita. The Skelly Oil team also continued to host the Kansas City Monarchs and other barnstorming teams. For a few games in 1932 Jesse Barnes pitched and played in the field for Skelly Oil. He was raised in northeastern Kansas and was the brother of major league pitcher Virgil "Zeke" Barnes. Like his sibling, Jess had pitched in the major leagues, hurling for the Boston Braves (now the Atlanta Braves), New York Giants (now the San Francisco Giants), and Brooklyn Robins (now the Los Angeles Dodgers) in 1915–1927. Nearly a decade after his stint with Skelly Oil in 1932, Jess returned to El Dorado in 1941 to manage the Skelly Oil team. He also joined the local police department in 1942, retiring in 1955. Jess moved to California in 1958 and died in 1961 of a heart attack in Santa Rosa, New Mexico, while traveling between Kansas and California. Joining the company teams around El Dorado from 1933 through 1935 was a team in the Kansas Ban Johnson League, which also had a connection to the oil companies. The Cities Service Colts represented El Dorado but played on the diamond at Oil Hill. The Colts struggled against other Ban Johnson teams, but were good enough to claim the county championship in a 1933 tournament. Perhaps feeling their oats the following summer, the Colts entered the state tournament in Wichita in 1934. In addition, the Colts, Oil Hill, and Skelly Oil vied for local bragging rights. In 1932 Skelly Oil lost a five-game series against Oil Hill and placed second in the local 1933 tournament, but they finally came out on top in the second annual Butler County Baseball Tournament in 1934. The following year the Cities Service Colts reclaimed the county championship in a five-game series, defeating an El Dorado team known as the Skelly Tagolenes (named for a brand of motor oil). The competition expanded in 1936, when the Skelly Oilers defeated the Skelly Tags for the championship of a Tri-County Baseball Tournament.[22]

During this time the Skelly Oilers continued to enter the state tournament in Wichita. In 1937 they claimed fourth place, despite injuries leaving them with only eleven players. Following the tournament, the Oilers continued to play a variety of teams. In August they defeated the Giant Collegians, an African American team from Mississippi, 14–13. Skelly was down one run in the ninth inning with a man on base when the next batter hit the ball "into the weeds in left field. Before the Giants could find the ball," both runners had scored. Later that month, Skelly defeated the Kansas City Booster Girls baseball team, with three male players—pitcher, catcher, and center fielder. Their pitcher was allowed to use an emery board to alter the baseball, which partly explains why nineteen Oilers struck out. In addition to their six regular female players, Helen Ralston of El Dorado played three innings for the Booster Girls. In 1938 the Skelly Oilers were members of the Kansas Semi-Pro League with Arkansas City, Emporia, Larned, Neodesha, and the Wichita Water baseball team, although Arkansas City later dropped out. No league games were scheduled between July 3 and 24 so the teams could enter the state semipro tournament in Wichita. The league was reorganized in 1939, with teams from Augusta, Colwich, El Dorado (Skelly Oilers), Emporia, Eureka, Neodesha, Wellington, and the Wichita All-Steel team, but Neodesha and Wellington later withdrew.[23]

In 1940, as war raged in Western Europe, a concerted effort was made to support baseball in El Dorado and Butler County through the organization of the Baseball and Softball Association. The group's plans included building the best baseball plant in Kansas and "trying to bring the national pastime back to its former standing in the community." The Skelly Oilers were renamed the El Dorado Oilers, and a second nine—playing for Stephens Auto Supply—was a member of the Central Kansas League. In addition, the association supported the Butler County Junior Baseball League, a church league, a city softball league, and an official Knot Hole Gang for young boys and girls, who received membership cards for free admission to ballgames. The Oilers finished in third place at the state tournament during July and were invited to the national semipro tournament in August, where they did not fare as well. The association's efforts continued through 1941, until the world of baseball and life in general changed dramatically in the United States.[24]

To support the variety of teams playing baseball in El Dorado, a new baseball park was constructed in 1940 as a Work Projects Administration (WPA) project. Babe Goff, manager of a local auto parts dealer and president of the Baseball and Softball Association, proposed that the new facility be constructed on land owned by the Missouri Pacific Railroad east of Griffith Street, south of the old fairgrounds (Wonderland Park). The railroad transferred the land to the city, and Goff lobbied the WPA to assist local volunteers with construction. Work initially focused on the playing fields and lights, beginning in March. To illuminate the field, 100 floodlights of 1,500 watts each were ordered. Where only single games had been possible each evening, the local leagues would now be able to play doubleheaders, making the new baseball facility a busy place most summer days as it accommodated the large number of teams. The baseball plant actually consisted of two fields—diamond 1 "inside the park" and diamond 2 "at the southeast corner of the park." Taking advantage of local expertise, Cities Service Company (now CITGO Petroleum) donated steel oil derricks to be used as poles for lights, and employees of Kansas Gas and Electric (now Westar Energy) installed the wiring. Local retailers provided other materials at cost. Financial support for the project came from local oil companies, banks, and donation cans placed around town. Construction on the grandstand did not begin until May, and it continued through the autumn. The grandstand eventually consisted of six sections of concrete seats forming an arc behind home plate. The first two sec-

Exterior of the concrete grandstand, built in 1940, at McDonald Stadium in El Dorado (2014). From the author's personal collection.

Seating in the grandstand, built in 1940, at McDonald Stadium in El Dorado (2014). The grandstand is unusual in that concrete also forms the roof. From the author's personal collection.

tions completed for the new grandstand were not opened to spectators until August 14, but the new baseball plant was dedicated in May with a doubleheader featuring the city's top two teams. Stephens Auto Supply played Augusta in the first game, and the score was tied when the game was stopped so the dedication ceremonies between the games could proceed. Following speeches and music provided by the El Dorado Band, the Stearman Aircraft team from Wichita defeated the Oilers in the nightcap. Even though the facility remained a work in progress through the season, an estimated 2,000 fans watched an Oilers game on July 4—"1,500 inside the park and 500 outside." The total cost of the stadium was $26,000 (equivalent to about $440,000 in 2016).[25]

In 1941 the main ballpark became known as Central Park Stadium, derived from the name given to the city park where the stadium is located. It began serving as the home field of El Dorado High School and American Legion baseball teams in the 1940s, when James McDonald organized a summer recreational program for local youths in 1943 and restarted baseball at the high school, serving as the head coach from 1944 to 1969. On July 27, 1972, the stadium was renamed for McDonald.[26] In the 1950s the minor league Wichita Indians of the Western League (Class A) played "home" games at Central Park Stadium during July and August as the National Baseball Congress state and national tournaments were conducted.[27] The baseball team at Butler County Community College also plays home games at the ballpark during the school year. In the summer, McDonald Stadium is now the home of the El Dorado Broncos (Jayhawk Collegiate Baseball League), who moved to El Dorado in 1996 from Hutchinson (1971–1984) by way of Wichita (1985–1995).

The grandstand at McDonald Stadium is unique among those in Kansas in that the concrete extends through the roof and its supports. In addition, the seating area is elevated fourteen steps above the playing field, making the front row of seats among the highest in the state. The infield grass was replaced with synthetic turf in 2012–2013, but the outfield fence consists of the traditional vertical planks painted green on the sides facing the field. The El Dorado Baseball Hall of Fame and Museum is housed in a newer building adjacent to the grandstand entrance.

CHAPTER 17

Larks Park, Hays

Hays City was founded in 1867, the same year Fort Hays was relocated to the south side of Big Creek. In November 1869 a Junction City newspaper reported, "Hays City has a base ball club. They played their first game on the 23d, beating the 'Eureka' club of the fort." Other reports from Hays for November 23 simply claimed that a "base ball club was organized to-day by Messrs. Ainslee and Keene, of the R. R. Company[,] Mr. Forshee, telegraph operator, and Tom Reilly, the Kansas Giant. They challenge to beat the Wagners [sic] of the Fort to-day." However, reports that a town team had been formed in Hays were quickly denied by J. M. Forshee, who wrote that it was "a false report, and has no foundation in fact."[1] At the time, some people viewed baseball as an unacceptable activity for respectable citizens (such as telegraph operators) in a frontier town that desired parity with older towns to the east.

Games between teams at the fort and the city were played into the 1880s, sometimes using the fort's parade ground as a ball diamond.[2] In 1877 a team at the fort was organized as the Vance Base Ball Club, named for the commanding officer. The Hays City Base Ball Club was also organized that year. The first game between the two teams was played at the post on May 12. Seats were provided, as was unspecified "conveyance to and from the grounds" (perhaps the fort's ambulance, which was sometimes used to carry healthy passengers). A "large crowd" watched the Vance BBC triumph 27–16. A few days later the Hays City BBC won a rematch 56–41. That same month, the Vance BBC narrowly defeated a picked team of Pawnee Scouts 18–16. The Pawnee had served with Major

Frank North in the wars with the Cheyenne and Lakota, and they were on their way south from Nebraska to the Indian Territory (Oklahoma).[3] The following summer, post commander Lieutenant Colonel Richard Dodge of the Twenty-Third US Infantry, who was apparently concerned about the appearance of the post, ordered that "enlisted men are prohibited from walking on the grass of the parade ground except on duty. This order is not intended to interfere with ball playing; but the base must be changed each time of playing."[4]

The fort was decommissioned in November 1889, but in 1903 baseball games returned to the parade ground as students attending the Western Branch of the State Normal School initially held classes in buildings at the decommissioned post. The school is now named Fort Hays State University, in recognition of the earlier tenant.[5]

Baseball was also played at various sites around Hays. One area that was used frequently for baseball games and other activities was nestled within a bend of Big Creek near the "old bridge" connecting the city with the fort at the southern ends of Ash and Fort Streets. It was referred to as the "base ball grounds south of town" or "Bussard's pasture south of town." The virtues of this area were touted on a poster announcing the first annual fair of the Western Kansas Fair Association to be held in September 1883. "The fair grounds are pleasantly located, Big Creek running on three sides, affording plenty of shade and water." In addition to the various races, exhibitions, brass band, and military review of soldiers from Fort Hays (to be followed by a "magnificent sham battle"), the fair included a baseball tournament with a substantial premium of $100 to be awarded to the winning team.[6]

Beginning in 1916 this area was developed as the Golden Belt Fair Grounds, with multistory exhibit buildings, a horse barn, a half-mile racetrack, and a covered wooden grandstand 192 feet long. The site continued to be used for baseball during the summer.[7] However, the Golden Belt Fair Association held its last fair in 1929 and ceased operations in June 1931. The university purchased the grandstand and other buildings the following year at a sheriff's sale and used it as the site of a new football field and student housing. The land had been part of the former military reservation and was officially transferred to the school in May 1936. The racetrack's wooden grandstand was soon replaced by a pair of limestone and concrete grandstands on opposing sides of the gridiron, which were constructed as part of a Works Progress Administration (WPA) project from 1935 to 1939.[8]

Another early baseball field was about one-half mile northwest of the Golden Belt Fair Grounds. In 1903 an eighty-acre site on the north side of Big Creek "west of Charley Reeder's field" at the west end of Floyd Jones Street (now 7th Street) was selected by the Kansas Board of Regents as the new normal school campus. In 1904 the first limestone building was constructed (the central section of the Academic Building, which was later renamed Picken Hall). "[In the] back of the school building [in what is now the campus quadrangle] are the Baseball and football grounds already laid out with [a] grand stand already built. It belonged to the town club but [the] Normals will buy it." Grainy photographs of ballgames taken in about 1905 seem to show spectators filling a straight bleacher section of perhaps three rows with no roof. By April 1907 the bleacher was referred to as an unsightly "kindling pile" that needed to be replaced.[9]

In 1914, with the addition of more campus buildings, the athletic field moved a short distance to the south, where Forsyth Library and Malloy Hall now stand, and an uncovered bleacher was in place by about 1916.[10] Men's baseball at the school took a hiatus after the 1917 season, as the United States entered the First World War.[11] In March 1920, as the city of Hays was arranging the purchase of its first "motor fire truck," improvements were made at the college Athletic Field. A quarter-mile oval track was constructed around the football field, and the ball diamond was placed "northwest and southeast diagonally across the field."[12] The "Normal Tigers" played various town teams beginning in 1920, but baseball ended at the school after 1924 and did not return until 1966. With no baseball team, the football field was enclosed by a white wooden fence, which constrained the available playing area and effectively precluded its use for baseball.[13]

In addition to the college students, local men and boys also played organized baseball in Hays City on these early diamonds. As elsewhere, the top adult team was referred to as the first nine, and the team of the youngest players—"the little boys"—was the third nine. Two picked teams at the high school even scheduled a game for Christmas afternoon in 1903 at the normal school grounds, with the 10¢ admission to be used for the purchase of "dazzling" new uniforms for the Hays second nine—the Eagles. In the earliest years, the normal school played the town teams in Hays and

Studio photograph of the 1904 men's baseball team at the Western Branch of the Kansas State Normal School (now Fort Hays State University), paired with the record of that spring's games written on a chalkboard—seven wins, one loss, and a fifteen-inning tie that exceeded the hours of daylight and the chalkboard's width. Competition among early college teams was less structured than it is today, partly because of the difficulty in traveling during that period. Thus, college teams often played town teams, and all of the school's opponents listed here represented nearby towns. Courtesy of the University Archives, Forsyth Library, Fort Hays State University, Hays.

other towns, as well as the high school team. The first, second, and third nines in Hays also played teams from nearby towns, including the Smoky Hill Township in southwestern Ellis County, site of the short-lived town of Smoky Hill City. Smoky Hill City was the product of the gold boom scam of 1897–1903, in which profitable quantities of gold could reportedly be extracted from shale deposits along the Smoky Hill River. The town faded away after 1903, when even the most gullible investors finally accepted the truth of the scam.[14]

Unlike many towns in Kansas, especially the relatively larger county seats, virtually all of the teams representing the town, the college, and the high school in Hays were composed of white males. There were no teams of African Americans or Mexican Americans, and there were only intra-mural teams of girls at the schools. A rare exception was a 1917 baseball game in Hays between a team of girls from Hays (with a pitcher from Ellis) and a WaKeeney girls' team (as opposed to their "regular team") viewed by a "large crowd" that raised funds for the Red Cross. "There [were] some good plays made and the young ladies showed that the national game was not entirely a man's game."[15] Hays also differed from most of its peers in that the town team did not join a league until 1928—no minor leagues and no local amateur leagues. However, the city hosted a variety of traveling teams with players who were not white males.

In 1905 the American Indians of Haskell Institute traveled to Hays for a week. On Monday they defeated the normal school team 1–0 before a crowd estimated at 2,000 spectators (1,361 paid adult admissions). Five years later, the population of Hays had only grown to 1,961. On the following Friday, the Haskell team lost to the Hays town team 9–7 in front of more than 800 fans.[16] In the autumn of 1906 the National Bloomer Girls from Kansas City, Kansas, played the Hays town team. The bloomer girls' team was composed mostly of female players supplemented by a few male players ("toppers"). One of the toppers who played in Hays was a young Howard "Smoky Joe" Wood (listed as Woods in the Hays newspaper), who was a recent recruit from the nearby Ness City town team. He later was a standout pitcher for the Boston Red Sox (1908–1915). The Hays town team defeated the National Bloomer Girls 5–2.[17]

During the late 1920s Hays teams began to participate in organized leagues. In 1926 the Hays American Legion sponsored a team of local teenagers in the national program's first year. The Hays Legion team finished their inaugural season in second place in the state behind El Dorado.

The Hays American Legion continued to sponsor a team each summer, except during much of the Great Depression (1930–1934 and 1937–1939), Second World War (1941–1945), and the flood year of 1951.[18]

The first league for the Hays town team was the Two-County League organized in 1928 by teams from Ellis County and adjacent Rush County. Organizing a league was viewed "as the solution of the baseball problem when expensive independent teams are out of the question." Hays had been represented by a salaried team earlier in the decade. A county-level league was seen as a way to generate fan interest through local rivalries and reduce travel expenses. In addition, the league would reduce costs for the teams because they would be limited to using only local players, not "star" players hired "to give genuine competition to strong opposing teams." However, news of the league all but disappeared from the local newspaper after early June (Ellis was the eventual league champion). The following year a town team was not organized until late June, and it played independently. However, Hays joined other local leagues periodically through the 1930s and after the Second World War.[19]

During the 1920s and 1930s teams representing Hays played most of their home games on the athletic field of what is now Thomas More Prep–Marian High School, just north of the university. In newspaper accounts of the 1920s, the site was referred to as the "College grounds," a reference to the Hays Catholic College, which was founded in 1908 in a building across the street from Saint Joseph's Catholic Church. In 1931 a new, larger school was built just north of the athletic field and renamed Saint Joseph's College. In 1932 it became Saint Joseph's College and Military Academy, when a Reserve Officers' Training Corps (ROTC) program was added. Consequently, the baseball field was often referred to as some variation of Saint Joseph's College Field or Saint Joseph's Academy Field in the 1930s.[20] (The school is now Thomas More Prep–Marian High School.) In 1932 and 1933 a second nine, the Saint Joseph's Alumni, represented Hays in the Central Kansas League, which included Russell and several smaller towns, while the first nine continued to play independently.[21]

Although the Catholic College ground was the primary ball field for two decades, other sites were occasionally used. The athletic field at the state college was used until it became unavailable in 1923, and a few games were still played at the fairgrounds during the 1920s, until that site was transformed into the Lewis Field football stadium. In 1932–1933, while the Saint Joseph's Alumni team used their alma mater's grounds, the Hays first nine had a ball diamond "just west of town" on US Highway 40 (8th Street). In 1939 the Hays first nine also played a few games against teams such as Russell, Larned, and the Coors Brewers of Golden, Colorado, at the Timken Park diamond, sometimes referred to as Tournament Park. The small town of Timken, which had its own team, is about thirty miles southeast of Hays (and about thirty-five miles southwest of Russell and twenty miles northwest of Larned).[22]

Through most of its early history, the independent baseball team representing Hays against outside competitors lacked a chosen name. In 1928 a local newspaper seems to have christened the town team as the Hays Fencebusters. Otherwise, the Hays City Base Ball Club of the 1870s simply became the Hays town team most years. In 1921–1922 and again in 1933 the Hays Veterans of Foreign Wars sponsored the team, as did the Central Kansas Power Company (now Midwest Energy) in 1931. It was not until after the Second World War that the town team finally received a perennial name, when it was christened the Hays Larks in May 1946 as part of a contest. The winning contestant received a season's pass to that summer's games.[23]

Hays continued to host a variety of traveling teams during the 1920s and 1930s. In 1926 (prior to the military being racially integrated), the Hays town team played a game against the African American baseball team from the Ninth US Cavalry stationed at Fort Riley, Kansas. Down 7–1 after seven innings, the Ninth Cavalry scored four runs in each of the last two innings to win the game 9–7.[24] In 1933 and 1934 Hays hosted a House of David barnstorming team, losing both times, 9–7 and 13–8, respectively. In the 1933 game, former major leaguer Grover Cleveland Alexander pitched the first two innings, and Mildred "Babe" Didrikson pitched the first inning of the 1934 game.[25]

The famed Kansas City Monarchs also barnstormed through northwestern Kansas prior to the Second World War, including a stop in Hays in September 1929 for a game at the Golden Belt Fair Grounds. By a score of 11–1, the Monarchs defeated an area "all-star" team with a pitcher and catcher from the Hays town team. The star pitcher of the Monarchs at the time was Wilber "Bullet" Rogan. He was one of the best pitchers and hitters of his time—and beyond—earning him a place in the National Baseball Hall of Fame. However, it was one of the Coopers (either Alfred "Army" Cooper or Andy Cooper) who pitched to catcher Frank Duncan that day in Hays.[26] The Kansas City Monarchs also played in Hays on

September 9, 1947, defeating the Hays Larks 7–3, with Satchel Paige pitching the first three innings for the Monarchs. After 1955 the Monarchs moved to Michigan and continued to barnstorm through rural communities, including Hays, where they played either the Larks or another barnstorming team into the 1960s. In Hays and elsewhere, Paige always drew crowds of fans.[27] An unconfirmed connection between Hays and Paige was based on the claim that he and Lahoma Jean Brown "ran over to Hays," about 270 miles west of Kansas City, on October 12 or 13, 1947, to be married in a civil ceremony (he said it was October 12; she said it was October 13). He was headed west to barnstorm against Bob Feller's all-star team and did not want to be separated from her for two months. Attempts to find evidence supporting this story have been unsuccessful, although the marriage license could have been obtained elsewhere. It is also possible he invented the story to protect their privacy.[28] October 12 seems an unlikely date for a civil ceremony. On October 6, President Harry S. Truman proclaimed October 12, 1947—a Sunday—to be the first Columbus Day.[29] Thus, Lahoma's recollection of October 13 seems more likely. The site of Paige's nuptials remains one of baseball's historical mysteries.

A more tangible connection shared by Hays and the Kansas City Monarchs occurred in 1940. After playing most of the 1920s and 1930s at the "College grounds," the Hays town team again had its own ballpark in 1940. A permanent baseball ground had been planned for what is now Frontier Park, a city park, since it was established in March 1905 as the Fort Hays State Park.[30] Thirty-five years later, that ballpark was finally constructed as a joint venture between the Work Projects Administration (WPA) and the city of Hays, beginning in February 1940 with the scraping of the ground. The outfield was eventually sodded, but the infield remained all dirt.[31] The first games were played on the field that spring, while construction of the grandstand was still under way. The light fixtures (but not the poles) were purchased from the Kansas City Monarchs.

In early 1930 the Monarchs' owners, J. L. Wilkinson and Thomas Y. Baird, purchased a system of portable lights on telescoping poles mounted to flatbed trucks and powered by a noisy portable generator. The lighting system cost an estimated $50,000–$100,000 (equivalent to about $710,000–$1,420,000 in 2016). Each pole held a set of floodlights forty-five to fifty feet above the field. Typically, trucks were stationed along each foul line and behind home plate, although lights were sometimes placed above a grandstand. The generator sat behind the center field fence, connected to the light trucks by cables that ran across the outfield, presenting a minor obstacle to players. To aid the depth perception of the hitters, a white canvas fence six feet tall was placed just inside the regular fence around the outfield. Most ballparks did not have lights in the 1930s; thus, the Monarchs used their portable lighting system at league games, both home and away, and at barnstorming games. In many towns these games were the first to be played under lights. The Monarchs left the Negro National League after the 1930 season, becoming a strictly barnstorming team, traveling with their lights, until joining the Negro American League in 1937. Although the initial cost was high, use of the portable lights increased attendance at games and helped the Monarchs survive financially during the Great Depression.[32]

The lights that Hays purchased from the Monarchs in 1940 were mounted on eight poles seventy feet tall and two poles sixty feet tall, and were installed during May and June. The sixty bulbs were 1,500 watts each (a total of 90,000 watts). The first night baseball game at Larks Park was played on Wednesday, June 26, 1940, as construction continued on the grandstand.[33] The seating and other external features of the grandstand were completed in August 1940, but additional work remained on the concession stands, showers, and dressing rooms under the grandstand, as did construction of dugouts and sodding of the outfield. The formal dedication of the completed ballpark preceded the "official opening contest" of the 1941 season on May 25. However, several of the team's starters who had played on the ball field in 1940 had begun military training and were unable to play during the official dedication.[34]

Although it was built specifically for a baseball field, the grandstand behind home plate is straight rather than curved toward the baselines, making it unique among the historical grandstands in Kansas. The fields at the other straight grandstands were also used for horse races or football games. The Hays grandstand was constructed of concrete faced with native limestone in six sections. It never had a roof. With lights installed during its first year, many games were anticipated to be played at night, when spectators would not need protection from the afternoon sun, and omitting a roof lowered the construction cost. The grandstand was estimated to seat 800 spectators on wooden planks mounted on each of the thirteen tiers of concrete.[35] The original wooden seats have been replaced with metal benches, and seatbacks are now attached to the benches in most of the central third of the grandstand.[36]

Early photograph of the concrete and limestone grandstand, built in 1940, at Larks Park in Hays. Whether any of the lights purchased from the Kansas City Monarchs are among those above the grandstand is unknown. Courtesy of Pete Felten, Hays.

The first outfield fence was constructed in late July 1940, of wood six and a half feet high and painted green. The city had underestimated the cost of constructing the ballpark, requiring the sale of bonds in July 1940 for $3,500 (equivalent to about $59,000 in 2016). This matching money was needed to receive the full allotment of WPA funds available to complete the work (minus $300 designated for a bandshell elsewhere in the city park). However, the city still lacked funds to pay for a fence around the ballpark, which would limit access to fans paying admission (25¢ plus tax in 1940 for a regular game featuring the town team).[37] The American Legion stepped in to construct the outfield fence and was granted the right to sell space for advertising signs on the fence to local businesses at $30 per year for up to five years, unless the city built a "suitable fence" and returned the original lumber to the Legion. The initial outfield distances from home plate were 320 feet down each line and an imposing 440 feet to center field.[38] The current distances down the lines are similar (322 feet in left field and 319 feet in right field), but the distance in center field is a more reasonable 405 feet.

At first, the baseball field was called the Hays Baseball Park or Hays Ball

Field at Larks Park in Hays viewed from the top of the concrete and limestone grandstand (2016).
The seatbacks fill only the central third of the seating area. From the author's personal collection.

Park, but the name slowly transitioned to Larks Park during the 1960s. During its first year the ballpark hosted both baseball and softball games. In addition to the independent Hays town team, there was an Ellis County League, with baseball teams from Emmeram, Gorham, Hyacinth, Munjor, Severin, Toulon, Victoria, and Walker. Area businesses also supported several softball teams. During the Second World War, Hays continued to support a town team, although only a few games were scheduled. In the final part of the war, they shared the ballpark with the team from Walker Army Air Field, about fifteen miles east of Hays. The Hays and Walker teams played each other as well as teams from other army airfields in Kansas.[39]

Periodic repairs and renovations have been made at Larks Park, with some projects being repeated every decade or two. However, the grandstand remains essentially the same as when it was originally built. The chain-link fence behind home plate was replaced with the fiber netting now widely used at ballparks. Unfortunately, the color of the concrete seating area and press box was changed from traditional green to a light gray. The current fence in the outfield and down the foul lines consists of sheets of wood painted dark green, eight feet high in the outfield and four feet high along the foul lines. The mature trees of the city park along Big Creek beyond the outfield fence extend this vertical green backdrop. In 1991 the first synthetic turf was installed on the infield, and it was replaced in 2003 and again in 2013, but the outfield is still natural grass. In 1997 an irrigation system was installed to allow the use of effluent water on the outfield in this semiarid region of the country.[40] The lights have been replaced twice since 1940.[41] Attempts to determine the fate of the original light fixtures purchased from the Kansas City Monarchs after they were removed have been unsuccessful.

The city still owns Larks Park, but it is operated under a multiyear lease by the athletic department at Fort Hays State University, which restarted its baseball program in 1966 and plays there during the academic year. The local American Legion teams also have used the ballpark during the summer. The senior Legion team is named the Eagles, the name of the city's second nine in 1903. The town team transitioned to a collegiate summer league team in the 1970s but retained the name Hays Larks, and they continue to be the primary tenant during the summer. Thus, from the town team's christening in 1946 through the transition to a collegiate summer league team, the Hays Larks have represented the city under that name for over seventy years, which is exceptional in the state.

Epilogue

History is part of baseball's soul, whether that history was last month, last year, or last century. The statistics, the records, and the predictions are all based on elements of the sport's history. Exploring the early history of baseball in Kansas and the ballparks built by communities for their teams more than seventy-five years ago raises different sorts of historical questions. How long will these stadiums remain in use? Is there any value in conserving these old baseball parks and their grandstands?

In larger cities, historical buildings, including sports venues, can be the focus of neighborhood revitalization programs, serving as an anchor for other businesses and residential development. For example, Lawrence-Dumont Stadium might serve as an integral component of the Riverwalk area and the Delano District in Wichita. As worthy as this goal is, it has little relevance to the smaller towns in Kansas with historical baseball parks. However, in all of these cases, there are costs associated with the maintenance, renovation, or restoration of historical structures such as the old grandstands. Replacing them also comes with a substantial cost.

The cost of maintaining components of a baseball field other than the grandstand could be set aside for this discussion because they would be the same regardless of the seating available. However, the costs associated with upkeep of the grandstand, playing field, and other structures are typically viewed as part of a single budget item. The way in which maintenance costs for the grandstands are viewed can also be misleading because projects undertaken once every several years are often viewed in the context of a particular budget year rather than averaged over multiple years. In a long-term view, the costs of doing regular maintenance, before costly damage occurs, are likely to be less than the cost of demolishing and replacing a grandstand with a comparably sized structure, which will also require periodic maintenance or replacement. The fact that all of these grandstands are more than seventy-five years old and still in use speaks to the overall quality of the original construction. It also suggests that they have the potential to be in use for decades to come, with proper maintenance.

Of course, buildings that are more than seventy-five years old eventually require more substantial renovation or restoration, which might carry costs that would constitute a sizable portion of the funds available in smaller towns for community facilities and services. As used here, *renovation* refers to changes in the structure, such as upgrading locker rooms or constructing a new concession area. Restoration, on the other hand, might include projects such as repairing or replacing damaged stone, concrete, or wood in a manner that maintains the historical features of the structure. For restoration projects, listing a grandstand as a historical property provides opportunities to obtain grants and other financial assistance through public sources and private philanthropies. Even property owned by a local government, such as a city, is eligible for much of this assistance, which would be combined with matching local funds, not unlike the combinations of funding sources that were used to construct most of these grandstands during the Great Depression. A few funding sources even provide money for projects in small communities with limited financial resources that are able to offer "sweat equity" from volunteers. In addition, a designation of a ballpark as a historical property could enhance opportunities to obtain donations from local businesses or external foundations. A combination of grants, public funds, and private donations would be the ideal way for communities to undertake the necessary projects to care for their historical ballparks.

There are two lists of historical places in Kansas. The National Park Service administers the National Register of Historic Places, which generally includes properties at least fifty years old that retain their historical appearance and are historically or architecturally important at the state or national level. The equivalent list at the state level is the Register of Historic Kansas Places. The listed properties on the state list must meet the same criteria as those on the federal list, but they are judged from a state perspective. Getting on either list requires documentation and paperwork. When developing a nomination, guidance is available through the State Historic Preservation Office at the Kansas Historical Society, and funding from outside sources is sometimes available to assist with the planning. The process to register a property, if successful, can take six to twelve months, followed by additional time to develop funding opportunities, but the benefits potentially have a much longer life.[1]

Preserving the historical ballparks and their grandstands is important because it speaks to a community's view of itself. Many small towns that supported town teams a century ago are gone, other than a house or two and perhaps a few old foundations. This loss of towns in rural Kansas is not simply an event from decades ago. Even today, smaller communities passionately resist the loss of their schools, their government offices, and their businesses. As modern automobiles and highways "shorten" the distances between towns and the internet increasingly provides access to education, government services, shopping, and even social engagement among neighbors, do the historical structures associated with these aspects of a community still have value? I would argue that they do, especially if they include a variety of sites important to a community's identity, such as a courthouse, retail stores, houses of worship, and social venues, including baseball parks, because they provide important opportunities for the kind of social interaction that defines a community. These group activities contribute to unity, just as they did in Mexican communities of the early 1900s. Today the entire community in a small rural town is strengthened through these interactions.

As I traveled to towns throughout Kansas to learn about the state's early baseball history, one of the most frequent stories I heard was about the day that the Kansas City Monarchs, Satchel Paige, or both played in their town. And they played in many Kansas towns on their barnstorming tours. It is natural and healthy for people to seek these sorts of waypoints in their history. They might be notable events such as a ballgame, but a patch of ground or a historical structure is an even more powerful waypoint. In the history presented here, these old ballparks are reminders of the successes and pleasures in a community's past. Just as importantly, these old ballparks—these historical waypoints—also help us to contemplate the misfortunes imparted by segregation, so that we may be guided with fuller awareness of others as we move toward a more truly inclusive community, both as individuals and as a society. They allow us to take measure of how far we have come and how far we have to go. As mentioned in the acknowledgments, we are "standing on the shoulders of giants." All of the accomplishments of human society are founded on the work of our predecessors. Their successes and their failures have much to teach us. Historical sites, such as the ballparks described here, are valuable waypoints because they not only commemorate those who came before us, they invite us to share the experience as they did and to reflect on our present and future actions. It is about more than just a ballgame.

As mentioned in the opening paragraph of the prologue, I grew up on the interface of the old rural landscape and the new suburban sprawl during the latter half of the twentieth century. Watching a baseball game while seated in one of the old grandstands in a small Kansas town is a chance to cross a historical interface and experience what one aspect of life—local, town team baseball—was like in these earlier communities, to experience something in a way that is nearly identical to the experience they had decades ago in that same spot (assuming you put your cell phone away).

The continued use of these historical ballparks also reflects the pride residents feel for their community and its history. It expresses an appreciation for the earlier residents of the community who constructed these facilities more than seventy-five years ago, when their towns were still young and struggling to survive. They are a tangible reminder—a memorial—to the earlier residents, and yet they are much more. These historical structures are still used for their original purpose. They are living history, still contributing essential services to their communities. Most such structures have been lost, and the few that remain in a city, in a state, or in a country take on even more value as touchstones of our history whenever one is lost. Yet they are also part of our future. Just as these ballparks have provided the mix of stories summarized in this book—stories about who we were and how we have grown—we can scarcely imagine what stories are yet to unfold on these diamonds and in these grandstands. They are living history in which everyone is still welcome to participate and to contribute to our collective story yet to be written.

Appendix

Three ballparks in Kansas have grandstands that were constructed for baseball fans after the Second World War that are at least fifty years old. Brief histories of these ballparks, along with information about earlier ballparks in these towns, are highlighted here for those who enjoy visiting such sites. To include other baseball grounds that lack historical grandstands would require more time to document than available for this project, but their histories are no less noteworthy. I encourage others to record their stories. For example, Griffith Park in Manhattan is still used for ballgames at two small diamonds and is surrounded by the wall of native stone built in 1936, but the baseball grandstand is gone. Similarly, a portion of the red brick wall built in 1940 by the Work Projects Administration (WPA) is still in place at Jaycee Ballpark in Pittsburg. Humboldt's Walter Johnson Athletic Field was constructed in 1920 with the aid of native son Walter Johnson, who was one of the first five players voted into the National Baseball Hall of Fame. The athletic field is used for both baseball and football. It still retains a diamond and its wall of native stone built by the WPA in 1936. The original baseball seating is gone, but the stone and concrete grandstand for the football field forms an attractive backdrop beyond center field. In Paola, new life was given to the stone and concrete grandstand constructed in 1934 at a former football stadium by replacing the football field with a pair of small ball diamonds. The baseball grounds at Jones Field in Soden's Grove Park in Emporia and Hobart-Detter Field in Hutchinson's Cary Park have been in use since the 1920s, but the current grandstands are much newer. The history of baseball at other sites within Soden's Grove goes back to 1885.

Perhaps the oldest historical baseball ground in Kansas maintained as a public park is Huron Park in Kansas City, Kansas (bounded on the west and east by the Seventh Street Trafficway and Sixth Street, and on the north and south by Minnesota and Ann Avenues). In 1867 the Wyandott Base Ball Club moved their baseball ground "from the levee to the Huron place," a public square filling an entire city block that included the Huron Indian Cemetery (established in 1843; now the Wyandot National Burying Ground).[1] The southeastern portion of the block that once made up

Huron Place is now Huron Park, landscaped with trees, flowerbeds, and walkways, with an open grass lawn in the southeastern corner. Although it now lacks a diamond, a baseball could be tossed across a field of grass. In addition to the public park, the old cemetery sits in the northwestern portion of the block, and the main branch of the Kansas City Public Library occupies the north-central part of the block. A few other buildings dot the periphery of the block on the north and west.

Municipal Stadium, Hobbs Park, Lawrence

BASEBALL GROUNDS FIRST USED: 1947

GRANDSTAND BUILT: 1947

Lawrence was founded in 1854, but the first town teams were not organized until 1866 and 1867. Even so, they were among the first in the state. As in most towns, several sites were used for baseball games. The first baseball ground in the 1860s was near the northwestern corner of South Park, described in newspapers as "in front of the Blakely House, near the Park" and "at the corner of Vermont and Quincy [11th] streets."[2] Being so close to the growing core of the city, this site was soon converted to other uses. Two Lawrence baseball clubs—the University BBC and the Kaw Valley BBC—also scheduled a game at the Lawrence fairgrounds for July 4, 1867.[3]

The first long-term site used for ballparks in Lawrence was at the intersection of 14th and Massachusetts Streets. Originally known as the Kaw Valley baseball grounds, it was described as "south of the Park" (South Park) on Massachusetts Street, the main north–south street across Lawrence at the time. The property used for "the grounds at the south end of Massachusetts street" was owned by Charles F. Garrett at the corner of Adams Street, which is now 14th Street.[4] The grounds had been used by the ball club since 1867, when a set of games was scheduled between the Kaw Valleys and the Frontier BBC of Leavenworth. "Arrangements have been made for the convenience of spectators, and comfortable seats for such as walk to the ground. . . . Citizens are requested not to encroach upon the ground set aside for play."[5] Although people were likely to walk to the ball grounds, transportation to the ballpark for special games sometimes was provided from the Eldridge House (now the Eldridge Hotel) on north Massachusetts Street.[6] In 1870 seating was available for 250 spectators, although about 800 people attended the holiday game with the Nasby BBC of Ottawa. The ballpark had also been fenced that year so tickets could be sold for admission to the game.[7] The following year, there was "a covered amphitheater on the ground . . . which is capable of accommodating one hundred and fifty ladies."[8] Although the Kaw Valley BBC held a lease for the ground, other teams in Lawrence were allowed to use the ballpark with prior permission, including some of the town's early African American teams.[9] By 1877 the ballpark was referred to as "the old Kaw Valley grounds," although it continued to be used by various teams.[10] In August 1879 the Brass Alleys of Lawrence played a Clinton team on the "Kaw Valley grounds," and "a keg of beer [was] to be the stakes."[11]

In early August 1886 the site at 14th and Massachusetts Streets was revived as a developed baseball park when the Lawrence Athletic Association "leased the grounds on South Massachusetts street for five years at $120 per year. . . . The diamond will be in the northeast corner, with the grand stand back of home plate about ninety feet." On August 24, a newspaper reported that the "new ball park on South Massachusetts street is almost finished. The fence is completed and the [grand]stand has reached such a point that it will accommodate from five to eight hundred people."[12] A tall wooden fence surrounded the South Massachusetts Street Ballpark, and by the spring of 1892, "the shade trees along the south side of the ball park [were] being ruined by the gamins who witness the games from them."[13] In the autumn of 1892 the south fence at the ballpark was a point of contention between those who said it should be removed so that the dirt street adjacent to the park could be widened and those who said that no street had been officially designated ("when it was wet the road was abandoned because it was so bad"). City employees tore down the fence and widened the street by plowing inside of the former fence line. The city had no easement allowing them to widen the street, however, and a complaint was filed in court on behalf of the new property owner, Helen Welch. The city employees responsible for these actions were convicted and fined $10 plus costs, a verdict subsequently upheld in district court. Nonetheless, the south fence was again removed in September 1893 as the city continued to pursue the street issue by legal means.[14]

Following the city's loss in court regarding the initial removal of the fence and the attempt to widen the road, the city engineer was asked in April 1893 "to survey both Adams street [14th Street] and University avenue from Massachusetts street to Connecticut street. . . . This is in regard to the street along the ball ground which another effort will be made to widen."[15] On the 1902 plat map of Lawrence, the street running along the southern side of this property is labeled as Morris Street, not University Avenue. The map lists the landowner as H. M. Welch, which matches the owner mentioned in the 1892 accounts of the trial, Helen Welch.[16] This map places the South Massachusetts Street Ballpark between Massachusetts and New Hampshire Streets on the west and east, and 14th and 15th Streets on the north and south, with the grandstand and diamond in the northeastern corner (14th and New Hampshire Streets). The property was still an open field fourteen years later, when a "trained animal exhibition" performed two shows at the "Old Ball Park, 1400 Mass. St." in May 1907.[17] The property is now occupied by a school.

An interesting successor to the South Massachusetts Street Ballpark was constructed on the east side of town in 1910 within Woodland Park, a large amusement park that also featured activities such as concerts, dances, shows, carnival rides, and horse races.[18] The park was north of the eastern end of Lee Street (now 13th Street). During the park's first year an exhibition baseball game featured an American Indian team that traveled with its own bleachers, canvas fence, and acetylene lamps for playing after sundown.[19] The resident bleacher at the ballpark originally seated about 450 people but was extended by 200 seats during the first year, and in 1912 promises were made to expand it to 2,000.[20] Beginning in that year, Woodland Park changed hands several times as attempts were made to maintain it as a park open to the public.[21] Baseball was interrupted in Lawrence, as elsewhere, during the First World War, but teams continued to play occasionally at Woodland Park through the postwar years, although interest in town teams declined.[22] The park's famed roller coaster—the Daisy Dozer—had blown down during a windstorm in March 1916.[23] What remained of Woodland Park slowly faded from use beginning in the 1920s, and parts of the property were developed for houses. However, a portion of the old park is now within Brook Creek Park.

The "community ballpark" at Hobbs Park in Lawrence was dedicated on July 9, 1947. The evening's ceremonies included a parade of local baseball teams, a concert, a speech by the mayor, a three-inning exhibition game by local all-stars, and a nine-inning game between the Lawrence

Seating in the concrete grandstand, built in 1947, at Hobbs Park in Lawrence (2015). From the author's personal collection.

Junior Legionnaires and the Topeka Mosby-Macks. About 2,500 people attended the dedication. Unfortunately, Topeka defeated Lawrence 13–4.[24] The seven sections of the concrete grandstand form an arc behind home plate similar to the grandstand in El Dorado that was built in 1940 (minus El Dorado's concrete roof). As part of Lawrence's sesquicentennial in 2004, the East Lawrence Neighborhood Association commemorated the event with a mural depicting the city's history painted on the exterior of the grandstand.[25] The park was converted from baseball to softball in 1973, and the concrete dugouts, locker rooms, concession stand, and manual scoreboard were removed.[26] The original green wooden fence, six feet tall, was removed, and the current fence along the outfield and foul lines is chain-link. With the conversion to softball, the outfield distances were shortened to 285 feet.

Hibbs-Hooten Field,
Sellers Park, Wellington

BASEBALL GROUNDS FIRST USED: 1909

GRANDSTAND BUILT: 1964

Since the late 1800s baseball in Wellington has been played periodically on grounds in or near the present Sellers Park, which was the site of a manufactured gas plant in 1886–1894. The first site used for baseball in this area, at least as early as 1892, was immediately west of the gas plant at the corner of Harvey Avenue and A Street (now a residential area about one block west of the current ballpark).[27] In 1893 a new baseball ground was constructed on the north side of town in a pasture owned by Henry Bowers on the north side of 16th Street (now a residential area north of US Highway 160). That December, the local constable executed a sale of the grandstand and fence at the ballpark, but the structures were left standing and the ballpark continued to be used.[28]

In 1895 a new ballpark at the corner of Harvey Avenue and Elm Street was proposed, although it apparently was not built. However, the issue of moving the ballpark closer to the center of town resurfaced in May 1896, when the north ball grounds were said to be "too far out." Consequently, "the commons just west of the gas works on Harvey avenue and A street" were fixed up again as a baseball park used for several years. Just prior to a game in 1905, the grandstand at the ballpark collapsed. Fortunately, the most serious injuries were one woman with a broken rib, a man with a damaged knee, and a smashed automobile. At a game later that summer it was apparent that the Wellington Sluggers were not named for their fielding skills. "At one time, when a fly was knocked into right field, the Wellington team, with a few exceptions, gathered in the vicinity and it looked like they expected to hold some kind of convention. The base runner trotted around with no one to disturb him."[29]

In 1906 the name of the town team was changed from the Sluggers to the Greys, and they constructed a new baseball park in the Woodlawn Second Addition north of the old ballpark in Bowers' Pasture. The team thought that the new site, which was farther away from the heart of town, was outside the city limits and beyond the municipal ban on Sunday baseball. It was not. Ironically, the site of the old ballpark in Bowers' Pasture had not yet been included within the city limits, which would have made it possible to play a little closer to town on Sundays.[30]

In 1909–1911, Wellington hosted a minor league team in the Kansas State League (Class D) that played its games on private property leased for the "League base ball park," which occupied the present site of Hibbs-Hooten Field. However, the Dukes of Wellington moved to Wichita partway through the 1911 season, and the lumber from the grandstand and fence were offered for sale later that year. In 1913–1916 a portion of the property around the league ballpark, but not the ballpark itself, was developed as a municipal park.[31] Ballgames were played on a site just south of Ninth Street at the northern end of what was initially named Community Park.[32]

In 1919, Lulu Planz Sellers (Mrs. Fred Sellers), the unpaid Wellington Park Commissioner from 1915 to 1921, made arrangements to purchase the property used for ballgames in 1909–1911 so it could be added to the existing Community Park. This allowed the ballpark to return from the northern end of the park to its former location.[33] The field was restored in time for games that summer, and Sellers purchased the unused "old airdome building" so it could be dismantled, with the lumber used for the construction of a covered grandstand. (An airdome was a venue for summer theatrical events, with a covered stage and open seating.) In the meantime, the seats and backstop were moved from the diamond at the northern end of the park to the restored ballpark.[34] Improvements at the park were slowed somewhat in 1919 by limited funds, needed in part to purchase additional lumber, but work on the grandstand began the following spring.[35] In 1938 the city changed the name of Community Park to Lulu P. Sellers Park, usually shortened to Sellers Park, to commemorate her energetic and creative leadership as a volunteer working on behalf of the city's parks.[36]

The wooden grandstand at Community Park Stadium built in 1920 consisted of three sections, with the shorter sections on each end angled toward the base paths. The outside of the grandstand was encased by horizontal wooden planks, with a single entrance in the center flanked by two ticket windows. The sections in the center and along the first base line were covered with a roof, open on the outside just below the roofline for ventilation. The section along the third base line had no roof. There were twelve rows of seats in the open section facing third base. The first rows under the roofed sections consisted of box seats, which were auctioned at one of the games to help raise money to pay for construction of the grandstand.[37]

The ballpark fell into disrepair during the mid-1900s. The local school district held an easement on the property, and the track used by the high school extended onto the field, making the playing surface uneven. In the spring of 1963 voters easily passed a $35,000 bond issue (equivalent to about $275,000 in 2016) to pay for improvements at the ballpark. However, during the long process of approvals and architectural design through the summer, costs rose for repairing the field, removing the old grandstand, and constructing a new grandstand. Thus, additional money was transferred from improvement funds slated for use at Lake Wellington. The diamond was repaired in time for the 1964 baseball season, but the grandstand was not completed until later in the year. The original ballpark had been named Community Park Stadium but was usually referred to by the general park name, Sellers Park. In May 1964 a petition was presented to name the new baseball stadium after Louis "L. E." Hooten, a veteran of the First World War who had founded youth baseball in Wel-

Seating in the concrete grandstand, built in 1964, at Hibbs-Hooten Field in Wellington (2015). From the author's personal collection.

lington in 1951. The name of Hooten Field was later amended to Hibbs-Hooten Field to honor Loren Hibbs, who served as a "coach, fundraiser, groundskeeper," and other roles to keep the sport viable in Wellington.[38]

The grandstand currently in use, built in 1964, is a concrete arc of three sections, with wooden benches and a metal roof. The outfield wall is constructed of cement blocks. The unpainted blocks in left field are partially covered by vines, while the rest of the outfield wall is painted dark green. It is a short 294 feet down the right field line, 316 feet down the left field line, and 403 feet in center field. The ballpark is the summer home of the Wellington Heat (Jayhawk Collegiate Baseball League), who moved from Haysville, Kansas (2010–2012), after relocating from Lake Havasu, Arizona (1993–2009).

Light Capital Baseball Diamond, McPherson

BASEBALL GROUNDS FIRST USED: 1919

GRANDSTAND BUILT: 1966

As in many Kansas towns, baseball took a few years to become established in McPherson, and games were often played at the local fairgrounds, where seating was available at the racetrack. In the 1880s the grounds of the McPherson Fair Association were on the east side of North Main Street in what is now a commercial and residential area. At the time it was north of the city limits. In 1887 the city considered purchasing the site for a public park, but the property was sold in August to private owners and became Olympian Park, which retained its half-mile racetrack and baseball diamond. Baseball continued to be played at the park through 1889, but games were also played that year on a new ball ground at the corner of Elizabeth Street and Grand Avenue. It was sometimes referred to as Fisher Ball Park (it was in the Fisher Addition to the city).[39]

Although teams occasionally played games during the early 1890s, interest in baseball in McPherson waned, and in 1893 a nice crop of wheat was harvested from the old fairground. The following year a game was played between a white team and an African American team, and interest in baseball was said to be awakening in midsummer. That interest peaked in 1895, when McPherson fielded an independent professional team. Games were played on the 1889 ball ground "east of the city on Elizabeth street."[40] However, in the years after the 1895 professional team disbanded interest in town team baseball once again waned, and local players used several baseball grounds, including the "east ball ground" and the "old show grounds," none of which was a fully developed ballpark.[41]

Calls for a sports facility to include a racetrack and baseball diamond returned at the turn of the century. After the 1902 season it was decided that a new, enclosed ballpark with a grandstand was needed to prevent people from watching games at a distance to avoid paying admission, as was done at the existing ball grounds. In addition, it was anticipated that McPherson would join a Central Kansas League in 1903, although this did not happen.[42] New fairgrounds for the County Fair Association were finally constructed in 1905 on a tract of land that included the site currently occupied by the Light Capital Baseball Diamond, but the fairgrounds extended farther north from Blaine Street (now A Avenue) to Hancock Street, just southwest of the old "east ball ground" on Elizabeth Street.[43]

Through the years, baseball diamonds were built at various sites within the new fairgrounds. McPherson had again hoped to join a Central Kansas League in 1905, but that goal would be postponed another three years. Nonetheless, plans in 1905 included building a ball ground either inside the half-mile oval racetrack or on a five-acre extension of the fairgrounds property on the northwestern corner. When it came time to construct the ball diamond in 1906, it was not placed inside the oval racetrack on the east side of the property, although racetrack infields were often used for baseball fields. The racetrack grandstand built in August 1905 was 160 feet long and seated about 1,500 spectators. Plans at the ball diamond called for a smaller grandstand to replace temporary seats that had been installed for the first games in the spring of 1906. This initial baseball field at the new fairgrounds was at the eastern end of Skancke Street between Fisher Street and Grand Avenue (north of the present diamond).[44]

McPherson had a successful town team in 1907, and the Merry Macks finally joined the Central Kansas League (Class D) in 1908. The baseball grandstand was considered insufficient, so it was enlarged to increase its seating capacity to almost 600 spectators. The following year, the Macks joined the Kansas State League (Class D), and their fans were accommodated in a new grandstand constructed behind home plate on the north side of the ball ground. Its seating capacity was 500 spectators, and a bleacher of similar size extended from its western end. The Macks played in the Kansas State League through early July in 1911, when the league folded due to inadequate revenue. The baseball grandstand was later torn down and sold as secondhand lumber.[45]

The ballpark at the fairgrounds continued in use after the end of minor league baseball, but in 1913 a complaint was made that there was no place to play. The fairgrounds had become unavailable because they had been leased to others, but arrangements were later made to play there. Other games were played at the "oil tanks diamond" in the western part of town in 1914 and early 1915. In the spring of 1915 a new baseball diamond was constructed at the fairgrounds on a site just west of the former state league diamond. It was used by the McPherson City Base Ball League and other teams, but only for two years.[46]

In early 1917 the McPherson County Agricultural Fair Association arranged to auction fourteen acres at the northern end of the fairgrounds to help settle its debts. This included the area occupied by the former league

The concrete grandstand and press box (on top of the third base dugout), built in 1966, at Light Capital Baseball Diamond in McPherson (2014). From the author's personal collection.

ballpark and the 1915 diamond at the eastern end of Skancke Street. Consequently, a new ballpark was constructed to the south on a site immediately north of the racetrack at the fairgrounds.[47] The First World War interrupted most baseball through 1918, but the diamond at the fairgrounds was still in use. After the war, a County Base Ball League was formed, and league games were played at various sites around town.[48]

In the autumn of 1919 a new baseball diamond was laid out in front of the grandstand at the fairgrounds, and plans were made to develop a multi-sport athletic park, on which a football field would overlap the baseball field and be surrounded by a cinder track for races.[49] In 1921 the orientation of the diamond (from home plate to second base) was changed from east to southeast to reduce the evening "sun field" for the outfielders, and the old judge's stand at the racetrack was moved behind the plate to be used by scorekeepers. Fences were installed along each foul line to protect cars and to keep people from driving onto the playing field. A new scoreboard was also installed that displayed the names and positions of the players, as well as the score by innings.

The current grandstand centered behind home plate and facing northeast was constructed of concrete blocks in 1966.[50] It has a metal roof and seats. The press box sits atop the third base dugout rather than the top of the grandstand behind home plate. The infield and outfield are grass. The outfield fence is chain-link. In recent years, local college and American Legion teams have used Light Capital Baseball Diamond. The ballpark was purchased from the city by Central Christian College in 2015.

The city's nickname, Light Capital, is derived from the numerous lights on the smokestacks and other structures at the National Cooperative Refinery Association oil refinery in McPherson, established in 1932 as the Globe Oil Refinery. The refinery was noted for the basketball teams it sponsored (the McPherson Globe Refiners), including the team that won the gold medal at the 1936 Olympic Games in Munich, Germany.

Notes

INTRODUCTION: GROUND RULES

Prologue Epigraph: Traubel (1908) 1961.

1. Block 2005; Morris 2003, 2008; Thorn 2011; Wright 2000. Early rules of base-ball are available in *Beadle's Dime Base-Ball Player* (http://dimenovels.lib.niu.edu /islandora/object/dimenovels%3A262). The national Vintage Base Ball Association was organized in 1996 for teams that play by rules of the 1850s–1880s (http://vbba .org/). Several vintage baseball teams play in Kansas.

2. Morris 2003.

3. Tygiel 2000.

4. Dodger Stadium in Los Angeles, California, opened in 1962 and is the third-oldest Major League Baseball stadium currently in use. Angel Stadium in Anaheim, California, and the Oakland County Coliseum in Oakland, California, were also opened in the 1960s. Kauffman Stadium in Kansas City, Missouri, was opened in 1973 and would advance to the fifth-oldest stadium in the major leagues if the Oak-land A's move (again).

PART I. EARLY HISTORY OF BASEBALL IN KANSAS

Epigraph: Graham 1909.

CHAPTER 1. TOWN TEAMS AND THE EARLY GAME

1. *Emporia Kansas News,* 1 January 1859.

2. Block 2005.

3. *Lawrence Daily Kansas Tribune,* 1 June 1870, 10 June 1870.

4. *White Cloud Kansas Chief,* 31 May 1860.

5. *Topeka Tribune,* 4 January 1860.

6. *Topeka Tribune,* 28 April 1860.

7. *Wyandotte Commercial Gazette,* 18 August 1866, 8 December 1866, 12 January 1867, 16 February 1867, 18 May 1867, 28 December 1867, 12 September 1868, 14 August 1869.

8. *Wyandotte Commercial Gazette,* 15 June 1867 (advertisement), 13 July 1867.

9. *Wyandotte Commercial Gazette,* 18 May 1867, 17 August 1867, 9 November 1867, 23 November 1867.

10. *Junction City (Weekly) Union,* 30 September 1871.

11. *Topeka Daily Commonwealth,* 24 March 1874, 18 April 1874, 23 May 1874.

12. *Topeka Daily Commonwealth,* 9 July 1874.

13. *Saline County Journal,* 24 September 1874.

14. *Lawrence Republican Daily Journal,* 3 September 1875, 16 September 1875.

15. *Emporia Weekly News*, 14 May 1885, 13 August 1885, 29 April 1886, 27 May 1886, 1 July 1886.

16. *Topeka Daily Capital*, 11 May 1886, 11 August 1895, 5 September 1895, 20 April 1907, 6 July 1914; *Topeka Daily Commonwealth*, 24 March 1874, 18 April 1874.

17. *Emporia Weekly News*, 1 July 1886; *Topeka Daily Capital*, 26 June 1886, 6 July 1914.

18. *Barber County Index*, 15 May 1889, 19 June 1889; *Clay Center Times*, 25 July 1889, 22 August 1889, 29 August 1889.

19. *Atchison Daily Champion*, 8 September 1900; *Topeka Daily Capital*, 6 September 1900.

20. *Topeka Daily Capital*, 11 August 1895.

21. Utley 1977, p. 152.

22. Lieutenant Beecher was post quartermaster and commissary officer at Fort Wallace from November 1866 through March 1868. Captain Keogh had been commanding officer at Fort Wallace from November 1866 through August 1867. Beecher was killed while serving with Forsyth's Scouts at what was later named Beecher Island in the Arikaree River in northeastern Colorado in September 1868. Keogh was killed at the Battle of Little Bighorn in June 1876, but his horse, Comanche, survived and was retired, passing away in 1891. Comanche's taxidermy mount was subsequently displayed at the University of Kansas Museum of Natural History in Lawrence.

23. *New York Clipper*, 18 April 1868, 5 September 1868.

24. Bohn 2014; Mills and Seymour 1990, p. 293. Dorothy Seymour Mills was not credited in the 1990 edition of *Baseball: The People's Game*, but was retroactively added as coauthor in 2010 to give her proper credit, correcting earlier gender bias. Although I used the 1990 edition of the work, I prefer to give credit where it is due.

25. *Kinsley Graphic*, 24 August 1878, 12 July 1879, 11 October 1879, 18 October 1879.

26. *New York Clipper*, 16 December 1865; Chadwick 1866.

27. *Lawrence Kansas Daily Tribune*, 25 July 1867, 3 August 1867, 5 September 1867.

28. Chadwick 1867.

29. *Fort Scott Weekly Monitor*, 7 August 1867, 4 September 1867.

30. *Lawrence Kansas Daily Tribune*, 26 October 1866; *Wyandotte Commercial Gazette*, 1 September 1866, 20 October 1866, 17 November 1866.

31. *Lawrence Kansas Daily Tribune*, 26 October 1866; *Wyandotte Commercial Gazette*, 20 October 1866, 3 November 1866.

32. *Wyandotte Commercial Gazette*, 15 June 1867.

33. *Wyandotte Commercial Gazette*, 1 September 1866, 17 November 1866, 26 January 1867, 23 February 1867, 24 August 1867, 23 November 1867; Mills and Seymour 1990, p. 213–217. The spellings of *Wyandotte* and *Wyandott*, with and without the *e*, were used interchangeably for the county and city names at the time.

34. *Kansas City Times*, 28 April 1927; Horner 2011; Kirkman 2012, p. 47–49; *Bio-*

graphical Directory of the United States Congress 1774–Present, s.v. "Pomeroy, Samuel Clarke (1816–1891)" 2015.

35. *Ferdinand Vandeveer Hayden and the Founding of the Yellowstone National Park* 1973; Goodwin 2005, p. 605–607.

36. *Kansas City Times*, 28 April 1927, 28 February 1964; Horner 2011; Kirkman 2012, p. 47–49.

37. Rosa 2011.

38. *Atchison Daily Champion*, 16 May 1867.

39. *Atchison Daily Champion*, 30 May 1867, 16 June 1867, 9 July 1867, 27 July 1867, 30 July 1867, 31 July 1867, 3 August 1867, 9 August 1867, 13 August 1867, 17 August 1867, 21 August 1867, 27 August 1867.

40. *Daily Atchison Patriot*, 5 July 1870, 23 July 1870, 4 August 1870, 10 August 1870, 27 August 1870, 29 August 1870, 31 August 1870, 10 October 1870; *Atchison Weekly Champion and Press*, 2 July 1870, 9 July 1870, 30 July 1870, 3 September 1870, 24 September 1870; *Lawrence Kansas Daily Tribune*, 23 June 1868; *Leavenworth Daily Times*, 1 October 1870, 2 October 1870, 8 October 1870.

41. *Atchison Globe*, 16 July 1883, 18 July 1883, 20 May 1884, 10 July 1884, 18 April 1885, 6 July 1886; *Brown County World*, 11 July 1885; *Leavenworth Daily Times*, 8 May 1885, 20 June 1885, 8 July 1885.

42. *Kansas City Times*, 28 April 1927; *New York Clipper*, 22 September 1866, 27 April 1867.

43. *Fort Scott Weekly Monitor*, 7 August 1867, 4 September 1867; *Junction City (Weekly) Union*, 11 May 1867, 25 May 1867; *Kansas City Daily Journal of Commerce*, 10 November 1867; *Lawrence Kansas Daily Tribune*, 9 June 1867, 28 July 1867, 7 August 1867, 29 October 1867; *Olathe Mirror*, 2 May 1867; Evans 1940.

44. *Fort Scott Weekly Monitor*, 26 February 1868.

45. *New York Clipper*, 28 September 1867 (Bradley listed as a colonel). Captain G. W. Bradley, AQM, was transferred from Fort Harker, Kansas, to Fort Union, New Mexico, in November 1867 (Special Orders Number 13, District of New Mexico, 18 November 1867).

46. *Lawrence Kansas Daily Tribune*, 11 August 1867.

47. *Olathe Mirror*, 25 June 1868.

48. *Fort Scott Weekly Monitor*, 7 August 1867, 18 September 1867, 23 October 1867; *Lawrence Kansas Daily Tribune*, 11 June 1867, 3 July 1867, 6 July 1867, 1 August 1867, 3 August 1867.

49. *Fort Scott Weekly Monitor*, 18 September 1867, 16 October 1867.

50. *Lawrence Kansas Daily Tribune*, 14 August 1867.

51. *Oskaloosa Independent*, 13 March 1861.

52. Becker 2002; Vaught 2013, p. 1–11.

53. Becker 2002.

54. *McPherson (Weekly) Republican*, 7 September 1894.

55. *Lawrence Daily Kansas Tribune*, 2 September 1868, 13 September 1868, 16 September 1868, 17 September 1868.

56. Gelber 1983.

57. *Leavenworth Daily Times*, 19 July 1870.

58. Morris 2010, p. 28.

59. Italics used in the original.

60. *Lawrence Daily Journal-World*, 12 August 1911; *Lawrence Daily World*, 29 June 1906; Chadwick 1867; Goldstein 1989, p. 48–53; Morris 2008, p. 65–73.

61. Chadwick 1867; Kansas Historical Society 2014a; Major League Baseball 2014.

62. Kansas Historical Society 2014b.

63. James and Neyer 2004, p. 68.

64. *Independence Evening Reporter*, 22 June 1887; "Baseball Rule Change Timeline" 2015.

65. *Lawrence Kansas Daily Tribune*, 3 August 1867.

66. *Lawrence Kansas Daily Tribune*, 4 September 1867, 23 June 1868.

67. *El Dorado Times*, 26 August 1920.

68. *Kinsley Graphic*, 1 August 1890.

69. Morris 2010, p. 382.

70. *Topeka Daily Capital*, 2 July 1897.

71. *Salina Evening Journal*, 10 August 1906, 17 August 1906.

72. *Emporia Gazette*, 3 August 1914, 25 July 1923; *Newton Evening Kansan-Republican*, 6 July 1908, 14 August 1908; *Olathe Mirror*, 19 August 1920; *Salina Daily Union*, 5 July 1905, 6 July 1908; *Wichita Daily Eagle*, 22 April 1914.

73. Morris 2010, p. 382.

74. *Wichita Eagle*, 11 August 1908.

75. *Walnut Valley Times* (El Dorado), 26 May 1911; *Wichita Daily Eagle*, 14 May 1912, 15 May 1912.

76. *Iola Register*, 14 August 1911.

77. *Iola Register*, 21 June 1911. For more about Pomp Reagor, see chapter 3.

78. *Chanute Daily Tribune*, 14 June 1920; *Iola Register*, 5 July 1913, 18 August 1913; *Lawrence Republican Daily Journal*, 11 September 1869.

79. *Chanute Daily Tribune*, 13 June 1921.

80. *Abilene Daily Reflector*, 22 June 1907.

81. Mills and Seymour 1990, p. 12–14.

82. *Chanute Daily Tribune*, 29 August 1904.

83. *Chanute Daily Tribune*, 19 July 1920.

84. *Onaga Herald*, 31 August 1911.

85. *Atchison Daily Champion*, 27 August 1867; *Belleville Telescope*, 23 May 1902; *Beloit Daily Call*, 27 June 1921; *Garden City Telegram*, 18 September 1924; *Kinsley Graphic*, 6 August 1881, 13 September 1907; *Lawrence Daily Kansas Tribune*, 6 May 1868; *Topeka Daily Capital*, 2 August 1885; Chadwick 1866.

86. *Beloit Daily Call*, 19 June 1919, 24 September 1919; Gerlach 2010.

87. *Atchison Daily Champion*, 27 August 1867; *Garden City Telegram*, 3 July 1924; *Hutchinson News*, 2 August 1894; *Kinsley Graphic*, 13 August 1881, 10 August 1882, 5 July 1883; *Lawrence Daily Journal*, 27 May 1892, 15 June 1892, 30 July 1892; *Lawrence Daily Kansas Tribune*, 16 May 1868; *Leavenworth Times and Conservative*, 12 September 1869; *Osage City Free Press*, 5 September 1901; *Troy Weekly Kansas Chief*, 19 September 1895; Chadwick 1866.

88. *Chanute Daily Tribune*, 29 August 1904; *Chanute Sun*, 29 August 1904, 17 March 1906; *Humboldt Union*, 17 July 1909; *Junction City (Daily) Union*, 19 April 1910; *Kinsley Graphic*, 21 June 1907; *Topeka Daily Capital*, 9 April 1905, 3 June 1906, 23 September 1917, 13 June 1921, 30 November 1921; *Topeka State Journal*, 22 April 1905; *Troy Weekly Kansas Chief*, 20 September 1894; *Wichita Daily Eagle*, 25 March 1908; Powers-Beck 2004c, p. 59.

89. Adelman 1980; Chadwick 1866, 1867, 1871; Schiff 2008, 2016; Schwarz 2006; "Boxscore" 2013.

90. *Lawrence Kansas Daily Tribune*, 28 September 1867, 2 October 1867; *Topeka Kansas Weekly Commonwealth*, 2 September 1869; Evans 1940; Kansas Historical Society 2014b; Kansas Historical Society 2014c.

91. Chadwick 1867.

92. *Lawrence Kansas Daily Tribune*, 4 October 1868, 10 October 1868.

93. *Lawrence Kansas Daily Tribune*, 21 February 1869, 8 April 1869, 28 May 1869, 18 June 1869, 26 August 1869, 2 September 1869, 11 September 1869; *Topeka Kansas Weekly Commonwealth*, 2 September 1869.

94. The silver ball was held by M. Newmark, an original Kaw Valley BBC team member. *Lawrence Daily Journal*, 2 October 1889, 23 July 1891; *Lawrence Daily Journal-World*, 12 August 1911, 16 September 1916; *Lawrence Daily World*, 12 February 1901; *Lawrence Kansas Daily Tribune*, 14 June 1870, 2 March 1871.

95. *Kinsley Mercury*, 29 September 1887, 5 June 1913; *Larned Tiller and Toiler*, 25 August 1905; *McPherson Republican and Weekly Press*, 1 July 1887.

96. *Chanute Daily Tribune*, 11 March 1907; *Holton Recorder*, 1 June 1882; *Hutchinson News*, 10 September 1914, 20 April 1922; *Saline County Journal*, 26 June 1879; *Wichita Daily Eagle*, 23 April 1912, 17 April 1914, 16 April 1922.

97. *Kinsley Graphic*, 22 April 1904.

98. *Kinsley Graphic*, 6 July 1882, 20 July 1882, 3 July 1891; *Kinsley Mercury*, 27 June 1885; Morris 2008, p. 142–146.

99. *Hays Free Press*, 27 May 1905; *Humboldt Union*, 1 August 1896; *Topeka Daily Commonwealth*, 27 July 1875.

100. This ruling is described more fully in chapter 4.

101. *Garden City Herald*, 24 July 1926; *Humboldt Union*, 6 July 1901; *Lawrence Kansas Daily Tribune*, 10 August 1867, 14 August 1867, 13 September 1868, 25 September 1868; Mills and Seymour 1990, p. 188–212.

102. "Lawrence . . . will soon be able to compete with New York city in everything." *Lawrence Kansas Daily Tribune*, 15 August 1867. Mills and Seymour 1990, p. 188–212; Morris 2008, p. 135–151.

103. Becker 2002.

104. DeArment 2006.

105. *Kinsley Graphic*, 28 March 1890, 4 April 1890; *Kinsley Mercury*, 17 May 1884, 18 June 1887; *Larned Tiller and Toiler*, 16 July 1909; *McPherson Daily Republican*, 25 April 1906.

106. *Junction City (Weekly) Union*, 7 May 1870; *Leavenworth Times and Conservative*, 26 April 1870.

107. *Atchison Daily Champion and Press*, 26 February 1870, 24 May 1883; *Daily Atchison Patriot*, 14 May 1870; *Emporia (Weekly) News*, 17 December 1869; *Fort Scott Daily Monitor*, 17 May 1870, 28 August 1870; *Lawrence Kansas Daily Tribune*, 7 October 1870, 6 December 1870; *Lawrence Republican Daily Journal*, 11 February 1870, 20 May 1870, 22 September 1870, 20 November 1870, 27 January 1871; *Leavenworth Times and Conservative*, 19 February 1870, 10 November 1870, 26 October 1871, 3 December 1871; *Topeka Daily Commonwealth*, 30 May 1876.

108. *Fort Scott Daily Monitor*, 17 May 1870; *Lawrence Kansas Daily Tribune*, 27 April 1870, 7 May 1870, 9 April 1871, 31 August 1871; *Lawrence Republican Daily Journal*, 29 June 1871; *Leavenworth Times and Conservative*, 26 April 1870, 28 April 1870; *Wyandotte Gazette*, 15 June 1871.

109. *Junction City (Weekly) Union*, 5 September 1885.

110. *McPherson Daily Republican*, 17 April 1916.

111. Mills and Seymour 1990, p. 194; Morris, 2008, p. 82.

112. *Leavenworth Daily Times*, 14 July 1907.

113. *Chanute Daily Tribune*, 17 May 1916, 24 May 1916, 26 April 1921; *Hutchinson News*, 17 March 1888; *Kinsley Graphic*, 4 April 1890; *Larned Tiller and Toiler*, 12 July 1907, 20 March 1908, 19 November 1909; *Lawrence Kansas Daily Tribune*, 6 May 1871; *Wellington Daily News*, 23 March 1909, 14 April 1909; *Wyandotte Commercial Gazette*, 26 January 1867.

114. *Leavenworth Daily Times*, 12 August 1905.

115. *Larned Tiller and Toiler*, 28 May 1909, 4 June 1909.

116. *Rossville Reporter*, 20 June 1929, 4 July 1929.

117. *Lawrence Kansas Daily Tribune*, 11 September 1867.

118. *Wichita Daily Beacon*, 11 July 1907.

119. *Brown County World*, 14 June 1889 (Johnstown flood victims); *Chanute Daily Tribune*, 3 August 1896 (local band), 21 May 1920 (ball diamond improvements); *Chanute Weekly Times*, 13 June 1889 (Johnstown flood victims); *Council Grove Republican*, 9 October 1903 (cemetery fund); *Fort Scott Daily Monitor*, 8 August 1891 (Tower Hill Park); *Humboldt Union*, 8 June 1889 (Johnstown flood victims); *Hutchin-*

son *News*, 11 June 1889 (Johnstown flood victims); *Independence Daily Reporter*, 16 August 1890 (baseball club); *Kinsley Mercury*, 28 July 1887 (band uniforms); *Newton Daily Republican*, 5 June 1888 (Women's Relief Corps); *Newton Daily Kansan*, 11 June 1892 (ballpark fence); *Ottawa Daily Republican*, 4 September 1885 (general statement about fund-raisers), 1 October 1888 (yellow fever sufferers); *Salina Daily Republican*, 30 April 1891 (YMCA); *Topeka Daily Capital*, 20 August 1885 (Grant Monument), 1 June 1886 (Ingleside Home for working women); *Topeka Daily Commonwealth*, 12 August 1875 (Library Association), 22 May 1886 (Ingleside Home); *Valley Falls New Era*, 1 June 1916 (baseball club); *Wichita Daily Beacon*, 19 April 1892 (baseball club); McCullough 1968.

120. *Chanute Daily Tribune*, 6 May 1915, 20 June 1921; *Humboldt Union*, 1 July 1920; *Hutchinson News*, 14 May 1907; *Kinsley Graphic*, 15 June 1916; *Kinsley Mercury*, 12 July 1911; *McPherson Weekly Republican*, 18 April 1919.

121. *Hays Free Press*, 22 July 1905.

122. Bevis 2003, p. 5–23.

123. Utley 1977, p. 152.

124. *Kinsley Graphic*, 21 June 1884, 8 September 1887; *Kinsley Mercury*, 28 June 1884.

125. Bevis 2003, p. 5–23.

126. *Atchison Daily Champion*, 29 August 1902. *Red Cloud Chief*, 25 July 1902.

127. Etcheson 2004, p. 50–68; Graham 1909.

128. *Atchison Globe*, 23 July 1883.

129. *Clay Center Times*, 9 May 1895.

130. *Hays Free Press*, 16 April 1904.

131. *Hays Free Press*, 18 June 1904, 27 May 1905.

132. *Chanute Sun*, 22 April 1904, 26 April 1904.

133. Graham 1909.

134. *Topeka Daily Capital*, 7 January 1909.

135. *Topeka Daily Capital*, 19 October 1910, 14 January 1911, 26 January 1911, 27 January 1911.

136. *Proceedings of the House of Representatives of the State of Kansas, Seventeenth Biennial Session* 1911.

137. *Topeka Daily Capital*, 6 February 1917; *Wichita Beacon*, 17 January 1913; Caldwell 1943.

138. *Chanute Daily Tribune*, 17 April 1915, 4 May 1915, 15 May 1915, 21 April 1921, 19 May 1921, 28 June 1921, 29 June 1922; *Topeka Daily Capital*, 5 August 1912, 27 March 1921; *Wellington Daily News*, 20 June 1922, 1 July 1922.

139. *Coffeyville Daily Journal*, 23 April 1913.

140. *Topeka Daily Capital*, 26 July 1912.

141. *Kinsley Graphic*, 29 May 1913.

142. *Beloit Daily Call*, 22 February 1919, 14 May 1919, 21 May 1919, 23 May 1919, 19 June 1919, 27 June 1919, 30 June 1919, 8 July 1919, 22 August 1919, 23 August 1919, 24 September 1919, 12 October 1919, 22 October 1919, 18 March 1920.

143. *Beloit Daily Call*, 26 April 1920, 27 April 1920, 8 July 1920, 21 July 1920, 16 September 1920, 22 September 1920, 30 September 1920, 4 December 1920, 9 April 1921, 23 May 1921, 25 June 1921, 12 June 1922, 14 July 1922, 17 July 1922, 20 July 1922.

144. *Lawrence Daily Journal-World*, 12 August 1913; *Leavenworth Daily Times*, 10 August 1912; *Ottawa Weekly Herald*, 28 August 1913.

145. *Arkansas City Daily Traveler*, 11 July 1905; *Chanute Daily Tribune*, 31 March 1914; *Coffeyville Daily Journal*, 17 July 1913; *Fort Scott Daily Tribune and Fort Scott Daily Monitor*, 19 June 1914; *Galena Weekly Republican*, 20 June 1913; *Iola Register*, 12 June 1912; *Kansas City Gazette Globe*, 15 April 1913; *Kinsley Graphic*, 20 May 1915; *Lawrence Daily Journal-World*, 20 April 1911; *Leavenworth Daily Times*, 17 July 1912; *Olathe Mirror*, 11 June 1914; *Ottawa Weekly Herald*, 24 April 1913; *Topeka Daily Capital*, 4 June 1914; *Wellington Daily News*, 13 July 1909, 16 July 1915; *Winfield Daily Free Press*, 16 July 1914.

146. *Lawrence Daily Journal-World*, 19 July 1912; *Osage City Free Press-Public Opinion*, 12 August 1912.

147. *Galena Weekly Republican*, 20 June 1913; *Wichita Beacon*, 12 October 1922.

148. *Hutchinson News*, 15 May 1913; *Kinsley Mercury*, 27 May 1915; *Ottawa Weekly Herald*, 5 June 1913.

149. *Chanute Sun*, 19 June 1905; *Hutchinson News*, 5 January 1909; *Kinsley Graphic*, 9 August 1907; *Topeka Daily Capital*, 7 January 1909, 9 January 1910, 23 May 1920.

150. *Chanute Daily Tribune*, 8 August 1900, 17 July 1909, 20 July 1909.

151. *Chanute Daily Tribune*, 8 March 1911, 17 March 1911, 30 March 1911, 10 April 1911, 12 April 1911, 17 April 1911, 25 April 1911.

152. Santillán 2008; Trembanis 2014, p. 25–26.

153. *Arkansas City Daily Traveler*, 17 April 1913; *Coffeyville Daily Journal*, 6 February 1914; *Leavenworth Daily Times*, 23 February 1912; *Topeka Daily Capital*, 6 February 1912, 29 March 1914, 22 April 1916, 13 May 1916.

154. *Leavenworth Daily Times*, 25 April 1912. Father Kelly also mentioned his acceptance of people attending "good, clean shows" on Sundays after church.

155. *Topeka Daily Capital*, 6 May 1912; *Wichita Beacon*, 14 May 1912; *Wichita Daily Eagle*, 12 May 1912, 14 May 1912.

156. *Topeka Daily Capital*, 16 August 1898, 20 August 1898; *Wichita Daily Eagle*, 16 August 1898.

157. Mills and Seymour 1990, p. 213–235.

158. *Wichita Eagle*, 19 April 1913, 30 July 1914, 10 August 1919.

159. *Hutchinson News*, 14 June 1902; *Topeka Daily Capital*, 5 January 1896.

160. *Arkansas City Daily Traveler*, 12 July 1905; *Lawrence Daily Journal*, 14 June

1899; *Newton Evening Kansan-Republican*, 21 June 1904; *Parsons Daily Sun*, 7 June 1905; *Topeka Daily Capital*, 10 July 1904; *Wichita Daily Eagle*, 30 May 1901.

161. *Humboldt Union*, 3 August 1907; *Iola Register*, 20 August 1907; *Kinsley Graphic*, 21 June 1907, 6 July 1911, 3 August 1911, 21 April 1921; *McPherson Daily Republican*, 12 May 1919, 24 April 1920; *Parsons Daily Sun*, 22 May 1913; *Pittsburg Daily Headlight*, 24 April 1913.

162. Mills and Seymour 1990, p. 363–364.

163. *Brown County World*, 12 December 1890, 26 December 1890; *Columbus Advocate*, 8 October 1903; *Lawrence Daily Journal*, 2 January 1900.

164. *Concordia Daily Blade*, 25 July 1905. Night baseball is covered in chapter 6.

165. *Emporia Daily Gazette*, 3 April 1908.

166. Greeley 1916.

167. *Hutchinson News*, 17 September 1908; *Junction City Daily Union*, 1 September 1908; *Parsons Daily Sun*, 17 July 1920, 19 July 1920.

CHAPTER 2. HOMETOWN WOMEN'S TEAMS AND BARNSTORMING
BLOOMER GIRLS

1. *Wakarusa Kansas Herald of Freedom*, 25 June 1859; *Holton Recorder*, 13 February 1879; Berlage 1994, 2000, p. 1–24; Forsythe 2002; Mills and Seymour 1990, p. 443–451.

2. Goldstein 1989, p. 38–39; Mills and Seymour 1990, p. 447, 459–460.

3. Mills and Seymour 1990, p. 447–451; Shattuck 2011.

4. Berlage 1994, 2000, p. 9–24; Mills and Seymour 1990, p. 447–451; Ring 2009, p. 33–39; Shattuck 2001, 2011; Smith 1994.

5. *Topeka Daily Capital*, 27 February 1886; "History of Washburn" 2015.

6. *Lawrence Daily Gazette*, 25 April 1894; *Leavenworth Daily Times*, 20 May 1897; *Ottawa Daily Republican*, 24 April 1894; *Ottawa Evening Herald*, 11 May 1897; Ottawa University 2016.

7. *Lawrence Daily Gazette*, 20 June 1894.

8. *Burlingame Enterprise*, 20 May 1897; Baker University 2015.

9. *Salina Daily Union*, 21 April 1899, 22 April 1899; Kansas Wesleyan University 2015.

10. *Emporia Daily Gazette*, 26 April 1906.

11. *Emporia Daily Gazette*, 12 April 1912.

12. Emporia State University 2016.

13. *Topeka Daily Capital*, 24 April 1911.

14. *Topeka Daily Capital*, 17 April 1913, 25 April 1920; *Walnut Valley Times* (El Dorado), 2 July 1915.

15. Forsythe 2002.

16. *Hays Free Press*, 27 May 1905, 19 May 1906.

17. *Hays Free Press*, 13 September 1902, 20 September 1902, 27 September 1902, 4 October 1902.

18. *Ellis County News*, 8 May 1903; *Hays Free Press*, 21 March 1903; Forsythe 2002.

19. *Reveille 1915*, p. 36, Fort Hays Kansas Normal School Yearbook.

20. *Hays Free Press*, 17 April 1915.

21. *Wichita City (Weekly) Eagle*, 13 February 1873; Shattuck 2011.

22. *Marion Record*, 22 February 1889.

23. *Abilene Daily Reflector*, 21 August 1903.

24. *Barber County Index*, 27 June 1894 (Atwood "female base ball club"); *Barton County Democrat*, 28 September 1906 (Dighton "ladies base ball team"); *Brown County World*, 3 July 1896 ("girls of Harper"), 4 September 1896 (Highland "young ladies base ball nine"); *Chanute Morning Sun*, 26 July 1899 (in Chanute, "eighteen charming young ladies have organized two base ball clubs"); *Chanute Sun*, 6 May 1904, 22 July 1904 ("two little girl base ball clubs" in Chanute); *Clay Center Times*, 20 April 1882 ("female base ball club"); *Coffeyville Daily Journal*, 20 June 1895, 21 June 1895 ("Ed. Rea is now posing as instructor to the young ladies' base ball team. He is also envied by all the young men of the town"), 6 August 1895 (Pleasanton "female base ball team" known as the "Pleasanton 'New Woman' Base Ball Team"); *Council Grove Republican*, 16 August 1895 ("female base ball club"); *Junction City (Weekly) Union*, 21 April 1877 ("girls of Neodesha have organized a base ball club"), 29 April 1882 ("female base ball club"); *Kinsley Graphic*, 22 April 1904 (Dodge City with "two base ball nines, composed entirely of young ladies"); *Marion Record*, 22 February 1889 (Newton high school girls); *McPherson Daily Republican*, 30 July 1889 (McPherson "female nine"), 6 August 1889 (McPherson "female base ball clubs"), 21 July 1902 (Red Poppies), 9 August 1906 (Fairies and Bonbons), 10 August 1906, 11 August 1906, 14 August 1906; *Newton Daily Republican*, 6 May 1893 ("ladies base ball club practices daily"), 17 July 1894 (Hope "female baseball club"); *Osawatomie Graphic*, 6 July 1888; *Ottawa Daily Republican*, 1 August 1885 ("girl base ball club met the boys . . . and played a friendly game"; "It ended in favor of the girls"); *Topeka Daily Capital*, 26 June 1888 (*Hope Dispatch*: "a lady base ball club" to challenge town teams); *Wichita Daily Beacon*, 2 November 1885 (Atchison "female base ball club"); *Wichita City (Weekly) Eagle*, 13 February 1873 ("young ladies of our city have organized a base ball club"), 29 August 1903 (Sedan has "two girl baseball teams").

25. *Topeka Daily Capital*, 25 July 1902.

26. *McPherson Daily Republican*, 30 July 1889, 6 August 1889, 26 August 1889.

27. *McPherson Daily Republican*, 4 June 1907, 8 June 1907, 2 July 1907, 8 July 1907, 22 July 1907, 25 July 1907, 27 July 1907, 29 July 1907, 30 August 1907; *Salina Daily Union*, 30 August 1907; *Windom Press*, 10 May 1907, 24 May 1907, 31 May 1907 (photo of Windom teams), 28 June 1907, 26 July 1907, 2 August 1907, 27 September 1907.

28. *Wichita Daily Eagle*, 25 March 1908.

29. *Independence Daily Reporter*, 4 April 1908, 6 April 1908, 7 April 1908.

30. Caldwell 1943.

31. *Louisville Lyre*, 4 August 1911, 11 August 1911.

32. *Onaga Herald*, 3 August 1911; *Westmoreland Recorder*, 20 July 1911, 5 October 1911.

33. *Wamego Reporter*, 6 July 1911, 27 July 1911, 17 August 1911.

34. *Wamego Reporter*, 13 July 1911, 20 July 1911; *Wamego Weekly Times*, 21 July 1911, 8 September 1911. The United States Department of Labor online inflation calculator (http://www.bls.gov/data/inflation_calculator.htm) was used to estimate all modern equivalent dollar values provided throughout this book.

35. *Alma Signal*, 21 September 1911; *Chanute Daily Tribune*, 28 August 1911; *Lawrence Daily Journal-World*, 1 September 1911; *Onaga Herald*, 13 July 1911, 3 August 1911; *Topeka Daily Capital*, 22 July 1911, 10 September 1911; *Wichita Daily Eagle*, 30 August 1911.

36. *Wamego Reporter*, 20 July 1911.

37. *Louisville Lyre*, 14 July 1911, 28 July 1911, 4 August 1911; *Wamego Reporter*, 20 July 1911, 27 July 1911; *Wamego Weekly Times*, 28 July 1911, 4 August 1911; *Westmoreland Recorder*, 13 July 1911.

38. *Onaga Herald*, 3 August 1911.

39. *Westmoreland Recorder*, 27 July 1911.

40. *Louisville Lyre*, 25 August 1911, 1 September 1911, 8 September 1911; *Wamego Weekly Times*, 1 September 1911, 8 September 1911.

41. *Onaga Herald*, 14 September 1911, 28 September 1911.

42. *Onaga Herald*, 21 September 1911 (Onaga team photo); *Topeka Daily Capital*, 20 August 1911 (Wamego team photograph), 17 September 1911 (Westmoreland team photograph), 29 October 1911 (Onaga team photograph); *Wamego Reporter*, 17 August 1911 (Wamego team photograph).

43. *Junction City (Daily) Union*, 22 August 1911; *Onaga Herald*, 21 September 1911 (Onaga team photo); *Wamego Reporter*, 17 August 1911 (Wamego team photo), 24 August 1911.

44. *Wamego Reporter*, 24 August 1911.

45. *Onaga Herald*, 14 September 1911; *Wamego Weekly Times*, 28 July 1911, 4 August 1911, 25 August 1911; *Westmoreland Recorder*, 3 August 1911, 17 August 1911, 31 August 1911.

46. *Onaga Herald*, 28 September 1911.

47. *Wamego Weekly Times*, 4 August 1911.

48. *Louisville Lyre*, 11 August 1911, 18 August 1911, 1 September 1911; *Westmoreland Recorder*, 10 August 1911, 31 August 1911; Blackmar 1912, p. 309.

49. *Westmoreland Recorder*, 31 August 1911.

50. *Onaga Herald*, 14 September 1911.

51. *Onaga Herald*, 28 September 1911.

52. *Salina Evening Journal*, 9 May 1912.

53. *Wichita Beacon*, 8 July 1918.

54. *Topeka Daily Capital*, 8 June 1905.

55. *Topeka Daily Capital*, 23 August 1919.

56. *Alma Signal*, 30 June 1927; *Hays Daily News*, 10 May 1933; *Junction City (Daily) Union*, 20 August 1921; *Lawrence Daily Journal-World*, 23 August 1934; *Rossville Reporter*, 22 August 1929, 29 August 1929.

57. *Salina Evening Journal*, 20 June 1921, 29 June 1921, 26 July 1921.

58. *Hays Daily News*, 9 June 1930.

59. *Columbus Advocate*, 19 November 1885; *Fort Scott Daily Monitor*, 14 November 1885; *Lawrence Daily Journal*, 8 November 1885; *Lawrence Gazette*, 12 November 1885; *Topeka Daily Capital*, 10 November 1885; *Topeka Daily Commonwealth*, 8 November 1885.

60. *Junction City (Weekly) Union*, 9 July 1892; *Kansas City Gazette*, 18 July 1892; *Leavenworth Daily Times*, 12 July 1892; *Ottawa Daily Republican*, 31 October 1892; *Topeka Daily Capital*, 12 July 1892; *Topeka State Journal*, 8 July 1892, 11 July 1892, 12 July 1892.

61. *Arkansas City Weekly Republican Traveler*, 15 September 1892; *Atchison Daily Champion*, 24 August 1892, 25 August 1892, 26 August 1892; *Lawrence Weekly World*, 1 September 1892; *Newton Daily Kansan*, 8 September 1892; *Salina Daily Republican*, 3 September 1892; *Wichita Daily Eagle*, 9 September 1892. The roster of the women's team at Arkansas City was Mollie Gorman (third base), Kittie Grant (catcher), May Howard (pitcher), Bessie Kirby (center field), Mabel Kirby (left field), Maud Nelson (second base), Maggie Spencer (shortstop), Ray Warren (first base), Maud Woods (right field), and Eva Wright (substitute).

62. *Wichita Daily Eagle*, 9 September 1892.

63. *Wichita Daily Eagle*, 9 September 1892.

64. *Salina Daily Republican-Journal*, 15 February 1898; *Wichita Daily Beacon*, 16 February 1898, 11 July 1898.

65. At the time, the number 4-11-44 was said to be lucky in a gambling lottery known as "policy" and later referred to as the "numbers" game. Numbers usually ranging from one to seventy-eight were drawn from a barrel, and a group of three correct numbers was known as a gig. The Boston Bloomer Girls apparently had that number painted on their railcar for fun and to attract attention. At least that seems to have been the result in McPherson and Wichita (Sweeney 2009, p. 73).

66. *Arkansas City Weekly Traveler*, 23 June 1898; *Lawrence Daily World*, 11 June 1898; *McPherson (Weekly) Republican*, 15 July 1898 (Pullman Palace Sleeper 4-11-44); *Osage City Free Press*, 16 June 1898; *Wichita Daily Beacon*, 12 July 1898 (Pullman Palace Sleeper 4-11-44).

67. *Holton Recorder*, 4 August 1898; *Ottawa Evening Herald*, 12 July 1898; *Pittsburg Daily Headlight*, 6 July 1898; *Salina Union*, 16 July 1898; *Wichita Daily Beacon*, 12 July 1898; *Wichita Daily Eagle*, 12 July 1898.

68. *Kansas City Gazette*, 22 June 1898.

69. *Brown County World,* 29 July 1898; *Fort Scott Weekly Monitor,* 9 July 1898; *Holton Recorder,* 28 July 1898; *Lawrence Daily World,* 21 June 1898; *Leavenworth Daily Times,* 2 August 1898; *Newton Daily Republican,* 13 July 1898; *Ottawa Daily Republican,* 12 July 1898; *Wichita Daily Beacon,* 12 July 1898.

70. *Lawrence Daily Journal,* 21 June 1898.

71. *Lawrence Daily World,* 21 June 1898.

72. *Brown County World,* 29 July 1898; *Fort Scott Weekly Monitor,* 9 July 1898; *Goodland Republic,* 3 May 1901, 10 May 1901; *Holton Recorder,* 4 August 1898; *Humboldt Union,* 19 October 1901; *Iola Register,* 15 October 1901; *Leavenworth Daily Times,* 2 August 1898; *Newton Daily Republican,* 13 July 1898; *Phillipsburg Herald,* 7 May 1901; *Pittsburg Daily Headlight,* 6 July 1898.

73. *Arkansas City Daily Traveler,* 27 June 1898; *Leavenworth Daily Times,* 2 August 1898; *McPherson (Weekly) Republican,* 15 July 1898; *Wichita Daily Beacon,* 11 July 1898, 12 July 1898. The team members playing in Kansas in 1898 listed in several newspapers were Nellie Bly, Brady (male catcher), Lucy Hall, Belle Jennings, Julia Marlowe, Montgomery (possibly a man; in center field at Wichita), Clara Moore, Morris (male catcher), Maud Nelson, Della Reid, Yeula Robertson, Carrie Rowe, Gertie Snow, Alice White, Nettie Woods, and someone named Lola (no last name given).

74. Berlage 1994, p. 35; Cohen 2009, p. 29–30; Gregorich 1993, p. 6–11; Shattuck 2001.

75. *Arkansas City Weekly Republican Traveler,* 15 September 1892.

76. Gregorich 1993, p. 6–11.

77. *Leavenworth Daily Times,* 2 August 1898.

78. *Wichita Daily Beacon,* 12 July 1898.

79. *Ellis County News,* 19 November 1909; Foster 2014; "Smoky Joe Wood" 2016; Wood 2013, p. 35–37.

80. *Chanute Daily Tribune,* 24 May 1911, 31 July 1915; *Coffeyville Daily Journal,* 19 July 1920; *Fort Scott Daily Tribune and Fort Scott Daily Monitor,* 26 May 1914; *Garnett Journal,* 4 July 1902; *Iola Register,* 14 June 1935; *Topeka Daily Capital,* 14 September 1911; *Valley Falls New Era,* 3 August 1911.

81. *Fort Scott Weekly Monitor,* 9 July 1898.

82. *Arkansas City Daily Traveler,* 3 September 1901, 6 September 1901, 7 September 1901, 12 September 1901, 16 September 1901, 18 September 1901, 4 October 1901.

83. *Wichita Beacon,* 2 August 1916.

84. *Chanute Daily Tribune,* 6 August 1915.

85. *Kansas City Kansas Globe,* 31 March 1909, 3 April 1909; *Kansas City Journal,* 19 November 1909; *Kansas City Star,* 14 November 1909; *Kansas City Times,* 16 May 1911; *Liberty Vindicator,* 3 July 1908; *Sporting Life,* 27 November 1909.

86. *Parsons Daily Sun,* 17 July 1920, 19 July 1920.

87. *Junction City Daily Union,* 1 September 1908.

88. *Belleville Telescope*, 14 October 1937; *Beloit Daily Call*, 9 September 1921; *Coffeyville Daily Journal*, 16 June 1921; *Galena Weekly Republican*, 13 April 1923; *Iola Register*, 13 May 1935; *Kansas City Kansan*, 7 June 1921, 23 June 1921; *Pittsburg Sun*, 19 May 1922; *Topeka Daily Capital*, 18 November 1913, 2 August 1914, 2 June 1916, 4 April 1920 (photograph of team at Lyman School), 14 April 1922; Berlage 2000; Ring 2009, p. 59–72.

89. *Topeka Daily Capital*, 24 April 1921.

CHAPTER 3. AFRICAN AMERICAN BASEBALL

1. Pendleton 1997.

2. Bruce 1985; Dixon 2010; Heaphy 2007; Lester and Miller 2000; Kansas Baseball History Project.

3. Bruce 1985, p. 72–80; Dixon 2010, p. 115–117, 141–147; Hawkins and Bertolino 2000.

4. Hawkins and Bertolino 2000.

5. *Wichita Beacon*, 27 August 1934, 28 September 1934; *Wichita Eagle*, 27 August 1934, 28 September 1934.

6. *Dodge City Journal*, 28 September 1933.

7. Bruce 1985, p. 68–73; Dixon 2010, p. 96–99; Hawkins and Bertolino 2000; Lester and Miller 2000, p. 31–32. The lights used by the Monarchs are discussed in chapters 6 and 17.

8. *Fort Scott Daily Monitor*, 10 March 1870; *Lawrence Republican Daily Journal*, 28 May 1870, 17 May 1873, 1 August 1878; *Lawrence Kansas Daily Tribune*, 23 June 1868, 10 July 1868, 17 June 1871; *Topeka Daily Commonwealth*, 14 April 1874, 26 June 1874, 26 July 1875, 30 June 1875; *White Cloud Kansas Chief*, 12 August 1869; *Wichita City (Weekly) Eagle*, 9 April 1874.

9. *White Cloud Kansas Chief*, 12 August 1869.

10. *Lawrence Kansas Daily Tribune*, 21 February 1869, 8 April 1869, 28 May 1869, 18 June 1869, 26 August 1869, 2 September 1869; *Topeka Kansas Weekly Commonwealth*, 2 September 1869.

11. *Lawrence Kansas Daily Tribune*, 3 September 1869.

12. *Lawrence Republican Daily Journal*, 25 May 1870, 28 May 1870.

13. *Fort Scott Daily Monitor*, 6 March 1870, 10 March 1870, 13 March 1870.

14. *Fort Scott Daily Monitor*, 4 April 1874.

15. *Wichita City (Weekly) Eagle*, 9 April 1874.

16. *Wichita City (Weekly) Eagle*, 18 June 1874.

17. *Wichita City (Weekly) Eagle*, 30 July 1874.

18. *Topeka Daily Commonwealth*, 26 June 1874, 10 July 1875, 11 July 1875.

19. *Chanute Daily Tribune*, 25 July 1904, 15 August 1906, 21 March 1907, 9 September 1907, 23 September 1907, 19 April 1908; *Chanute Sun*, 14 June 1904, 25 June 1904, 18 May 1905.

20. *Chanute Daily Tribune*, 29 August 1904; *Chanute Sun*, 29 August 1904.

21. *Chanute Daily Tribune*, 24 May 1911.

22. *Chanute Daily Tribune*, 10 June 1911, 12 June 1911.

23. *Iola Register*, 23 May 1908, 30 April 1909, 17 July 1909, 23 September 1911, 25 September 1911, 26 September 1911, 9 October 1911, 5 July 1912, 12 August 1912, 2 September 1912, 15 September 1913, 22 September 1913, 20 July 1914, 7 September 1914, 14 September 1914, 28 September 1914, 3 October 1914, 26 June 1915, 28 June 1915, 6 July 1915, 20 June 1919, 31 August 1925, 26 July 1926, 7 July 1927, 9 July 1927, 8 September 1927, 10 October 1927, 27 March 1928, 16 April 1928, 20 April 1928, 21 June 1929, 6 August 1929, 27 June 1930; Greeley 1916.

24. *Iola Register*, 10 October 1927, 27 March 1928, 16 April 1928, 20 April 1928, 29 June 1928.

25. *Iola Register*, 20 August 1906, 26 August 1912, 1 April 1931, 22 April 1931, 8 May 1931, 24 June 1931, 17 August 1931, 20 August 1931, 22 August 1931, 24 August 1931, 25 August 1931, 26 August 1931, 27 August 1931, 5 March 1932, 23 August 1932, 24 August 1932, 25 August 1932, 26 August 1932, 27 August 1932, 6 September 1932.

26. *Iola Register*, 8 March 1933, 20 March 1933, 8 April 1933, 20 April 1933, 1 September 1933.

27. *Iola Register*, 23 April 1934, 5 June 1934, 28 June 1934, 5 July 1934, 16 July 1934, 20 July 1934, 22 August 1934.

28. *Iola Register*, 19 March 1935, 28 March 1935, 8 April 1935, 13 July 1935, 18 July 1935, 1 August 1935, 16 April 1936, 18 March 1937.

29. *Atchison Daily Champion*, 5 February 1887; *Collyer Advance*, 30 July 1931; *Hutchinson News*, 4 August 1939; *Nicodemus Enterprise*, 24 August 1887 (roster), 31 August 1887; *Nicodemus Cyclone*, 10 August 1888; *Western Cyclone*, 27 January 1887, 10 February 1887, 24 February 1887 (roster), 24 March 1887, 19 May 1887, 22 July 1887, 29 July 1887, 26 August 1887, 2 September 1887; O'Brien 1996; Painter 1986.

30. *Fort Scott Daily Monitor*, 23 September 1879; *Humboldt Union*, 27 September 1879; *Iola Register*, 29 September 1877; *Lawrence Kansas Daily Tribune*, 12 September 1871; *Topeka Daily Commonwealth*, 23 September 1879; *Troy Weekly Kansas Chief*, 11 September 1879.

31. *Arkansas City Daily Traveler*, 4 August 1899; *Brown County World*, 20 August 1897; *Chanute Daily Tribune*, 21 September 1920; *Clay Center Times*, 8 August 1895 (baseball); *Coffeyville (Weekly) Journal*, 27 July 1878; *Council Grove Republican*, 29 September 1910; *Fort Scott Daily Monitor*, 2 August 1872, 22 September 1887; *Holton Recorder*, 18 July 1878; *Junction City (Weekly) Union*, 5 August 1871; *Larned Weekly Eagle-Optic*, 7 August 1885; *Lawrence Republican Daily Journal*, 30 July 1871; *Leavenworth Daily Times*, 2 August 1871, 2 August 1879; *Ottawa Evening Herald*, 1 August 1901; *Topeka Daily Capital*, 23 September 1893; *Topeka Daily Commonwealth*, 2 August 1879, 23 September 1879; *Wichita Daily Eagle*, 2 August 1885.

32. *Garden City Herald*, 28 July 1921.

33. *Collyer Advance*, 30 July 1931.

34. Arthur John "Jack" Johnson, the "Galveston Giant," was the first African American to hold the title of World Heavyweight Champion (1908–1915). He lost his title to a white boxer, Kansan Jess Willard, in the twenty-sixth round of a scheduled forty-five-round bout in Havana, Cuba.

35. "Jack Johnson" 2016.

36. *Topeka Daily Capital*, 1 April 1905; "Jack Johnson" 2016.

37. *Topeka Daily Capital*, 8 July 1905, 8 March 1906, 26 March 1906, 18 April 1906, 19 April 1906, 22 April 1906, 23 April 1906, 27 April 1906, 30 April 1906, 5 May 1906, 15 May 1906, 17 May 1906, 18 May 1906, 20 May 1906, 24 May 1906, 28 May 1906, 14 June 1906, 15 June 1906, 17 June 1906, 19 June 1906, 20 June 1906, 21 June 1906, 22 June 1906, 23 June 1906, 24 June 1906, 25 June 1906, 28 June 1906, 1 July 1906, 7 July 1906 (record 30–7), 8 July 1906, 9 July 1906, 11 July 1906, 12 July 1906, 15 July 1906, 17 July 1906, 18 July 1906, 20 July 1906, 21 July 1906, 23 July 1906, 24 July 1906, 25 July 1906, 26 July 1906, 27 July 1906, 31 July 1906, 1 August 1906, 2 August 1906, 6 August 1906, 8 August 1906 (record 66–10), 9 August 1906, 11 August 1906, 13 August 1906, 21 August 1906, 24 August 1906, 26 August 1906, 29 August 1906, 31 August 1906, 3 September 1906, 4 September 1906, 7 September 1906, 9 September 1906, 10 September 1906, 15 September 1906, 30 September 1906, 1 October 1906.

38. *Indianapolis Freeman*, 5 March 1910; *Kansas City Gazette Globe*, 14 June 1909; *Kansas City Kansas Globe*, 10 October 1908; *Kansas City Times*, 4 August 1908, 12 May 1910; *Topeka Daily Capital*, 7 December 1906, 8 February 1907, 15 April 1907, 29 April 1907, 29 May 1907, 30 May 1907, 20 June 1907, 1 July 1907, 15 July 1907, 18 July 1907, 9 September 1907, 3 August 1908, 13 September 1912; Lester and Miller 2000, p. 12–14; Peterson 2010, p. 70–71.

39. *Indianapolis Freeman*, 5 March 1910; *Kansas City Gazette Globe*, 24 April 1909, 6 May 1909, 14 June 1909, 22 June 1909, 28 June 1909, 30 June 1909, 14 August 1909, 21 August 1909 (photo of KCK Giants), 25 August 1909, 28 August 1909, 30 August 1909, 7 September 1909, 15 September 1909, 17 September 1909, 7 October 1909.

40. *Indianapolis Freeman*, 19 February 1910, 26 February 1910, 5 March 1910, 16 April 1910, 17 June 1911; *Kansas City Gazette Globe*, 14 May 1910, 23 July 1910, 8 August 1910, 29 August 1910; *Kansas City Times*, 23 September 1909, 25 September 1909, 1 April 1910, 11 April 1910, 14 April 1910, 23 April 1910, 4 May 1910, 12 May 1910, 13 June 1910, 14 June 1910, 30 June 1910 ("KCK Giants to play at Riverside Park under electric lights at 8:00 p.m. on July 2"), 1 March 1911, 29 May 1911, 2 October 1911, 7 October 1911, 9 October 1911, 10 October 1911.

41. *Indianapolis Freeman*, 16 March 1912, 30 March 1912, 8 June 1912.

42. *Topeka Daily Capital*, 7 July 1913, 15 December 1913, 29 July 1914, 3 August 1914, 6 August 1914, 7 August 1914, 29 August 1914, 2 September 1914, 6 Septem-

ber 1914, 7 September 1914, 4 October 1914, 9 April 1915, 17 April 1915, 20 April 1915, 31 December 1915, 17 May 1916, 10 May 1917, 16 May 1917, 17 May 1917, 18 May 1917, 31 May 1917, 3 June 1917, 4 June 1917, 10 June 1917, 18 June 1917, 20 June 1917, 23 June 1917, 25 June 1917, 9 July 1917, 16 July 1917, 24 July 1917, 13 August 1917, 26 August 1917, 30 August 1917, 31 August 1917, 2 September 1917, 3 September 1917, 4 September 1917, 5 September 1917, 9 September 1917, 11 September 1917, 19 September 1917, 23 September 1917, 24 September 1917, 8 October 1917, 30 June 1918, 27 February 1919, 10 July 1920, 12 July 1920, 19 July 1920, 25 July 1920, 5 August 1920, 10 August 1920, 11 August 1920, 13 August 1920, 7 September 1920, 13 September 1920, 20 September 1920, 10 November 1920, 26 November 1920, 30 April 1921, 30 May 1921, 4 June 1922, 7 June 1922, 8 July 1922; Peterson 1970, p. 147–148.

43. *Wichita Beacon*, 3 April 1921.

44. *Wichita Beacon*, 17 July 1920, 20 July 1920; *Wichita Daily Eagle*, 17 July 1920, 20 July 1920.

45. *Wichita Daily Eagle*, 5 June 1921.

46. *Wichita Daily Eagle*, 10 May 1921.

47. *Wichita Beacon*, 18 April 1921; *Wichita Daily Eagle*, 18 April 1921.

48. *Wichita Daily Eagle*, 5 April 1921, 18 April 1921, 11 May 1921, 15 May 1921, 4 June 1921, 28 July 1921, 30 August 1921; Pendleton 1997.

49. *Wichita Beacon*, 19 July 1932; *Wichita City (Weekly) Eagle*, 18 June 1874; Carroll 2011; Pendleton 1997.

50. Mexican and Mexican American teams, and the challenges they faced, are described in chapter 5.

51. *Wichita Beacon*, 30 April 1922, 6 May 1922, 4 June 1922.

52. *Nashville Globe*, 10 June 1910.

53. *Leavenworth Post*, 18 July 1910.

54. *Leavenworth Daily Times*, 30 March 1916, 20 April 1916, 29 April 1916, 16 May 1916, 23 May 1916, 11 June 1916, 18 June 1916, 8 July 1916, 12 July 1916, 16 July 1916, 23 July 1916.

55. *Indianapolis News*, 3 July 1920, 17 July 1920; *Indianapolis Star*, 27 June 1920, 2 July 1920, 4 July 1920, 7 July 1920, 11 September 1920.

56. *Kansas City Kansan*, 30 June 1921, 6 July 1921, 12 July 1921, 13 July 1921, 21 July 1921, 24 July 1921; *Lawrence Daily Journal-World*, 23 May 1921, 26 May 1921, 10 June 1921, 5 July 1921, 7 July 1921, 9 July 1921, 11 July 1921, 22 July 1921, 29 September 1921; *Topeka Daily Capital*, 31 July 1921, 14 August 1921, 5 September 1921, 6 September 1921.

57. *Wichita Daily Eagle*, 11 April 1922, 28 April 1922.

58. *Coffeyville Daily Journal*, 4 May 1922; *Independence Evening Star*, 4 May 1922; *Morning Tulsa Daily World*, 3 May 1922; *Topeka Daily Capital*, 29 July 1914, 3 May 1922; *Topeka State Journal*, 27 July 1914; *Wichita Beacon*, 23 April 1922, 30 April 1922, 5 May 1922; *Wichita Daily Eagle*, 28 April 1922, 2 May 1922.

59. *Wichita Beacon*, 2 June 1922, 20 July 1922.

60. *Oklahoma City Oklahoma Leader*, 5 June 1922; *Wichita Beacon*, 2 June 1922, 4 June 1922.

61. *Wichita Beacon*, 4 June 1922; *Wichita Daily Eagle*, 11 April 1922.

62. *Kansas City Kansan*, 3 May 1922.

63. *Topeka Daily Capital*, 22 July 1922; *Wichita Beacon*, 20 June 1922, 21 June 1922.

64. *Chanute Daily Tribune*, 11 May 1922, 19 June 1922; *Coffeyville Daily Journal*, 3 June 1922, 7 June 1922.

65. *Morning Tulsa Daily World*, 3 June 1922.

66. *Chanute Daily Tribune*, 19 June 1922, 24 June 1922, 26 June 1922, 15 July 1922, 17 July 1922; *Coffeyville Daily Journal*, 7 June 1922, 10 June 1922, 12 June 1922, 22 June 1922, 23 June 1922, 29 June 1929, 11 August 1922, 12 August 1922; *Independence Evening Star*, 4 May 1922; *Oklahoma City Black Dispatch*, 18 May 1922, 1 June 1922, 8 June 1922, 17 August 1922; *Oklahoma City Oklahoma Leader*, 1 June 1922, 2 June 1922; *Topeka Daily Capital*, 8 July 1922; *Morning Tulsa Daily World*, 3 June 1922, 8 June 1922, 25 July 1922, 26 July 1922, 27 July 1922, 28 July 1922; *Wichita Beacon*, 4 June 1922, 5 June 1922, 18 June 1922, 19 June 1922, 20 June 1922, 1 July 1922, 2 July 1922, 3 July 1922, 4 July 1922, 16 July 1922, 17 July 1922, 18 July 1922, 20 July 1922, 21 July 1922, 27 August 1922, 28 August 1922, 3 September 1922, 10 September 1922; *Wichita Daily Eagle*, 3 July 1922.

67. *Morning Tulsa Daily World*, 4 September 1922.

68. *Wichita Beacon*, 2 September 1922, 10 September 1922.

69. *Wichita Beacon*, 20 July 1922.

70. *Wichita Beacon*, 6 June 1922, 11 July 1922, 26 September 1922; *Wichita Daily Eagle*, 8 June 1922, 9 July 1922, 23 September 1922, 26 September 1922.

71. Described in chapter 8.

72. *Bismarck Tribune*, 18 July 1935; *Cheney Sentinel*, 31 May 1923; *Emporia Daily Gazette*, 29 July 1937, 31 July 1937, 4 August 1937, 5 August 1937, 6 August 1937; *Hutchinson News*, 13 August 1924, 23 July 1937; *Larned Tiller and Toiler*, 6 September 1923; *Pampa Daily News*, 20 June 1937, 22 June 1937, 23 June 1937; *Topeka Daily Capital*, 3 May 1922; *Wichita Beacon*, 4 June 1922, 20 June 1922, 25 June 1922; Pendleton 1997.

73. *Emporia Daily Gazette*, 5 August 1937.

74. *Wichita Beacon*, 21 June 1925, 23 June 1925; Carroll 2008; Pendleton 1997; Price 2003, p. 124.

75. *Atchison Globe*, 7 July 1883.

76. *Topeka Daily Capital*, 25 May 1917, 10 June 1917, 11 June 1917, 25 June 1917; Johnson 2016c.

77. Laing 2013; McKenna 2015.

78. *Topeka Daily Capital*, 8 April 1886.

79. *Topeka Daily Capital*, 18 May 1886, 16 June 1886, 24 July 1886, 13 August 1886, 11 September 1886, 24 September 1886, 19 April 1887; *Topeka Daily Commonwealth*, 8 April 1886, 24 July 1886, 10 August 1886, 3 September 1886, 15 September 1886, 23 March 1887; *Topeka Weekly Commonwealth*, 10 June 1886; Laing 2013, p. 89; McKenna 2015.

80. Bond 2003.

81. Bond 2004.

82. Woods 1983; *Plessy v. Ferguson* 1986.

83. Bond 2003.

84. *Coffeyville Daily Journal*, 22 August 1896, 11 September 1896, 21 June 1899, 31 August 1900, 21 July 1901; *Coffeyville (Weekly) Journal*, 6 June 1889, 29 July 1892, 20 August 1897; *Independence Daily Reporter*, 23 June 1894, 7 July 1896, 15 July 1896, 29 May 1897, 2 August 1898, 12 August 1899; *Independence Evening Star*, 21 July 1906; *Iola Register*, 28 July 1899; *Olathe Mirror*, 6 June 1889, 13 June 1889, 15 August 1889; *Topeka Daily Capital*, 13 May 1896; *Wichita Daily Beacon*, 29 June 1909.

85. *Abilene Daily Chronicle*, 10 May 1898, 18 June 1898; *Abilene Daily Reflector*, 23 June 1897, 29 June 1897, 6 July 1897, 8 July 1897, 13 July 1897, 21 July 1897, 31 May 1898, 4 June 1898; *Atchison Daily Champion*, 6 May 1896, 30 June 1896, 13 August 1896, 18 August 1896, 25 August 1896, 1 September 1896, 25 September 1896, 7 October 1896; *Brown County World*, 17 July 1896, 7 August 1896, 5 July 1901, 2 July 1915; *Salina Daily Republican-Journal*, 20 June 1898, 22 June 1898, 25 June 1898; *Troy Weekly Kansas Chief*, 23 December 1886, 13 June 1889, 21 November 1889, 23 November 1893, 12 July 1894, 19 July 1894, 26 July 1894, 9 August 1894, 23 August 1894, 20 September 1894, 27 September 1894, 18 October 1894, 15 August 1895, 2 July 1896, 20 May 1897, 11 August 1898, 16 February 1899, 23 February 1899, 4 May 1899, 12 October 1899.

86. *Atchison Daily Champion*, 9 September 1896, 22 September 1896, 30 September 1896, 21 April 1897, 12 June 1897, 31 August 1897, 20 April 1898, 12 June 1898, 20 June 1898, 24 June 1898, 26 June 1898, 27 July 1898, 28 July 1898, 13 August 1898; *Brown County World*, 2 August 1895, 9 August 1895, 16 August 1895, 6 September 1895, 13 September 1895, 20 September 1895; *Topeka Daily Capital*, 3 May 1903; Bond 2003.

87. *Arkansas City Daily Traveler*, 5 August 1899, 9 August 1899, 11 August 1899, 19 August 1899, 23 August 1899; *Iola Register*, 7 July 1899, 10 July 1899; *Ottawa Daily Republican*, 1 May 1899; *Ottawa Evening Herald*, 1 May 1899; *Topeka Daily Capital*, 1 April 1900, 23 September 1900, 26 September 1900, 28 August 1903, 29 March 1905, 9 April 1905, 14 April 1905, 8 July 1905, 8 March 1906, 22 April 1906, 3 June 1906; *Topeka State Journal*, 26 May 1897, 20 May 1899, 1 June 1901, 22 May 1903, 30 March 1905, 22 April 1905, 7 July 1905, 28 May 1906; Washburn University 2015.

88. Bond 2003.

89. Campney 2015.

90. *Garnett Journal*, 9 August 1895, 16 August 1895, 25 October 1895.

91. *Humboldt Union*, 18 December 1924, 2 August 1928, 9 August 1928; Ancestry .com, "Kansas State Census Collection" 1905, 1915.

92. *Humboldt Union*, 12 May 1888.

93. *Humboldt Union*, 20 July 1895, 28 June 1902, 9 August 1928.

94. *Chanute Daily Tribune*, 9 September 1907; *Chanute Sun*, 15 May 1905, 23 June 1908; *Humboldt Union*, 11 July 1896; *Iola Register*, 15 June 1908, 14 June 1909.

95. *Humboldt Union*, 1 August 1896, 26 August 1899.

96. *Humboldt Union*, 17 August 1895, 1 August 1896, 21 August 1899, 26 August 1897, 23 June 1900, 14 July 1900, 20 July 1901, 14 May 1904; *Topeka Daily Capital*, 9 September 1902.

97. *Chanute Daily Tribune*, 6 August 1900, 8 August 1900; *Chanute Morning Sun*, 10 August 1900; *Iola Register*, 6 August 1908.

98. *Humboldt Union*, 14 April 1900, 25 October 1902, 24 February 1912.

99. *Fredonia Alliance Herald*, 11 October 1901; *Topeka Daily Capital*, 10 October 1901, 11 October 1901.

100. *Chanute Daily Tribune*, 29 August 1906, 29 June 1908; *Chanute Sun*, 30 June 1908; *Humboldt Union*, 26 May 1894, 29 July 1905; *Iola Register*, 15 February 1895, 16 December 1898.

101. *Humboldt Union*, 26 May 1894.

102. *Humboldt Union*, 7 November 1896.

103. *Chanute Daily Tribune*, 12 December 1908.

104. *Chanute Daily Tribune*, 10 June 1909.

105. *Humboldt Union*, 17 July 1909.

106. *Iola Register*, 21 April 1899.

107. *Iola Register*, 5 August 1901.

108. *Humboldt Union*, 6 September 1902.

109. *Humboldt Union*, 6 July 1901.

110. *Chanute Daily Tribune*, 31 May 1902; *Humboldt Union*, 26 May 1894, 21 August 1897; *Iola Register*, 16 December 1898.

111. *Iola Register*, 5 August 1901.

112. *Chanute Daily Tribune*, 28 June 1920.

113. *Chanute Daily Tribune*, 27 August 1906.

114. *Humboldt Union*, 2 August 1928.

115. Thomas 1995.

116. *Chanute Daily Tribune*, 29 August 1906.

117. *Humboldt Union*, 30 May 1912, 13 June 1912, 27 June 1912; *Iola Register*, 2 August 1912, 12 August 1912, 5 July 1913, 18 August 1913.

118. *Humboldt Union*, 18 July 1912, 18 June 1914, 15 July 1915, 9 September 1915; *Iola Register*, 15 July 1912, 20 October 1915. His occupation as an automobile repairman was listed on his draft registration.

119. *Humboldt Union*, 27 June 1918; *Iola Register*, 25 July 1918; Rinaldi 2005; "George Sweatt" 2015.

120. *Humboldt Union*, 29 July 1920, 5 August 1920, 26 August 1920, 9 September 1920, 16 September 1920, 23 September 1920.

121. *Chanute Daily Tribune*, 5 May 1921, 16 May 1921, 26 September 1921; "George Sweatt Register Statistics and History" 2015.

122. *Coffeyville Daily Journal*, 2 September 1922; *Iola Register*, 17 September 1930, 22 September 1930; *Pittsburg Morning Sun*, 18 October 2006; Lester and Miller 2000, p. 18; Moore 1924.

123. Revel and Munoz 2014.

124. Revel and Munoz 2010.

125. Rice 2016.

126. Dixon 2010, p. 6.

127. The tournament is described in chapter 8.

128. *Wichita Negro Star*, 25 January 1935; "Bingo DeMoss" 2016; Carroll 2011; "Dink Mothell" 2016; Dixon 2010, p. 57; Dunkel 2013; Pendleton 1997; Revel and Munoz 2010, 2014; Rice 2016.

129. Campney 2015.

130. Campney 2015; Woods 1983.

CHAPTER 4. AMERICAN INDIAN BASEBALL

1. *Dodge City Times*, 2 June 1877.

2. *Holton Recorder*, 14 August 1879.

3. *Holton Recorder*, 28 August 1879.

4. *Brown County World*, 21 April 1911; *Carpenter's Kansas Lyre* (Rossville), 26 June 1885; *Holton Recorder*, 30 August 1900; *Topeka Daily Capital*, 26 July 1920, 30 August 1920; *Pittsburg Daily Headlight*, 4 May 1897.

5. Unrau 2007.

6. *Brown County World*, 2 August 1895, 3 July 1896, 11 June 1897, 16 July 1897, 23 July 1897, 20 August 1897, 4 February 1898, 15 July 1898, 27 July 1900, 5 June 1903, 7 August 1903, 18 September 1903, 15 July 1904, 22 July 1904, 5 August 1904, 19 August 1904, 26 August 1904, 11 November 1904, 18 August 1905, 25 August 1905, 4 May 1906, 8 June 1906, 22 June 1906, 20 July 1906, 19 June 1908, 14 August 1908, 2 September 1910, 12 July 1912, 13 September 1912, 15 September 1916; *Holton Recorder*, 2 July 1896, 12 August 1897, 13 August 1897; *Troy Weekly Kansas Chief*, 25 August 1898; James 1897; Wilson 1897.

7. Mills and Seymour 1990, p. 385. The reference to Haskell Institute in Haskell, Nebraska, should be Lawrence, Kansas.

8. *Topeka Daily Capital*, 16 March 1890; Anderson 2009, p. 151.

9. *Hays Free Press*, 27 May 1905; *Topeka Daily Capital*, 10 September 1901; Evans 1940; Powers-Beck 2004c, p. 52.

10. *Salina Evening Journal,* 25 August 1908.

11. *Lawrence Journal-World,* 25 May 1980.

12. Stout 2012, p. 61.

13. *Arkansas City Daily Traveler,* 9 June 1894, 31 May 1899, 31 May 1902, 5 September 1905, 15 June 1906, 8 March 1907; *Belle Plaine News,* 17 May 1900; *McPherson Daily Republican,* 29 April 1914; *Meade County News,* 16 July 1903; *Wellington Daily News,* 20 May 1920; *Wichita Daily Eagle,* 28 April 1901, 31 July 1904, 11 May 1912; *Winfield Daily Free Press,* 2 May 1922; *Winfield Evening News,* 8 May 1899.

14. *Topeka Daily Capital,* 12 June 1918.

15. Stout 2012, p. xviii.

16. *Beloit Daily Call,* 22 August 1919, 4 September 1919 (roster); *Holton Recorder,* 30 August 1900; *Onaga Herald,* 19 June 1913, 19 August 1915; *Saint Marys Star,* 28 July 1910; *Topeka Daily Capital,* 20 April 1906, 11 June 1906, 24 June 1906, 28 June 1906, 8 July 1906, 15 March 1908 (incorrectly listed as the Kickapoo Reservation in the Shawnee County League), 14 October 1908, 31 May 1909, 9 May 1910, 13 August 1911, 1 June 1914, 15 July 1917, 16 July 1917, 9 September 1917, 10 September 1917, 14 July 1919, 24 July 1919 (Charles Menninger was mentioned as possible umpire in a Topeka game that took place in the same year he founded the Menninger Clinic), 22 August 1919, 25 August 1919, 30 August 1920, 4 October 1920, 11 October 1920, 25 July 1921, 10 October 1921, 27 October 1921, 31 October 1921, 12 June 1922, 3 July 1922; *Valley Falls New Era,* 7 June 1906, 18 July 1912.

17. *Brown County World,* 15 September 1916; *Topeka Daily Capital,* 25 August 1915, 7 September 1916, 9 September 1917, 31 August 1919, 4 September 1920, 3 September 1922.

18. *Concordia Blade-Empire,* 6 January 1923; *Salina Evening Journal,* 16 January 1923; *Topeka Daily Capital,* 13 June 1921, 30 November 1921; *Wichita Beacon,* 7 January 1923; Moore 1923.

19. *Brown County World,* 10 May 1901, 6 May 1904; *Chanute Daily Tribune,* 9 June 1916, 10 June 1916; *Hoisington Dispatch,* 22 June 1916; *Lawrence Daily Journal-World,* 6 June 1912; *Lawrence Daily World,* 24 May 1905; *Lawrence Jeffersonian Gazette,* 19 April 1905; *McPherson Daily Republican,* 9 June 1916; *Ottawa Evening Herald,* 18 May 1915; Green 2010; Powers-Beck 2004a, 2004c, p. 51–66.

20. *Brown County World,* 24 July 1908; *Chanute Sun,* 18 April 1906, 12 May 1908; *Fort Scott Daily Tribune and Fort Scott Daily Monitor,* 30 June 1908; *Garnett Journal,* 12 August 1910; *Humboldt Union,* 6 August 1910; *Larned Tiller and Toiler,* 22 June 1906, 29 June 1906, 21 August 1908; *Newton Evening Kansan-Republican,* 16 August 1900; *Osage City Free Press,* 19 August 1910; *Ottawa Evening Herald,* 21 May 1904; *Parsons Daily Sun,* 16 April 1906; *Salina Evening Journal,* 9 May 1904, 26 June 1906; *Wichita Daily Beacon,* 2 August 1894, 3 May 1895.

21. *Fort Scott Daily Tribune and Fort Scott Daily Monitor,* 7 May 1908; *Garden City*

Evening Telegram, 25 April 1908; *Junction City Daily Union*, 20 April 1906, 21 April 1906; *Wellington Daily News*, 29 April 1906; Green 2010, p. xxxi–xxxiii.

22. *Fort Scott Daily Tribune and Fort Scott Daily Monitor*, 11 May 1908; *Garden City Evening Telegram*, 16 April 1908.

23. *Barton County Democrat*, 8 May 1908; *Emporia Daily Gazette*, 2 May 1908; *Fort Scott Daily Tribune and Fort Scott Daily Monitor*, 7 May 1908, 9 May 1908, 11 May 1908; *Garden City Evening Telegram*, 16 April 1908, 27 April 1908, 28 April 1908; *Kansas City Kansas Globe*, 18 May 1908; *Larned Tiller and Toiler*, 24 April 1908, 1 May 1908, 8 May 1908; *Newton Evening Kansan-Republican*, 5 May 1908; *Olathe Mirror*, 14 May 1908, 21 May 1908; *Topeka Daily Capital*, 30 April 1908.

24. *Fort Scott Daily Tribune and Fort Scott Daily Monitor*, 7 May 1908, 11 May 1908; *Garden City Evening Telegram*, 27 April 1908.

25. *Kinsley Mercury*, 15 May 1908.

26. *Emporia Daily Gazette*, 2 May 1908.

27. *Lawrence Daily Journal-World*, 12 May 1911; *Saint Marys Star*, 11 May 1911; *Topeka Daily Capital*, 11 May 1911; *Wichita Beacon*, 15 May 1911; Green 2010, p. xxxi–xxxiii.

28. *Iola Register*, 22 July 1920; *Lawrence Daily Journal-World*, 29 June 1920; Powers-Beck 2004a, 2004b.

29. *Brown County World*, 23 July 1897.

30. *Olathe Mirror*, 23 May 1901.

31. *Hays Free Press*, 27 May 1905.

32. *Hays Free Press*, 27 May 1905.

33. *Hays Free Press*, 3 June 1905.

34. *Hays Free Press*, 3 June 1905.

35. Mills and Seymour 1990, p. 386. The game in Blue Rapids is described in chapter 7.

36. *Great Bend Tribune*, 25 July 1921, 1 August 1921, 18 August 1921, 22 August 1921, 29 August 1921, 2 September 1921, 6 September 1921, 12 September 1921, 19 September 1921, 23 September 1921, 28 September 1921, 3 October 1921, 25 March 1922, 1 May 1922, 8 May 1922, 22 May 1922, 5 June 1922, 12 June 1922, 15 June 1922, 19 June 1922, 26 June 1922, 5 July 1922, 13 July 1922, 24 July 1922, 31 July 1922, 5 August 1922, 14 August 1922, 30 September 1922, 6 October 1922, 9 October 1922, 24 October 1924, 28 October 1922; *Hoisington Dispatch*, 4 September 1919; *Hutchinson News*, 17 May 1922, 19 May 1922, 23 May 1922, 24 October 1922; *Larned Tiller and Toiler*, 21 July 1921, 4 August 1921, 18 August 1921, 15 September 1921; "Emmett Bowles" 2016; Sargent 2004.

37. *Emporia Daily Gazette*, 30 July 1924, 9 August 1924, 11 August 1924; *Hutchinson News*, 10 July 1924, 14 July 1924, 24 July 1924, 30 July 1924, 2 May 1925; *Larned Tiller and Toiler*, 26 April 1923, 3 May 1923, 17 May 1923, 31 May 1923, 7 June 1923,

14 June 1923, 21 June 1923, 28 June 1923, 5 July 1923, 12 July 1923, 19 July 1923, 26 July 1923, 2 August 1923, 9 August 1923, 16 August 1923, 23 August 1923, 30 August 1923, 6 September 1923, 13 September 1923, 20 September 1923, 27 September 1923; Sargent 2004; Sutter 2010, p. 65.

38. *Coffeyville Daily Journal*, 14 June 1920, 6 July 1920, 25 September 1920, 27 September 1920, 4 October 1920; *El Dorado Daily Republican*, 1 September 1919, 2 September 1919; *Independence Daily Reporter*, 16 August 1920, 2 November 1920; *Iola Register*, 22 September 1919, 6 October 1919, 3 May 1920, 22 July 1920, 24 July 1920, 26 August 1920; *Lawrence Daily Journal-World*, 25 August 1915, 28 August 1915, 11 April 1916, 13 April 1916, 5 May 1916, 19 May 1916, 25 May 1916, 31 March 1917, 11 April 1917, 20 April 1917, 20 July 1917, 16 May 1918, 10 June 1918, 12 June 1918, 9 August 1918, 23 April 1919, 28 April 1919, 7 May 1919, 26 December 1919, 29 June 1920; Parr 2004.

39. "Ike Kahdot" 2016; Parr 2004; Spencer 1993.

40. *Pittsburg Daily Headlight*, 18 April 1921; "Ike Kahdot" 2016; Parr 2004; Spencer 1993.

41. Bak 1991, p. 251–259; Costello 2014.

42. Bak 2014; Burgos 2007.

43. "Chief Hogsett Career Stats" 2014.

44. Costello 2014.

45. "Chief Hogsett Career Stats" 2014.

46. Kaufman and Kaufman 1995.

47. "Chief Hogsett" 2014.

48. Costello 2014.

49. Powers-Beck 2004c, p. 101.

CHAPTER 5. MEXICAN AND MEXICAN AMERICAN BASEBALL AND SOFTBALL

1. Oppenheimer 1985; Quastler 2004; Rutter 1972, p. 45; Santillán 2008.

2. *Chanute Daily Tribune*, 20 May 1905, 22 February 1906; *Chanute Sun*, 21 October 1905.

3. *Pittsburg Daily Headlight*, 14 April 1916; Ávila 1997; Laird 1975; Oppenheimer 1985; Rutter 1972, p. 20–28; Smith 1981.

4. *Newton Evening Kansan-Republican*, 26 May 1910, 4 June 1911; Ávila 1997; Mendoza 1993; Oppenheimer 1985; Rutter 1972, p. 45–48; Smith 1981.

5. *Chanute Daily Tribune*, 17 March 1905, 22 March 1905, 1 August 1905, 22 October 1905, 18 December 1905, 21 April 1906, 25 April 1907, 3 December 1907; *Chanute Sun*, 11 March 1907; Iber 2014.

6. *Chanute Daily Tribune*, 21 February 1907, 5 June 1916.

7. *Chanute Daily Tribune*, 22 July 1920.

8. Rutter 1972, p. 66.

9. *Topeka Capital Journal*, 1 September 1917 (drawing of a boxcar residence).

10. *Chanute Daily Tribune*, 17 March 1905, 25 August 1909, 31 January 1910; *Newton Evening Kansan-Republican*, 19 February 1913; *Topeka Daily Capital*, 8 February 1907; Rutter 1972, p. 76–77; Fiftieth Annual Mexican-American Softball Tournament Program, 3–5 July 1998, Harvey County Historical Museum archives.

11. *Garden City Herald*, 17 September 1925.

12. *Emporia Daily Gazette*, 16 March 1907; *Hutchinson News*, 13 December 1904; *Lawrence Daily World*, 4 June 1910; *Topeka Daily Capital*, 8 December 1904; *Wichita Daily Beacon*, 8 December 1904.

13. *Chanute Daily Tribune*, 19 May 1914.

14. Garcia 1973.

15. Santillán 2008.

16. Santillán 2008; Santillán et al. 2013, p. 99.

17. Laird 1975.

18. Santillán 2008.

19. *Chanute Daily Tribune*, 18 September 1922; *Hutchinson News*, 9 August 1910; *Lawrence Daily Journal-World*, 20 April 1915; *Ottawa Herald*, 24 January 1920; *Parsons Daily Sun*, 12 October 1915; *Topeka Daily Capital*, 22 October 1916, 20 November 1916, 17 September 1919, 27 June 1920; *Wyandott Herald*, 20 September 1906.

20. Iber 2014; Santillán 2008.

21. *Wichita Beacon*, 30 July 1917.

22. *Olathe Mirror*, 20 July 1922.

23. *Chanute Daily Tribune*, 12 September 1921.

24. *Olathe Mirror*, 13 April 1922.

25. *Olathe Mirror*, 27 April 1922.

26. *Hutchinson News*, 23 July 1926, 8 July 1927, 30 August 1927, 5 September 1927, 6 September 1927.

27. Quastler 2004 (photo of game at Tweentracks).

28. Ávila 1997; Oppenheimer 1985.

29. *Emporia Daily Gazette*, 5 August 1938; *Hutchinson News*, 22 July 1933.

30. *Emporia Daily Gazette*, 13 September 1933, 19 September 1934, 20 September 1934; *Hutchinson News*, 31 July 1936; *Iola Register*, 17 August 1934; *Newton Journal*, 11 September 1930.

31. *Emporia Daily Gazette*, 17 August 1932, 18 May 1933, 4 May 1935, 27 May 1935, 31 May 1940; *Hutchinson News*, 30 July 1932, 29 April 1933, 22 July 1933, 2 August 1933, 7 August 1933, 16 April 1934.

32. *Wichita Beacon*, 19 July 1932; Carroll 2011; Pendleton 1997.

33. *Emporia Daily Gazette*, 11 May 1935, 31 May 1935, 2 June 1935, 21 May 1936; Santillán 2008.

34. *Emporia Daily Gazette*, 22 April 1932.

35. *Hutchinson News*, 5 August 1932.

36. *Hutchinson News*, 17 March 1920.

37. *Emporia Daily Gazette*, 22 April 1932, 7 May 1932; *Hutchinson News*, 17 March 1920, 29 July 1933, 31 July 1936, 4 August 1936, 5 August 1936; *Wichita Beacon*, 12 June 1932, 19 July 1932.

38. *Emporia Daily Gazette*, 22 April 1932, 29 April 1932, 6 May 1932, 10 May 1932, 13 May 1932, 20 May 1932, 25 May 1932, 3 June 1932, 11 June 1932, 17 June 1932, 18 June 1932, 30 June 1932, 12 July 1932, 14 July 1932, 4 August 1932, 27 April 1933, 29 April 1933, 4 May 1933, 27 May 1933, 4 May 1935, 8 May 1935, 25 May 1935, 27 May 1935, 1 June 1935, 8 June 1935, 15 June 1935, 18 June 1935, 27 June 1935.

39. *Emporia Daily Gazette*, 31 May 1940.

40. Burgos 2007, p. 34–46; McKenna 2016; Nowlin 2016.

41. Martinez 2015.

42. Iber 2014.

43. Sutter 2010, p. 156–173; Tenney 2016, p. 101–117.

44. Santillán 2008.

45. Santillán 2008.

46. *Newton Evening Kansan-Republican*, 5 July 1946, 3 July 1947, 5 July 1950; *Newton Kansan*, 7 July 1952, 3 July 1953; Santillán 2008; Fiftieth Annual Mexican-American Softball Tournament Program 1998.

CHAPTER 6. MINOR LEAGUES AND THE ESTABLISHMENT OF NIGHT BASEBALL

1. Mills and Seymour 1990, p. 205–208.

2. Fleitz 2004; "Jake Beckley" 2015; Kansas Baseball History Project; Madden and Stewart 2002, p. 13–20; "Western League (A) Encyclopedia and History" 2015.

3. *Topeka Daily Capital*, 4 October 1887, 24 June 1906 (Golden Giants team photo); Kansas Baseball History Project; Madden and Stewart 2002, p. 20–28; "Western League (A) Encyclopedia and History" 2015.

4. *Pittsburg Sun*, 26 January 1921.

5. Dickson and McAfee 2009, p. 546; "General History" 2015; Johnson and Wolff 2007, p. 15–16; Morris 2010, p. 344–345.

6. Cronin 2013; "Teams by Classification" 2016.

7. Kansas Baseball History Project; "Wichita, Kansas Register City Encyclopedia" 2015.

8. "American Association (Independent) Encyclopedia and History" 2015; *Independent Professional Baseball Federation* 2016; "History" 2015; "Important Dates in Wingnuts History" 2016.

9. "Pecos League (Independent) Encyclopedia and History" 2015; *Official Website of the Pecos League* 2015.

10. Kansas Baseball History Project.

11. Simon 2016; "1907 Western Association" 2015; "Top 100 Teams" 2015.

12. *Junction City (Daily) Union*, 22 July 1901, 25 April 1910, 27 May 1910, 23 June 1910; *Topeka Daily Capital*, 30 June 1914, 5 August 1914; "Jimmy Whelan" 2016.

13. *New Philadelphia (OH) Daily Times*, 23 February 1931; "Les Barnhart" 2016.

14. *Coffeyville Daily Journal*, 28 March 1906; *Iola Register*, 11 June 1906, 16 April 1907, 26 April 1907, 29 April 1907, 8 June 1907, 13 June 1907, 25 June 1907, 1 July 1907, 10 July 1907, 13 July 1907, 15 July 1907, 23 July 1907, 8 August 1907, 14 August 1907, 11 March 1908, 28 March 1908, 27 April 1908, 4 May 1908, 8 July 1908, 10 July 1908, 19 October 1908, 10 April 1909; "Ad Brennan" 2016; Wiggins 2016.

15. *Wichita Daily Eagle*, 30 June 1907; Lamb 2016.

16. "Art Weaver" 2016; Lamb 2016.

17. "Joe Wilhoit" 2016; Rives 2016.

18. "Nick Allen" 2016; Sandoval 2016.

19. "Roy Garvin Sanders" 2016 ; "Roy Lee Sanders" 2016.

20. *Emporia Gazette*, 2 June 1914, 12 January 1915, 10 May 1915; *Fort Scott Tribune and Fort Scott Monitor*, 28 August 1911, 12 August 1913, 18 June 1919, 29 June 1920, 14 February 1923; *Iola Register*, 6 November 1918, 26 May 1928, 9 December 1933; *Kansas City Kansan*, 10 May 1921, 4 July 1921, 7 July 1921; *Topeka Daily Capital*, 30 January 1916, 14 July 1916, 15 February 1918, 21 April 1918, 16 July 1919; *Wichita Beacon*, 13 March 1911; "Otis Lambeth" 2016.

21. "Bill Burwell" 2016; Wolf 2013.

22. Eddleton 1980; Pietrusza 1997.

23. *Pittsburgh Post*, 8 July 1909; Eddleton 1980; Pietrusza 1997.

24. Eddleton 1980; Pietrusza 1997; Skelton 2016.

25. *Concordia Daily Blade*, 25 July 1905; Bowman 1995.

26. *Kansas City Times*, 30 June 1910.

27. *Junction City Daily Union*, 1 September 1908.

28. *Garnett Journal*, 12 August 1910; *Lawrence Daily World*, 12 August 1910; *Osage City Free Press*, 19 August 1910.

29. *Parsons Daily Sun*, 17 July 1920, 19 July 1920.

30. Metcalf 2016.

31. *Independence Daily Reporter*, 10 June 1886, 17 August 1886, 17 September 1886, 18 June 1887, 19 May 1888, 11 June 1889, 27 May 1890, 20 June 1894, 26 June 1894, 8 August 1894, 2 June 1895, 26 June 1895, 3 April 1896, 5 April 1896, 15 May 1896, 4 December 1896, 21 August 1897, 14 July 1898, 13 March 1899, 30 September 1904, 3 July 1905; *Independence (Weekly) Star and Kansan*, 18 September 1885, 11 June 1886, 20 August 1886, 27 August 1886, 14 June 1889, 22 May 1891, 21 July 1893, 4 August 1893; Edwards 1881; Richmond 1916; Kansas Baseball History Project.

32. *Independence Daily Reporter*, 13 April 1906, 14 June 1906, 16 March 1907, 11 June 1907, 6 July 1907, 3 April 1908; *Independence Evening Star*, 11 April 1906, 7 May 1906, 21 June 1906, 27 June 1906, 2 June 1907; Edwards 1881; Richmond 1916; Kansas Baseball History Project.

33. *Independence Daily Reporter*, 29 January 1909, 16 March 1910, 26 March 1910,

13 March 1911; *Independence Evening Star*, 29 April 1909, 3 June 1909, 10 March 1910, 16 March 1911, 16 April 1912; Kansas Baseball History Project.

34. *Independence Daily Reporter*, 9 April 1913; *Independence Evening Star*, 21 June 1913.

35. *Independence Daily Reporter*, 9 June 1913, 11 June 1913, 5 July 1913, 14 July 1913, 10 June 1915, 11 October 1915; *Independence Evening Star*, 14 October 1915.

36. Brown 1980, p. 15; Duncan 1903, p. 489–490.

37. *Independence Daily Reporter*, 6 July 1918, 30 July 1918, 25 November 1918, 12 May 1919, 16 June 1920, 30 July 1920; *Independence Evening Star*, 25 March 1920.

38. *Independence Daily Reporter*, 26 February 1921, 4 March 1921, 21 May 1921, 25 May 1921, 4 June 1921, 5 August 1921.

39. *Independence Daily Reporter*, 15 March 1922.

40. *Independence Daily Reporter*, 29 December 1922.

41. *Independence Daily Reporter*, 17 June 1937.

42. Kansas Baseball History Project; "Top 100 Teams" 2015.

43. Kansas Baseball History Project; "Mickey Mantle" 2015.

44. Bowman 1995.

45. The Ban Johnson League is described in chapter 8.

46. Described in chapter 17.

47. Bowman 1996; Lester 2015.

48. *Independence Daily Reporter*, 13 March 1930, 17 March 1930, 28 March 1930, 10 April 1930, 16 April 1930, 18 April 1930; *Independence Evening Star*, 1 June 1906, 29 April 1922; Bowman 1995.

49. Bowman 1995.

50. *Independence Daily Reporter*, 29 April 1930; Bowman 1995, 1996; Kansas Baseball History Project.

51. Bowman 1996.

52. Bowman 1995; "Pioneer Night Baseball in Des Moines," 1963.

53. *Independence Daily Reporter*, 5 September 1930; Bowman 1996.

54. *Independence Daily Reporter*, 29 April 1930, 1 May 1930, 12 May 1930, 17 May 1930, 26 May 1930, 27 May 1930, 2 June 1930, 3 June 1930, 7 June 1930, 23 June 1930, 30 June 1930, 12 July 1930, 21 July 1930, 26 July 1930, 1 August 1930, 2 August 1930, 9 August 1930, 14 August 1930, 26 August 1930.

55. *Independence Daily Reporter*, 20 March 1931, 28 April 1931.

CHAPTER 7. MAJOR LEAGUE EXHIBITION GAMES AND TOURS

1. Carey 2016; Thomas 1995.

2. Skelton 2016.

3. Costello 2014.

4. Anderson 2015b.

5. Johnson 2016b, 2016c.

6. Foster 2014; Wood 2013.

7. Dunkle 2016.

8. Pomrenke 2016.

9. The National Baseball Congress is discussed in chapter 8.

10. Louisa 2016.

11. Jacobsen 2016.

12. Nitz 2015.

13. Lowry 2006, p. 196–197.

14. McMahon 2015; Nitz 2015.

15. *Lawrence Daily Kansas Tribune*, 19 April 1870; *Leavenworth Times and Conservative*, 16 April 1870, 24 April 1870.

16. *Lawrence Daily Kansas Tribune*, 19 April 1870; *Leavenworth Times and Conservative*, 22 April 1870, 4 May 1870.

17. *Fort Scott Daily Monitor*, 6 May 1870; *Lawrence Republican Daily Journal*, 4 May 1870, 13 May 1870; *Lawrence Daily Kansas Tribune*, 14 May 1870; *Leavenworth Times and Conservative*, 12 May 1870; *Weekly Osage Chronicle*, 7 May 1870.

18. Fleitz 2015; McMahon 2015.

19. *Lawrence Republican Daily Journal*, 23 June 1871, 28 June 1871, 29 June 1871; *Lawrence Daily Kansas Tribune*, 23 June 1871, 24 June 1871.

20. "1871 National Association Team Statistics and Standings" 2015.

21. During this first attempt to organize the Nebraska State League, three teams had African American players in what would be the closing decade of integration in organized baseball—William Castone and Bud Fowler played for the Lincoln team, which moved to Kearney; Frank Maupin, John Patterson, and John Reeves played for Plattsmouth; and George Taylor played for Beatrice (Bond 2004).

22. *Hastings Gazette-Journal*, 5 July 1887; *Omaha Daily Bee*, 27 October 1888; *Parsons Daily Sun*, 20 October 1888; Burton and Lewis 1916, p. 302–306; Fleitz 2015; Lamster 2006, p. 70; McMahon 2015.

23. *Emporia Weekly News*, 29 April 1886; *Leavenworth Daily Times*, 25 April 1886, 27 April 1886; *Topeka Daily Capital*, 22 April 1886, 23 April 1886, 24 April 1886; *Topeka Daily Commonwealth*, 22 April 1886, 23 April 1886, 24 April 1886; Kansas Baseball History Project.

24. *Fort Scott Daily Monitor*, 3 November 1889, 5 November 1889, 6 November 1889; *Hutchinson News*, 7 November 1889, 8 November 1889, 9 November 1889, 10 November 1889; *Wichita Daily Eagle*, 6 November 1889, 7 November 1889; "1889 American Association Team Statistics and Standings" 2015; Kansas Baseball History Project.

25. *Topeka Daily Capital*, 26 July 1893, 5 October 1893, 18 October 1894, 19 October 1895, 25 October 1898, 2 April 1906; *Topeka State Journal*, 19 June 1891, 9

May 1892; "Duff Cooley" 2015; Kansas Baseball History Project; Leerhsen 2015, p. 94.

26. *Newton Evening Kansan-Republican*, 23 October 1902, 24 October 1902; *Topeka Daily Capital*, 22 October 1902, 23 October 1902.

27. *Leavenworth Daily Times*, 1 April 1903, 2 April 1903, 3 April 1903, 4 April 1903, 5 April 1903, 7 April 1903, 8 April 1903, 9 April 1903, 10 April 1903, 11 April 1903, 14 April 1903, 15 April 1903, 16 April 1903, 17 April 1903, 18 April 1903, 21 April 1903; "1903 Chicago White Sox" 2015.

28. *Parsons Daily Sun*, 12 March 1917, 14 March 1917, 19 March 1917, 20 March 1917, 23 March 1917, 26 March 1917, 28 March 1917, 29 March 1917, 2 April 1917, 4 April 1917.

29. *Parsons Daily Sun*, 21 January 1918, 30 January 1918, 16 February 1918, 2 April 1918, 3 April 1918, 4 April 1918, 10 April 1918, 11 April 1918; Kansas Baseball History Project.

30. *Wichita Daily Beacon*, 29 March 1909, 3 April 1911; Kansas Baseball History Project; Thomas 1995; Wood 2013.

31. Elfers 2003, p. xxi–xxiii; Lamster 2006, p. 287–291.

32. Elfers 2003, p. xxi–xxiii, 21–33.

33. *Blue Rapids Times*, 1 September 1913, 8 September 1913, 20 October 1913; Elfers 2003, p. xxi.

34. *Blue Rapids Times*, 2 October 1913.

35. *Concordia Daily Blade*, 8 October 1913.

36. *Blue Rapids Times*, 16 October 1913, 20 October 1920. The stone building that housed the State Bank on the town square in Blue Rapids still houses a bank, but the adjacent building used for the "base ball headquarters" is gone.

37. *Blue Rapids Times*, 2 October 1913, 9 October 1913, 16 October 1913, 20 October 1913, 23 October 1913.

38. *Blue Rapids Times*, 9 October 1913, 13 October 1913. The Blue Rapids Historical Society has an original ticket and poster. Copies of the poster are used for displays in the museum.

39. *Blue Rapids Times*, 2 October 1913, 23 October 1913.

40. *Atchison Daily Champion*, 3 October 1913; *Blue Rapids Times*, 20 October 1913, 23 October 1913; *Concordia Daily Blade*, 21 October 1913, 25 October 1913; *Junction City (Daily) Union*, 20 October 1913; *Salina Daily Union*, 24 October 1913.

41. *Beloit Daily Call*, 23 March 1914, 29 April 1915; *Clay Center Times*, 24 December 1914, 13 May 1915; *Lawrence Daily Journal-World*, 9 June 1914, 2 December 1914; *Topeka Daily Capital*, 9 May 1914, 22 May 1914, 8 June 1914, 8 February 1915, 12 February 1915, 30 April 1915, 9 May 1915, 20 May 1915, 26 May 1915; Weingroff 2015.

42. *Atchison Daily Champion*, 3 October 1913; *Clay Center Times*, 16 October 1913, 30 October 1913, 6 November 1913; *Concordia Daily Blade*, 25 October 1913; *Junction City (Daily) Union*, 20 October 1913, 22 October 1913, 23 October 1913, 25 October

1913; *Olsburg Gazette*, 24 October 1913; *Onaga Herald*, 30 October 1913; *Salina Daily Union*, 22 October 1913; *Topeka Daily Capital*, 17 August 1913; Elfers 2003, p. 51; Swan 2013.

43. *Wichita Daily Eagle*, 20 November 1913.

44. *Nineteenth Biennial Report of the Kansas State Board of Agriculture to the Legislature of the State for the Years 1913 and 1914* 1915.

45. *Blue Rapids Times*, 27 October 1913; *Concordia Daily Blade*, 25 October 1913; *Topeka Daily Capital*, 25 October 1913; *Wichita Beacon*, 25 October 1913.

46. *Blue Rapids Times*, 27 October 1913.

47. *Chicago Tribune*, 28 October 1913.

48. Association Park in Kansas City, Missouri, the second ballpark by that name, was used by the Kansas City Blues minor league team from 1903 through 1922. The Kansas City Monarchs also used the ballpark in 1920–1922. The two teams played for the city championship at the ballpark in 1921 (won by the Blues) and 1922 (won by the Monarchs). There were no more games between the two teams (Dixon 2010, p. 45–48). A portion of the site is now Blues Municipal Park, which has a small baseball diamond (Lowry 2006, p. 111). It is about half a mile east and two blocks south of the Negro Leagues Baseball Museum.

49. *New York Times*, 27 October 1913.

50. Elfers 2003, p. 55–56.

51. *Chicago Tribune*, 28 October 1913, 29 October 1913; *New York Times*, 29 October 1913; Elfers 2003, p. 57–58.

52. *New York Times*, 25 October 1913.

53. *Chicago Tribune*, 25 October 1913.

54. *Blue Rapids Times*, 23 October 1913; Anderson 2015a; "Bill Klem" 2015; Elfers 2003, p. 48–52.

55. *Chicago Tribune*, 25 October 1913.

56. *Blue Rapids Times*, 27 October 1913.

57. Elfers 2003, p. 51.

58. *Chicago Tribune*, 25 October 1913; *New York Times*, 25 October 1913; *Pittsburgh Gazette Times*, 25 October 1913, 16 November 1913; *San Francisco Call*, 25 October 1913.

59. *Topeka Daily Capital*, 25 October 1913.

60. *Salina Evening Journal*, 24 October 1913; Elfers 2003, p. 58.

61. *Topeka Daily Capital*, 28 October 1913; *Wichita Beacon*, 31 October 1913.

62. *Blue Rapids Times*, 27 October 1913.

63. *Blue Rapids Times*, 20 October 1913.

64. *Atchison Daily Champion*, 25 October 1913; *Junction City (Daily) Union*, 25 October 1913.

65. Elfers 2003, p. xxi–xxiii; Lamster 2006, p. 287–291.

66. Barthel 2007; Fountain 2009; Francis 2016.

CHAPTER 8. THE GAME GOES ON

1. *Leavenworth Daily Times*, 11 May 1882; *Topeka Daily Capital*, 29 February 1876.

2. Mills and Seymour 1990, p. 76–77.

3. *Chanute Daily Tribune*, 17 April 1900; *Chanute Morning Sun*, 26 February 1898; *Kansas City Gazette*, 21 February 1900, 27 April 1900; *Parsons Daily Sun*, 13 April 1898; *Pittsburg Daily Headlight*, 25 March 1899; *Valley Falls New Era*, 22 April 1899; *Wichita Daily Beacon*, 15 April 1898.

4. *Coffeyville Daily Journal*, 26 May 1922.

5. Evans 1940; "History of American Legion Baseball" 2014; Mills and Seymour 1990, p. 85–89.

6. Berlage 1994, p. 90–96; Evans 1940; "History of American Legion Baseball" 2014; Mills and Seymour 1990, p. 88.

7. Discussed more fully in chapter 16.

8. American Legion 2016.

9. *Topeka Daily Capital*, 31 May 1933; Corbett 2015; "Murry Dickson" 2015; Nowlin 2008.

10. "History of Little League" 2014.

11. Babe Ruth League 2015; "Kansas State" 2015.

12. *Kansas NBC Hap Dumont Youth Baseball* 2016.

13. Peterson and Tomashek 2006; Thornley 2006, p. 3–11, 124–142.

14. Minnesota Baseball Association 2016.

15. Dickinson Press Staff 2011; South Dakota Amateur Baseball Association 2016.

16. *Nebraska Baseball Association* 2014.

17. *Dodge County Baseball League* 2016; *Lincoln Adult Baseball League* 2016; *Omaha Adult Baseball League* 2016. Populations given are from 2010.

18. Kansas Department of Agriculture 2016; Wuthnow 2011, 2016.

19. *Ellis County News*, 14 June 1928; *Hays Daily News*, 10 May 1940.

20. *Atchison Daily Champion*, 1 June 1888; *Hays Daily News*, 11 June 1937; *McPherson Daily Republican*, 6 June 1908; *Parsons Daily Sun*, 22 March 1917; *Pittsburg Daily Headlight*, 18 May 1921; *Wellington Daily News*, 10 October 1923, 17 October 1925; *Wichita Daily Beacon*, 24 June 1909; *Wichita Daily Eagle*, 7 May 1905.

21. *Chanute Tribune and Daily Timesett*, 28 September 1936, 2 October 1936.

22. *Wellington Daily News*, 10 October 1923; Vecsey 2006, p. 97–106; Walker 2015, p. 15–16, 21–41.

23. Peterson 2003, p. 50.

24. Walker and Bellamy 2008, p. 3–42.

25. *Kansas City Star*, 29 March 2002; Evans 1940; *Ban Johnson Amateur League Baseball* 2014.

26. *Salina Journal*, 28 March 28 1933.

27. *Iola Register*, 28 February 1938; Evans 1940.

28. *Emporia Daily Gazette*, 11 March 1939.

29. *Hutchinson News*, 3 May 1951; *Junction City (Daily) Union*, 18 February 1947, 21 February 1947, 25 February 1947, 27 February 1947, 3 March 1947, 29 March 1947, 8 May 1947.

30. *Garden City Telegram*, 11 July 1957.

31. *Hays Daily News*, 7 March 1960.

32. *Jayhawk Baseball League* 2016; *Kansas Collegiate League Baseball* 2016; *Mid-Plains League* 2016; *M.I.N.K. Collegiate Baseball League* 2016.

33. Broeg 1989, p. 32–34.

34. *American Amateur Baseball Congress* 2016.

35. Mills and Seymour 1990, p. 281–284.

36. Mills and Seymour 1990, p. 286.

37. Broeg 1989, p. 32–33; Dunkel 2013, p. 174–177.

38. The stadium is covered in more detail in chapter 11.

39. Broeg 1989, p. 33–36; Dunkel 2013, p. 179–182; Larsen 2007a, 2007b.

40. Broeg 1989, p. 37–49, 187–188; Dunkel 2013, p. 189–238; Larsen 2007a, 2007b.

41. Broeg 1989, p. 142–145; Evans 1940.

42. *Hays Daily News*, 26 May 1968, 18 May 1969.

43. The reference to the golden age of town team baseball is from Phil Dixon in a 2016 documentary on Kansas town teams—*Town Teams: Bigger than Baseball*.

PART II. HISTORICAL BASEBALL PARKS IN KANSAS

1. *Final Report on the WPA Program, 1935–43* 1947.

2. Major League Baseball 2016, p. 2.

CHAPTER 9. JOE CAMPBELL MEMORIAL STADIUM, ROSSVILLE

1. *Carpenter's Kansas Lyre* (Rossville), 31 July 1885, 21 May 1886, 4 June 1886, 11 June 1886, 18 June 1886, 16 July 1886, 23 July 1886, 6 August 1886, 13 August 1886, 13 May 1887, 1 July 1887, 8 July 1887; *Rossville News*, 18 August 1883, 11 May 1900, 15 June 1900, 29 June 1900, 3 August 1900, 31 August 1900, 7 September 1900; *Rossville Reporter*, 21 June 1907, 5 July 1907, 5 June 1908, 19 June 1908, 4 June 1909, 27 May 1910, 3 June 1910, 9 June 1911, 7 June 1912, 15 August 1913, 11 June 1914, 10 June 1915, 12 August 1915, 8 June 1916, 22 June 1916, 14 June 1917, 28 June 1917, 16 August 1917, 5 June 1919, 12 June 1919, 26 June 1919, 10 July 1919, 31 July 1919, 7 August 1919; *Rossville Times*, 20 July 1894, 5 July 1895; *Topeka Weekly Commonwealth*, 19 July 1877, 1 May 1879.

2. *Rossville Reporter*, 14 October 1920, 21 October 1920, 18 November 1920, 16 June 1921; *Topeka Daily Capital*, 17 October 1920.

3. *Rossville Reporter*, 2 June 1911, 17 July 1919, 12 January 1922, 26 January 1922, 28 February 1922, 9 March 1922, 6 April 1922, 20 April 1922, 27 April 1922, 4 May 1922; *Topeka Daily Capital*, 30 April 1922.

4. *Rossville Reporter*, 16 November 1922, 15 February 1923, 1 March 1923; *Topeka Daily Capital*, 19 November 1922.

5. *Rossville Reporter*, 5 April 1923, 12 April 1923.

6. *Rossville Reporter*, 25 June 1931.

7. *Rossville Reporter*, 12 April 1923 (illustration of the original park layout), 1 May 1924.

8. *Rossville Reporter*, 11 June 1925.

9. *Rossville Reporter*, 1 May 1924, 8 May 1924.

10. *Rossville Reporter*, 15 May 1924, 22 May 1924.

11. *Rossville Reporter*, 12 June 1924.

12. *Rossville Reporter*, 5 June 1924.

13. *Rossville Reporter*, 4 June 1925, 30 May 1929.

14. *Carpenter's Kansas Lyre* (Rossville), 1 July 1887; *Rossville Reporter*, 19 September 1923, 2 April 1925.

15. *Rossville Reporter*, 7 August 1924, 14 August 1924.

16. *Rossville Reporter*, 9 July 1925.

17. *Rossville Reporter*, 18 June 1925, 30 July 1925, 20 August 1925.

18. *Rossville Reporter*, 23 July 1925, 6 August 1925.

19. *Rossville Reporter*, 1 September 1932, 14 September 1933; *Topeka Daily Capital*, 10 June 1917.

20. *Rossville Reporter*, 3 July 1924.

21. *Rossville Reporter*, 5 July 1928.

22. *Rossville Reporter*, 5 April 1934, 26 April 1934, 17 May 1934, 7 June 1934.

23. *Rossville Reporter*, 1 May 1930, 11 June 1936, 20 August 1936.

24. *Rossville Reporter*, 9 June 1938.

25. *Rossville Reporter*, 13 April 1939.

26. *Rossville Reporter*, 25 June 1936, 16 July 1936, 15 October 1936, 12 November 1936, 31 December 1936.

27. *Rossville Reporter*, 15 May 1924, 22 May 1924, 21 July 1938.

28. *Rossville Reporter*, 15 April 1954, 22 April 1954, 13 May 1954, 3 June 1954, 17 June 1954, 12 August 1954.

29. *Rossville Reporter*, 17 March 1955, 24 March 1955, 7 April 1955, 14 April 1955, 28 April 1955, 9 June 1955, 16 June 1955, 23 June 1955, 30 June 1955; *Rossville Centennial Booklet* 1971, p. 147.

CHAPTER 10. SOUTH PARK FIELD, KINSLEY

1. *Edwards County Leader*, 21 June 1877, 28 June 1877, 12 July 1877, 2 August 1877, 9 August 1877, 30 August 1877.

2. *Edwards County Leader*, 11 July 1878; *Kinsley Graphic*, 1 June 1878, 13 July 1878; *Valley Republican* (Kinsley), 20 April 1878.

3. *Kinsley Graphic*, 24 August 1878, 12 July 1879, 11 October 1879, 18 October 1879.

4. *Kinsley Graphic*, 10 July 1880.

5. *Kinsley Graphic*, 2 July 1881, 9 July 1881, 16 July 1881, 23 July 1881, 6 August 1881.

6. *Kinsley Graphic*, 15 June 1882, 29 March 1890; *Kinsley Mercury*, 7 August 1886.

7. *Kinsley Graphic*, 26 April 1889, 4 April 1890; *Kinsley Mercury*, 6 June 1885, 7 August 1886, 13 November 1886, 18 June 1887, 11 August 1887, 29 March 1890, 21 August 1890.

8. *Kinsley Graphic*, 7 December 1878.

9. *Kinsley Graphic*, 14 June 1879, 6 September 1879.

10. *Kinsley Graphic*, 12 July 1879.

11. *Kinsley Graphic*, 14 June 1917, 6 June 1917, 16 September 1920, 23 September 1920, 7 October 1920, 28 July 1921; *Kinsley Mercury*, 31 August 1916, 24 May 1917, 14 June 1917, 28 June 1917, 30 September 1920, 9 June 1921, 16 June 1921, 20 July 1922, 27 July 1922, 10 August 1922.

12. *Kinsley Graphic*, 9 July 1886, 23 July 1886, 30 July 1886, 10 August 1888, 21 September 1888, 27 September 1889, 12 August 1892, 28 June 1895; *Kinsley Mercury*, 26 June 1886, 10 July 1886, 17 July 1886, 31 July 1886, 21 August 1886, 16 July 1887, 23 July 1887, 8 September 1887, 22 September 1887, 29 September 1887, 21 September 1888, 26 September 1889, 21 August 1890, 27 June 1895.

13. *Kinsley Graphic*, 11 September 1885, 23 October 1885; *Kinsley Mercury*, 12 September 1885, 19 September 1885, 17 October 1885, 31 October 1885, 16 January 1886, 14 August 1886, 2 October 1886, 9 October 1886.

14. *Kinsley Mercury*, 5 September 1889.

15. *Kinsley Graphic*, 17 May 1895, 26 June 1903; *Kinsley Mercury*, 30 May 1885, 13 June 1889.

16. *Kinsley Graphic*, 28 February 1896; *Kinsley Mercury*, 27 August 1896.

17. *Kinsley Graphic*, 15 April 1898, 10 June 1898, 12 May 1899, 9 June 1899, 16 June 1899, 23 June 1899, 14 June 1901, 13 June 1902; *Kinsley Mercury*, 13 February 1896, 22 April 1897, 19 June 1903; Ogle and Company 1906a.

18. *Kinsley Graphic*, 20 May 1904, 10 June 1904, 17 June 1904.

19. *Kinsley Graphic*, 10 June 1904.

20. *Kinsley Graphic*, 17 June 1904.

21. *Kinsley Graphic*, 2 June 1910.

22. *Kinsley Graphic*, 16 September 1920; *Kinsley Mercury*, 23 April 1914.

23. *Kinsley Graphic*, 21 June 1907, 16 April 1908, 28 May 1908, 5 May 1910, 18 August 1910, 15 September 1910, 6 July 1911, 3 August 1911.

24. *Kinsley Graphic*, 6 May 1915, 29 July 1915, 30 March 1916, 15 June 1916, 31 August 1916, 24 May 1917, 7 June 1917, 14 June 1917, 21 June 1917, 28 June 1917,

6 September 1917, 5 June 1919, 26 May 1921, 16 June 1921, 22 April 1926; *Kinsley Mercury*, 6 May 1915, 27 May 1915, 22 June 1916, 5 July 1916, 21 April 1921, 26 May 1921, 5 July 1923.

25. *Kinsley Graphic*, 8 February 1923; *Kinsley Mercury*, 8 September 1921, 8 February 1923, 15 February 1923.

26. *Kinsley Mercury*, 4 March 1920.

27. *Kinsley Graphic*, 6 May 1920, 27 May 1920, 10 June 1920, 17 June 1920, 24 June 1920, 1 July 1920, 8 July 1920, 15 July 1920, 29 July 1920, 12 August 1920, 19 August 1920, 26 August 1920, 2 September 1920, 9 September 1920, 23 September 1920, 7 October 1920, 28 July 1921; *Kinsley Mercury*, 30 September 1920, 2 June 1921, 16 June 1921, 28 July 1921, 20 July 1922, 27 July 1922, 10 August 1922.

28. *Kinsley Graphic*, 21 April 1921, 26 May 1921, 16 June 1921, 4 August 1921, 25 August 1921, 27 July 1922; *Kinsley Mercury*, 30 March 1922, 7 June 1923.

29. *Kinsley Graphic*, 17 April 1924, 11 September 1924, 18 September 1924, 23 April 1925, 30 April 1925, 13 May 1926, 20 May 1926, 27 May 1926, 21 April 1927, 19 April 1928, 2 May 1929, 23 May 1929, 27 June 1929, 25 July 1929; *Kinsley Mercury*, 21 June 1923, 25 July 1929.

30. *Kinsley Graphic*, 15 May 1930, 5 June 1930, 12 June 1930; *Kinsley Mercury*, 15 May 1930, 22 May 1930.

31. *Dodge City Globe-Republican*, 22 June 1894.

32. *Kinsley Graphic*, 8 April 1904.

33. *Barton County Democrat*, 24 September 1909.

34. *Kinsley Graphic*, 4 June 1931; *Kinsley Mercury*, 21 May 1931.

35. *Kinsley Graphic*, 23 April 1931, 30 April 1931, 7 May 1931, 14 May 1931, 21 May 1931, 4 June 1931, 11 June 1931, 21 April 1932, 28 April 1932, 5 May 1932, 12 May 1932, 26 May 1932, 2 June 1932, 16 June 1932, 7 July 1932, 21 July 1932, 28 July 1932, 4 August 1932, 11 August 1932, 18 August 1932, 25 August 1932, 1 September 1932, 8 September 1932, 15 September 1932, 6 April 1933, 27 April 1933, 4 May 1933, 11 May 1933, 18 May 1933, 25 May 1933, 8 June 1933, 15 June 1933, 22 June 1933, 29 June 1933, 3 August 1933, 10 August 1933, 17 August 1933.

36. *Kinsley Graphic*, 22 February 1934; *Kinsley Mercury*, 15 February 1934.

37. *Kinsley Graphic*, 1 March 1934, 8 March 1934, 15 March 1934; Kinsley Board of Commissioners, *Minutes of the Regular Meetings*, 5 March 1934, transcript, Kinsley Public Library; Kinsley Board of Commissioners, *Minutes of the Regular Meetings*, 19 March 1934, transcript, Kinsley Public Library.

38. *Kinsley Graphic*, 24 May 1934; *Kinsley Mercury*, 24 May 1934.

39. *Kinsley Mercury*, 24 May 1934.

40. *Kinsley Mercury*, 8 March 1934.

41. *Kinsley Graphic*, 18 April 1935, 25 April 1935, 2 May 1935, 9 May 1935, 16 May 1935, 23 May 1935, 30 May 1935, 6 June 1935, 13 June 1935, 20 June 1935, 27 June 1935, 4 July 1935, 18 July 1935, 25 July 1935, 1 August 1935, 15 August 1935, 22 August

1935, 29 August 1935, 5 September 1935, 12 September 1935, 19 September 1935, 26 September 1935, 3 October 1935.

42. *Kinsley Graphic*, 14 May 1936, 21 May 1936, 28 May 1936, 18 June 1936, 25 June 1936, 2 July 1936, 9 July 1936, 16 July 1936, 27 August 1936, 3 September 1936, 13 May 1937, 27 May 1937, 24 June 1937, 15 July 1937; *Kinsley Mercury*, 7 May 1936, 14 May 1936, 21 May 1936, 13 August 1936, 27 August 1936, 13 May 1937, 17 June 1937, 24 June 1937, 8 July 1937, 22 July 1937, 12 August 1937, 19 August 1937, 26 August 1937, 2 September 1937, 16 September 1937.

43. *Kinsley Mercury*, 12 May 1938, 19 May 1938, 2 June 1938, 9 June 1938, 23 June 1938, 14 July 1938, 21 July 1938, 28 July 1938, 4 August 1938, 11 August 1938, 28 August 1938, 1 September 1938, 22 September 1938, 29 September 1938, 27 April 1939, 4 May 1939, 11 May 1939, 18 May 1939, 25 May 1939, 1 June 1939, 8 June 1939, 15 June 1939, 22 June 1939, 29 June 1939, 6 July 1939, 13 July 1939, 20 July 1939, 27 July 1939, 3 August 1939, 10 August 1939, 17 August 1939, 24 August 1939, 31 August 1939, 7 September 1939, 14 September 1939, 21 September 1939.

44. *Kinsley Mercury*, 9 May 1940, 16 May 1940, 23 May 1940, 30 May 1940, 6 June 1940, 20 June 1940, 27 June 1940, 11 July 1940, 18 July 1940, 25 July 1940, 1 August 1940, 8 August 1940, 15 August 1940, 22 August 1940, 5 September 1940, 12 September 1940.

CHAPTER 11. LAWRENCE-DUMONT STADIUM, WICHITA

1. *Wichita City (Weekly) Eagle*, 13 February 1873, 13 March 1873, 20 March 1873; Price 2003, p. 55; Rives 2004, p. 11–12.

2. *Wichita City (Weekly) Eagle*, 9 April 1874, 23 April 1874, 28 May 1874, 4 June 1874, 18 June 1874.

3. *Wichita City (Weekly) Eagle*, 30 July 1874, 6 August 1874, 13 August 1874, 20 August 1874, 10 September 1874, 15 October 1874.

4. Rives 2004.

5. *Wichita Daily Beacon*, 25 May 1887, 27 May 1887, 2 June 1887, 4 June 1887; Kansas Baseball History Project.

6. This game is also described in chapter 2.

7. *Wichita Daily Beacon*, 20 May 1891, 25 April 1892, 20 August 1892, 9 September 1892, 11 July 1902; *Wichita Daily Eagle*, 6 June 1890, 1 July 1890, 4 September 1892, 8 September 1892, 16 May 1894.

8. *Wichita Daily Beacon*, 10 March 1898, 26 March 1898; *Wichita Daily Eagle*, 2 March 1898, 10 March 1898, 20 March 1898, 3 April 1898, 8 September 1898, 6 April 1900; Kansas Baseball History Project.

9. *Wichita Daily Eagle*, 16 April 1901, 18 April 1901, 5 July 1901.

10. *Wichita Daily Eagle*, 4 April 1901, 21 April 1901.

11. *Wichita Beacon*, 21 March 1916; *Wichita Daily Eagle*, 7 January 1906, 20 August 1911, 22 March 1916.

12. *Wichita Daily Eagle*, 4 April 1920.

13. *Wichita Daily Beacon*, 16 October 1902, 26 August 1909, 27 December 1909, 14 August 1911, 24 April 1912; *Wichita Daily Eagle*, 8 May 1900, 30 April 1903, 3 October 1903, 30 April 1905, 19 November 1905, 7 January 1906, 5 October 1906, 17 October 1907.

14. *Wichita Daily Eagle*, 11 September 1915.

15. *Wichita Daily Beacon*, 31 August 1901; *Wichita Daily Eagle*, 6 September 1901.

16. *Wichita Beacon*, 2 February 1914, 8 April 1914; *Wichita Daily Eagle*, 16 April 1932, 17 April 1932.

17. *Wichita Daily Beacon*, 5 July 1909, 12 May 1910; *Wichita Daily Eagle*, 29 April 1916, 19 May 1917.

18. *Wichita Beacon*, 29 August 1917; *Wichita Daily Eagle*, 30 August 1917, 30 September 1917.

19. The origin of the devastating "Spanish flu" pandemic associated with the First World War, which killed millions of people around the world, is still uncertain, but it has been linked to influenza outbreaks in Haskell County in southwestern Kansas and Camp Funston at Fort Riley near Junction City (Barry 2004a, p. 91–97, 2004b; Humphries 2014).

20. *Wichita Daily Eagle*, 31 March 1920, 4 April 1920, 21 April 1920.

21. *Wichita Daily Eagle*, 1 November 1922, 16 April 1932, 17 April 1932.

22. *Wichita Beacon*, 28 May 1922, 31 May 1922, 5 June 1922, 6 June 1922; Pendleton 1997.

23. *Wichita Beacon*, 21 July 1922, 1 August 1922, 7 August 1922, 24 August 1922, 17 September 1922; Pendleton 1997.

24. Kansas Baseball History Project.

25. *Wichita Daily Beacon*, 11 March 1905, 21 March 1905, 4 April 1905, 20 April 1905; *Wichita Daily Eagle*, 12 March 1905, 18 March 1905, 19 March 1905, 22 March 1905, 20 April 1911; Ogle and Company 1905c.

26. *Wichita Daily Beacon*, 19 April 1905, 26 April 1905; *Wichita Daily Eagle*, 8 April 1905, 7 May 1905, 10 May 1905, 24 May 1905, 28 May 1905, 30 May 1905.

27. *Wichita Daily Eagle*, 8 September 1905, 4 October 1905, 6 October 1905, 7 October 1905, 15 October 1905, 17 October 1905.

28. *Wichita Daily Beacon*, 1 November 1909; *Wichita Daily Eagle*, 13 December 1908.

29. *Wichita Beacon*, 11 May 1911, 8 June 1911, 10 June 1911, 24 June 1911, 27 July 1911, 5 September 1911; *Wichita Daily Eagle*, 21 May 1911, 20 August 1911, 20 September 1911, 11 October 1911, 29 December 1911.

30. *Wichita Daily Beacon*, 12 July 1892, 16 August 1905, 31 January 1917, 15 August 1917, 13 March 1918, 1 March 1920; *Wichita Daily Eagle*, 20 August 1905, 20 October 1905, 10 March 1918, 21 September 1918.

31. *Wichita Beacon*, 17 January 1912, 20 February 1912, 19 March 1912 (photo of

grandstand), 19 April 1912, 1 June 1912; *Wichita Daily Eagle*, 21 January 1912, 3 April 1912, 5 April 1912, 11 April 1912, 1 May 1912, 5 March 1914, 2 August 1920, 31 March 1921.

32. *Wichita Beacon*, 20 July 1918; *Wichita Daily Eagle*, 17 September 1915, 15 July 1919, 22 November 1921.

33. *Wichita Beacon*, 29 May 1920.

34. *Wichita Daily Eagle*, 2 July 1912, 17 August 1919.

35. Strecker 2015.

36. *Wichita Daily Eagle*, 3 June 1930, 16 April 1932, 17 April 1932, 22 April 1932, 30 November 1933; Carroll 2011; Rives 2004, p. 22–23.

37. *Wichita Beacon*, 22 July 1934, 24 July 1934; *Wichita Eagle*, 1 February 1934, 26 March 1934 (stadium construction photo), 2 July 1934 (grandstand construction photo), 22 July 1934, 24 July 1934 (stadium photo), 29 July 1934 (stadium photo); Broeg 1989.

38. *Wichita Beacon*, 1 August 1924, 3 August 1934, 15 August 1934, 18 August 1934, 19 August 1934; *Wichita Eagle*, 3 July 1934.

39. *Wichita Beacon*, 22 July 1934, 22 November 1934; *Wichita Eagle*, 17 September 1934, 22 November 1934.

40. The teams for these periods are listed in chapter 6.

CHAPTER 12. CLINT LIGHTNER FIELD, GARDEN CITY

1. *Garden City Herald*, 27 April 1886, 29 April 1886, 5 May 1886, 14 June 1886, 15 June 1886.

2. *Garden City Herald*, 2 June 1887, 6 June 1887, 11 June 1887, 24 June 1887, 25 June 1887, 27 June 1887, 28 June 1887, 5 July 1887, 9 July 1887, 13 July 1887, 16 July 1887, 29 July 1887, 3 August 1887, 8 August 1887, 11 August 1887, 16 August 1887, 17 August 1887, 25 August 1887.

3. Thomas 2004.

4. *Garden City Herald*, 11 May 1888, 21 June 1888, 28 June 1888, 12 July 1888, 27 July 1888, 28 July 1888, 16 July 1889, 17 July 1889, 18 July 1889, 20 July 1889, 22 July 1889, 23 July 1889, 24 July 1889, 25 July 1889, 27 July 1889, 29 July 1889, 3 August 1889, 8 August 1889, 19 August 1889, 26 June 1890, 14 August 1890, 28 August 1890, 18 September 1890, 16 October 1890, 30 October 1890, 21 May 1891, 28 May 1891, 3 June 1893, 8 July 1893, 15 July 1893, 29 July 1893, 5 August 1893, 12 August 1893, 2 September 1893, 9 September 1893, 16 September 1893, 19 May 1894, 2 June 1894, 23 June 1894, 30 June 1894, 7 July 1894, 28 July 1894, 25 August 1894.

5. *Garden City Herald*, 18 May 1895, 22 June 1895, 13 July 1895, 20 July 1895, 19 June 1897, 10 July 1897, 31 July 1897, 14 August 1897, 13 August 1898, 13 May 1899, 20 May 1899, 27 May 1899, 3 June 1899, 8 July 1899, 22 July 1899, 29 July 1899, 5 August 1899, 16 September 1899, 30 September 1899.

6. *Garden City Herald*, 2 August 1902, 23 August 1902.

7. *Garden City Evening Telegram*, 11 April 1907, 3 June 1907, 6 June 1907, 12 June 1907, 15 June 1907, 22 June 1907, 25 June 1907, 5 July 1907, 6 July 1907, 10 July 1907, 12 July 1907, 20 July 1907, 3 August 1907, 5 August 1907, 6 August 1907, 26 August 1907, 16 November 1907.

8. *Garden City Herald*, 20 June 1912, 27 June 1912, 18 July 1912, 25 July 1912, 31 July 1913, 16 July 1914, 23 July 1914, 30 July 1914, 6 August 1914, 13 August 1914, 24 June 1915, 26 August 1915; *Garden City Evening Telegram*, 21 April 1908, 25 April 1908, 27 April 1908, 28 April 1908, 5 May 1908, 28 May 1908, 1 June 1908, 4 June 1908, 5 June 1908, 15 June 1908, 22 June 1908, 3 July 1908, 8 July 1908, 11 July 1908, 10 August 1908, 17 August 1908, 24 August 1908, 31 May 1909, 4 June 1909, 18 June 1909, 28 June 1909, 5 July 1909, 24 July 1909, 4 August 1909, 6 September 1909, 8 September 1909, 9 May 1910, 1 June 1910, 2 June 1910, 5 July 1910, 18 July 1910, 21 July 1910, 1 May 1911, 15 May 1911, 20 May 1911, 22 May 1911, 5 June 1911, 10 July 1911, 19 August 1911, 31 August 1911; *Garden City Telegram*, 21 May 1915, 11 June 1915.

9. *Garden City Herald*, 8 May 1919, 14 August 1919; *Garden City Telegram*, 7 August 1919, 18 September 1919, 2 October 1919, 5 October 1922, 23 November 1922.

10. *Garden City Herald*, 27 May 1920, 17 June 1920; "History" 2014.

11. *Garden City Herald*, 1 July 1920.

12. *Garden City Herald*, 3 June 1920, 17 June 1920, 24 June 1920, 7 July 1920, 15 July 1920, 22 July 1920, 29 July 1920, 5 August 1920, 12 August 1920, 19 August 1920, 26 August 1920, 23 September 1920.

13. *Garden City Herald*, 19 May 1921, 2 June 1921, 30 June 1921, 14 July 1921, 21 July 1921, 18 August 1921, 25 August 1921; *Garden City Telegram*, 5 October 1922.

14. *Garden City Herald*, 8 June 1922, 18 July 1922; *Garden City Telegram*, 5 July 1923, 12 July 1923, 19 July 1923, 26 July 1923, 2 August 1923, 16 August 1923, 23 August 1923, 30 August 1923, 6 September 1923, 27 September 1923.

15. *Garden City Telegram*, 24 April 1924, 22 May 1924, 5 June 1924, 19 June 1924, 3 July 1924, 10 July 1924, 24 July 1924, 14 August 1924, 21 August 1924, 28 August 1924, 4 September 1924, 11 September 1924, 18 September 1924.

16. *Garden City Telegram*, 31 August 1917, 14 June 1918, 9 May 1919, 20 November 1919, 25 December 1919, 8 January 1920, 26 July 1923.

17. *Garden City Herald*, 28 July 1921; *Garden City Telegram*, 29 May 1924, 12 June 1924, 26 June 1924, 7 August 1924.

18. *Garden City Herald*, 30 April 1925, 7 May 1925, 14 May 1925, 21 May 1925, 4 June 1925, 11 June 1925, 18 June 1925, 25 June 1925, 2 July 1925, 9 July 1925, 23 July 1925, 30 July 1925, 6 August 1925, 13 August 1925, 20 August 1925, 27 August 1925, 3 September 1925, 10 September 1925, 17 September 1925, 24 September 1925, 1 October 1925.

19. *Garden City Herald*, 1 April 1926, 22 April 1926, 29 April 1926, 6 May 1926, 13 May 1926, 20 May 1926, 27 May 1926, 10 June 1926, 17 June 1926, 24 June 1926,

1 July 1926, 8 July 1926, 15 July 1926, 22 July 1926, 29 July 1926, 5 August 1926, 12 August 1926, 19 August 1926, 19 August 1926, 26 August 1926, 2 September 1926, 9 September 1926, 16 September 1926, 23 September 1926, 7 October 1926, 21 October 1926, 21 April 1927.

20. *Garden City Herald*, 9 June 1927, 16 June 1927, 23 June 1927, 21 July 1927, 4 August 1927, 11 August 1927, 18 August 1927, 15 September 1927, 22 September 1927, 29 September 1927.

21. *Garden City Telegram*, 24 May 1928, 31 May 1928, 7 June 1928, 14 June 1928 19 July 1928, 30 August 1928, 20 September 1928, 11 October 1928, 9 May 1929, 16 May 1929, 13 June 1929.

22. The lights are discussed in chapter 17.

23. Ban Johnson teams are covered in chapter 8.

24. *Garden City Telegram*, 17 April 1930, 30 April 1930, 21 May 1930, 28 May 1930, 4 June 1930, 25 June 1930, 9 July 1930, 16 July 1930, 23 July 1930, 24 September 1930, 8 October 1930, 27 April 1931, 18 May 1931, 8 June 1931, 22 June 1931, 6 July 1931, 13 July 1931, 17 August 1931, 2 May 1932, 9 May 1932, 16 May 1932, 31 May 1932, 13 June 1932, 27 June 1932, 18 July 1932, 12 September 1932, 19 September 1932, 26 September 1932, 10 October 1932, 19 June 1933, 5 July 1933, 24 July 1933, 7 August 1933, 21 August 1933, 2 October 1933, 19 May 1934, 2 June 1934, 4 June 1934, 18 June 1934, 2 July 1934, 5 July 1934, 23 July 1934, 30 July 1934, 6 August 1934, 20 August 1934, 4 September 1934, 17 September 1934, 24 September 1934, 3 June 1935, 7 June 1935, 10 June 1935, 17 June 1935, 24 June 1935, 27 June 1935, 8 July 1935, 22 July 1935, 5 August 1935, 19 August 1935, 26 August 1935.

25. *Garden City Telegram*, 2 May 1936, 4 May 1936, 13 August 1936, 10 October 1936, 27 November 1936; Steve Cottrell, Garden City engineer, personal communication, 8 October 2014 (grandstand blueprints on file).

26. *Garden City Telegram*, 4 May 1936, 11 May 1936, 18 May 1936, 1 June 1936, 8 June 1936, 15 June 1936, 22 June 1936, 29 June 1936, 6 July 1936, 13 July 1936, 20 July 1936, 27 July 1936, 3 August 1936, 10 August 1936, 17 August 1936, 24 August 1936, 31 August 1936, 7 September 1936, 9 September 1936, 12 September 1936, 21 September 1936, 3 May 1937, 10 May 1937, 17 May 1937, 24 May 1937, 29 May 1937, 31 May 1937, 1 June 1937, 7 June 1937 (*Daily Telegram* Resource Edition: photo of grandstand), 12 June 1937, 14 June 1937, 17 June 1937, 21 June 1937, 28 June 1937, 3 July 1937, 6 July 1937, 12 July 1937, 19 July 1937, 24 July 1937, 26 July 1937, 31 July 1937, 2 August 1937, 9 August 1937, 13 August 1937, 16 August 1937, 23 August 1937, 30 August 1937, 6 September 1937, 13 September 1937, 20 September 1937, 26 September 1937, 23 April 1938, 25 April 1938, 26 April 1938, 2 May 1938, 9 May 1938, 16 May 1938, 23 May 1938, 30 May 1938, 6 June 1938, 13 June 1938, 20 June 1938, 27 June 1938, 5 July 1938, 11 July 1938, 16 July 1938, 18 July 1938, 25 July 1938, 1 August 1938, 8 August 1938, 15 August 1938, 22 August 1938, 29 August 1938, 5 September 1938, 12 September 1938, 19 September 1938, 20 September 1938, 21 April 1939, 1

May 1939, 8 May 1939, 15 May 1939, 22 May 1939, 29 May 1939, 5 June 1939, 12 June 1939, 19 June 1939, 26 June 1939, 5 July 1939, 8 July 1939, 10 July 1939, 17 July 1939, 24 July 1939, 31 July 1939, 7 August 1939, 14 August 1939, 21 August 1939, 28 August 1939, 4 September 1939, 11 September 1939, 18 September 1939, 6 May 1940, 13 May 1940, 20 May 1940, 27 May 1940, 3 June 1940, 10 June 1940, 17 June 1940, 8 July 1940, 15 July 1940, 22 July 1940, 29 July 1940, 5 August 1940, 12 August 1940, 19 August 1940, 26 August 1940.

27. *Garden City Telegram*, 27 July 1955, 24 August 1955.

28. *Garden City Telegram*, 27 July 1955, 9 November 1955, 19 March 1956, 10 May 1956.

29. *Garden City Telegram*, 27 July 1955.

30. *Garden City Telegram*, 27 July 1955, 19 March 1956.

31. *Garden City Telegram*, 21 August 1936, 25 August 1936, 7 June 1948, 21 April 1951, 9 May 1951; *Garden City Herald*, 14 August 1919, 30 April 1925, 8 July 1926, 24 July 1926; "*Discover Southwest Kansas, 2014–2015 Resource Guide,*" *Garden City Telegram*, 92.

32. *Garden City Telegram*, 21 April 1951, 9 May 1951.

33. *Garden City Telegram*, 16 March 1960, 11 April 1960, 25 April 1960, 31 May 1960.

34. *Garden City Telegram*, 20 May 1960, 24 May 1961.

35. *Garden City Telegram*, 16 April 1962, 25 April 1962, 26 April 1962, 31 May 1962, 7 June 1962.

36. *Garden City Telegram*, 27 March 1968; "*Discover Southwest Kansas, 2014–2015,*" 92.

CHAPTER 13. KATY STADIUM, CHANUTE

1. *Chanute Times*, 23 June 1887, 21 July 1887, 4 August 1887, 25 August 1887; *Chanute Weekly Times*, 26 July 1888, 2 August 1888, 16 August 1888, 8 August 1889.

2. *Chanute Weekly Times*, 11 July 1890.

3. *Chanute Daily Tribune*, 4 August 1893, 10 August 1893, 20 June 1894, 5 July 1894, 5 July 1895, 17 July 1895, 22 August 1895, 24 September 1895.

4. *Chanute Daily Tribune*, 13 April 1896, 17 April 1896, 25 April 1896, 28 April 1896, 12 May 1896, 18 May 1896, 22 May 1896, 25 May 1896, 29 May 1896, 24 June 1896, 25 June 1896.

5. *Chanute Daily Tribune*, 29 June 1896, 3 July 1896, 8 July 1896, 28 August 1896, 29 August 1896.

6. *Chanute Daily Tribune*, 4 September 1896, 29 September 1896.

7. *Chanute Daily Tribune*, 17 December 1897; *Chanute Morning Sun*, 12 March 1897.

8. *Chanute Morning Sun*, 7 May 1897, 8 May 1897, 26 May 1897.

9. *Chanute Morning Sun*, 27 February 1898, 6 March 1898, 9 April 1898, 25 September 1898.

10. *Chanute Morning Sun*, 4 June 1899, 25 June 1899, 12 July 1899, 30 July 1899.

11. *Chanute Morning Sun*, 29 July 1899, 16 August 1899, 19 August 1899.

12. *Chanute Daily Tribune*, 2 June 1900, 28 June 1901, 3 September 1901; *Chanute Morning Sun*, 28 June 1901, 20 August 1901.

13. *Chanute Daily Tribune*, 10 October 1900; *Chanute Morning Sun*, 10 October 1900.

14. *Chanute Morning Sun*, 4 August 1901.

15. *Chanute Daily Tribune*, 17 May 1902, 22 May 1902, 4 June 1902, 6 June 1902, 9 June 1902, 10 June 1902, 11 June 1902, 17 June 1902, 23 June 1902, 26 June 1902; *Chanute Daily Sun*, 22 May 1902, 21 June 1902.

16. *Chanute Daily Sun*, 14 June 1902.

17. *Chanute Daily Tribune*, 29 September 1902.

18. *Chanute Daily Tribune*, 9 January 1903, 16 February 1903.

19. *Chanute Daily Tribune*, 19 January 1904, 29 February 1904; *Chanute Sun*, January 1904.

20. *Chanute Daily Tribune*, 30 April 1904, 14 May 1904, 5 July 1904, 23 September 1904; *Chanute Sun*, 14 May 1904, 16 May 1904, 7 June 1904, 3 August 1904.

21. *Chanute Sun*, 17 February 1906, 9 July 1906; Kansas Baseball History Project.

22. *Chanute Sun*, 6 May 1907, 23 May 1907.

23. *Chanute Sun*, 10 August 1907, 21 August 1907, 26 August 1907, 25 September 1907, 30 September 1907.

24. *Chanute Daily Tribune*, 26 July 1894, 8 August 1900, 11 July 1902, 15 August 1906, 21 March 1907, 19 April 1908, 20 July 1909, 22 June 1911, 17 August 1912, 16 June 1913, 28 June 1913, 29 August 1913, 19 September 1914, 29 June 1916, 30 June 1916, 20 August 1917, 14 July 1920; *Chanute Sun*, 14 June 1904, 25 June 1904, 18 May 1905.

25. *Chanute Daily Tribune*, 29 August 1904, 10 June 1911, 12 June 1911, 21 April 1921, 16 May 1921, 23 May 1921, 5 July 1921; *Chanute Sun*, 29 August 1904.

26. *Chanute Daily Tribune*, 20 August 1917, 22 August 1917, 27 August 1917, 26 August 1919.

27. *Chanute Daily Tribune*, 11 May 1922, 18 June 1922, 24 June 1922.

28. *Chanute Times*, 27 July 1905.

29. *Chanute Daily Tribune*, 8 February 1894.

30. *Chanute Daily Tribune*, 30 July 1894, 31 July 1894.

31. *Chanute Daily Tribune*, 3 August 1894.

32. *Chanute Daily Tribune*, 11 October 1894.

33. *Chanute Daily Tribune*, 21 December 1894, 31 January 1895, 2 February 1895.

34. *Chanute Daily Tribune*, 13 June 1895, 7 August 1895, 21 September 1895, 24 September 1895.

35. *Chanute Sun*, 8 August 1904.

36. *Chanute Morning Sun*, 7 May 1897.

37. *Chanute Daily Tribune*, 17 April 1906, 6 September 1906, 28 March 1907, 20 April 1908, 1 May 1909, 29 May 1911, 26 June 1911, 15 July 1911.

38. *Chanute Daily Tribune*, 30 September 1907, 20 May 1915, 10 June 1916, 2 September 1916; Ogle and Company 1906b.

39. *Chanute Sun*, 7 June 1904, 18 June 1904, 24 June 1904.

40. *Chanute Daily Tribune*, 10 June 1916, 8 March 1921.

41. *Chanute Daily Tribune*, 3 July 1911, 17 July 1912.

42. *Chanute Times*, 11 March 1911, 7 August 1911, 21 October 1911, 11 November 1911, 11 January 1912, 13 January 1912, 27 February 1912, 14 June 1912.

43. *Chanute Times*, 12 March 1912; *Chanute Weekly Times*, 15 March 1912, 29 March 1912, 5 April 1912, 26 April 1912, 31 May 1912, 14 June 1912.

44. *Chanute Daily Tribune*, 31 May 1913.

45. *Chanute Daily Tribune*, 12 May 1913, 31 May 1913; *Chanute Times*, 23 May 1913.

46. *Chanute Daily Tribune*, 16 June 1913, 22 July 1913; *Chanute Times*, 16 June 1913.

47. *Chanute Daily Tribune*, 17 April 1915, 4 May 1915, 15 May 1915, 21 April 1921, 19 May 1921, 28 June 1921, 29 June 1922.

48. *Chanute Daily Tribune*, 28 May 1921, 13 June 1921, 13 August 1921, 27 August 1921, 13 October 1921.

49. *Chanute Daily Tribune*, 21 April 1921, 16 May 1921, 23 May 1921, 5 July 1921.

50. George Sweatt's story is told in more detail in chapter 3.

51. *Chanute Daily Tribune*, 10 April 1922, 17 April 1922, 18 April 1922, 11 May 1922, 10 June 1922.

52. *Chanute Daily Tribune*, 24 June 1922.

53. *Chanute Daily Tribune*, 7 June 1922, 13 June 1922, 14 June 1922, 5 May 1923, 14 May 1923, 13 June 1923, 15 June 1923, 12 May 1924, 19 May 1924, 14 June 1924, 12 August 1924, 28 August 1924, 19 May 1925, 25 May 1925, 2 July 1925, 15 May 1926, 3 July 1926, 6 July 1926; *Iola Register*, 23 April 1923, 30 April 1923, 1 May 1923, 4 May 1923.

54. *Chanute Daily Tribune*, 30 April 1927, 28 May 1927, 6 June 1927, 13 June 1927, 20 June 1927, 11 July 1927, 18 July 1927, 7 May 1928, 14 May 1928, 23 July 1928, 3 June 1929, 1 July 1929, 5 July 1929, 12 August 1929, 19 August 1929, 26 August 1929, 10 May 1930, 23 June 1930, 7 July 1930, 18 August 1930, 2 May 1931, 4 May 1931, 2 May 1932, 9 May 1932, 13 June 1932, 20 June 1932, 27 June 1932, 11 July 1932, 18 July 1932, 25 July 1932, 1 August 1932, 8 August 1932, 13 August 1932, 15 August 1932, 22 August 1932, 6 September 1932, 12 September 1932, 8 May 1933, 19 June 1933, 9 June 1934, 18 June 1934, 10 May 1935, 27 May 1935.

55. *Chanute Tribune and the Daily Timesett*, 27 May 1935, 10 September 1935, 16 September 1935, 7 October 1935, 14 October 1935; *Iola Register*, 10 April 1935, 14 June 1935, 23 July 1935.

56. *Chanute Tribune and the Daily Timesett,* 20 November 1935, 21 November 1935, 27 February 1936.

57. *Chanute Tribune and the Daily Timesett,* 9 April 1936 (grandstand construction photo), 22 June 1936, 27 June 1936, 2 July 1936, 3 July 1936, 27 July 1936, 6 August 1936, 7 August 1936, 12 August 1936, 13 August 1936, 18 August 1936, 21 August 1936, 28 August 1936.

58. *Chanute Tribune and the Daily Timesett,* 16 September 1936, 1 October 1936.

59. *Chanute Tribune and the Daily Timesett,* 24 April 1937, 26 April 1937, 3 May 1937, 10 May 1937, 17 May 1937, 24 May 1937, 9 June 1937, 14 June 1937, 21 June 1937, 25 June 1937, 28 June 1937, 6 July 1937, 9 July 1937, 10 July 1937, 12 July 1937, 13 July 1913, 16 July 1937, 19 July 1937, 26 July 1937, 2 August 1937, 9 August 1937, 16 August 1937, 19 August 1937, 23 August 1937, 24 August 1937, 27 August 1937, 31 August 1937, 7 September 1937, 15 September 1937, 20 September 1937, 18 April 1938, 2 May 1938, 9 May 1938, 16 May 1938, 25 May 1938, 30 May 1938, 6 June 1938, 8 June 1938, 13 June 1938, 2 July 1938, 16 July 1938, 22 August 1938, 25 August 1938, 5 May 1939, 6 May 1939, 2 June 1939, 3 July 1939, 31 July 1939, 29 September 1939, 7 May 1940, 22 May 1940, 22 July 1940, 27 July 1940, 26 May 1941, 30 May 1941.

60. *Chanute Tribune and the Daily Timesett,* 8 March 1937, 24 April 1937, 26 April 1937, 3 May 1937, 10 May 1937, 17 May 1937, 24 May 1937, 9 June 1937, 14 June 1937, 21 June 1937, 25 June 1937, 28 June 1937, 6 July 1937, 9 July 1937, 10 July 1937, 12 July 1937, 13 July 1937, 16 July 1937, 19 July 1937, 23 July 1937, 26 July 1937, 2 August 1937, 9 August 1937, 16 August 1937, 19 August 1937, 23 August 1937, 24 August 1937, 27 August 1937, 30 August 1937, 18 April 1938, 2 May 1938, 9 May 1938, 16 May 1938, 25 May 1938, 30 May 1938, 6 June 1938, 8 June 1938, 13 June 1938, 2 July 1938, 16 July 1938, 25 July 1938, 22 August 1938, 8 May 1939, 2 June 1939, 3 July 1939, 24 July 1939, 11 August 1939, 23 August 1939, 7 May 1940, 22 May 1940, 30 May 1940, 22 July 1940, 27 July 1940, 29 July 1940; *Iola Register,* 8 March 1937, 13 April 1937, 26 April 1937, 22 April 1938, 21 April 1939, 29 March 1940.

61. *Emporia Gazette,* 27 July 1938, 24 September 1938; *Iola Register,* 4 June 1938, 24 July 1939, 14 March 1940, 29 March 1940, 18 April 1940, 9 April 1941; "Claude Willoughby" 2016.

62. *Chanute Tribune and the Daily Timesett,* 5 May 1939, 6 May 1939, 31 July 1939.

63. *Emporia Gazette,* 23 April 1946; *Iola Register,* 18 March 1946, 7 February 1947; Hall 2004, p. 117.

64. Hofmann 2015, 2016.

CHAPTER 14. MOFFET FIELD STADIUM, LARNED

1. *Dodge City Times,* 23 March 1878; *Larned Optic,* 12 September 1879, 5 August 1881, 19 August 1881, 9 September 1881, 16 September 1881; *Larned Weekly Eagle-Optic,* 17 September 1886, 10 June 1887, 26 June 1891, 1 July 1892, 21 June 1895, 12 July 1895, 19 June 1896, 25 June 1897, 20 August 1897, 22 July 1898, 30 June 1899;

Pawnee County Herald, 4 August 1877, 18 August 1877, 8 September 1877, 14 May 1878, 23 July 1878.

2. *Dodge City Times*, 25 May 1882; *Kinsley Graphic*, 10 August 1882; *Larned Optic*, 11 August 1882, 7 September 1883; *Larned Weekly Eagle-Optic*, 18 February 1898.

3. *Larned Weekly Eagle-Optic*, 7 August 1885.

4. *Barton County Democrat*, 9 June 1887, 13 August 1891, 5 April 1894, 8 September 1898, 28 July 1899; *Hutchinson News*, 19 August 1903; *Kinsley Graphic*, 5 October 1894, 31 May 1895, 28 August 1896, 18 September 1896, 26 June 1903; *Kinsley Mercury*, 17 October 1895; *Larned Weekly Chronoscope*, 15 July 1898; *Larned Tiller and Toiler*, 29 June 1906; *Larned Weekly Eagle-Optic*, 17 June 1887, 1 July 1887; *Topeka Daily Capital*, 20 August 1903, 25 August 1903.

5. *Larned Tiller and Toiler*, 18 August 1905, 19 July 1907.

6. *Larned Tiller and Toiler*, 21 June 1907, 20 September 1907, 27 September 1907, 4 October 1907.

7. *Larned Tiller and Toiler*, 22 May 1908.

8. *Larned Tiller and Toiler*, 1 May 1908, 8 May 1908.

9. *Larned Tiller and Toiler*, 16 July 1909, 14 July 1911; Kansas Baseball History Project.

10. Johnson 2016a.

11. *Larned Tiller and Toiler*, 30 August 1907, 1 May 1908, 15 May 1908, 30 July 1909, 19 November 1909, 24 June 1910, 22 July 1910; Johnson 2016a.

12. Johnson 2016a.

13. *Larned Tiller and Toiler*, 22 May 1903, 19 June 1903, 20 May 1904, 25 August 1905, 1 September 1905, 19 July 1907, 13 September 1907, 4 October 1907, 17 April 1908, 24 April 1908, 8 May 1908, 15 May 1908, 26 June 1908, 17 July 1908, 21 August 1908, 4 September 1908, 11 September 1908, 18 September 1908, 11 June 1909, 25 June 1909, 23 July 1909, 30 July 1909, 6 August 1909, 13 August 1909, 19 November 1909, 18 February 1910, 4 March 1910, 18 March 1910, 25 March 1910, 8 April 1910, 6 May 1910, 22 July 1910, 12 August 1910, 18 November 1910, 28 November 1935; *Wichita Beacon*, 15 January 1917; *Plat Book of Pawnee County, Kansas* 1902.

14. *Larned Tiller and Toiler*, 29 October 1909, 11 August 1911, 24 May 1912, 28 June 1912.

15. *Hutchinson News*, 4 June 1918; *Larned Tiller and Toiler*, 15 January 1920, 10 June 1920, 29 July 1920, 15 June 1922, 13 June 1929, 10 October 1929, 24 April 1930, 22 May 1930, 10 July 1930, 7 May 1931; "The Larned Trust Fund Case" 1926, 32–33.

16. *Larned Tiller and Toiler*, 12 June 1914, 3 July 1914, 20 September 1917, 1 May 1919, 22 May 1919, 5 June 1919, 12 June 1919, 26 June 1919, 3 July 1919, 24 July 1919, 31 July 1919, 7 August 1919, 14 August 1919, 21 August 1919, 28 August 1919, 11 September 1919, 18 September 1919, 25 September 1919, 2 October 1919, 9 October 1919.

17. *Larned Tiller and Toiler*, 6 May 1920, 13 May 1920, 20 May 1920, 27 May 1920, 3 June 1920, 17 June 1920, 1 July 1920, 8 July 1920, 5 August 1920, 12 August 1920, 19 August 1920, 26 August 1920, 2 September 1920, 9 September 1920, 7 October 1920.

18. *Larned Tiller and Toiler*, 22 April 1920, 27 May 1920, 15 July 1920, 22 July 1920, 29 July 1920, 23 September 1920, 25 May 1922, 22 June 1922, 13 July 1922, 3 August 1922.

19. *Larned Tiller and Toiler*, 21 April 1921, 28 April 1921, 5 May 1921, 16 June 1921, 7 July 1921, 14 July 1921, 1 September 1921, 8 September 1921, 15 September 1921, 22 September 1921, 8 June 1922.

20. For more on Emmett "Chief" Bowles, see chapter 4.

21. *Great Bend Tribune*, 2 September 1921, 12 September 1921, 19 September 1921, 25 March 1922; *Hoisington Dispatch*, 4 September 1919; *Larned Tiller and Toiler*, 21 July 1921, 4 August 1921, 18 August 1921, 15 September 1921, 13 October 1921, 20 October 1921; "Emmett Bowles" 2016; Sutter 2010, p. 65–74.

22. *Larned Tiller and Toiler*, 4 May 1922, 15 June 1922, 22 June 1922, 21 September 1922, 26 April 1923, 3 May 1923, 17 May 1923, 31 May 1923, 7 June 1923, 14 June 1923, 21 June 1923, 28 June 1923, 5 July 1923, 12 July 1923, 19 July 1923, 26 July 1923, 2 August 1923, 9 August 1923, 16 August 1923, 23 August 1923, 30 August 1923, 6 September 1923, 13 September 1923, 20 September 1923, 27 September 1923.

23. *Larned Tiller and Toiler*, 10 April 1924, 1 May 1924, 8 May 1924, 15 May 1924, 22 May 1924, 29 May 1924, 5 June 1924, 12 June 1924, 19 June 1924, 26 June 1924, 3 July 1924, 10 July 1924, 17 July 1924, 24 July 1924, 31 July 1924, 7 August 1924, 14 August 1924, 21 August 1924, 28 August 1924, 4 September 1924, 11 September 1924, 18 September 1924, 25 September 1924.

24. *Larned Tiller and Toiler*, 23 April 1925, 7 May 1925, 14 May 1925, 21 May 1925, 28 May 1925, 4 June 1925, 11 June 1925, 18 June 1925, 25 June 1925, 2 July 1925, 9 July 1925, 16 July 1925, 23 July 1925, 30 July 1925, 6 August 1925, 13 August 1925, 20 August 1925, 27 August 1925, 10 September 1925, 8 April 1926; *Wichita Beacon*, 21 June 1925, 23 June 1925.

25. *Larned Tiller and Toiler*, 17 September 1925, 24 September 1925, 1 October 1925; "Thomas Blodgett" 2016; "Joe Bloomer" 2016; "Roy Garvin Sanders" 2016.

26. *Larned Tiller and Toiler*, 1 April 1926, 15 April 1926, 22 April 1926, 29 April 1926, 6 May 1926, 13 May 1926, 20 May 1926, 27 May 1926, 3 June 1926, 10 June 1926, 17 June 1926, 24 June 1926, 1 July 1926, 8 July 1926, 15 July 1926, 22 July 1926, 29 July 1926.

27. *Larned Tiller and Toiler*, 5 August 1926, 12 August 1926, 19 August 1926, 26 August 1926, 9 September 1926, 23 September 1926.

28. *Larned Tiller and Toiler*, 7 April 1927, 21 April 1927, 28 April 1927, 5 May 1927, 12 May 1927, 19 May 1927, 26 May 1927, 2 June 1927, 16 June 1927, 23 June 1927,

30 June 1927, 7 July 1927, 14 July 1927, 21 July 1927, 28 July 1927, 4 August 1927, 11 August 1927, 18 August 1927, 25 August 1927, 1 September 1927, 15 September 1927, 4 April 1929.

29. *Larned Tiller and Toiler*, 5 April 1928, 12 April 1928, 19 April 1928, 26 April 1928, 3 May 1928, 10 May 1928, 17 May 1928, 24 May 1928, 31 May 1928, 7 June 1928, 14 June 1928, 21 June 1928, 28 June 1928, 5 July 1928, 12 July 1928, 19 July 1928, 26 July 1928, 2 August 1928, 9 August 1928, 16 August 1928, 23 August 1928, 30 August 1928, 6 September 1928, 13 September 1928.

30. *Larned Tiller and Toiler*, 18 April 1929, 25 April 1929, 2 May 1929, 9 May 1929, 16 May 1919, 23 May 1929, 30 May 1929, 6 June 1929, 13 June 1929, 20 June 1929, 4 July 1929, 11 July 1929, 18 July 1929, 25 July 1929, 1 August 1929, 8 August 1929, 15 August 1929, 22 August 1929, 29 August 1929, 19 September 1929, 26 September 1929, 3 April 1930, 10 April 1930, 17 April 1930, 24 April 1930, 1 May 1930, 8 May 1930, 15 May 1930, 22 May 1930, 29 May 1930, 5 June 1930, 12 June 1930, 19 June 1930, 26 June 1930, 3 July 1930, 10 July 1930, 17 July 1930, 24 July 1930, 31 July 1930, 7 August 1930, 14 August 1930, 21 August 1930, 28 August 1930, 4 September 1930, 11 September 1930, 18 September 1930, 25 September 1930, 2 October 1930, 9 April 1931, 16 April 1931, 30 April 1931, 7 May 1931, 14 May 1931, 21 May 1931, 28 May 1931, 4 June 1931, 11 June 1931, 18 June 1931, 9 July 1931, 23 July 1931, 30 July 1931, 6 August 1931, 13 August 1931.

31. The Ban Johnson League is described in chapter 8.

32. *Larned Tiller and Toiler*, 20 August 1931, 14 April 1932, 28 April 1932, 5 May 1932, 12 May 1932, 19 May 1932, 26 May 1932, 16 June 1932, 23 June 1932, 28 July 1932, 4 August 1932, 11 August 1932, 18 August 1932, 25 August 1932, 1 September 1932, 15 September 1932, 29 September 1932, 27 April 1933, 4 May 1933, 11 May 1933, 18 May 1933, 25 May 1933, 1 June 1933, 8 June 1933, 15 June 1933, 22 June 1933, 29 June 1933, 6 July 1933, 20 July 1933, 27 July 1933, 3 August 1933, 10 August 1933, 17 August 1933, 24 August 1933, 31 August 1933, 7 September 1933, 14 September 1933, 3 May 1934, 10 May 1934, 24 May 1934, 31 May 1934, 7 June 1934, 14 June 1934, 28 June 1934.

33. *Larned Tiller and Toiler*, 10 July 1903, 23 September 1910, 6 December 1934, 15 June 1939.

34. *Larned Tiller and Toiler*, 14 September 1934, 17 September 1934, 2 October 1934, 3 October 1934.

35. *Larned Tiller and Toiler*, 5 December 1934, 1 February 1935, 5 March 1935, 25 March 1935, 3 April 1935, 9 April 1934.

36. *Larned Tiller and Toiler*, 12 April 1935, 13 May 1935, 29 May 1935, 4 June 1935, 10 June 1935, 22 July 1935, 29 July 1935, 21 August 1935, 1 May 1936, 5 June 1936, 23 June 1936, 22 March 1938, 10 May 1938.

37. *Larned Tiller and Toiler*, 29 April 1935, 30 April 1935, 3 May 1935, 29 July 1935, 2 August 1935, 6 September 1935, 10 September 1935, 25 November 1935.

38. *Larned Tiller and Toiler*, 16 August 1935, 19 August 1935.

39. *Larned Tiller and Toiler*, 25 November 1935, 10 April 1936, 24 April 1936.

40. *Larned Tiller and Toiler*, 9 June 1936, 4 August 1936, 17 August 1936, 23 September 1936, 13 October 1936, 2 November 1936 (drawing of grandstand), 27 November 1936, 29 December 1936, 11 January 1937, 12 February 1937, 19 February 1937.

41. *Larned Tiller and Toiler*, 28 November 1935, 8 March 1938, 24 June 1938, 11 July 1938, 21 July 1939.

42. *Hutchinson News*, 18 June 1937; *Larned Tiller and Toiler*, 3 May 1937, 18 June 1937, 21 June 1937.

43. *Larned Tiller and Toiler*, 4 April 1938, 13 April 1938, 30 May 1938, 29 May 1939, 5 June 1939, 10 July 1939, 14 July 1939, 31 July 1939, 7 August 1939, 23 August 1939, 28 August 1939, 29 May 1940.

44. *Larned Tiller and Toiler*, 12 September 1939, 22 September 1939.

45. *Larned Tiller and Toiler*, 22 August 1939.

CHAPTER 15. RATHERT STADIUM, JUNCTION CITY

1. *Junction City (Weekly) Union*, 11 May 1867, 25 May 1867, 21 May 1870, 8 April 1871, 29 April 1871, 22 July 1871, 29 August 1882, 30 April 1887, 30 August 1890, 16 July 1892.

2. *Junction City (Weekly) Union*, 21 April 1877.

3. *Junction City (Weekly) Union*, 1 June 1872, 15 June 1872, 19 June 1875, 24 July 1875, 21 April 1877, 26 May 1877, 9 June 1877, 30 June 1877, 7 July 1877, 31 May 1879, 7 August 1880, 8 July 1882, 29 July 1882, 19 August 1882, 7 June 1884, 4 July 1885, 11 July 1885, 11 June 1887, 29 September 1888, 22 June 1889, 20 July 1889, 10 August 1889, 24 August 1889, 28 June 1890, 26 July 1890, 2 May 1891, 11 July 1891, 9 July 1892.

4. *Junction City (Weekly) Union*, 26 July 1879, 16 August 1879, 13 September 1879, 6 May 1882, 22 August 1885, 12 September 1885, 10 August 1889, 17 August 1889, 31 August 1889, 3 May 1890, 16 May 1891, 28 May 1892, 9 July 1892, 30 July 1892, 27 May 1893, 17 June 1893.

5. *Junction City (Weekly) Union*, 11 May 1895.

6. *Junction City (Weekly) Union*, 18 May 1895.

7. *Junction City (Weekly) Union*, 29 June 1895.

8. *Junction City (Weekly) Union*, 6 July 1895.

9. *Junction City (Weekly) Union*, 13 July 1895, 20 July 1895, 3 August 1895, 26 October 1895, 9 May 1896.

10. *Junction City (Weekly) Union*, 28 December 1895, 11 April 1896, 2 May 1896, 9 May 1896, 16 May 1896.

11. *Coffeyville Daily Journal*, 13 July 1896, 17 July 1896; *Junction City (Weekly) Union*, 26 June 1896, 17 July 1896, 24 July 1896, 31 July 1896, 15 January 1897; *Topeka Daily Capital*, 25 June 1896.

12. *Junction City (Weekly) Union*, 28 December 1895, 4 April 1896, 14 August 1896, 11 June 1897, 25 June 1897, 2 July 1897, 9 July 1897, 23 July 1897, 6 August 1897; Anderson 2015b; Lahman 2004; "Dummy Taylor" 2015.

13. *Junction City (Weekly) Union*, 12 August 1898, 21 October 1898, 28 October 1898.

14. *Junction City (Weekly) Union*, 9 June 1899, 23 June 1899.

15. *Junction City (Weekly) Union*, 10 June 1904.

16. *Junction City (Daily) Union*, 13 February 1909; *Junction City (Weekly) Union*, 22 July 1904, 29 June 1906, 29 August 1907.

17. *Junction City (Daily) Union*, 1 April 1909.

18. *Junction City (Daily) Union*, 13 April 1909, 26 May 1909.

19. *Junction City (Daily) Union*, 16 April 1909.

20. *Junction City (Daily) Union*, 15 April 1909, 21 April 1909, 27 April 1909, 8 June 1909.

21. *Junction City (Daily) Union*, 15 April 1909, 4 April 1910.

22. *Junction City (Daily) Union*, 8 April 1909, 19 January 1910, 1 August 1911, 30 December 1911, 2 February 1913; Kansas Baseball History Project.

23. *Junction City (Daily) Union*, 12 January 1915, 17 February 1915, 18 February 1915, 23 February 1915.

24. *Junction City (Daily) Union*, 17 June 1916, 19 June 1916, 29 June 1916, 13 April 1917, 16 May 1918, 12 February 1919, 17 February 1919, 18 April 1919, 7 May 1921, 14 May 1921, 12 May 1922; *Junction City (Weekly) Union*, 31 October 1918, 27 February 1919.

25. *Junction City (Daily) Union*, 17 August 1922; *Junction City (Weekly) Union*, 5 April 1923, 12 April 1923, 3 May 1923, 5 June 1924, 20 June 1929.

26. Kansas Baseball History Project.

27. *Junction City (Daily) Union*, 28 April 1936; *Junction City (Weekly) Union*, 23 July 1925.

28. *Junction City (Daily) Union*, 14 March 1936, 16 March 1936, 19 March 1936, 21 March 1936, 30 March 1936, 17 April 1936, 18 April 1936, 20 April 1936, 22 August 1936; *Junction City (Weekly) Union*, 14 May 1936, 9 July 1936.

29. *Junction City (Daily) Union*, 24 June 1936, 17 August 1936, 20 August 1936; *Junction City (Weekly) Union*, 2 July 1936, 20 August 1936, 27 August 1936, 8 October 1936.

30. In August 1937 the WPA granted permission for this unbuilt bleacher to be "relocated" to the southern side of Fegan Field, where the football field was moved south to be closer to the new seating. The limestone and concrete structure with no roof still stands at Fegan Field.

31. *Junction City (Daily) Union*, 16 July 1937; *Junction City (Weekly) Union*, 24 September 1936, 1 October 1936, 22 October 1936, 25 March 1937, 6 May 1937, 15 July 1937, 12 August 1937.

32. *Junction City (Daily) Union*, 12 July 1937, 17 July 1937, 19 July 1937; *Junction City (Weekly) Union*, 8 October 1936, 17 December 1936, 13 May 1937, 24 June 1937, 15 July 1937.

33. *Junction City (Daily) Union*, 3 August 1937, 20 September 1937, 21 September 1937; Kansas Baseball History Project.

CHAPTER 16. MCDONALD STADIUM, EL DORADO

1. *Walnut Valley Times* (El Dorado), 10 March 1871, 19 May 1871, 2 August 1872, 16 August 1872, 23 August 1872, 6 September 1872, 20 September 1872.

2. *El Dorado (Weekly) Republican*, 10 June 1887, 17 January 1890; *Walnut Valley Times* (El Dorado), 31 July 1874, 7 August 1874, 9 July 1875, 13 August 1880, 28 July 1882, 4 August 1882, 25 August 1882, 10 July 1885, 19 August 1887, 7 September 1888, 27 July 1894, 10 August 1894, 19 July 1895, 2 August 1895, 23 August 1895, 6 August 1897, 13 August 1897, 20 August 1897, 27 August 1897, 3 September 1897, 10 September 1897, 26 August 1898, 14 July 1899; Ogle and Company 1905a.

3. *Walnut Valley Times* (El Dorado), 3 August 1900, 19 July 1901, 11 July 1902, 17 July 1903, 12 August 1904, 7 April 1905, 5 May 1905, 12 May 1905, 2 June 1905, 9 June 1905, 29 June 1905, 23 June 1905, 13 April 1906, 15 June 1906, 22 June 1906, 17 August 1906, 12 July 1907, 18 March 1908, 20 August 1910.

4. *Walnut Valley Times* (El Dorado), 8 November 1910, 12 November 1910, 23 November 1910, 14 April 1911, 16 June 1911, 30 June 1911, 14 July 1911, 21 July 1911; Kansas Baseball History Project.

5. *Walnut Valley Times* (El Dorado), 24 May 1912, 14 June 1912, 21 June 1912, 5 July 1912, 12 July 1912, 9 August 1912, 16 August 1912, 23 August 1912, 30 August 1912, 13 September 1912, 27 September 1912, 11 October 1912, 4 April 1913, 17 April 1913, 12 June 1913, 26 June 1913, 28 June 1913, 8 July 1913, 9 July 1913, 11 July 1913, 14 July 1913, 24 July 1913, 27 September 1913, 16 March 1914, 6 April 1914, 13 May 1914, 6 August 1914, 8 October 1914.

6. *Walnut Valley Times* (El Dorado), 26 June 1919; "Beals Becker" 2015; "Top 100 Teams" 2015.

7. *Walnut Valley Times* (El Dorado), 7 May 1915, 14 May 1915, 21 May 1915, 28 May 1915, 4 June 1915, 11 June 1915, 18 June 1915, 25 June 1915, 23 July 1915, 6 August 1915, 13 August 1915, 3 September 1915, 24 September 1915.

8. *Walnut Valley Times* (El Dorado), 4 June 1915, 30 July 1915, 17 September 1915.

9. *Walnut Valley Times* (El Dorado), 29 January 1915, 2 July 1915, 16 July 1915, 23 July 1915, 6 August 1915, 20 August 1915, 27 August 1915, 1 October 1915.

10. *Walnut Valley Times* (El Dorado), 9 July 1915, 6 August 1915, 13 August 1915, 20 August 1915, 3 September 1915, 10 September 1915, 17 September 1915.

11. *Walnut Valley Times* (El Dorado), 14 January 1916 (Clover moves to Arkansas City), 21 January 1916, 28 January 1916, 18 February 1916, 25 February 1916, 17 March 1916, 24 March 1916, 31 March 1916, 7 April 1916, 14 April 1916, 5 May 1916,

12 May 1916, 19 May 1916, 2 June 1916, 9 June 1916, 16 June 1916, 23 June 1916, 30 June 1916. Clover's wife's maiden name was Eberle, but she is no relation to my family.

12. *El Dorado Daily Republican*, 16 January 1917; *Walnut Valley Times* (El Dorado), 21 July 1916, 28 July 1916, 4 August 1916, 11 August 1916, 18 August 1916, 25 August 1916, 1 September 1916, 15 September 1916, 22 September 1916, 29 September 1916, 6 October 1916; Price 2005.

13. *El Dorado Daily Republican*, 9 April 1917, 13 April 1917, 16 April 1917, 23 April 1917, 27 April 1917, 7 May 1917, 14 May 1917, 4 June 1917, 11 June 1917, 18 June 1917, 25 June 1917, 2 July 1917, 6 July 1917, 9 July 1917, 16 July 1917, 23 August 1917, 27 August 1917, 17 April 1918, 2 May 1918, 9 May 1918, 13 May 1918, 20 May 1918, 27 May 1918, 28 May 1918, 21 June 1918, 22 June 1918, 11 July 1918, 16 September 1918.

14. *El Dorado Daily Republican*, 6 May 1918, 10 June 1918, 17 July 1919, 6 August 1919, 22 September 1919, 12 March 1920, 25 June 1920, 2 July 1920, 22 April 1921, 13 May 1921, 3 June 1921, 15 July 1921, 26 August 1921, 16 June 1922, 29 September 1922, 8 June 1923, 6 July 1923, 20 July 1923, 31 August 1923, 5 October 1923, 30 May 1924.

15. *El Dorado Daily Republican*, 19 April 1919, 2 May 1919, 10 May 1919, 19 May 1919, 28 May 1919, 12 June 1919, 13 June 1919, 20 June 1919, 23 June 1919, 25 June 1919, 28 June 1919, 2 July 1919, 3 July 1919, 11 July 1919, 26 July 1919, 28 July 1919, 4 August 1919, 11 August 1919, 18 August 1919, 23 August 1919, 25 August 1919, 28 August 1919, 1 September 1919, 15 September 1919, 29 September 1919; *Walnut Valley Times* (El Dorado), 2 May 1919, 12 May 1919, 16 May 1919, 19 May 1919, 28 May 1919, 10 June 1919, 20 June 1919, 23 June 1919, 28 June 1919, 30 June 1919, 2 July 1919, 17 July 1919, 24 July 1919, 26 July 1919, 13 August 1919.

16. *El Dorado Daily Republican*, 25 June 1919, 30 June 1919, 2 July 1919, 24 July 1919; *Walnut Valley Times* (El Dorado), 26 April 1919, 19 May 1919, 9 June 1919, 25 June 1919, 30 June 1919; Price 2005.

17. *El Dorado Daily Republican*, 28 July 1919, 2 August 1919, 4 August 1919, 11 August 1919, 15 August 1919, 18 August 1919, 25 August 1919; *Walnut Valley Times* (El Dorado), 28 July 1919, 2 August 1919, 5 August 1919, 25 August 1919.

18. *El Dorado Daily Republican*, 1 September 1919, 2 September 1919, 8 September 1919, 15 September 1919, 27 September 1919, 30 September 1919.

19. *El Dorado Times*, 6 July 1920, 3 August 1920, 16 August 1920, 26 August 1920, 13 September 1920, 20 September 1920, 25 September 1920, 27 September 1920, 4 July 1921, 9 July 1921, 25 July 1921, 1 August 1921, 22 August 1921, 29 August 1921, 5 September 1921, 6 September 1921, 12 September 1921, 10 October 1921, 1 July 1922, 3 July 1922, 6 July 1922, 17 July 1922, 14 August 1922, 11 September 1922, 6 July 1923, 16 July 1923, 23 July 1923, 6 August 1923, 13 August 1923, 20 August 1923, 5 July 1924, 28 July 1924, 23 August 1924, 25 August 1924, 1 September 1924, 6 September 1924, 29 September 1924, 13 October 1924, 13 July 1925, 2 July 1932.

20. *El Dorado Times*, 17 April 1926, 19 April 1926, 29 April 1926, 25 May 1926, 6 July 1926, 12 July 1926, 2 August 1926, 7 August 1926, 12 August 1926, 16 August 1926, 24 August 1926, 25 August 1926, 11 September 1926, 14 September 1926, 12 October 1926.

21. *El Dorado Times*, 5 July 1927, 19 July 1927, 20 August 1927, 9 July 1928, 13 August 1928, 3 September 1928, 10 September 1928, 17 September 1928, 1 October 1928, 8 July 1929, 15 July 1929, 22 July 1929, 29 July 1929, 26 August 1929, 30 August 1929.

22. *El Dorado Times*, 7 July 1930, 14 July 1930, 21 July 1930, 28 July 1930, 18 August 1930, 1 September 1930, 6 July 1931, 20 July 1931, 3 August 1931, 21 September 1931, 28 September 1931, 16 July 1932, 6 August 1932, 22 August 1932, 6 September 1932, 19 September 1932, 26 September 1932, 1 October 1932, 3 October 1932, 10 October 1932, 16 October 1932, 10 July 1933, 17 July 1933, 24 July 1933, 7 August 1933, 25 September 1933, 2 July 1934, 3 August 1934, 6 August 1934, 3 September 1934, 22 October 1934, 13 July 1935, 15 July 1935, 7 October 1935, 9 July 1936, 20 July 1936, 12 October 1936.

23. *El Dorado Times*, 12 July 1937, 27 July 1937, 2 August 1937, 23 August 1937, 1 July 1938, 5 July 1938, 7 July 1938, 11 July 1938, 20 July 1938, 25 July 1938, 1 May 1939, 5 May 1939, 8 July 1939, 18 July 1939, 22 July 1939; *Emporia Gazette*, 20 April 1938, 3 July 1938, 3 May 1939, 3 June 1939.

24. *El Dorado Times*, 8 February 1940, 19 April 1940, 10 May 1940, 28 May 1940, 17 June 1940, 29 July 1940, 15 August 1940, 19 May 1941, 12 July 1941, 25 July 1941, 4 August 1941.

25. *El Dorado Times*, 8 February 1940, 16 February 1940, 12 March 1940, 26 March 1940, 19 April 1940, 10 May 1940, 22 May 1940, 24 May 1940, 28 May 1940, 7 June 1940, 17 June 1940, 5 July 1940, 29 July 1940, 14 August 1940, 15 August 1940, 19 May 1941, 12 July 1941, 25 July 1941, 4 August 1941; *El Dorado Baseball Hall of Fame and Museum* 2016; "McDonald Stadium" 2014.

26. *El Dorado Baseball Hall of Fame and Museum* 2016; "McDonald Stadium" 2014.

27. *El Dorado Times*, 10 July 1952, 14 July 1952, 11 August 1952.

CHAPTER 17. LARKS PARK, HAYS

1. *Junction City (Weekly) Union*, 27 November 1869; *Leavenworth Times and Conservative*, 24 November 1869, 26 November 1869; *Topeka Kansas Weekly Commonwealth*, 2 December 1869.

2. *Hays City Sentinel*, 16 September 1887; *Junction City (Weekly) Union*, 3 August 1872.

3. *Dodge City Times*, 2 June 1877; *Hays City Sentinel*, 4 May 1877, 11 May 1877, 18 May 1877, 8 June 1877.

4. Special Orders Number 4 (II), Headquarters, Fort Hays, Kansas, 31 July 1878. The orders were later marked "Cancelled."

5. *Hays Free Press*, 9 June 1921; Edwards 1991.

6. *Ellis County News*, 1 June 1901; *Hays Free Press*, 8 March 1902, 11 June 1904, 31 July 1909; Ogle and Company 1905b; Kansas Historical Society, *Kansas Memory: Hays City Fair* (poster), Item Number 212371.

7. *Hays Free Press*, 19 August 1916, 23 September 1916, 7 July 1917, 24 April 1919, 22 September 1921.

8. *Ellis County News*, 17 July 1930; *Hays Daily News*, 19 June 1931; Dickey 1942, p. 75–77; Rogers 1984, p. 14–17.

9. *Hays Free Press*, 13 September 1902, 28 March 1903, 18 April 1903, 20 April 1907.

10. *Reveille 1914*, p. 105, and *Reveille 1917*, p. 156, Fort Hays Kansas Normal School Yearbooks.

11. *Hays Free Press*, 26 May 1917; *Reveille 1918–1919*, p. 124–136, Fort Hays Kansas Normal School Yearbook.

12. *Hays Free Press*, 18 March 1920.

13. *Hays Daily News*, 9 September 1965, 20 March 1966; *Hays Free Press*, 27 May 1920; *Reveille 1924*, p. 70, 84, Kansas State Teachers College at Hays Yearbook; *Reveille 1966*, p. 112–115, Fort Hays Kansas State College Yearbook.

14. *Hays Free Press*, 6 September 1902, 13 September 1902, 20 September 1902, 11 April 1903, 2 May 1903, 23 May 1903, 30 May 1923, 20 June 1903, 11 July 1903, 19 December 1903, 25 June 1904, 15 April 1905, 22 April 1905, 25 April 1905, 6 May 1905, 13 May 1905, 20 May 1905, 27 May 1905, 8 July 1905, 22 July 1905, 2 September 1905, 19 May 1906, 2 June 1906, 1 September 1906, 2 February 1907, 20 April 1907, 27 April 1907, 11 May 1907, 1 June 1907, 25 April 1908, 2 May 1908, 16 May 1908, 23 May 1908, 30 May 1908, 7 May 1910, 9 August 1913, 26 May 1917; Plazak 2007.

15. *Ellis Review Headlight*, 7 September 1907.

16. *Hays Free Press*, 3 June 1905; Thirteenth Census of the United States 1910.

17. *Hays Free Press*, 1 September 1906; Foster 2014; Wood 2013, p. 35–37.

18. "1926 American Legion" 2014; "A Brief History of Hays Eagles Baseball" 2014.

19. *Ellis County News*, 17 May 1928, 24 May 1928, 31 May 1928, 14 June 1928, 13 September 1928, 27 June 1929, 4 July 1929, 11 July 1929, 25 July 1929, 1 August 1929, 8 July 1929, 22 August 1929, 29 August 1929, 5 September 1929, 19 September 1929, 3 July 1930, 21 August 1930; *Hays Daily News*, 14 May 1934.

20. *Ellis County News*, 31 May 1923, 29 May 1924, 25 June 1925, 24 June 1926, 29 June 1927, 7 June 1928, 25 July 1929; *Hays Daily News*, 30 May 1931, 6 June 1931, 28 April 1934, 29 June 1935, 13 June 1936, 16 May 1938, 10 June 1939; *Hays Free Press*, 22 June 1922; Farber 1991.

21. *Hays Daily News*, 13 June 1932, 29 April 1933.

22. *Hays Daily News*, 7 May 1932, 30 May 1933, 5 June 1939, 21 June 1939; *Hays Free Press*, 24 April 1919, 22 September 1921; *Larned Tiller and Toiler*, 19 June 1939, 26 June 1939.

23. *Hays Daily News*, 1 June 1931, 6 June 1931, 19 April 1933, 1 June 1933, 9 May 1946, 27 May 1946; *Hays Free Press*, 3 March 1921, 22 June 1922, 21 September 1922; Thompson and Hays Public Library 2010, p. 75.

24. *Ellis County News*, 3 June 1926, 10 June 1926.

25. *Hays Daily News*, 1 June 1933, 17 May 1934, 18 May 1934.

26. *Ellis County News*, 5 September 1929, 19 September 1929; Kansas Baseball History Project.

27. *Hays Daily News*, 10 September 1947, 20 July 1961, 27 July 1962, 1 August 1963, 12 August 1963; Bruce 1985, p. 124–126.

28. *Hays Daily News*, 10 March 1961, 18 June 2004; Paige 1962; Tye 2009.

29. Truman 1947.

30. *Hays Free Press*, 18 March 1905.

31. *Hays Daily News*, 1 March 1940, 8 August 1940.

32. Bowman 1996; Bruce 1985, p. 68–73; Lester 2015.

33. *Hays Daily News*, 14 May 1940, 22 June 1940.

34. *Hays Daily News*, 8 August 1940, 23 May 1941.

35. *Hays Daily News*, 1 March 1940, 23 July 1940, 8 August 1940.

36. City of Hays Parks Department Invitation to Bid, Aluminum Seating for the Grandstands at Larks Park, 2008; Hays City Commission Work Session Notes, 2 February 2010.

37. *Hays Daily News*, 23 August 1940.

38. *Hays Daily News*, 16 July 1940, 17 July 1940, 23 July 1940, 2 August 1940.

39. *Hays Daily News*, 10 May 1940, 12 July 1943, 19 May 1944, 16 June 1944, 27 May 1945, 28 May 1945.

40. *Hays Daily News*, 13 March 1964, 28 September 1975, 10 February 1977, 18 February 1977, 29 June 2003; Hays City Commission Meeting Minutes, 25 September 1997, 27 March 2008, 23 December 2008, 10 September 2009, 28 June 2012, 11 October 2012; City of Hays Parks Department Invitation to Bid, Scoreboard for Larks Park, 2008.

41. *Hays Daily News*, 29 June 2003, 13 May 2004; Hays City Commission Meeting Minutes, 23 November 1999.

EPILOGUE. WAIT TILL NEXT YEAR
1. Kansas State Historical Society 2016.

APPENDIX. EXTRA INNINGS
1. *Wyandotte Commercial Gazette*, 15 June 1867.

2. *Lawrence Kansas Daily Tribune*, 4 October 1866, 29 November 1866, 17 May 1867.

3. *Lawrence Kansas Daily Tribune*, 3 July 1867.

4. *Lawrence Republican Daily Journal*, 2 August 1870; *Lawrence Kansas Daily Tribune*, 3 August 1867, 22 September 1867, 13 May 1880; Beers 1873.

5. *Lawrence Kansas Daily Tribune*, 2 August 1867.

6. *Lawrence Republican Daily Journal*, 3 July 1870, 11 August 1875.

7. *Lawrence Republican Daily Journal*, 3 July 1870, 6 July 1870; *Lawrence Kansas Daily Tribune*, 14 June 1870.

8. *Lawrence Kansas Daily Tribune*, 25 May 1871.

9. *Lawrence Republican Daily Journal*, 2 August 1870, 4 June 1873.

10. *Lawrence Republican Daily Journal*, 8 May 1877.

11. *Lawrence Daily Journal*, 9 August 1879.

12. *Lawrence Daily Journal*, 10 August 1886, 24 August 1886.

13. *Lawrence Daily Journal*, 12 May 1892, 1 July 1892, 11 February 1893, 23 September 1893.

14. *Lawrence Daily Journal*, 1 July 1892, 4 October 1892, 14 October 1892, 17 October 1892, 18 October 1892, 24 October 1892, 11 February 1893, 14 February 1893, 4 April 1893, 27 July 1893, 23 September 1893; *Lawrence Gazette*, 27 October 1892.

15. *Lawrence Daily Journal*, 8 April 1893.

16. Ogle and Company 1902a.

17. *Lawrence Daily Journal*, 27 April 1907.

18. *Lawrence Daily Journal*, 25 August 1910, 8 October 1910; *Lawrence Jeffersonian Gazette*, 15 March 1911.

19. *Lawrence Daily World*, 12 August 1910.

20. *Lawrence Daily World*, 6 July 1910; *Lawrence Jeffersonian Gazette*, 31 January 1912.

21. *Lawrence Daily Journal-World*, 20 March 1912, 14 April 1915, 21 April 1915, 22 May 1915, 26 May 1915, 23 July 1919.

22. *Lawrence Daily Journal-World*, 17 May 1922, 24 June 1922, 29 July 1922.

23. *Lawrence Jeffersonian Gazette*, 22 March 1916.

24. *Lawrence Daily Journal-World*, 3 July 1947, 8 July 1947, 9 July 1947, 10 July 1947.

25. *Lawrence Journal-World*, 7 March 2004.

26. *Lawrence Journal-World*, 16 July 1993, 5 August 1996, 16 June 2003.

27. *Wellington People's Voice*, 15 July 1892, 21 April 1893; Junge and Cook 2008; Ogle and Company 1902b; Kansas State Historical Society 1991. Manufactured gas consisted of volatile gases, such as hydrogen derived from coal, and was used to generate light and heat. The stone gashouse in Wellington has variously served as a community center, art gallery, and museum.

28. *Wellington People's Voice*, 16 June 1893, 23 June 1893, 30 June 1893, 29 December 1893.

29. *Wellington Daily News*, 2 September 1902, 18 July 1905, 19 July 1905; *Wellington People's Voice*, 28 March 1895, 14 May 1896, 9 July 1896; Edwards 1883.

30. *Wellington Daily News*, 7 July 1906, 3 June 1907, 12 April 1919; Ogle and Company 1902b.

31. Van Deventer 1981.

32. *Wellington Daily News*, 20 April 1909, 1 May 1911, 12 April 1919; Kansas Baseball History Project.

33. *Wellington Daily News*, 12 April 1919; Van Deventer 1981.

34. *Wellington Daily News*, 9 June 1919, 16 September 1919, 28 June 1922; Van Deventer 1981.

35. *Wellington Daily News*, 16 September 1919, 14 April 1920; Van Deventer 1981.

36. *Woman's Home Companion Picture Section*, "These Kansas Folks Hold a New Record," May 1922, 60; Van Deventer 1981.

37. *Wellington Daily News*, 28 June 1922; Van Deventer 1981.

38. *Wellington Daily News*, 7 March 1963, 19 March 1963, 3 April 1963, 27 September 1963, 13 May 1964, 28 May 1964; Van Deventer 1981.

39. *McPherson Daily Republican*, 8 March 1887, 22 June 1887, 27 June 1887, 15 July 1887, 26 July 1887, 30 July 1887, 10 August 1887, 14 October 1887, 14 June 1888, 15 June 1888, 17 July 1888, 2 February 1889, 22 February 1889, 15 April 1889, 24 May 1889, 29 May 1889, 12 June 1889, 22 June 1889, 22 July 1889, 10 August 1889, 23 November 1889; *McPherson (Weekly) Republican*, 4 September 1885; *McPherson Republican and Weekly Press*, 19 November 1886; Edwards 1884.

40. *McPherson Daily Republican*, 21 July 1891, 21 July 1893, 3 July 1894, 7 July 1894 (roster), 14 July 1894, 23 July 1894, 11 September 1894, 3 April 1895, 7 September 1895, 28 September 1895; *McPherson Republican and Weekly Press*, 25 August 1893, 15 June 1894.

41. *McPherson Daily Republican*, 11 June 1898, 19 July 1899, 1 August 1899, 1 September 1899, 21 April 1900, 11 May 1900, 28 May 1901, 26 August 1902, 20 May 1905.

42. *McPherson Daily Republican*, 4 July 1895, 19 July 1899, 12 September 1901, 18 September 1902.

43. *McPherson Daily Republican*, 6 May 1904, 18 April 1905.

44. *McPherson Daily Republican*, 13 May 1905, 17 May 1905, 18 May 1905, 23 May 1905, 24 May 1905, 13 July 1905, 7 August 1905, 18 August 1905, 19 April 1906, 8 May 1906, 10 May 1906, 11 May 1906, 12 May 1906, 21 June 1906, 15 May 1909, 21 February 1912.

45. *McPherson Daily Republican*, 29 May 1908, 25 June 1908, 26 June 1908, 19 August 1908, 5 January 1909, 27 February 1909, 13 March 1909, 25 March 1909, 8 April 1909, 16 August 1909, 18 June 1910, 28 August 1910, 11 July 1911, 7 June 1912, 11 June 1912; Kansas Baseball History Project.

46. *McPherson Daily Republican*, 29 May 1912, 8 March 1913, 10 July 1913, 2 June 1914, 6 June 1914, 20 July 1914, 11 April 1916, 18 April 1916, 8 May 1917; *McPherson Weekly Republican*, 23 April 1915, 30 April 1915.

47. *McPherson Daily Republican*, 28 February 1917, 2 March 1917, 15 March 1917, 21 March 1917, 29 March 1917, 8 May 1917.

48. *McPherson Daily Republican*, 6 June 1918, 23 April 1919, 14 May 1919, 26 July 1919, 2 August 1919, 6 September 1919, 8 September 1919; Ogle and Company 1921.

49. *McPherson Daily Republican*, 9 September 1919, 16 September 1919, 23 September 1919, 26 May 1920, 27 July 1920, 16 August 1920.

50. *McPherson Sentinel*, 24 May 1966.

Sources

NEWSPAPERS

Published in Kansas, except where noted. Indented entries are either the weekly version of the daily newspaper (usually a collection of stories from the daily) or minor name changes in the newspaper title.

Abilene Daily Chronicle
Abilene Daily Reflector
Alma Signal
Arkansas City Daily Traveler
   Arkansas City Weekly Republican
     Traveler
Atchison Daily Champion
   Atchison Weekly Champion and Press
Atchison Globe
Barber County Index
Barton County Democrat
Belle Plaine News
Belleville Telescope
Beloit Daily Call
Bismarck (ND) Tribune
Blue Rapids Times
Brown County World
Burlingame Enterprise
Carpenter's Kansas Lyre (Rossville)
Chanute Daily Tribune
Chanute Morning Sun
   Chanute Daily Sun
   Chanute Sun
Chanute Times
   Chanute Weekly Times
Chanute Tribune and Daily Timesett
Cheney Sentinel
Chicago (IL) Tribune
Clay Center Times
Coffeyville Daily Journal
   Coffeyville (Weekly) Journal
Collyer Advance
Columbus Advocate

Concordia Daily Blade
Council Grove Republican
Daily Atchison Patriot
Dickinson (SD) Press
Dodge City Globe-Republican
Dodge City Journal
Dodge City Times
Edwards County Leader
El Dorado Daily Republican
   El Dorado (Weekly) Republican
El Dorado Times
Ellis County News
Ellis Review Headlight
Emporia Daily Gazette
Emporia Kansas News
   Emporia Weekly News
Fort Scott Daily Monitor
   Fort Scott Weekly Monitor
Fort Scott Daily Tribune and Fort Scott
   Daily Monitor
Fredonia Alliance Herald
Galena Weekly Republican
Garden City Herald
Garden City Telegram
   Garden City Evening Telegram
Garnett Journal
Goodland Republic
Great Bend Tribune
Hastings (NE) Gazette-Journal
Hays City Sentinel
Hays Daily News
Hays Free Press
Hoisington Dispatch

Holton Recorder
Humboldt Union
Hutchinson News
Independence Daily Reporter
    Independence Evening Reporter
Independence Evening Star
    Independence (Weekly) Star and
        Kansan
Indianapolis (IN) Freeman
Indianapolis (IN) News
Indianapolis (IN) Star
Iola Register
    Iola Daily Register
Junction City (Daily) Union
    Junction City Daily Union
    Junction City (Weekly) Union
Kansas City Gazette
Kansas City Gazette Globe
Kansas City Kansan
Kansas City Kansas Globe
Kansas City (MO) Daily Journal of
    Commerce
Kansas City (MO) Journal
Kansas City (MO) Star
Kansas City (MO) Times
Kinsley Graphic
Kinsley Mercury
Larned Optic
Larned Tiller and Toiler
Larned Weekly Chronoscope
Larned Weekly Eagle-Optic
Lawrence Daily Journal
    Lawrence Republican Daily Journal
Lawrence Daily Journal-World
    Lawrence Journal-World
Lawrence Daily Kansas Tribune
Lawrence Daily World
    Lawrence Weekly World
Lawrence Gazette
    Lawrence Jeffersonian Gazette

Leavenworth Daily Times
    Leavenworth Times and Conservative
Leavenworth Post
Liberty (TX) Vindicator
Louisville Lyre
Marion Record
McPherson Daily Republican
    McPherson Republican and Weekly
        Press
    McPherson Weekly Republican
    McPherson (Weekly) Republican
Meade County News
Morning Tulsa (OK) Daily World
Nashville (TN) Globe
New Philadelphia (OH) Daily Times
Newton Daily Kansan
Newton Daily Republican
Newton Evening Kansan-Republican
Newton Journal
New York (NY) Clipper
New York (NY) Times
Nicodemus Enterprise
Oklahoma City (OK) Black Dispatch
Oklahoma City (OK) Oklahoma Leader
Olathe Mirror
Olsburg Gazette
Omaha (NE) Daily Bee
Onaga Herald
Osage City Free Press
    Osage City Free Press-Public Opinion
Osawatomie Graphic
Oskaloosa Independent
Ottawa Daily Republican
Ottawa Herald
    Ottawa Evening Herald
    Ottawa Weekly Herald
Pampa (TX) Daily News
Parsons Daily Sun
Pawnee County Herald
Phillipsburg Herald

Pittsburg Daily Headlight
Pittsburgh (PA) Gazette Times
Pittsburgh (PA) Post
Pittsburg Sun
   Pittsburg Morning Sun
Red Cloud (NE) Chief
Rossville News
Rossville Reporter
Rossville Times
Saint Marys Star
Salina Daily Republican
Salina Daily Republican-Journal
Salina Daily Union
   Salina Union
Salina Evening Journal
Saline County Journal
San Francisco (CA) Call
Topeka Daily Capital
Topeka Daily Commonwealth
   Topeka Kansas Weekly Commonwealth
   Topeka Weekly Commonwealth
Topeka State Journal
Topeka Tribune
Troy Weekly Kansas Chief

Valley Falls New Era
Valley Republican (Kinsley)
Wakarusa Kansas Herald of Freedom
Walnut Valley Times (El Dorado)
Wamego Reporter
Wamego Weekly Times
Weekly Osage Chronicle (Burlingame)
Wellington Daily News
Wellington People's Voice
Western Cyclone
   Nicodemus Cyclone
Westmoreland Recorder
White Cloud Kansas Chief
Wichita Beacon
   Wichita Daily Beacon
Wichita Eagle
   Wichita City (Weekly) Eagle
   Wichita Daily Eagle
Wichita Negro Star
Windom Press
Winfield Daily Free Press
Winfield Evening News
Wyandotte Commercial Gazette
Wyandott Herald

ARTICLES, BOOKS, AND DISSERTATIONS

"1871 National Association Team Statistics and Standings." 2015. *Baseball-Reference .com*. Accessed 12 September. http://www.baseball-reference.com/leagues/NA /1871.shtml.

"1889 American Association Team Statistics and Standings." 2015. *Baseball-Reference.com*. Accessed 12 September. http://www.baseball-reference.com/leagues /AA/1889.shtml.

"1903 Chicago White Sox." 2015. *Baseball-Reference.com*. Accessed 7 December. http://www.baseball-reference.com/teams/CHW/1903.shtml.

"1907 Western Association." 2015. *Baseball-Reference.com*. Accessed 29 October. http://www.baseball-reference.com/register/league.cgi?id=497175fe.

"1926 American Legion." 2014. *El Dorado Baseball Hall of Fame and Museum*. Accessed 5 October. http://www.eldoradobaseballhof.org/hall/1926-american-le gion.php.

"Ad Brennan." 2016. *Baseball-Reference.com*. Accessed 13 July. http://www.baseball -reference.com/register/player.cgi?id=brennao01add.

Adelman, Melvin L. 1980. "The First Baseball Game, the First Newspaper References to Baseball, and the New York Club: A Note on the Early History of Baseball." *Journal of Sport History* 7 (3): 132–135.

American Amateur Baseball Congress. 2016. Accessed 21 July. http://aabc.us/.

"American Association (Independent) Encyclopedia and History." 2015. *Baseball-Reference.com*. Accessed 8 June. http://www.baseball-reference.com/minors /league.cgi?code=AA&class=Ind.

American Legion. 2016. *American Legion Baseball National Champions*. Accessed 17 July. http://www.legion.org/documents/baseball/national_champions.pdf.

Anderson, David W. 2015a. "Bill Klem." *Society for American Baseball Research (SABR) Baseball Biography Project*. Accessed August 23. http://sabr.org/bioproj/person /31461b94.

———. 2015b. "Dummy Taylor." *Society for American Baseball Research (SABR) Baseball Biography Project*. Accessed July 11. http://sabr.org/bioproj/person/14fca2f4.

Anderson, Eric P. 2009. "Reformers Revealed: American Indian Progressives at Haskell Institute, Lawrence, Kansas, 1884–1909." PhD diss., University of Kansas.

"Art Weaver." 2016. *Baseball-Reference.com*. Accessed 13 July. http://www.baseball -reference.com/register/player.cgi?id=weaver001art.

Ávila, Henry J. 1997. "Immigration and Integration: The Mexican American Community in Garden City, Kansas, 1900–1950." *Kansas History* 20 (Spring): 22–37.

Babe Ruth League. 2015. *2015 Babe Ruth League Media Guide*. Accessed 7 May. https:// baberuthleague.org/sitemedia/2015%20MediaGuide.pdf.

Bak, Richard. 1991. *Cobb Would Have Caught It: The Golden Age of Baseball in Detroit*. Detroit, MI: Wayne State University Press.

———. 2014. "My Day with Chief Hogsett, Detroit's First Bullpen Ace." *Detroit Athletic Co.* November 7. http://blog.detroitathletic.com/2014/11/07/day-chief -hogsett-detroits-first-bullpen-ace/.

Baker University. 2015. "A History of Excellence & Support." *Baker University*. Accessed 16 August. http://www.bakeru.edu/about/history.

Ban Johnson Amateur League Baseball. 2014. Accessed 10 September. http://www .bjbaseball.com/.

Barry, John M. 2004a. *The Great Influenza: The Epic Story of the Deadliest Plague in History*. New York: Viking.

———. 2004b. "The Site of Origin of the 1918 Influenza Pandemic and Its Public Health Implications." *Journal of Translational Medicine* 2. doi:10.1186/1479 -5876-2-3.

Barthel, Thomas. 2007. *Baseball Barnstorming and Exhibition Games, 1901–1962: A History of Off-Season Major League Play*. Jefferson, NC: McFarland.

"Baseball Rule Change Timeline." 2015. *Baseball Almanac*. Accessed 19 July. http://www.baseball-almanac.com/rulechng.shtml.

"Beals Becker." 2015. *Baseball-Reference.com*. Accessed 27 November. http://www.baseball-reference.com/players/b/beckebe01.shtml.

Becker, Carl M. 2002. "Crossing Bats: Baseball in the Villages of the Upper Miami Valley, 1865–1900." *NINE: A Journal of Baseball History and Culture* 10 (2): 46–70.

Beers, F. W. 1873. *Atlas of Douglas Co., Kansas*. New York: F. W. Beers.

Berlage, Gai Ingham. 1994. *Women in Baseball: The Forgotten History*. Westport, CT: Praeger.

———. 2000. "Transition of Women's Baseball: An Overview." *NINE: A Journal of Baseball History and Culture* 9 (1–2): 72–81.

Bevis, Charlie. 2003. *Sunday Baseball: The Major Leagues' Struggle to Play Baseball on the Lord's Day, 1876–1934*. Jefferson, NC: McFarland.

"Bill Burwell." 2016. *Baseball-Reference.com*. Accessed 3 October. http://www.baseball-reference.com/players/b/burwebi01.shtml.

"Bill Klem." 2015. *National Baseball Hall of Fame*. Accessed 23 August. http://baseballhall.org/hof/klem-bill.

"Bingo DeMoss." 2016. *Baseball-Reference.com*. Accessed 1 October. http://www.baseball-reference.com/bullpen/Bingo_DeMoss.

Biographical Directory of the United States Congress 1774–Present, s.v. "Pomeroy, Samuel Clarke (1816–1891)." 2015. Accessed 1 March. http://bioguide.congress.gov/scripts/biodisplay.pl?index=P000423.

Blackmar, Frank W., ed. 1912. *Kansas: A Cyclopedia of State History, Embracing Events, Institutions, Industries, Counties, Cities, Towns, Prominent Persons, Etc.* Chicago, IL: Standard.

Block, David. 2005. *Baseball before We Knew It: A Search for the Roots of the Game*. Lincoln: University of Nebraska Press.

Bohn, Terry. 2014. "'Many Exciting Chases after the Ball': Nineteenth Century Base Ball in Bismarck, Dakota Territory." *Baseball Research Journal* 43 (1): 48–53.

Bond, Gregory. 2003. "The Segregation of Professional Baseball in Kansas, 1895–1899: A Case Study in the Rise of Jim Crow during the Gilded Age." In *The Cooperstown Symposium on Baseball and American Culture, 2002*, edited by William M. Simons, p. 61–78. Jefferson, NC: McFarland.

———. 2004. "'Too Much Dirty Work': Race, Manliness and Baseball in Gilded-Age Nebraska." *Nebraska History* 85: 172–185.

Bowman, Larry G. 1995. "'I Think It Is Pretty Ritzy, Myself': Kansas Minor League Teams and Night Baseball." *Kansas History* 18: 248–257.

———. 1996. "The Monarchs and Night Baseball." *National Pastime* 16: 80–84.

"Boxscore." 2013. *Baseball-Reference.com*. Last modified 24 May. http://www.baseball-reference.com/bullpen/Boxscore.

"A Brief History of Hays Eagles Baseball." 2014. *Hays Eagles.* Accessed 19 October. http://www.hayseagles.com/history.

Broeg, Bob. 1989. *Baseball's Barnum: Ray "Hap" Dumont, Founder of the National Baseball Congress.* Wichita, KS: Center for Entrepreneurship, W. Frank Barton School of Business Administration, Wichita State University.

Brown, Ken D. 1980. *Independence: The Way We Were.* Independence, KS: published by the author.

Bruce, Janet. 1985. *The Kansas City Monarchs: Champions of Black Baseball.* Lawrence: University Press of Kansas.

Burgos, Adrian, Jr. 2007. *Playing America's Game: Baseball, Latinos, and the Color Line.* Berkeley: University of California Press.

Burton, William R., and David J. Lewis, eds. 1916. *Past and Present of Adams County, Nebraska.* Vol. 1. Chicago, IL: S. J. Clarke.

Busch, Thomas S. 1988. "Sunflower Stars: Big Leaguers from Kansas." *Kansas History* 11 (2): 80–92.

Caldwell, Martha B. 1943. "The Woman Suffrage Campaign of 1912." *Kansas Historical Quarterly* 12 (3): 300–326.

Campney, Brent M. S. 2015. *This Is Not Dixie: Racist Violence in Kansas, 1861–1927.* Urbana: University of Illinois Press.

Carey, Charles. 2016. "Walter Johnson." *Society for American Baseball Research (SABR) Baseball Biography Project.* Accessed June 30. http://sabr.org/bioproj/person/0e5ca45c.

Carroll, Brian. 2008. "Beating the Klan: Baseball Coverage in Wichita before Integration, 1920–1930." *Baseball Research Journal* 37: 51–61.

———. 2011. "'Praising My People': Newspaper Sports Coverage and the Integration of Baseball in Wichita, Kansas." *Kansas History* 33: 240–255.

Chadwick, Henry, ed. 1866. *Beadle's Dime Base-Ball Player.* New York: Beadle. http://dimenovels.lib.niu.edu/islandora/object/dimenovels%3A6838#page/1/mode/1up.

———, ed. 1867. *Beadle's Dime Base-Ball Player.* New York: Beadle. http://dimenovels.lib.niu.edu/islandora/object/dimenovels%3A6840#page/1/mode/1up.

———, ed. 1871. *Beadle's Dime Base-Ball Player.* New York: Beadle. http://dimenovels.lib.niu.edu/islandora/object/dimenovels%3A6843#page/1/mode/1up.

"Chief Hogsett." 2014. *Baseball-Reference.com.* Accessed 28 December. http://www.baseball-reference.com/players/h/hogsech01.shtml.

"Chief Hogsett Career Stats." 2014. *Major League Baseball.* Accessed 28 December. http://mlb.mlb.com/team/player.jsp?player_id=116052#gameType='R'&sectionType=career&statType=2&season=2014&level='ALL'.

"Claude Willoughby." 2016. *Baseball-Reference.com.* Accessed 26 May. http://www.baseball-reference.com/players/w/willoc101.shtml.

Cohen, Marilyn. 2009. *No Girls in the Clubhouse: The Exclusion of Women from Baseball.* Jefferson, NC: McFarland.

Corbett, Warren. 2015. "Murry Dickson." *Society for American Baseball Research (SABR) Baseball Biography Project.* Accessed January 6. http://sabr.org/bioproj/person/1bb26f23.

Costello, Raymond. 2014. "Chief Hogsett." *Society for American Baseball Research (SABR) Baseball Biography Project.* Accessed December 28. http://sabr.org/bioproj/person/29ac1752.

Cronin, John. 2013. "Truth in the Minor League Class Structure: The Case for the Reclassification of the Minors." *Baseball Research Journal* 42 (1): 87–91.

DeArment, Robert K. 2006. *Ballots and Bullets: The Bloody County Seat Wars of Kansas.* Norman: University of Oklahoma Press.

Dickey, Otis M. 1942. "A History of the Fort Hays Kansas State College." MS thesis, Fort Hays Kansas State College.

Dickinson Press Staff. 2011. "Times Changing for SD Amateur Baseball." *Dickinson Press,* 14 May. http://www.thedickinsonpress.com/content/times-changing-sd-amateur-baseball.

Dickson, Paul, and Skip McAfee. 2009. *The Dickson Baseball Dictionary.* 3rd ed. New York: W. W. Norton.

"Dink Mothell." 2016. *Baseball-Reference.com.* Accessed 8 June. http://www.baseball-reference.com/register/player.cgi?id=demoss000.

Dixon, Phil S. 2010. *Wilber "Bullet" Rogan and the Kansas City Monarchs.* Jefferson, NC: McFarland.

Dodge County Baseball League. 2016. Last updated 28 June. http://www.leaguelineup.com/welcome.asp?url=dcbl&sid=346249534.

"Duff Cooley." 2015. *Baseball-Reference.com.* Accessed 13 September. http://www.baseball-reference.com/players/c/cooledu01.shtml.

"Dummy Taylor." 2015. *Baseball-Reference.com.* Accessed 11 July. http://www.baseball-reference.com/players/t/taylodu01.shtml.

Duncan, L. Wallace. 1903. *History of Montgomery County.* Iola, KS: Press of Iola Register.

Dunkel, Tom. 2013. *Color Blind: The Forgotten Team That Broke Baseball's Color Line.* New York: Atlantic Monthly Press.

Dunkle, Jonathan. 2016. "Claude Hendrix." *Society for American Baseball Research (SABR) Baseball Biography Project.* Accessed June 30. http://sabr.org/bioproj/person/fca42ef7.

Eddleton, Oscar. 1980. "Under the Lights." *Baseball Research Journal* 9: 37–42.

Edwards, John P. 1881. *Historical Atlas of Montgomery County, Kansas.* Philadelphia, PA: published by the author.

———. 1883. *Historical Atlas of Sumner County, Kansas.* Philadelphia, PA: published by the author.

———. 1884. *Edward's Atlas of McPherson County, Kansas.* Quincy, IL: John P. Edwards.

Edwards, Reginald. 1991. "Theory, History, and Practice of Education: Fin de Siècle and a New Beginning." *McGill Journal of Education* 26 (3): 237–266.

El Dorado Baseball Hall of Fame and Museum. 2016. Accessed 26 May. http://www .eldoradobaseballhof.org/.

Elfers, James E. 2003. *The Tour to End All Tours: The Story of Major League Baseball's 1913–1914 World Tour.* Lincoln: University of Nebraska Press.

"Emmett Bowles." 2016. *Baseball-Reference.com.* Accessed 8 March. http://www .baseball-reference.com/players/b/bowleem01.shtml.

Emporia State University. 2016. "A Brief History of Emporia State University." *Emporia State University.* Accessed 16 July. http://www.emporia.edu/about/history .html.

Enders, Eric. 2004. "Zachariah Davis Wheat." In *Deadball Stars of the National League,* edited by Tom Simon, p. 287–290. Dulles, VA: Brassey's.

———. 2015. "Zack Wheat." *Society for American Baseball Research (SABR) Baseball Biography Project.* Accessed May 19. http://sabr.org/bioproj/person/c914 f820.

Etcheson, Nicole. 2004. *Bleeding Kansas: Contested Liberty in the Civil War Era.* Lawrence: University Press of Kansas.

Evans, Harold C. 1940. "Baseball in Kansas, 1867–1940." *Kansas Historical Quarterly* 9 (2): 175–192.

Farber, Alan. 1991. "Thomas More Prep–Marian High School, Hays." In *At Home in Ellis County, 1867–1992,* p. 218–220. Hays, KS: History Book Committee, Ellis County Historical Society.

Ferdinand Vandeveer Hayden and the Founding of the Yellowstone National Park. 1973. Washington, DC: United States Department of the Interior Geological Survey.

Final Report on the WPA Program, 1935–43. 1947. Washington, DC: US Government Printing Office.

Fleitz, David. 2004. "Jacob Peter Beckley." In *Deadball Stars of the National League,* edited by Tom Simon, p. 231–232. Dulles, VA: Brassey's.

———. 2015. "Cap Anson." *Society for American Baseball Research (SABR) Baseball Biography Project.* Accessed September 12. http://sabr.org/bioproj/person /9b42f875.

Forsythe, James L. 2002. *Lighthouse on the Plains: Fort Hays State University, 1902–2002.* Hays, KS: Fort Hays State University.

Foster, Michael. 2014. "Smoky Joe Wood." *Society for American Baseball Research (SABR) Baseball Biography Project.* Accessed October 5. http://sabr.org/bioproj /person/9f244666.

Fountain, Charles. 2009. *Under the March Sun: The Story of Spring Training.* New York: Oxford University Press.

Francis, Bill. 2016. "At Home on the Road." *National Baseball Hall of Fame.* Accessed 10 June. http://baseballhall.org/barnstorming-tours.

Garcia, Jose M. 1973. "History of the Mexicans in Topeka—1906–66." Unpublished manuscript, Topeka and Shawnee County Public Library, Topeka, Kansas.

Gelber, Steven M. 1983. "Working at Playing: The Culture of the Workplace and the Rise of Baseball." *Journal of Social History* 16 (4): 3–22.

"General History." 2015. *Minor League Baseball*. Accessed 25 August. http://www .milb.com/milb/history/general_history.jsp.

"George Sweatt." 2015. *Baseball-Reference.com*. Accessed 5 August. http://www.base ball-reference.com/bullpen/George_Sweatt.

"George Sweatt Register Statistics and History." 2015. *Baseball-Reference.com*. Accessed 20 June. http://www.baseball-reference.com/nlb/player.cgi?id=sweatt00geo.

Gerlach, Larry R. 2010. "Ernie Quigley: An Official for All Seasons." *Kansas History* 33 (4): 218–239.

Goldstein, Warren. 1989. *Playing for Keeps: A History of Early Baseball*. Ithaca, NY: Cornell University Press.

Goodwin, Doris Kearns. 2005. *Team of Rivals*. New York: Simon and Schuster.

Graham, Llewellyn James, reporter. 1909. *The State of Kansas v. Earnest Prather*. In *Reports of Cases Argued and Determined in the Supreme Court of the State of Kansas*, vol. 79, p. 513–520. Topeka, KS: State Printing Office.

Greeley, A. T., ed. 1916. *Spalding's Official Indoor Base Ball Guide, Containing the Constitution, By-Laws and Playing Rules of the National Indoor Base Ball Association of the United States, 1917*. New York: American Sports Publishing Company.

Green, Guy W. 2010. *The Nebraska Indians and Fun and Frolic with an Indian Ball Team: Two Accounts of Baseball Barnstorming at the Turn of the Twentieth Century*. Edited by Jeffrey Powers-Beck. Jefferson, NC: McFarland.

Gregorich, Barbara. 1993. *Women at Play: The Story of Women in Baseball*. San Diego: Harcourt Brace and Company.

Hall, John G. 2004. *The KOM League Remembered*. Charleston, SC: Arcadia.

Hall, Tony. 2014. *Home, Home Plate on the Range: Historical Guide of Major League Players from Kansas and Baseball in the Sunflower State*. Emporia, KS: Spiritheart.

Hawkins, Joel, and Terry Bertolino. 2000. *The House of David Baseball Team*. Charleston, SC: Arcadia.

Heaphy, Leslie A., ed. 2007. *Satchel Paige and Company: Essays on the Kansas City Monarchs, Their Greatest Star and the Negro Leagues*. Jefferson, NC: McFarland.

"History." 2014. *The American Legion*. Accessed 29 September. http://www.legion .org/history.

"History." 2015. *Kansas City T-Bones*. Accessed 8 June. http://www.tbonesbaseball .com/team/history/.

"History of American Legion Baseball." 2014. *The American Legion*. Accessed 9 September. http://www.legion.org/baseball/history.

"History of Little League." 2014. *Little League Baseball and Softball*. Accessed 10 September. http://www.littleleague.org/learn/about/historyandmission.htm.

Hofmann, Paul. 2015. "Paul Lindblad." In *Mustaches and Mayhem: Charlie O's Three-Time Champions—The Oakland Athletics, 1972–74,* edited by Chip Greene, p. 443–448. Phoenix, AZ: Society for American Baseball Research.

———. 2016. "Paul Lindblad." *Society for American Baseball Research (SABR) Baseball Biography Project.* Accessed July 24. http://sabr.org/bioproj/person/1278 ab6d.

Horner, John Arthur. 2011. "Know Your KC History: Strange Goings on at Exposition Fair, 1872, Part 2." *Kansas City Public Library,* October 7. http://www.kclibrary .org/blog/kc-unbound/know-your-kc-history-strange-goings-exposition-fair -1872-pt-2.

Humphries, Mark Osborne. 2014. "Paths of Infection: The First World War and the Origins of the 1918 Influenza Pandemic." *War in History* 21 (1): 55–81.

Iber, Jorge. 2014. "The Early Life and Career of Topeka's Mike Torrez, 1946–1978: Sport as a Means for Studying Latino/a Life in Kansas." *Kansas History* 37 (3): 164–179.

"Ike Kahdot." 2016. *Baseball-Reference.com.* Accessed 12 February. http://www.base ball-reference.com/players/k/kahdoiko1.shtml.

"Important Dates in Wingnuts History." 2016. *Wichita Wingnuts Baseball.* Accessed 3 October. http://wichitawingnuts.com/about/important-dates-in-wingnuts-his tory/.

Independent Professional Baseball Federation. 2016. Accessed 19 July. http://www.inde pendentprofessionalbaseballfederation.com/.

"Jack Johnson." 2016. *Seamheads.com Negro Leagues Database.* Accessed 31 January. http://www.seamheads.com/NegroLgs/player.php?ID=1328.

Jacobsen, Lenny. 2016. "Joe Tinker." *Society for American Baseball Research (SABR) Baseball Biography Project.* Accessed June 30. http://sabr.org/bioproj/person /bc0df648.

"Jake Beckley." 2015. *National Baseball Hall of Fame.* Accessed 28 October. http:// baseballhall.org/hof/beckley-jake.

James, Bill, and Rob Neyer. 2004. *The Neyer/James Guide to Pitchers: An Historical Compendium of Pitching, Pitchers, and Pitches.* New York: Fireside.

James, George W. 1897. "Report of Pottawatomie and Great Nemaha Agency." In *Report of Agent in Kansas, Report of the Commissioner of Indian Affairs, Annual Reports of the Department of the Interior, for the Fiscal Year Ended June 30, 1897,* p. 151–156. Washington, DC: Government Printing Office.

Jayhawk Baseball League. 2016. Accessed 20 July. http://www.jayhawkbaseballleague .pointstreaksites.com/view/jayhawkbaseballleague.

"Jimmy Whelan." 2016. *Baseball-Reference.com.* Accessed 13 July. http://www.base ball-reference.com/register/player.cgi?id=whelan001jam.

"Joe Bloomer." 2016. *Baseball-Reference.com.* Accessed 21 March. http://www.base ball-reference.com/register/player.cgi?id=bloome001jos.

"Joe Wilhoit." 2016. *Baseball-Reference.com.* Accessed 13 July. http://www.baseball-reference.com/register/player.cgi?id=wilhoi001jos.

Johnson, Janice. 2016a. "Farmer Weaver." *Society for American Baseball Research (SABR) Baseball Biography Project.* Accessed June 30. http://sabr.org/bioproj/person/2c20717c#_edn31.

———. 2016b. "Jesse Barnes." *Society for American Baseball Research (SABR) Baseball Biography Project.* Accessed June 30. http://sabr.org/bioproj/person/cd4085a8.

———. 2016c. "Virgil Barnes." *Society for American Baseball Research (SABR) Baseball Biography Project.* Accessed June 30. http://sabr.org/bioproj/person/3492f328.

Johnson, Lloyd, and Miles Wolff, eds. 2007. *Encyclopedia of Minor League Baseball.* 3rd ed. Durham, NC: Baseball America.

Junge, Aspen, and John Cook. 2008. *The Manufactured Gas Industry in Kansas.* Kansas Department of Health and Environment, Bureau of Environmental Remediation. June 30. http://www.kdheks.gov/remedial/articles/FMGP_History.pdf.

Kansas Collegiate League Baseball. 2016. Accessed 20 July. http://www.kclbonline.com/.

Kansas Department of Agriculture. 2016. *Kansas Farm Facts.* Accessed 21 July. http://agriculture.ks.gov/docs/default-source/Kansas-Farm-Facts-2015/kansasfarmfacts2014final.pdf?sfvrsn=4.

Kansas Historical Society. 2014a. "Baseball Bat." *Kansas Memory.* Accessed 26 December. http://www.kansasmemory.org/item/221126.

———. 2014b. "Baseball Trophy." *Kansas Memory.* Accessed 26 December. http://www.kansasmemory.org/item/221667.

———. 2014c. "Cool Things—Baseball Trophy and Bat." *kansapedia.* Accessed 26 December. http://www.kshs.org/kansapedia/cool-things-baseball-trophy-and-bat/10283.

———. 2016. "Preserve." *Kansas Historical Society.* Accessed 18 March. http://www.kshs.org/p/preserve/19387.

Kansas NBC Hap Dumont Youth Baseball. 2016. Accessed 20 July. http://kansashapdumontbaseball.com/.

"Kansas State." 2015. *Babe Ruth League.* Accessed 7 May. http://ks.baberuthonline.com/.

Kansas State Historical Society. 1991. *Park House Gallery Certificate of State Register Listing, Register of Historic Kansas Places.* http://www.kshs.org/resource/national_register/nominationsNRDB/Sumner_ParkHouseGallerySR.pdf.

Kansas Wesleyan University. 2015. "History and Faith." Accessed 16 August. http://www.kwu.edu/about-kwu/history-faith.

Kaufman, James C., and Alan S. Kaufman. 1995. *The Worst Baseball Pitchers of All Time: Bad Luck, Bad Arms, Bad Teams, and Just Plain Bad.* New York: Citadel Press.

Kirkman, Paul. 2012. *Forgotten Tales of Kansas City.* Charleston, SC: History Press.

Lahman, Sean. 2004. "Luther Haden 'Dummy' Taylor." In *Deadball Stars of the National League,* edited by Tom Simon, p. 37–38. Dulles, VA: Brassey's.

Laing, Jeffrey Michael. 2013. *Bud Fowler: Baseball's First Black Professional*. Jefferson, NC: McFarland.

Laird, Judith Fincher. 1975. "Argentine, Kansas: The Evolution of a Mexican-American Community, 1905–1940." PhD diss., University of Kansas.

Lamb, Bill. 2016. "Art Weaver." *Society for American Baseball Research (SABR) Baseball Biography Project*. Accessed July 13. http://sabr.org/bioproj/person/17f71fc5.

Lamster, Mark. 2006. *Spalding's World Tour: The Epic Adventure That Took Baseball around the Globe—And Made It America's Game*. New York: Public Affairs.

"The Larned Trust Fund Case." 1926. In *Twenty-Sixth Biennial Report of the Attorney-General of Kansas*, p. 32–33. Topeka: Kansas State Printing Plant.

Larsen, Travis. 2007a. "Baseball Can Survive: How Semi-Pro Baseball Thrived in Wichita during the 1930s and 1940s." *Heritage of the Great Plains* 40 (Spring–Summer): 29–40.

———. 2007b. "Satchel Paige and Hap Dumont: The Dynamic Duo of the National Baseball Congress Tournament." In *Satchel Paige and Company: Essays on the Kansas City Monarchs, Their Greatest Star and the Negro Leagues*, edited by Leslie A. Heaphy, p. 89–96. Jefferson, NC: McFarland.

"Leagues." 2016. *Baseball-Reference.com*. Accessed 22 October. http://www.baseball-reference.com/minors/league.cgi.

Leerhsen, Charles. 2015. *Ty Cobb: A Terrible Beauty*. New York: Simon and Schuster.

"Les Barnhart." 2016. *Baseball-Reference.com*. Accessed 3 October. http://www.baseball-reference.com/players/b/barnhle01.shtml.

Lester, Larry. 2015. "Only the Stars Come Out at Night: The Story of J. L. Wilkinson." *Black Ball: A Negro Leagues Journal* 8: 54–81.

———, and Sammy J. Miller. 2000. *Black Baseball in Kansas City*. Charleston, SC: Arcadia.

Lincoln Adult Baseball League. 2016. Last updated 28 June. http://www.leaguelineup.com/welcome.asp?url=labl.

Louisa, Angelo. 2016. "Fred Clarke." *Society for American Baseball Research (SABR) Baseball Biography Project*. Accessed June 30. http://sabr.org/bioproj/person/6f6673ea.

Lowry, Philip J. 2006. *Green Cathedrals: The Ultimate Celebration of Major League and Negro League Ballparks*. New York: Walker.

Madden, W. C., and Patrick J. Stewart. 2002. *The Western League: A Baseball History, 1885 through 1999*. Jefferson, NC: McFarland.

Major League Baseball. 2014. *Official Baseball Rules, 2014 Edition*. http://mlb.mlb.com/mlb/downloads/y2014/official_baseball_rules.pdf.

Major League Baseball. 2016. *Official Baseball Rules, 2016 Edition*. http://mlb.mlb.com/mlb/downloads/y2016/official_baseball_rules.pdf.

Martinez, Rod. 2015. "A Young Man's Baseball Journey." *Latino Baseball History Project Newsletter* 5 (1): 6–7. http://scholarworks.lib.csusb.edu/lbhp/11.

McCullough, David. 1968. *The Johnstown Flood*. New York: Simon and Schuster.

"McDonald Stadium." 2014. *El Dorado Main Street*. Accessed 7 December. http://eldoradomainstreet.org/mcdonald-stadium.

McKenna, Brian. 2015. "Bud Fowler." *Society for American Baseball Research (SABR) Baseball Biography Project*. Accessed May 22. http://sabr.org/bioproj/person/200e2bbd.

———. 2016. "Sandy Nava." *Society for American Baseball Research (SABR) Baseball Biography Project*. Accessed March 5. http://sabr.org/bioproj/person/1ac63c02.

McMahon, George. 2015. "Al Spalding." *Society for American Baseball Research (SABR) Baseball Biography Project*. Accessed September 12. http://sabr.org/bioproj/person/b99355e0.

Mendoza, Valerie M. 1993. "They Came to Kansas Searching for a Better Life." *Kansas Quarterly* 25 (2): 97–106.

Metcalf, Mark. 2016. "Organized Baseball's Night Birth." *Baseball Research Journal* 45 (2): 47–49.

"Mickey Mantle." 2015. *Baseball-Reference.com*. Accessed 12 October. http://www.baseball-reference.com/register/player.cgi?id=mantleoo1mic.

Mid-Plains League. 2016. Accessed 20 July. http://midplainsleague.com/.

Mills, Dorothy Seymour, and Harold Seymour. 1990. *Baseball: The People's Game*. New York: Oxford University Press.

M.I.N.K. Collegiate Baseball League. 2016. Accessed 12 July. http://www.minkleaguebaseball.com/.

Minnesota Baseball Association. 2016. Accessed 28 June. http://www.mnbaseball.org/.

Moore, Oscar Leopold, reporter. 1923. *Charles Cooney, Manager of the Mayetta Indian Baseball Club of Mayetta v. Lou Hauck, Manager of the Valley Falls Baseball Club of Valley Falls*. In *Reports of Cases Argued and Determined in the Supreme Court of the State of Kansas*, vol. 112, p. 562–565. Topeka, KS: State Printing Office.

———, reporter. 1924. *Celia Thurman-Watts v. Board of Education of the City of Coffeyville and A.I. Decker, as Superintendent of Public Schools etc.* In *Reports of Cases Argued and Determined in the Supreme Court of the State of Kansas*, vol. 115, p. 328–333. Topeka, KS: State Printing Office.

Morris, Peter. 2003. *Baseball Fever: Early Baseball in Michigan*. Ann Arbor: University of Michigan Press.

———. 2008. *But Didn't We Have Fun?: An Informal History of Baseball's Pioneer Era, 1843–1870*. Chicago, IL: Ivan R. Dee.

———. 2010. *A Game of Inches: The Story Behind the Innovations That Shaped Baseball*. Rev. ed. Chicago, IL: Ivan R. Dee.

"Murry Dickson." 2015. *Baseball-Reference.com*. Accessed 6 January. http://www.baseball-reference.com/players/d/dicksmu01.shtml.

Nebraska Baseball Association. 2014. Last updated 4 August. http://www.leaguelineup.com/welcome.asp?url=nebraskabaseballassociation.

"Nick Allen." *Baseball-Reference.com*. Accessed 13 July. http://www.baseball-refer
ence.com/players/a/allenni01.shtml.

*Nineteenth Biennial Report of the Kansas State Board of Agriculture to the Legislature of
the State for the Years 1913 and 1914*. 1915. Topeka: Kansas Department of Agriculture.

Nitz, Jim. 2015. "Fair Grounds (Rockford, IL)." *Society for American Baseball Research
(SABR) Baseball Biography Project*. Accessed September 12. http://sabr.org/bio
proj/park/f3c1ca83.

Nowlin, Bill. 2008. "Murry Dickson, from One Life-Threatening Experience to Another." In *When Baseball Went to War*, edited by Todd Anton and Bill Nowlin,
p. 87–90. Chicago, IL: Triumph Books.

———. 2016. "Mel Almada." *Society for American Baseball Research (SABR) Baseball Biography Project*. Accessed February 23. http://sabr.org/bioproj/person
/1797ed2c.

O'Brien, Claire. 1996. "'With One Mighty Pull': Interracial Town Boosting in Nicodemus, Kansas." *Great Plains Quarterly* 16: 117–129.

Official Website of the Pecos League. 2015. Accessed 20 October. http://www.pecos
league.com/.

Ogle, George A., and Company. 1902a. *Standard Atlas of Douglas County, Kansas,
including a Plat Book*. Chicago, IL: George A. Ogle and Company.

———. 1902b. *Standard Atlas of Sumner County, Kansas, including a Plat Book*. Chicago, IL: George A. Ogle and Company.

———. 1905a. *Standard Atlas of Butler County, Kansas, including a Plat Book*. Chicago, IL: George A. Ogle and Company.

———. 1905b. *Standard Atlas of Ellis County, Kansas, including a Plat Book*. Chicago,
IL: George A. Ogle and Company.

———. 1905c. *Standard Atlas of Sedgwick County, Kansas, including a Plat Book*.
Chicago, IL: George A. Ogle and Company.

———. 1906a. *Standard Atlas of Edwards County, Kansas, including a Plat Book*.
Chicago, IL: George A. Ogle and Company.

———. 1906b. *Standard Atlas of Neosho County, Kansas, including a Plat Book*. Chicago, IL: George A. Ogle and Company.

———. 1921. *Standard Atlas of McPherson County, Kansas, including a Plat Book*. Chicago, IL: George A. Ogle and Company.

Omaha Adult Baseball League. 2016. Accessed 28 June. http://oabl.org/.

Oppenheimer, Robert. 1985. "Acculturation or Assimilation: Mexican Immigrants
in Kansas, 1900 to World War II." *Western Historical Quarterly* 16 (4): 429–
448.

"Otis Lambeth." 2016. *Baseball-Reference.com*. Accessed 3 October. http://www.base
ball-reference.com/players/l/lambeot01.shtml.

Ottawa University. 2016. "Ottawa University History and Ottawa Tribe Heritage." Accessed 12 March. http://www.ottawa.edu/about-us/history-and-heritage.

Paige, Leroy (Satchel). 1962. *Maybe I'll Pitch Forever*. Garden City, NY: Doubleday.

Painter, Nell Irvin. 1992. *Exodusters: Black Migration to Kansas after Reconstruction*. New York: W. W. Norton. First published 1986 by University Press of Kansas.

Parr, Royse. 2004. "Isaac Leonard 'Ike' 'Chief' Kahdot." In *Native Americans in Sports*, vol. 1, edited by C. Richard King, p. 167. Armonk, NY: Sharpe Reference.

"Pecos League (Independent) Encyclopedia and History." 2015. *Baseball-Reference.com*. Accessed 8 June. http://www.baseball-reference.com/minors/league.cgi?code=PECO&class=Ind.

Pendleton, Jason. 1997. "Jim Crow Strikes Out: Interracial Baseball in Wichita, Kansas, 1920–1935." *Kansas History* 20: 86–101.

Peterson, Armand, and Tom Tomashek. 2006. *Town Ball: The Glory Days of Minnesota Amateur Baseball*. Minneapolis: University of Minnesota Press.

Peterson, John E. 2003. *The Kansas City Athletics: A Baseball History, 1954–1967*. Jefferson, NC: McFarland.

Peterson, Robert. 1970. *Only the Ball Was White: A History of Legendary Black Players and All-Black Professional Teams*. New York: Oxford University Press.

Peterson, Todd. 2010. *Early Black Baseball in Minnesota: The St. Paul Gophers, Minneapolis Keystones and Other Barnstorming Teams of the Deadball Era*. Jefferson, NC: McFarland.

Pietrusza, David. 1997. *Lights On! The Wild Century-Long Saga of Night Baseball*. Lanham, MD: Scarecrow Press.

"Pioneer Night Baseball in Des Moines." 1963. *Annals of Iowa* 37 (1): 1–8.

Plat Book of Pawnee County, Kansas. 1902. Minneapolis, MN: North West.

Plazak, Dan. 2007. "The Imaginary Gold Mines of Kansas." *Mining History Journal* 14: 11–22.

Plessy v. Ferguson. 1986. Judgment, Decided 18 May 1896, Records of the Supreme Court of the United States, Record Group 267, Plessy v. Ferguson, 163, no. 15248, National Archives.

Pomrenke, Jacob. 2016. "Fred McMullin." *Society for American Baseball Research (SABR) Baseball Biography Project*. Accessed June 30. http://sabr.org/bioproj/person/7d8be958.

Powers-Beck, Jeffrey. 2004a. "'A Role New to the Race': A New History of the Nebraska Indians." *Nebraska History* 85: 187–199.

———. 2004b. "Nebraska Indians Profiles." *Nebraska History* 85: 200–203.

———. 2004c. *The American Indian Integration of Baseball*. Lincoln: University of Nebraska Press.

Price, Jay M. 2003. *Wichita, 1860–1930*. Charleston, SC: Arcadia.

———. 2005. *El Dorado: Legacy of an Oil Boom*. Charleston, SC: Arcadia.

Proceedings of the House of Representatives of the State of Kansas, Seventeenth Biennial Session. 1911. 10 January to 15 March. Topeka: State Printing Office.

Quastler, I. E. 2004. "'Emphatically a Rock Island Town': The Railroad Legacy of Horton, Kansas, 1887–1946." *Kansas History* 27 (4): 232–249.

Revel, Layton, and Luis Munoz. 2010. *Forgotten Heroes: Oscar "Heavy" Johnson*. Center for Negro League Baseball Research. http://www.cnlbr.org/Portals/0/Hero/Oscar-Heavy-Johnson.pdf.

———. 2014. *Forgotten Heroes: Chet Brewer*. Center for Negro League Baseball Research. http://www.cnlbr.org/Portals/0/Hero/Chet-Brewer.pdf.

Rice, Stephen V. 2016. "Frank Wickware." *Society for American Baseball Research (SABR) Baseball Biography Project*. Accessed June 8. http://sabr.org/bioproj/person/200cf3c2#sdendnote4sym.

Richmond, H. J. 1916. *Atlas and Plat Book of Montgomery County, Kansas*. Des Moines, IA: Kenyon Company.

Rinaldi, Richard A. 2005. *The United States Army in World War I: Orders of Battle: Ground Units, 1917–1919*. Takoma Park, MD: Tiger Lily Publications.

Ring, Jennifer. 2009. *Stolen Bases: Why American Girls Don't Play Baseball*. Urbana: University of Illinois Press.

Rives, Bob. 2004. *Baseball in Wichita*. Charleston, SC: Arcadia.

———. 2016. "Joe Wilhoit." *Society for American Baseball Research (SABR) Baseball Biography Project*. Accessed July 13. http://sabr.org/bioproj/person/f460 1077.

Rogers, Katherine L. 1984. *Grit, Spirit and Character: A Story of the Lewis Field Housing Project*. Topeka: State of Kansas Division of Printing.

Rosa, Joseph G. 2011. "Was Wild Bill Ever an Ump?" *Wild West* 24 (1): 43.

Rossville Centennial Booklet. 1971. Rossville Community Library. Transcribed and published online 2013. http://www.rossvillelibrary.org/wp-content/uploads/2013/03/Rossville-Centennial-Booklet-final.pdf.

"Roy Garvin Sanders." 2016. *Baseball-Reference.com*. Accessed 13 July. http://www.baseball-reference.com/register/player.cgi?id=sander002roy.

"Roy Lee Sanders." 2016. *Baseball-Reference.com*. Accessed 13 July. http://www.baseball-reference.com/register/player.cgi?id=sander003roy.

Rutter, Larry G. 1972. "Mexican Americans in Kansas: A Survey and Social Mobility Study, 1900–1970." Master's thesis, Kansas State University.

Sandoval, James. 2016. "Nick Allen." *Society for American Baseball Research (SABR) Baseball Biography Project*. Accessed July 10. http://sabr.org/bioproj/person/8e64df2e.

Santillán, Richard. 2008. "Mexican Baseball Teams in the Midwest, 1916–1965: The Politics of Cultural Survival and Civil Rights." In *Sports and the Racial Divide: African American and Latino Experience in an Era of Change*, edited by Michael E. Lomax, p. 146–165. Jackson: University Press of Mississippi.

————, Susan C. Luévano, Luis F. Fernández, and Angelina F. Veyna. 2013. *Mexican American Baseball in Orange County*. Charleston, SC: Arcadia.

Sargent, Kelly Boyer. 2004. "Emmet [*sic*] Jerome Bowles." In *Native Americans in Sports*, vol. 1, edited by C. Richard King, p. 58–59. Armonk, NY: Sharpe Reference.

Schiff, Andrew J. 2008. *"The Father of Baseball": A Biography of Henry Chadwick*. Jefferson, NC: McFarland.

————. 2016. "Henry Chadwick." *Society for American Baseball Research (SABR) Baseball Biography Project*. Accessed July 23. http://sabr.org/bioproj/person/436e570c.

Schwarz, Alan. 2006. "Take Me Out to the Box Score." *New York Times*, 2 April.

Shattuck, Debra. 2001. "Playing a Man's Game: Women and Baseball in the United States, 1866–1954." In *Baseball History from Outside the Lines: A Reader*, edited by John E. Dreifort, p. 195–215. Lincoln: University of Nebraska Press.

————. 2011. "Women's Baseball in the 1860s: Reestablishing a Historical Memory." *NINE: A Journal of Baseball History and Culture* 19 (2): 1–26.

Simon, Tom. 2016. "Clyde Milan." *Society for American Baseball Research (SABR) Baseball Biography Project*. Accessed February 27. http://sabr.org/bioproj/person/a1651456.

Skelton, David E. 2016. "Joe Bowman." *Society for American Baseball Research (SABR) Baseball Biography Project*. Accessed July 15. http://sabr.org/bioproj/person/aa4eed26.

Smith, Gene. 1994. "The Girls of Summer." *American Heritage* 45: 110–111.

Smith, Michael M. 1981. "Beyond the Borderlands: Mexican Labor in the Central Plains, 1900–1930." *Great Plains Quarterly* 1 (4): 239–251.

"Smoky Joe Wood." 2016. *Baseball-Reference.com*. Accessed 18 October. http://www.baseball-reference.com/players/w/woodjo02.shtml.

South Dakota Amateur Baseball Association. 2016. *South Dakota Amateur Baseball*. Accessed 28 June. http://www.sdaba.com/.

Spencer, Burl. 1993. "Oldest Living Cleveland Indian Remembers the Good Year: 1922." *Tulsa World*, September 22. http://www.tulsaworld.com/archives/oldest-living-cleveland-indian-remembers-the-good-year/article_1a42d1f0-ef5b-5b87-9217-de429ba91b66.html.

Stout, Mary A. 2012. *Native American Boarding Schools*. Santa Barbara, CA: ABC-CLIO.

Strecker, Trey. 2015. "Frank Isbell." *Society for American Baseball Research (SABR) Baseball Biography Project*. Accessed April 26. http://sabr.org/bioproj/person/88d6e6dd.

Sutter, L. M. 2010. *New Mexico Baseball: Miners, Outlaws, Indians, and Isotopes, 1880 to the Present*. Jefferson, NC: McFarland.

Swan, Tony. 2013. "Ford's Assembly Line Turns 100: How It Really Put the World on Wheels." *Car and Driver*, April. http://www.caranddriver.com/features/fords-assembly-line-turns-100-how-it-really-put-the-world-on-wheels-feature.

Sweeney, Matthew. 2009. *The Lottery Wars: Long Odds, Fast Money, and the Battle over an American Institution*. New York: Bloomsbury.

"Teams by Classification." 2016. *Minor League Baseball*. Accessed 27 August. http://www.milb.com/milb/info/classifications.jsp.

Tenney, John Darrin. 2016. *Baseball in Territorial Arizona: A History, 1863–1912*. Jefferson, NC: McFarland.

Thirteenth Census of the United States. 1910. United States Census Bureau. Accessed 9 June 2015. http://www.census.gov/prod/www/decennial.html.

Thomas, Henry W. 1995. *Walter Johnson: Baseball's Big Train*. Washington, DC: Phenom Press.

Thomas, Phillip Drennon. 2004. *Buffalo Jones: Citizen of the Kansas Frontier*. Garden City, KS: Finney County Historical Society.

"Thomas Blodgett." 2016. *Baseball-Reference.com*. Accessed 21 March. http://www.baseball-reference.com/register/player.cgi?id=blodgeo01tho.

Thompson, Mary Ann, and Hays Public Library. 2010. *Hays: The 1930s*. Charleston, SC: Arcadia.

Thorn, John. 2011. *Baseball in the Garden of Eden: The Secret History of the Early Game*. New York: Simon and Schuster.

Thornley, Stew. 2006. *Baseball in Minnesota: The Definitive History*. Saint Paul: Minnesota Historical Society Press.

"Top 100 Teams." 2015. *Minor League Baseball History*. Accessed 19 October. http://www.milb.com/milb/history/top100.jsp.

Town Teams: Bigger than Baseball. 2016. Digital video recording. Shawnee, KS: Destination Hope.

Traubel, Horace. (1908) 1961. *With Walt Whitman in Camden*. Vol. 2, *July 16, 1888–October 31, 1888*. Reprint, New York: Rowman and Littlefield.

Trembanis, Sarah L. 2014. *The Set-Up Men: Race, Culture and Resistance in Black Baseball*. Jefferson, NC: McFarland.

Truman, Harry S. 1947. "Proclamation 2749—Columbus Day, 1947." Online by Gerhard Peters and John T. Woolley, *American Presidency Project*, University of California, Santa Barbara. Accessed 31 October 2014. http://www.presidency.ucsb.edu/ws/?pid=87118.

Tye, Larry. 2009. *Satchel: The Life and Times of an American Legend*. New York: Random House.

Tygiel, Jules. 2000. *Past Time: Baseball as History*. New York: Oxford University Press.

United States Department of Labor. 2016. "Consumer Price Index Inflation Calculator, 1913 to Current Year." *Bureau of Labor Statistics*. http://www.bls.gov/data/inflation_calculator.htm.

Unrau, William E. 2007. *The Rise and Fall of Indian Country, 1825–1855*. Lawrence: University Press of Kansas.

Utley, Robert M., ed. 1977. *Life in Custer's Cavalry: Diaries and Letters of Albert and Jennie Barnitz, 1867–1868*. New Haven, CT: Yale University Press.

Van Deventer, Marie Sellers. 1981. *Community Park, 1913–1921: Currently Known as Sellers Park (since July 31, 1939)*. Wellington, KS: Privately published.

Vaught, David. 2013. *The Farmers' Game: Baseball in Rural America*. Baltimore: Johns Hopkins University Press.

Vecsey, George. 2006. *Baseball: A History of America's Favorite Game*. New York: Modern Library.

Walker, James R. 2015. *Crack of the Bat: A History of Baseball on the Radio*. Lincoln: University of Nebraska Press.

———, and Robert V. Bellamy Jr. 2008. *Center Field Shot: A History of Baseball on Television*. Lincoln: University of Nebraska Press.

Washburn University. 2015. "History of Washburn." *Washburn University*. Accessed 4 September. http://www.washburn.edu/about/history.html.

Weingroff, Richard F. 2015. *From Names to Numbers: The Origins of the U.S. Numbered Highway System*. US Department of Transportation, Federal Highway Administration, Highway History. Last updated 18 November. http://www.fhwa.dot.gov /infrastructure/numbers.cfm.

"Western League (A) Encyclopedia and History." 2015. *Baseball-Reference.com*. Accessed 28 October. http://www.baseball-reference.com/register/league.cgi?code =WL&class=A.

"Wichita, Kansas Register City Encyclopedia." 2015. *Baseball-Reference.com*. Accessed 8 June. http://www.baseball-reference.com/minors/team.cgi?city=Wichita& state=KS&country=US.

Wiggins, Robert Peyton. 2016. "Ad Brennan." *Society for American Baseball Research (SABR) Baseball Biography Project*. Accessed July 13. http://sabr.org/bioproj /person/4afa5984.

Wilson, H. E. 1897. "Report of Superintendent of Kickapoo School." In *Report of Agent in Kansas, Report of the Commissioner of Indian Affairs, Annual Reports of the Department of the Interior, for the Fiscal Year Ended June 30, 1897*, p. 156–157. Washington, DC: Government Printing Office.

Wolf, Gregory. 2013. "Bill Burwell." In *Sweet '60: The 1960 Pittsburgh Pirates*, edited by Clifton Blue Parker and Bill Nowlin, p. 231–236. Phoenix, AZ: Society for American Baseball Research.

Wood, Gerald C. 2013. *Smoky Joe Wood: The Biography of a Baseball Legend*. Lincoln: University of Nebraska Press.

Woods, Randall B. 1983. "Integration, Segregation, or Exclusion? The 'Color Line' in Kansas, 1878–1900." *Western Historical Quarterly* 14 (2): 181–198.

Wright, Marshall D. 2000. *The National Association of Base Ball Players, 1857–1870*. Jefferson, NC: McFarland.

Wuthnow, Robert. 2011. *Remaking the Heartland: Middle America since the 1950s.* Princeton, NJ: Princeton University Press.

———. 2016. "Rural Depopulation." In *The Routledge History of Rural America*, edited by Pamela Riney-Kehrberg, p. 260–273. New York: Routledge.

ARCHIVES

Blue Rapids Historical Society, Blue Rapids, Kansas
City of Garden City, Kansas
City of Hays, Kansas
El Dorado Baseball Hall of Fame, El Dorado, Kansas
Ellis County Historical Society, Hays, Kansas
Finney County Historical Museum, Garden City, Kansas
Forsyth Library, Fort Hays State University, Hays, Kansas
Harvey County Historical Museum, Newton, Kansas
Hays Public Library, Hays, Kansas
Independence Museum and Art Center, Independence, Kansas
Jordaan Memorial Library, Larned, Kansas
Kansas Baseball History Project, unpublished reports compiled by Jan Johnson, Topeka, Kansas
Kansas Oil Museum, El Dorado, Kansas
Kansas State Historical Society, Topeka, Kansas
Kaufman Museum, Bethel College, North Newton, Kansas
Kinsley Public Library, Kinsley, Kansas
McPherson Public Library, McPherson, Kansas
Wamego Public Library, Wamego, Kansas

WEBSITES

American Legion. http://www.legion.org/
Ban Johnson Amateur Baseball League. http://www.bjbaseball.com/
Baseball-Reference.com. http://www.baseball-reference.com/
El Dorado Baseball Hall of Fame and Museum. http://www.eldoradobaseballhof.org/
Fold3 by Ancestry.com. http://www.fold3.com
Gateway to Oklahoma History. http://gateway.okhistory.org/
Illinois Digital Newspaper Collections. http://idnc.library.illinois.edu/
Kansas NBC Hap Dumont Youth Baseball. http://kansashapdumontbaseball.com/
Library of Congress, Chronicling America: Historic American Newspapers. http://chroniclingamerica.loc.gov/newspapers/
Little League. http://www.littleleague.org/
Major League Baseball. http://mlb.mlb.com/
M.I.N.K. Collegiate Baseball League. http://www.minkleaguebaseball.com/

National Baseball Congress. http://www.nbcbaseball.com/
Newspaper Archive. http://newspaperarchive.com/us/
Newspapers.com. http://www.newspapers.com/
Protoball. http://protoball.org/
Seamheads.com Negro Leagues Database. http://www.seamheads.com/NegroLgs/
Society for American Baseball Research. http://sabr.org/
State Historical Society of Missouri. http://statehistoricalsocietyofmissouri.org/cdm/
Wamego Public Library. http://wamego.lib.nckls.org/

Index

Teams and ballparks of towns in Kansas and adjacent states are listed with their cities.

Hart, Robert Lee "Billy," 151
Hartford, CT, 5, 134
Haskell, Dudley, 18, 22, 98
Haskell Indian Nations University. *See*
    Haskell Institute (KS)
Haskell Institute (KS), x, 41, 44, 46, 98–99,
    103–107, 135, 285
Hastings, NE, 123, 147, 150, 159
Hays, KS, xx–xxi, 33, 170, 178, 184, 240, 254,
    276, 281–292
    American Indian baseball, 104–105,
        108–109
    Golden Belt Fairgrounds, 282–283, 287
    Hays Catholic (St. Joseph's) College
        grounds, 286
    Hays City Base Ball Club, 281, 287
    Hays Eagles, 283, 292
    Hays Larks, xxi, 178, 287–288, 292
    Larks Park, xx, 175, 182, 185, 187,
        289–292
    Sunday baseball, 37–38
    women's sports, 47–48, 57, 61
Hendrix, Claude, 145–146
Herington, KS, 49
Herron, Larkin "Curley," 61
Hiawatha, KS, 86, 131
Hibbs, Harry, 227
Hickok, James Butler "Wild Bill," 16–17
Highland, KS, 66
Hodgeman County, KS, 56, 207
Hodgeman–Pawnee–Edwards County
    League, 207
Hogsett, Elon "Chief," 108–109, 144
Hoover, Daisy, 62
Horton, KS, 82, 97, 99, 103, 115
House of David (barnstorming team), x,
    64–65, 141, 203, 240, 287
Humboldt, KS, 25–26, 70, 88–93, 128, 144,
    195, 233–234, 237–238
    Walter Johnson Athletic Field, 297
Huron Indian Cemetery. *See* Wyandot
    National Burying Ground
Hutchinson, KS, 73, 151, 176, 198, 200, 280
    Hobart-Detter Field, Carey Park, 297
    Mexican American teams, 115–116,
        120–121
    minor league teams, 78, 106–107, 123,
        139, 268

Independence, KS, 22, 85–86, 107, 133,
    136–143, 233, 241–242, 260, 276
    African American teams, 78–81, 91, 235
    Independence Producers, 106–107,
        138–139, 141
    Independence Shamrocks, 51
    Shulthis Stadium, 133, 136, 138–140, 142
    See also Shulthis Stadium
Independent Baseball League, 275–276
Indian baseball. *See* lacrosse
indoor ball. *See* softball
Ingram, Monroe, 85, 87–88
Iola, KS, 38–39, 67–71, 89, 91–92, 94, 107,
    133, 234, 237–238
    Iola Go-Devils, 67–69, 89, 92, 94, 234
    Iola Ramblers, 69–71, 94
    Iola White Sox (Boosters), 67–69, 92
    minor league teams, 25–26, 73, 129
Iowa, 76, 79, 106, 124, 126, 132–133, 140–
    143, 147, 154, 172, 175, 217, 241, 260
Iowa Tribe, 97, 100
Isbell, William Frank "Izzy," 217–218

Jackson, Clifford, 275
Jayhawk League, 175, 280, 305
Jetmore, KS, 56
Johnson, Arthur John "Jack," 324n34
Johnson, John Thomas "Topeka Jack," 73–75,
    77, 79–81
Johnson, Oscar "Heavy," 94
Johnson, Walter, 92, 107, 128, 144, 147, 153,
    159, 272, 297
Jones, Bert, 86–88
Jones, C. J. "Buffalo," 222
Joplin, MO, 24, 61, 142, 159, 174
    minor league teams, 107, 130–131, 133,
        139, 153
Junction City, KS, 13, 34–35, 62, 94, 128, 136,
    157, 174, 184, 258–266
    Athletic Park, 260–261, 263
    Fegan Field, 261, 263, 358n30
    Junction City Base Ball Club, 17
    Junction City Brigade, 266
    Junction City Generals, 266
    Rathert Stadium, 175, 182–184, 187,
        265–266
    Y Ballpark, 259, 261–263
    See also Y Ballpark